Dreams & Dead Ends

JACK SHADOIAN

SECOND EDITION

Dreams & Dead Ends

THE AMERICAN GANGSTER FILM

OXFORD
UNIVERSITY PRESS

2003

OXFORD

UNIVERSITY PRESS

Oxford   New York

Auckland   Bangkok   Buenos Aires   Cape Town   Chennai
Dar es Salaam   Delhi   Hong Kong   Istanbul   Karachi   Kolkata
Kuala Lumpur   Madrid   Melbourne   Mexico City   Mumbai   Nairobi
São Paulo   Shanghai   Taipei   Tokyo   Toronto

Copyright © 2003 by Oxford University Press

Published by Oxford University Press, Inc.
198 Madison Avenue, New York, New York 10016
www.oup.com

This volume is a revised edition of *Dreams and Dead Ends: The American Gangster/Crime Film*
published 1977 by MIT Press.

Library of Congress Cataloging-in-Publication Data
Shadoian, Jack.
Dreams and dead ends : the American gangster film / Jack Shadoian.— 2nd ed.
p.   cm.
Includes bibliographical references and index.
ISBN: 0-19-514291-8; 0-19-514292-6 (pbk.)
1. Gangster films—United States—History and criticism.   I. Title.
PN1995.9.G3   S5   2001
791.43'655—dc21   2001035081

9 8 7 6 5 4 3 2 1

Printed in the United States of America
on acid-free paper

To Christopher and Jessica,

in whom the passion

for film lives on

A large percentage of feature films are genre films. Filmmakers do not normally proceed without an awareness of the kind of film their time and money is being used to create. The decision they arrive at becomes a basic controlling factor for the film. Viewers use genres to help themselves determine the kind of evening they would prefer to spend at the movies. Critics use genre as a method of organization, as a term and a concept that serves their discourse and allows for particular kinds of discoveries. Since genre considerations figure so importantly in the production and the viewing of so many films, the direction for critical thought that genre supplies is central to the attempt at understanding them.

Criticism of film genres has largely been concerned with systematizing what most filmgoers haphazardly discern, with placing and classifying films on the evidence of descriptive definition. This is of course necessary, but both classification and description are open to dispute, despite claims to objectivity. More to the point, however, is that thinking about film genres should go beyond stressing their repetitive iconographical, situational, and narrative elements. Genres persist, change, and overlap, and we must ask questions about both their persistence and their evolution. If they persist, they must be useful, but useful for what? Observation must be incorporated into argument, into theory and interpretation. We must ponder the *meaning* of genres.

In dealing with the American gangster/crime film, I have posed to myself this question: What does the genre do that can't be done as well elsewhere? This seems to me the large question necessary to genre definition. What does the framework of any particular genre allow the expression of? I think, also, that we are well aware that the bare bones of generic description do not adequately account for the complexities of any given film, that infinite qualifications as to how generic elements function are required before our perception and experience of the film can proceed toward a criticism capable of exploring the film's value, meaning, and impact. Resemblances are often enough superficial and/or merely serviceable. It goes without saying that a genre critic is obliged to see a great number of films before attempting discriminations of kind, likeness, similarity. However, it is not enough to see a sufficient number of films. The critic is also obliged to think them through, if only to make classification, and designation of patterns and qualities, reasonably accurate.[1] Even genre criticism that is predicated upon an intellectual grasp of a distinct and distinguishable *body* of work must ultimately rise to the challenge of understanding specific works, not only because a film addresses us in its totality but also to ensure the flexibility and credibility of its generalizations.

The gangster/crime genre is an involved system of family relationships.

Specific films tend to violate, extend, adapt, and sometimes dismiss the conventions that in part color and motor them even as they are evoked and put into play. Paring down the complexity of the genre is no solution, whatever the advantage to critical convenience and efficiency. A theory of the genre that does it justice should be capable of elucidating its most complex manifestations as they occur in individual films. Whatever general ideas and implications can be drawn from the films of the genre, they must be shown to emerge from the films themselves. My discussion, therefore, centers on key, representative films, from which theory is derived and developed. Undertaking theory and close analysis in conjunction will, I hope, prevent theory from limiting and misrepresenting the films and advance criticism of the genre toward a complex consideration of works in relation to their informing structures. An activity it has been reluctant to perform.

Genres are cultural metaphors and psychic mirrors. We don't know of what until we study the films that comprise them. In varying degrees, each film genre offers an account of the life we lead, wish to lead, or ought to lead. To study a sequence of films that use similar frameworks allows us to think about the utility and potential of those frameworks. The sequence should be chronological so that changes may be perceived in their proper relation to so-cial/historical factors and advances in the medium itself and, more fundamentally, because films must be understood as standing in a line of influence. There remains the problem of which films belong in which genres. We all make hurried, though generally pretty reliable, distinctions—we know, more or less. what musicals, westerns, gangster films, soap operas, horror films, and war films are. (Comedy is notoriously amorphous and is not really a genre at all but a sensibility, a way of looking at the world.) In the five years or so that I have applied concentrated (as opposed to random) thought to the gangster/ crime film, several writers have charted out some possibilities and there seems to be a general consensus as to the outer limits of what films can be included. I stand indebted to all those writers—Lawrence Alloway, John Baxter, John Ga-bree, Stuart Kaminsky, and Colin McArthur, in particular—for their thoughts on the matter, although my personal sense of the continuity of the genre ap-proximates Baxter's and McArthur's most closely. That is to say. my view of the genre is rather a wide one: it embraces a great many films. In terms of their purpose, and their visual-iconic organization, the genre includes not only those works obviously concerned with the character and fate of the gangster hero but also certain *films noirs, policiers,* juvenile delinquent films, private eye films, and syndicate films.

The film critic operates under some disadvantages. He must depend too often on memory, he does not have a vast body of knowledge to support him, existing methodologies offer only minimal entry into the subject, and the complex factors of moviemaking are inhospitable to critical security. (A picture may be proverbially worth a thousand words, but our ability to read it, taken for granted, remains practically and theoretically underdeveloped in an icon-dominated culture.) Everything in a film is there because somebody wanted it there, although it is often hard to know why or even who that somebody was. There is far too much in any single film for a critic to discover on his own; moreover, some factors operate invisibly, and the critic may simply be blind to yet others. Movie "magic" is the result of the effective combination of numerous elements, and critical pursuit of these combinations is quite frustrating. An art director might have an idea about this or that, which may end up only half realized in the finished film, or even inverted. Meanings are never stable. No filmmaker can ever be certain that what he intends is what is communicated, and movies come and go so fast that there is little time or opportunity to arrive at a knowledgeable consensus. And then, watching movies is one thing, writing about them another. We are too quick, too self-protective in arranging experience into abstractions. Films have been both damned and praised because of the emotional force of their images, their immediate, nonverbal impact.

Given how movies work, the call to demystify them is at once romantic, impertinent, and necessary. Criticism has not progressed very far in accounting for how we are "spellbound in darkness," for how movies exert their control. Even at mundane, nonphilosophical levels, we operate in a half-light. We have no means to describe long-term rhythms, for example, nor are we clear about such simple matters as what "establishing shots" establish or what is signified by camera movements from the periphery of a location to the center—as in the conclusion of *The Line-Up*—or vice versa. Moreover, modern scientific and aesthetic theory points to the delusory nature of objective systems, and films themselves are beginning to work with the assumption that it is impossible to define anything as distinct from our perception of it[2] (what the Cubists incorporated into their paintings over six decades ago). This obviously puts into question the idea of critical "proof."

Assuming that criticism cannot hope to "prove" anything, it is still a formal and refined version of a natural human tendency to be curious about the works of art one has been affected by, and, to be manageable, criticism must, to some extent, be reductive. One cannot hope to say everything one feels and knows about a subject all at once, in one book. Nor can one risk being despotically conclusive about so young a field of inquiry and practice as film. No one critic can be the measure of any film, and certainly not of a cycle of films. The elucidation of films must proceed on as many fronts as possible, but in a measured, cautious, tentative, provisional way. The closing of any subject is always premature, and the desire that would have it so always pernicious. There isn't any aspect of film that doesn't require further opening up. Given the vast amount of work to be done, the following chapters may best be regarded as only a beginning. If the book is successful, it will provoke other critics to take up where I have left off.

Film criticism is in a primitive stage because we know very little about film—very little about the intricacies of intent and reception for any given film. It is in a primitive stage because the medium itself makes evident the obsolescence of our critical language. The history of film theory is a catalog of conflicting intellectual misadventures, and there is no secure and shared sense about when film criticism is actually talking about its subject matter and when not. In general, a relaxed, intelligent speculation that takes its time and weighs changes in the medium and new information into its consideration has not been the rule. Rather, there has been a rage for order, a hurry to nail things down, an urgent, sometimes desperate invasion of other disciplines for their methodologies. We should before we make dubious alignments to any critical or scholarly system, patiently discuss with each other and inform each other of what we have seen on the screen and provide different kinds of ordered presentations of the thoughts our experience has induced. In writing and thinking about film, we must be content to make slow, small, and partial gains. We must proceed using what we know, but with a healthy awareness also of all that we don't know.

I have voiced these (perhaps unnecessary) admonitions to ensure that these pages not be misunderstood in spirit. A pessimism about critical language—and the nature of the film medium gives it plenty of fuel—may on occasion seek to overcompensate by aggression and assertion. The same may be said for one's enthusiasm—which film also can provoke to excess. If I err in either direction, it is not from a wish to compel authority but to compel attention to the importance of the subject, to make the reader want to see or resee the films and think about them so that he or she, in turn, may provide new ways by which a viewer's receptivity to the medium and its works can be increased. One dilemma of film criticism is that the immediacy of films is often too matter-of-factly put aside in the interests of manageability. One's discontent with the detachment that accompanies any orderly critical investigation may, however, be tempered by the belief that there is a genuine, if limited, relation between our preconceptual, quirky, individualized apprehension of films and the reasoned discourse we apply to them.

The gangster/crime film is difficult to write about, to hold in view as a unity, because it shifts gears so frequently. Perhaps a small army of film critics is ultimately what is required to come fully to terms with it. My study must inevitably fall short of raising all the issues and questions pertinent to an examination of the genre and obviously cannot conduct analyses of all its films. If what I have written will hasten badly needed studies of films like *The Big*

House, Quick Millions, The Secret Six, T-Men, Raw Deal, Criss-Cross, Brute Force, Machine-Gun Kelly, Angels with Dirty Faces, The Line-Up, Bloody Mama, Dillinger, The Roaring Twenties, Party Girl, The Enforcer, Mean Streets, He Walked by Night, and many others, it will in large part have fulfilled its aim. Further insight into the genre is seriously hampered by the almost utter absence of responsible attention to films such as these. Whether the careful study of such films will produce evidence that confirms, alters, or negates the conceptual apparatus I provide remains to be seen.

The gangster crime genre is of course not exclusive to film. Film does not exist in isolation from other media. My interest, though, is in following the drift of the genre in film, a large enough task for one book. To attempt to include, say, the hard-boiled school of fiction or the enormous number of crime comics in the discussion would be to complicate matters unduly and nearly double the length of the book. (Moreover, access to the relevant pulp fiction and comic books is by no means easy.) This material is complementary and would no doubt prove mutually illuminating, but it merits a separate inquiry. The protean, unruly nature of the genre, besides, is never more apparent than when we observe its treatment in various media. It conforms to both appropriate and necessary contexts of production, materials, audience, and morality.

Thus, to take one example for illustration, the depiction given of Pretty Boy Floyd as a brutal psychopath reveling in sadistic violence in the Fawcett Publications' 1948 comic book one-shot entitled *On the Spot* could not then have been the attitude adopted by a movie biography of Floyd. It would have been modified and softened considerably, the violence kept proportionately in balance with a characterization developed through social/personal relationships. Interestingly enough, the 1970 movie *A Bullet for Pretty Boy* and the 1974 made-for-TV movie *Pretty Boy Floyd* show the figure as a warmhearted, misunderstood boy forced reluctantly into crime. One cannot study the minutiae of these interrelationships idly or parenthetically. It is not from lack of interest that they are excluded from this book. To limit oneself to a perception of a genre as it evolves in one medium and cohabits with the mores, speech, feelings, and general concerns of a society through several decades of time is a necessary confinement if one hopes to get anything done at all.

In preparing the bibliography, I was surprised to find that so little has been written about so important a body of films and that individual films, especially, have been neglected to such a sad degree. Discounting a stray paragraph or sentence here and there, my writing is the only sustained work done on *The Public Enemy, High Sierra, Kiss of Death, Force of Evil, D.O.A., White Heat, 99 River Street,* and *The Brothers Rico.* Several of the other films I treat are represented by one sometimes inadequate essay apiece. The lack of critical acknowledgment of so many rich films helped determine my focus, but that still left me with the problem of which films could best serve as paradigms of the genre's range and achievement. The genre is, of course, more diversified than my small selection of films for analysis may unwittingly imply. Nonetheless, my choices followed from a desire to show the genre's variety and versatility in its curvy, bumpy route over half a century of time. A films and B films, films celebrated and films *maudit*, classic films that had to be written on and curiosities that otherwise seemed destined to a premature oblivion, each a serviceable index to the directions the genre was taking at the time of its release, and each proving substantial upon reviewing.

I'd like first to thank—if it can be done unfacetiously—the city of New York, whose many theaters and movie-saturated TV programming allowed for a youth (some would say) misspent gorging happily on these films and countless others. I'd also like to thank everyone who has done his bit to keep me honest on this subject: several of my English Department colleagues at the University of Massachusetts, Amherst, and mainly my students, who provided the interest, support, and intellectual challenges that made this study possible. Special thanks to Professor Charles Eidsvik for ideas on *D.O.A.* and to Les Perlman for spotting additional Christological references in *Kiss of Death*. To my wife Carol I owe many debts—intellectual and otherwise—that go beyond what words can say.

Preface to the Second Edition

Back in 1973, around the time pursuit of theory was promising a purge of our critical sins—privileged interpretations, unacknowledged subjectivity, a toothless pluralism, watery logic, myopic burrowing, and a naive indolence in tracking the inevitable presence and diffusion of cultural forces—was when I first began writing about these "underworld" films that seemed, by and large, to be of a piece, often telling the same story for the same purpose with different "replacement" surfaces. I did so with some trepidation, as the rising young stars of academia were busy "getting at" works and movements and history with some new and critically glittering artillery—a cadre of young, excitable Turks brandishing procedures and assumptions like cutlasses; the uninitiated, at best uninstructed and at worst recalcitrant, remained, thanks to tenure, immovably there, identifiably dowdy and frumpy, clutching frayed manila folders, inside which lay a lifetime of now discredited notions fading and flaking. And so, feeling unprepared to launch an entire book without the rudiments of what currently was being embraced as the last words in critical sophistication, I set about getting some of the material under my belt. By the time I thought to bring it as far up as my brain, I had decided that under my belt was probably the best place for it. Well-meaning advocacy from disparate sites couldn't dispel my accelerating fear that those continental waters were too murky and chilly to swim in. I didn't see any point in trying my hand at writing so rapt as to forego being understood and which manufactured additional obfuscating jargon whenever it pleased, as though showing off a nimble intellect was what this newfangled logorrhea was all about. Writing is hard enough, and mine faulty enough, not to need assistance toward a more thorough incomprehensibility—plenty of that had gushed forth already, and even the "good" writing was so formidably arcane that I couldn't see any pedagogical payoff either. The initial concern over exposing professional shortsightedness and imprecision has, not surprisingly, subsided, and the zealous rainbow visions of a critical promised land have turned disappointingly monochrome. For a while, it seemed like a matter of life and death for the critical *arriere-garde* (or, at the least, some ill-conceived hiring and firing). Here was a fresh horde of barbarians at the gate; there was headhunting and caterwauling, and there were bench-clearing brawls. All that seems on the wane and critical writing is once again less severe and more versatile, and that is good, though irate professors can be very entertaining.

Dreams and Dead Ends, in that context, was surprisingly well received. There was some chiding of its limitations—critical looseness, a shying away from theoretical challenges, leaky categories, indiscreet enthusiasms—though many reviews didn't seem to mind any of that. (If there were some things wrong with the book, there must also have been more than a few things right with it—hence its current resurrection.) One expected point of debate was over the accommodatingly huge umbrella I had constructed for the genre. The definition was too broad, letting in all sorts of questionable films. I had foisted too many illegitimate children on the mother genre, more than she could handle. The reader was forced to proceed bereft of that most welcome of critical companions, clarity. In 1973, it now becomes clear, I was struck by all the similarities, even the most far-flung, between the gangster, cop, and noir cycles, all the ways in which they touched base and seemed to be expressing mutual (if different-natured) critiques of society and its institutions. Of late, it is the differences that strike me as perhaps more interesting, and I'll let that unexpected "fact" serve as a starting point for this reissue.

I'm not talking a turnaround here that negates what I wrote in 1973. If anything, these unshared qualities make for even more thoroughly cemented "connections," in the sense that the heads and tails of coins have remarkable differences, yet are strongly bonded materially and symbolically. If the ease with which we travel and "click in" to links on the Internet has shown us anything it is that everything is, or could be, connected, and that isolated disciplines can supply only a frail account of the meaning, range, and effect of whatever it is they may be holding under scrutiny. Not until all the disciplines have established their way of understanding text and context of any given work can we really feel how much elasticity, how much stretch, can be brought into play. These, then, are additional remarks not aiming to expunge the blunders of my youth, nor to expose the lazy contradictions of floppy-minded dotage. I aim merely to get the coin, lying flat so many years, turning again. Reissues cannot help being reconsiderations.[1]

If we say reissues are opportunities to present material that has been reconsidered, it sounds like something hardly worth saying. But in preparing this edition, I realized it was an important distinction to make. The 1977 *Dreams and Dead Ends* grew out of what seemed like considerations triggered by conversations with colleagues, friends and family, and countless students (who weren't shy about telling me which films still had plenty of pop to them and what that pop consisted of) over years of teaching. This time around was clearly different: I was having conversations with *myself*, that other, younger (and probably more foolish) person who wrote this book. It was a strange feeling to write as if I were interpreting, explaining, cautioning, commiserating, or otherwise chatting with the author, noting what ideas and opinions we still had in common or what needed refining or correcting or dumping. Conversations with myself is what the new writing I've added *felt* like, anyway, whatever its value might be for another reader. So if certain pages sometimes seem to be going over the same material, that's just my attempt to clarify or expand what was left too sketchy in my original comments. For the record, the additional material generally supports the positions taken twenty-plus years ago. Some quibbling, yes, some instances of "I beg to differ" but hardly any of "get out of town," and nothing requiring a prior tarring and feathering. The films described and assessed and evaluated remain as compelling as ever.

Assessment and evaluation both are two-way streets. The films of the last twenty-nine or so years shed light on their predecessors, and they in turn help clarify our contemporary fare. There is change but also continuity. Some emphases are dictated by technological advances in the medium (no film *looks* like those exemplary productions of the past). What is curious to see in the gangster/crime film is that most of its key scenes and pivots and formal patterns have survived, but only because they have withstood increasing intensifications.

The early gangster-crime films display, until the encroachment of *noir*, with its more variegated criminal types and societies, an easily readable curve. The gangster's life is noisy but short. As soon as he gets to the top, he gets to confront an inexplicable (to him) death. Then G-men and the like chase him and destroy him. By the late 1930s he becomes something of an endangered species and we grow a bit misty-eyed at his extinction, but we understand that *he* understands the nobility of gestures that make him our superior—in essence, if not earthly fortune. Transformed, he rises to a better place than our mean earth. And that's it. The figure is keyed exactly to our social history, most tightly to Prohibition, and the arrival and departure of the Depression. As the economy rebounds in preparation for the war against fascism, the gangster is forgiven, his brutal skills suddenly assets in a unified patriotic fervor, ready to use any means to preserve the zenith of civilized government—a cherished democracy. In war, it's pretty easy to know what to do; peace, on the other hand, can easily be a worrisome, now-what-do-I-do? state, especially if you're out of work, there's a recession, and the girl you used to date has your old job. With *noir*, the branching begins, and with it, surfaces and depths more difficult to read. And it never eases up, for as more and more films continue to articulate the milieu, iconography, and obligatory emphases of this genre, a thick, complex layering results, strange attitudes evolve, and unpredictable qualities enter into the mix. The final chapter tries to get a grip on all that, but for now, at points embarrassingly intact, here is *Dreams and Dead Ends* (following two new short essays), as it first came out in 1977.

Acknowledgments

First, a deep-breath release of thanks to the merry-go-round of editors who helped give this work new life—Elissa Morris and Jeremy Lewis above all, both of whom put me on a less zig-zag course and prevented additional waywardness. Jeremy Lewis, in particular, kept close watch on an admittedly over-eager style, one that required some timely chastening. I, of course, must take the blame for any incorrigibly unexpungeable blemishes remaining, either from having gone undetected or by obdurate override. Thanks also to Christine Sanmartin at MIT Press for her tireless responses to my mostly dumb questions and for engineering a smooth and gracious transfer of rights to OUP. Prompt last-minute help in procuring stills and permissions was provided by Mary Corliss, curator of the Film Stills Archive at the Museum of Modern Art in New York City.

Contents

Dreams & Dead Ends

Introduction (1977/2001 — Still Going Strong)

Gangster/crime films continue to be made and hold their own in the marketplace. The genre remains a viable framework for getting something important said. Its basic material continues to attract talented people who give it expressive force and creative shape. Its durability attests to its cultural importance. The genre has survived because the issues it addresses have always been central to the American experience, because its formal properties have given them a clarity of outline and lucidity of exposition, and because it has been infinitely flexible in adapting itself to shifting social and cultural conditions. It has played an important role in both forming and reflecting the American imagination.

Despite the excellence and popularity of its films, the genre has been generally held in low esteem. Critics and reviewers, high of tone and brow, have in the main been hostile. Even within the industry, until very recently, its prestige has not run parallel to its proven effectiveness. The reaction seems illogical. It is perhaps the danger of the gangster/crime film that has enforced a defensive distance and a refusal to acknowledge it. It has been troubled by censorship, a sure sign that people have been afraid of what it aims to accomplish and of its power.

The gangster/crime film is a genre like pornography and the horror film, held in contempt socially and intellectually not because it may corrupt and not because it is artistically inferior to other kinds of film but because it realizes our dreams, exposes our deepest psychic urges. Its imperative has been, as well, to stick close to the tawdry, unpleasant, ugly aspects of American life. Shunned by critics for its cheap-thrill sensationalism and muzzled by the industry's sparing financial support, its resiliency is instructive. The genre speaks not merely to our fascination/repulsion with aspects of our socioeconomic milieu that we prefer to shut our eyes to but also to our fascination/repulsion with the most haunting depths of ourselves. We tend to disown and discredit its films because to deal with them means facing those contradictions in ourselves that we evade by our adherence to social norms and to appeasing self- and national conceptions. We sense, instinctively, the threat they pose, and for half a century they have been rated an invisible "X" in our consciousness. While it may be true that individual films in the genre offer differing perspectives on American life, ranging from the explicitly apologetic to the harshly critical, the genre as a whole depicts America as a place of perpetual and violent conflict. It is always sinking its teeth into matters most other "entertainment" films gloss over or relegate to a safe historical past.

The gangster is a paradigm of the American dream. The gangster film is a vehicle that responds to our wish to have our dreams made visible to us in a form that retains their dreamlike qualities but contains a narrative that is the living dream of its hero who makes it happen, actualizes it. One can never be entirely certain about the precise analogies between films and dreams, but the condition of presence-in-absence is common to them both. It is our psyche that we watch—displaced, dislocated, alien yet familiar. Our involvement with the gangster rests on our identification with him as the archetypal American dreamer whose actions and behavior involve a living out of the dream common to most everyone who exists in the particular configurations and contradictions of American society, a dream in conflict with the society.[1] The gangster's death is a rude awakening. The world closes in; we see it close in. We can back away, break the identification pattern. But this does not mean the dream ends. It continues from film to film because all the films can ever do is return us back to our world, and we want to live the dream again and again because our ambivalence toward society's restrictions has become psychologically deep-rooted.

The genre may be defined by what its succession of films continuously expresses, and films may be generically aligned by determining whether their structures contain the possibility of that expression. The nature of what the gangster/crime film expresses will be argued throughout, but it may be useful at this point to provide the broad outlines of a theory. The gangster/crime film has a structure ready-made for certain kinds of concerns. Inherent to the genre's structuring and patterning are the following:

1. A man, a woman, or a group in opposition to the society. The term *versus* is built into the genre. Every instance of the genre poses an opposition, the conflict it gives rise to, and, by extension, the likelihood of violence. (The precise nature of the conflict, the ground on which it takes place, the location of opposing forces, the attitudes, values, and statements it provokes shift unceasingly from 1930 to the present. Observing the shifts illumines our history, psychology, and the aesthetics of film.)

2. That the conflict is societal—pivots around what people are and do in relation to society—is a given (although both society and its opponents may be used metaphorically and be taken to another plane of argument). The gangster is not the same as an outlaw; he specifically violates a system of rules that a group of people lives under. He is a product of an advanced, urban civilization. In westerns, by contrast, the conflict is often outside the realm of a social system as such, although it may bear upon it. It concerns the individual versus the land, or civilized versus uncivilized forces. In the gangster/crime film meanings emerge, whether deliberately or not, about the nature of the society and the kind of individual it creates. By definition, the genre must shed light on either the society or the outcasts who oppose it, and by definition the gangster is outside, or anti-, the legitimate social order. The gangster/crime film is

therefore a way of gaining a perspective on society by creating worlds and figures that are outside it. Its basic situation holds that distinction, and the meanings it continues to produce rest on that distinction. (In the thirties, the distinction is clear-cut, unquestionable, visible. As the genre evolves, it becomes less so. As a culture becomes more complex, so do its products.)

3. The gangster film was generated by the historical appearance of the gangster, but it rapidly became a metaphor.[2] Whether the gangster film was actually suppressed after *Scarface* (1932), or whether it simply became no longer profitable or pertinent to continue the model established by *Little Caesar* (1930), is a moot point. What is more important is that its structure, which manifests distinctions between insider and outsider (however each is defined), survived and is still highly serviceable. This structure makes it possible to handle virtually anything the culture is concerned or distressed about. The genre can particularize, through the contrast, comparison, analogy, and juxtaposition of characters and milieu on the inside with those on the outside, numerous issues and concerns (communism, mental abnormality, nuclear anxieties, the role of women). Usually, but not always, it is the gangster as such that is utilized. If there is a problem the society is worried about or a fantasy it is ready to support, odds are it can be located in the gangster. To take what's within and place it without is to create a context for observing it with a minimum of interfering clutter, and the gangster, by definition, is "without."

4. Most of us are law-abiding citizens who conduct our lives legitimately. Normally, few opportunities are extended that would help us gain perspective or insight into the nature of our lives, our law-abidingness and legitimacy. We remain busily—or even lazily—in the thick of existence, where the clearest view of any number of things is prohibited. It is necessary to get outside our life, our culture, our society, to see it. The gangster/crime film looks at a world that is opposed to legitimate society. Focusing there, it can make discoveries not possible from within, make us see things that would otherwise be hard to see. It locates an *under*world, a world beneath the surface, and shows it to us—a literal embodiment of those things that exist but are difficult to see in American life. It makes visual what is not visual; it gives us a picture of our world in microcosm. Its stylizations and contrasts play off meaningfully against the sense of the world we bring to the theater. (From the late 1950s on, the underworld becomes less visually and conceptually specifiable as it is shown merging into the world at large. What were formerly used as conventions that signified qualities in opposition to the macrocosm are either dropped or transformed. Replacing them are new conventions that thematically revolve around the difficulty of perceiving the differences.)

The above are offered as proposals of generic requirements. They are the ingrained factors of the gangster/crime film's operation, that which its structure and situation inevitably express. This does not mean that the genre is restricted to these concerns. What the genre *can* do is not the same as what it habitually appears to do. It becomes, as a problem of definition, a matter of proportion. For example, certain films in the genre may be interested more in love relationships between men and women, but their primary functions cannot be overridden by a disproportionate attention to love relationships. The gangster/crime film may contain a love story, but for the most subtle exploration of the emotions surrounding love, we must seek out another kind of film.

The genre is partial to certain explicit and implicit themes and issues that are not exclusive to it but that are well suited to be carried by its structure. The list that follows isolates what I consider prominent matters and is not meant to be exhaustive. The concluding item is a brief digression on the political aspects of the genre.

1. Central to the thematic substratum of the gangster/crime film is its exposition of two fundamental and opposing American ideologies. There is an inherent contradiction in American thought between America as a land of opportunity and the vision of a classless, democratic society. Both beliefs are deeply held, and the contradiction cannot be resolved. It's fine to get ahead, but it's wrong to get ahead. It's good to be an individual, but then you're set apart from others. The gangster is a vehicle to expose this central problem of the American people.

2. The most apparent surface manifestation of this theme is the notion of success—the urge for it, the fear of it, the consequences that both having it and not having it entail. The theme of success is perhaps the most insistent in American cinema, a cinema that reflects, whether it means to or not, this crucial dilemma of a capitalist democracy. The illusion of unlimited possibility for achieving wealth and position (power) and the culture's inducement of individual triumph create severe moral and psychological strains. The gangster film contains the clearest exposition of this disturbance, the extremities of success and failure—exhilarating, top-of-the-heap life and brutal death—being its (initial) stock in trade. The gangster's continued popularity and his transformation from a figure reasonably close to historical actuality to a near-mythic condensation of forces is a sign of an entrenched moral/ethical confusion of the culture.

American films tend to show self-advancement as an explicit or implicit criminal process. The gangster functions as the scapegoat for such desire. The equation of crime and business (a common motif) further supports the view that crime films are often disguised parables of social mobility as a punishable deviation from one's assigned place. The American cinema is one of unrelieved class conflict, infinitely covert and less clearheaded in comparison to the revolution genre of the early Russian cinema but of equal importance.

Class conflicts are demonstrated but are usually either salved by apology or obscured by melodramatic solutions—the killing or court conviction of the monstrous emblem of the capitalist, the gangster. Ideological anxieties are transferred to emotional/dramatic planes and thus prevented from leading to a logical criticism. The gangster doesn't suffer guilt or second thoughts, because there is no disjunction between what he professes to be and what he is and does. We know why he must die—he kills people.[3]

3. The majority of gangster/crime films make implicit commentary on the nature and power of cities. The city rarely plays a neutral role; it is generally seen as a virulent environment. To choose it as one's base of operations is to make a fatal choice, and since the gangster always comes there (or being there, either cannot or chooses not to leave it), the city is pictured as the end of the line. The darkest westerns are invariably about the closing of the frontier. All gangster films are set in the period when the frontier has long been closed, and all possibilities for heroic progress but one—making it in the city—have shriveled away. The city, with its cramped, explosive life, becomes the arena to work out one's ambitions and test one's ability. In the spacious landscapes of the western, decisions become of immense moral and psychological importance because they make a difference. One can always move on somewhere else—another state, "up North"; the world and society are still in the process of becoming. Staying and moving are real options, and the choice signifies a frame of mind (usually constructive) instrumental to the reordering of the status quo. The city, however, the creation of industrial man, is often seen as a place beyond the control of its inhabitants, a place that imposes its own harsh will. It beckons and destroys. As the place where *things happen*, it draws whoever dreams of making it big into its dangerous labyrinths and claims them all as victims. The city is the broadest icon of the gangster film, and it is a death trap (the dominant impression over hundreds of films is of the termination of set after set of expendable lives in rapid turnover). It is the seat of large-scale crime and violent death. Moral choice is an illusion because the city is a prison. As it evolves, the gangster/crime film extends its prison metaphor to include everything. The society as a whole, and not just cities where gangsters tend to congregate, is a prison. *High Sierra* (1941) provides the strongest visual representation. The wide expanses of space through which Roy Earle races his car toward a dead end are an illusion. The beautiful, open country promises freedom, but there is none left to give. Nor can all the hectic crossing of state lines alter the fate of Bonnie and Clyde.

4. So much has been written about violence that one is loath to raise the issue once again, but there is no doubt that one of the genre's keenest pleasures is in its depiction of violence. Obviously, one can abhor violence in principle and still enjoy gangster/crime films. The genre has been taken to task for its

profit-minded emphasis on violence, but the subject unarguably demands that violence be portrayed, often extensively, and it must be remembered that movies are a mass art not primarily designed for a refined audience with an intellectually humanist bias. Movies enforce a closer, more face-to-face encounter with violence than any other medium in history (except perhaps some recent theater and shows the Romans are reputed to have put on), and the gangster film is the most violent of genres. The conventions of screen violence are controlled by what the society will accept in kind and degree, although industry trial balloons may create new appetites. Each period of the genre (for a complex of reasons) has sought to intensify, refashion, embellish, and make more vivid its drawing card of violence. From the late sixties on, in a permissive climate, violence has escalated to an extreme. Whereas in the past violence was used to punctuate and heighten the story line, in a film like John Milius's *Dillinger* (1973) a minimum of narrative intrudes upon and barely holds together a continuous violence. The brutalization of the audience, which took on systematic form in the 1950s, has detached itself from urgent content and become an aesthetic factor with its own logic of communication. It has become the genre's core experience, and its ultimate statement.

Since the genre seems to have run its course in "explaining" the underworld, and since the analogies between the nature of underworld goals and power with those of business can no longer be put in opposition—having been gradually visualized as undifferentiated—audiences appear to want the gangster/crime film to unleash the full force of its violence, as if that were the one basic truth it had left to express and the only meaningful statement that can be made about power to the powerless. Granting its commercial motivations (all feature films hope to make money), the present onslaught of screen violence is not gratuitous when seen as part of the development of the genre. The genre has evolved to this method of persuasion and articulation; it is its response to the deepening currents of pessimism within the society. As *Little Caesar* did many years ago, the genre is still discovering ways to speak to its audience's desires.

5. A common theme of the gangster/crime film is the disintegration and destruction of the family, and on occasion the substitution of a "false" family (the gang, and especially the syndicate, which resembles large corporations and institutions in its unfeeling attitude toward its own members). Gangsters often have wives, brothers, sisters, nieces, and mothers but (almost) never fathers. Fathers are simply not mentioned, or we are told they died long ago. The idea of rejecting the father runs through much American art; it can only be briefly touched on here. Put simply, the son has to kill the father to become his own man. The father represents the past, the old world, Europe. He has nothing to say and nothing to do in the dynamic progress of America; he is in the

way. The hero's mobility must be untrammeled; he must prove himself an *American* by dealing successfully with the emerging realities of modern American life. Films register the dangers of this rootless individualism that turns its back on all the values of the past by incorporating, in the forties, the figure of the psychiatrist. He is sometimes ridiculed and made ominous, but his presence signifies both the awareness and the fear that things have gotten out of control. He steps in as the father figure, a means of bringing an order to human life. The need to push the father away has put an enormous burden on the self. Relief is necessary, hence the hero's marked proclivity toward substitute fathers. The mother is usually the icon of the family and of its troubles and distress. She is ineffectual and typically ignored or overpowered by the son-hero. (Interestingly, in Roger Corman's *Bloody Mama* [1970]—a title that suggests women as feared menstrual creatures—Ma Barker's sons want to kill the mother but aggress against others because that is impossible. At the end, Herman even points the gun at Kate, but then turns it around and uses it upon himself. Kate orders them to kill a middle-aged man, their captive, whose blue eyes remind the sons of their father, and they refuse. The reversal is significant in a feminist climate.)

6. Attitudes toward the police and law enforcement agencies in general vary considerably, but the virtual absence of police in many films creates nasty implications. Even in films that celebrate law enforcement, there are strong undercurrents of corruption and brutality. As the gangster's opponents, the police are generally colorless and/or unsympathetic. It is a given that the police cannot stop the gangster from getting to the top or the syndicate from being powerfully, and nationally, organized. Their function is rarely preventive. They fail to anticipate; they must hunt and catch, or kill. Flaherty corners Rico (in *Little Caesar*) only at the end, after all the damage has been done and when the character, down and out, has no reason to live. He does Rico a favor by raising his mettle.

Both gangster and cop abide by codes that are neither logical nor philosophical. They draw hard lines of antagonism from their respective imperatives, and the combination of iron commitment and personal initiative results in a deadlock usually resolved by the gangster's death or capture (a concession to morality). The gangster's lifestyle induces in the restricted, underpaid cop feelings of impotence, frustration, fatigue, and impatience and creates the desire for revenge (sometimes sharpened by envy) as well as for justice. The automatic opposition is fatalistic. Neither cop nor gangster can become other than what they are, despite, as in later films, the human resemblance. Don Siegel's *The Line-Up* (1958) is keyed to the character Julian's maxim: "Crime is aggressive. So is the law." This is offered as both fact and explanation, and it has nothing to do with moral positions or separate poles of belief. A violent pre-credit set piece uses a dolly-in to a dead cop. It is the death of one of their own that gives motive and resolution to Lieutenant Guthrie and Inspector Quine. The police routines they go through have no public dimension at all. There isn't the slightest mention of the evils of heroin. Admittedly, the film is an extreme version of this view, but it is pertinent to the genre as a whole.

Ultimately, generalizations are inadequate for this matter. The question of how police are presented in the genre must be individually treated since each film displays differences, however minute. As with other aspects of the genre, one needs, for example, to make the large distinction whether the depiction of the police is part of an attempt to reflect reality or whether it is dominated by other—moral, aesthetic, or human—concerns. The difficulties of adequate assessment may be represented by the following example. The identical insert of a police dragnet appears in *He Walked by Night* (1948), *Gun Crazy* (1949), and *The Big Combo* (1955), but it conveys different meanings and feelings in each case that are determined by the general context of the film and the immediate context of what precedes and follows the insert.

7. The politics of the genre is a very murky area that needs precise investigation. Roughly speaking, I find that the bias of the 1930s is toward the left, of the 1950s toward the right, and that the contemporary period, after a very brief flourish of revolutionary idealism in the late 1960s, is by and large conservative. The wary cynicism of the 1940s seems to extend into politics, and I sense no clear trend there. These distinctions must be understood as vague indeed; more explicit studies may, in fact, find them totally wrongheaded. The problem is that the tendency of American films is either to play naive or suppress political dimensions. Political *issues* aren't raised. Although all kinds of cinema are informed by politics, we have no tradition of a political cinema. The films register what is felt as insidious in any period, or their action subtly supports the existing ideology. One thing is certain: the genre offers no alternative to the American way of life. America's political, social, and economic flaws are not hidden, but the system, in principle, is never seriously argued with. Upper-middle-class, middle-class, or working-class heroes continue in the same system after convulsing it. In the end, they act on behalf of its *ideal* nature. If it could only work the way it is supposed to, there would be no problems. When it doesn't work the way it is supposed to, or working as it should it produces more ill than good, then one must either force it to work right or accept its imperfections as less ruinous to the conduct of life than those of other systems.

One valuable result of studying the nature and development of a particular genre is that one is forced to perceive, as well, the evolution of the medium as a narrative form. Since they go hand in hand, one makes discoveries about two things at once. One might say that discoveries arise from the circumstance of a localized attention and that by observing changes in the genre the functionality of developments in the medium assumes a degree of specificity it might not attain in a wider context of critical investigation. I have kept in mind throughout the necessity of integrating assumptions of form and technique with assumptions of content. What is being said is never static and is always seeking the proper way of saying it. Cinema-television still remains the last stronghold of the narrative tradition (excluding perhaps the denigrated practice of popular fiction and comic books), but, as a study of the genre shows, even the commercial feature film has come a long way toward matching the self-involved sophistication of the other, more "advanced" arts. Through the examination of a film genre one is made aware, almost of necessity, of what happens to *film*.

While the other arts were, each in its own way, groping toward modernism, which involved making a clean break from the past, the movies transferred to a new medium the traditional emphases that were impeding the progress of other arts—the classical perspective and figure grouping of paintings, the storytelling of narrative fiction, theatrical acting styles and naturalistic decor. For the general public, the innovation of the medium itself made for a fascinating reprise of the kinds of pictures and human behavior they liked to see and the stories they liked to be told. The technology was novel and intricate, but the content it communicated was, if anything, simplified. This is not the place to go into the explanations that have been given as to why the movies took on what the other arts abandoned. One suspects, in addition, though, a deeper logic: the movies could not enter into modernism without first undergoing an encapsulated version of the development of the other, long-established arts. At any rate, early attempts to bring film into the ongoing activity of modernism (the work of Richter, Eggeling, and Leger, for example) did not prevent the dominance of the commercial feature film, and it is only recently that movies have projected a noticeable sense that they can no longer assume a stance of artistic innocence, that their strategies must proceed from a knowledge about themselves, that each film must announce a reason for its being and an awareness about its nature and procedures. An overview of the gangster/crime film shows, with some inevitable differences, an approximation of the development of other arts. The genre's phases parallel, in abbreviated fashion, the periods through which literature, painting, and music progressed.

Little Caesar (1930)—rigid, reserved, formally elegant—and *The Public Enemy* (1931)—more seasoned, slightly warmer, less severely constructed, more tonally flexible—epitomize the spectrum of the early classicism. The genre then turns lyrical, romantic, and sentimental with films like *The Roaring Twenties* (1930) and *High Sierra* (1941). The range broadens, the construction is looser, and these films take their time. The rhythms are less formalized and impatient; they adapt to the need of savoring human emotions. These films strike an indulgent, expansive note in comparison with their predecessors. With *film noir* (*The Killers* [1946], *T-Men* [1947], *He Walked by Night* [1948]) we get the beginnings of modernism—a refined technique, a disenchanted irony, self-conscious creation of filmic worlds, a metaphorical level of action, a greater degree of compositional abstraction, a photographic virtuosity with light and shadow that calls specific attention to itself as a *tour de force* (as in the remarkable conclusion of *He Walked by Night*), and an increased philosophical flavor and control (perhaps caused by the indirect impact of existentialism), as in, most notably, the metaphysical pessimism of Robert Siodmak's *Criss Cross* (1949). The claim for an incipient modernist phase is also supported by the marked attention to style. Style itself becomes a value; when all else fails, it must assume the burden of establishing a meaning to existence and to art. (In *noir* revisited movies like Roman Polanski's *Chinatown* [1974] and Arthur Penn's *Night Moves* [1975], lifestyle and film style are coordinates of a more overt metaphysics, as could be expected when an extra layer of self-consciousness is superimposed on an already self-conscious mode.) The expressionist style of *noir* is, in the 1950s crime film, joined to a moral dynamism and an emotional primitivity to produce an intense paradox of style clashing with and outdistancing content, until this conflicting way of feeling the world burns itself out and the paradox is resolved by truly modernist films like *Point Blank* (1967). *Point Blank* invites our investigation of it as a text; it is a film whose identity is determined by the necessity of acknowledging its conventions as conventions and by using them as a formal means of articulation. This does not mean that the film is stripped of the content usually carried by conventions; rather, the typical content is subsumed under the self-referring attitude to produce a new content that transfers the force and purpose of thematic meanings to aesthetic ones.

The genre may of course satisfy many kinds of interests, some of them so idiosyncratic as to be beyond any one critic's ken or research possibilities. Cultists and fetishists of various persuasions may discover numerous special thrills the majority of people may remain inert to. The mere travelogue aspects of the genre—the underworld as a place of fascination, with fascinating local inhabitants; the anxiety and excitement of this milieu and the behavior it generates and requires—may be a major source of appeal. Some may find the tough-talk–tough-gesture repertoire of tough guys and flinty dames irresistible. The underworld has a look, shape, and texture peculiar to itself, and paraphernalia (cars, clothes, guns) and settings (nightclubs, city streets, nocturnal asphalt, concrete, and neon) that may exert an independent delight. I believe, though, that however powerful and stimulating these ingredients may be, the most interesting and important aspects of the genre do not lie on so surface a level. The genre itself rather quickly exhausts a direct interest in documenting the gangster and his world. The history of the genre I am most concerned with is the history of the *uses* to which the gangster figure, and his milieu, have been put.

How the gangster is conceived, or what he wants, varies from film to film and corresponds to what the culture needs to have expressed at any given time. The gangster is a creature who wants, and though he shares this trait with characters in other genres, the degree of his compulsion is probably unique. (In certain films—*The Killers* [1946], for example—it almost doesn't matter what he wants; it's *that* he wants that is important.) In *Machine-Gun Kelly* (1958) the gangster wants to achieve a self-respect and dignity that the film says is impossible for him. In *High Sierra* (1941) the gangster has the dignity and wants only to be able to live a simple, decent life. The film says *that* is impossible. (As a rule, the gangster cannot have what he wants. When he gets what he wants, his success is paradoxically a downfall of another kind.) The point, though, is that there is no way that either film can be received as an analysis of an actual gangster's actual way of life. Our interest is not, as it is in the early films, in being informed of how gangsters operate, what they look like, or in a literal depiction of their criminality.

The genre today (2002) continues potent, but where it's coming from and how it goes about its business is a freewheeling, hit-and-run, different-each-time affair that lacks the expected presence and distribution of generic traits we are accustomed to taking in through eye and ear. All kinds of gangster/crime films coexist, infringe, overlap, and mix it up, making it harder than ever to bestow upon them a reliable definition, one both accurate and comprehensive. One might wisely forego the effort, just accept and enjoy the variety. But the genre both gimps and gallops on, often revitalized by particular films, and some thoughts on how and why its formulaic patterns persist seem in order. It has certainly not been idle, and its features remain generally recognizable. *Dreams and Dead Ends* closed (in 1977) with a few suggestions about where these kinds of films were heading. It claimed that the gangster/crime film went through, only in accelerated fashion, the various stages of literary history and was left with an open field to cavort in, with styles and approaches ranging from the self-consciously naive to the self-consciously sophisticated and post-modern. Anything goes. A safe enough prediction, as it could hardly have avoided doing that. Like many kinds of films, it has gone international, relaxed its generic borders and requirements, rested securely on its traditions, made its peace with television and video, and attracted new talent that would revitalize its gestural and iconographic storehouse.

The chance to make a second stab at what the jumble of possibilities for defining the gangster/crime film can be boiled down to was instructive. It began to look like there were contrasting plots and passions coming from all over the place, and without any interest in converging; imaginations ignite from diverse, and sometimes unknowable, causes, from cloud nine happiness to hellhole misery. It is clear that the gangster figure ranks high among icons of ambivalence in American culture. His alluring criminality, capitalist pluck, manly fearlessness, emotional simplicity, oversized ego, childlike trust, glee, cluelessness, and eventual downfall (often marked by both pathos and tragedy) have combined to keep him in cinematic view some three-quarters of a century. How could he not have been fascinating given the incessant counterpoint of negative and positive traits that make up his screen identity? Whatever he is shown to abstractly stand for is always seriously altered and compromised by what we see him do: kill people. That's the bottom line, the line that cannot be crossed, and just about always is. When and where this happens is usually a reliable index of what the film wants us to feel or understand.

In the twenty-first century the genre seems temporarily suspended, cut off from its ancient source (Prohibition) of nurture. The Little Caesar type of troublemaker has been absorbed into the culture and replaced by once marginal aberrations: serial killers, psychopaths, drug gangs, outlaw couples, overworked cops with families. Somewhere along that sort of spectrum may be found what the genre wants to say to us, or be for us. But since it can be whatever the genre in the past has been, and what it could additionally come to be, in any combination, a critical grasp of it is tough. (Yet in trying to cope with the genre's present protean unpredictability, a comforting thought arrived: *It's much more interesting to get lost than to know exactly where you are and how you got there.* Perhaps the truth about criticism, the routes it takes to discovery, lies in its outtakes. And that experience of criticism, whereby it becomes a process not of recording what you know but rather something like a "live report" of something you are about to know. All those cherishable flubbed notes and false starts that we get to know in Charlie Parker's alternate takes, or those shocking miss-hits by which astonishing tennis pros reveal their mere mortality.)

The hard-nosed lyricism of *Point Blank* and the embittered nostalgia of *The Godfather* and *The Godfather II* ran the spectrum of the genre's output at the time of their release. In retrospect, Coppola's reach and passion, and his complex grasp of the material, are impressive, and the first two parts of his family saga seem less sentimental and softheaded than when they were first released. They share some common ground with *Point Blank*. Walker, for all his brutality, is something of a hero in his battle against anonymous corporate crime, so legitimized and ordinary that it scarcely sees itself as criminal. *Point Blank* no longer feels like the antithesis, or even the distant cousin, of the Corleones' weddings and funerals. Walker annexes our energies in his futile quest for justice. The single-minded intensity with which he rights wrongs is gripping and even terrifying, but we support all his annihilation of the facades and hypocrites, even as we feel it come to naught in the film's cryptic conclusion. In the Godfather films the appreciation for family loyalties and rituals and respect for honorable dealing begins to seriously sag under the weight of an enveloping pessimism. These films depend, as well, on an escalation and fresh applications of violence. Such intensification is crucial to the survival of the genre, as it always has been, but films like these and *Bonnie and Clyde* raised the stakes considerably and made a mainstay of this level of violence.

Most of the differences between the films of 1929 to 1959 and those from 1960 to the present are changes of degree rather than kind, and that includes the idea of criminality as a form of madness. *Film noir* gave us a slew of psychopaths, and there continues to be a very high count in 2002. The difference?—the newer ones are more horrible. The broadness of the genre allows all kinds of opportunity for all kinds of mental irregulars to run amok. The early gangsters are made demented by having a screw or two too tight (inflexibility both helping a rapid rise to the top and hastening their downfall; their *noir* successors have the more traditional "screw loose" and a far greater range of aberration). It's within the *noir* phase that the crazy individual gets permanently inscribed in the genre, never to disappear. One is hard put to think of any film within the category (since 1945) that isn't enlivened by one or another psycho. The deranged person (male, as a rule) as staple indicates an apparently fixed component of existence. Without fail, we can expect him to make some kind of contribution to what's going on. At times, indeed, society seems like a large psycho ward and is literally so in M-G-M's (!) *High Wall* (1947), some of which takes place in a mental institution that seems to house a multitude of incurable zanies, among which the likes of *D.O.A.*'s Chester and *Kiss of Death*'s Tommy Udo might easily be imagined strolling about while exchanging psychotic growls and grunts. Madness is emblematic of reality's core. It represents the human enigma.

The crazy person's graph does not resemble the gangster's. We can't note any real advance or rise. Criminals of every kind battle treadmill repetitions of their psychotic traits; trapped in circles of frustrated frenzy, they cannot go backward or forward or up or down. Plots often stand frozen while they run through what they need to express (invariably via violence). They have to be killed, or at least held down, if only so the story may continue. But they instruct how any of us could get so intensely and injuriously locked in. The *locus classicus* is in *Raw Deal* where, fairly deep into the film, a character played by Whit Bissell totally and gratuitously goes berserk. No apparent reason, just, at last, a refusal to go on in the face of meaningless misery. This little terrified mouse, the object of a massive manhunt, is finally cornered by cops, where, it happens, Jim Sullivan (also being hunted, but far bigger game) is also hiding out. He wails how he doesn't know why he killed his wife, and that he loved her. The cops show their usual understanding by blasting away. The film then resumes, content to have shown us this glimpse of how things are (including almost comically clueless cops, guilty of absurd overkill). The change we see in this "nut" figure is a change from pathetic to dangerous, although these are often combined—brilliantly in the central figure of Edward Dmytryk's *The Sniper* (1952); surrendering to helplessness is replaced by administrating terror (as though that were a life-sustaining dictate of a psychological diet). The embrace of the gangster as a kind of patron protecting the interests of capitalist enterprise, and Mafia families as guardians and caretakers of disappearing values, invites sentiment we are reluctant to grant to the psycho in his throes. For while the gangster goes through his poses of respectability, some social misfit or scourge is devising new methods of heartless torture and murder. Those *noir* heavies weren't exactly Florence Nightingales, but they didn't alienate us by graphic enactments of distasteful carnage. This is no longer true. In *Kiss of Death* (1947) Tommy Udo speaks of how he was arrested for "shovin' a guy's ears off his head . . . traffic-ticket stuff," and, later, speaking of some utter stranger says his desire is to "stick both thumbs right in his eyes, hang on till he drops dead." This is not pretty, but now we get to see such events and worse. Playing in a theater near you is some hideously disturbed criminal busy collecting fingers and nipples and ears and penises with a kind of mandated maniacal giggle or the satisfied look belonging to a job well done. There seems to be a prodigious demand for grisly graphic violence of the wildest and most innovative kind, and filmmakers seem all too eager to supply it. *Hoodlum* (1997), for example, serves up severed fingers and testicles for our entertainment dollar, as it keeps returning to scenes of torture to drive home its point and create anticipation for the next atrocity.

Madness is both a state and a theme that undergoes transformations. At first the property of the overachieving gangster that blinds him to his own mortality, it finds a different resonance among the gallery of amoral, often vicious urban creeps of *noir* melodramas, and functions now as a kind of vague but handy explanation for the brutal doings of a horde of sadistic misfits, icons of ineradicable evil. This tendency made it a natural move for the crime film to usurp some of the horror film's territory, utilize its suspense and gore and frissons to remain economically competitive. *Seven* (1995) is perhaps the most notable example.

An excess of madness and violence, then, along with a sexual and social abusiveness rarely held in check, and a gargantuan greed accompany the gangster's fall from our favor. These worsening characterizations simply magnify what was evident long ago from Little Caesar's behavior. The gangster is gluttonous for success; scenes of graphic violence serve his ends better than evenings of steamy sex, an activity that can weaken him and hinder his compulsive advance. Better that than the more dubious satisfactions of tumescence without love. To stick a knife in someone's gut is an accomplishment that says you're going somewhere, or at least protecting your territory. Sticking your penis into another human being is not nearly as impressive an act; not only does it not signify getting anywhere, but it can only lead to costly and irreparable derailments of *your* goal to accumulate power, rise above others, reach the top. Sex is in 'ɛd too "common" a denominator. No wonder the gangster's sexuality is most urgently activated by deviance, underscoring the perverse nature of his entire enterprise.

The female gangster also made a (somewhat awkward) dive into the widening pool of reconstructed identities. Taking the cue from Roger Corman's exploitative outlines, she became a fiercely individual social scourge, either by "sticking by her man" or going on an individual rampage of lawlessness. She still looks like an anomaly. These obstreperous and dangerous ladies are around a lot more these days, but the occasional majestic gargoyle like Judith Anderson's *Lady Scarface* (1941), or the chipper confidence of Joan Blondell's gang boss in *Blondie Johnson* (1933), seems out of reach. Contemporary versions have gained some more space perhaps, but at the cost of grandeur and dignity.

It's not that difficult to see where the gangster/crime film has gone since *Dreams and Dead Ends* was published. In 1977 my best guess was that the films would be increasingly inclined to stage the most violent actions and they have indeed turned to this, their omnipresent trump card, with regularity. The string of gangland killings that served as climax for the extraordinary trailer of *The Godfather*, was like a highlight reel of its commitment to both athletic and aesthetic violence; it was like a World Series of gangland, a spectacle to watch from a safe distance, and the film, despite its *longueurs*, delivered the goods, its blood-splattered set pieces lingering in the mind long after its more restrained episodes had receded (excepting the inspired opening).

The new technology spurs a lust for visual bravura, which, in this genre, means more convincingly realistic bloodbaths; it welcomes innovative gestures and the staging of complex action. In *The Godfather* the almost continuous violence (as in, say, John Woo's films or Tom and Jerry cartoons also) has a charged atmosphere. Part frolic, part roller coaster, part the urge toward extremes dictated by an appetite whetted by real-world craziness and slaughter, the filmmaker's compulsion to push at existing limits produces orgies of violence, the quiet moments serving as no real respite or contrast and more like opportunities to reload. Audiences have been known to laugh at head-to-toe enactments of screen blood lust. It's something of a game. No surprise, then, that the most grotesquely violent film ever made (*In Bad Taste*, 1997) is a hilarious send-up of the audience's pathological connoisseurship of the ultimate in imaginative maiming and killing. Films with more bulging budgets can manage to lay it on more, but no other film has risked being so wickedly *ultimate*.

I don't mean to imply the new's obliteration of the old. We're talking reasonable upgrading and upstaging here. The genre's foundations exert a strong undertow of discipline that makes even the most bizarre and recalcitrant variations feel grounded by surrounding echoes of the past and the genre's still-accumulating history. Although sometimes appearing to covet the cachet of the unique, genre films do not forsake the advantages of "belonging." They tend to stay "home" at crunch time, but what "home" is keeps changing. We usually know the kind of film we're dealing with by its look, its iconography, and how its environment dictates both screen behavior and audience expectations. The gangster/crime film isn't hard to spot. We can recognize it instantly and can usually predict what's likely to happen. It has been subject to major testing of its limits after the studios' long history of nurture and manipulation, and it has retained enough characteristic obduracies to survive even the most disproportionate mixes of echo and innovation. Having, so to speak, held out or hung on, the underworld denizen is still a viable option for screen treatment and continues to occupy the attention of both critics and filmmakers—and, now and again, paying customers. Film *categories* have multiplied to permit a narrowing of focus, but the large genres still have an Olympian presence among people involved in making, studying, or more than casually watching films, and this genre is too firmly anchored in the American psyche to be dislodged by any postmodern change of wind or fashion. (It's worth checking the Category Index in *Video Hound's Golden Movie Retriever* for amusing subdivisions galore. Thus, something like "Hide the Dead Guy," which might have once served as the title of a particular film, now takes on the less humble aura of a mini-genre.)

The extension of a genre's range does not portend its dissipation, but it does make it difficult to offer a controlling definition. It was a problem twenty years ago, and it is a worse problem now. "So big deal," the smart critic might contend. Does it really matter to anyone who isn't an academic? If you don't leave the genre loose and open, you'll lose many a treasure to some lurking opportunist. You don't want a critical apparatus that stagnates or ossifies groups of films so casually by theoretical fiat, or one that must end up excluding its liveliest material for the principle of tidiness. What made viewers feel *like* genres had disintegrated by the late 1950s were the many different ways one could now treat the material. Genres became politicized, neuroticized, eroticized, europisized, and thematically overworked. One could use them to say more things in more ways than ever before, which gave them a novel feel and perhaps reduced their predictability. This is very much the case today. If a single filmmaker wants to trash, or say a fond farewell to, a genre, it does not mean the genre is dead, only that he/she is through with it. Clint Eastwood's *True Crime* (1999) does for the lone wolf hero of the urban crime melodrama what his *Unforgiven* (1992) does for the laconic "stranger with a gun" hero of the western. *True Crime* derails at the end, switching to romance and a wish-fulfilling happiness that refuses to close the book on *our* lives (though we're given the choice to entertain a direr course of events). *Unforgiven* is willing to close the book on the western. We don't live there anymore. It was heroic, it was murderous, but it is past. I doubt that Eastwood will ever do another western, as *Unforgiven* can serve as that genre's funeral rite. *True Crime* seems to imply we need some more time to figure out the problems it saturates us with—hence the concluding upbeat segue to unlikely survival, which surely taxes credibility. But it's obviously, for Eastwood, a genre he can still work to good purpose.[4]

The "gangster" is tragic-heroic; the term itself carries some weight. He's at the top of his league of miscreants. There are terms for lawbreakers of lesser stature: hood, punk, thief, grifter, stoolie, and the like. Whenever a touch of dignity is called for, "gangster" serves just fine. One of the differences between early crime films and our current batch is how thoroughly the term has elapsed in referring to postwar equivalents. It crops up only in period reconstructions of the 1920s and 1930s. Even 1940s films use the term rarely and by the 1950s more demeaning terms like mobster, crook, Mr. Big, and killer have taken over. "Gangster," then, retains a special flavor, in part nostalgic, and, as an example of the successful, self-made man, not entirely negative. Moreover, a certain grandeur overwhelms ironic leveling in his dramatic rise/fall pattern, and his free swagger lets him avoid the lessons *noir* would have him learn. The black/white, shades-of-gray polarities that so aptly attire *noir* narratives are not his preferred atmosphere. (He wears the *noir* shroud most expressively, and in a way climactically, in Gordon Wiles's *The Gangster*, novelist Daniel Fuchs's morbidly pessimistic take on how the urge for respectability combined with an insufficient ruthlessness leaves his old-style gangster hero without the instinct to protect his territory, and a sitting duck for unsentimental elimination by a new-style mob.). The gangster is a showy sort and likes to be seen; his *noir* cousins are often hiding in shadows, on the lam, or just plain huddling in darkness. (The elderly inmate will often prefer staying on than testing his luck outside as a free man.) The gangster's colorful accomplishments can be given bright, ego-swelling depictions, gaudily externalized celebrations of his charisma. Quite a few period reconstructions are boldly extrovert and rather cheerful, for example, Roger Corman's *The St. Valentine's Day Massacre* (1967) and John Milius's *Dillinger* (1973). (The nonachieving, all-fall/no-rise tale of the *noir* hero has its power dissipated in color; the film seems inappropriately garbed.) The gangster gets to run, if only for a while, "the big show." The gangster hero feels he has mastered reality; his *noir* equivalent is, often messily, trying to grasp what it is (his is not a situation that promises thrills of triumph and increasing power but rather vicious beatings, sleazy detours, sinister undercurrents, and misplaced hopes). Even the "coolest" *noir* hero, one strong enough not to buckle under the revelation of all manner of deceit, treachery, hypocrisy, dysfunction, and plain old evil (Mitchum, say, in *Out of the Past*), remains, first and last, a victim, his sometimes ingenious sleuthing more disillusioning than illuminating. The gangster does get to do his thing and thereby gets his kicks (like Richard III, who has a Little Caesar moment of weakened psyche but goes to his bloody death snarling and unpenitent). The *noir* character, finding human nature unsavory, human society unjust, and human relationships unreliable, is, or becomes, too psychologically damaged to initiate some compensatory vigor or rebelliousness; he is more likely to succumb to hopeless inaction or weary extinction. Frank Bigelow's crazed zest in *D.O.A.* is an exception for "looniness," but his floundering tough-guy borderline dementia is not only an impersonation but is being conveyed via his own dying breaths, which interferes with any possible note of triumph.

(Should critics, like filmmakers, be granted use of the *long take*—what you have just endured, perhaps with some discomfort? There should be one on the house, I suppose, after which the critic would be on a kind of probation.)

American optimism is not likely to capitulate to *noir*'s more European fears and sorrows without soon reasserting its wired-in, defeat-denying dynamism. Yet one could say that *noir*, too, was also not to be denied, as its dark spell infiltrated across-the-board industry releases; troubled psyches trebled, and benign outlooks began to lose credibility. One look at the films from 1945 to 1960 should indicate that *noir* gained significant ground, waving its banners of doom and pain and paranoia from the depths of the American mainstream. Eventually, *noir*'s adversarial moods and techniques would settle within an aesthetic governed by a kind of partnership with more sanguine hopes and expectations. (Things are bad, yes, but . . . .) Resistance could be found in other, more genial, genres the studios continued to count on to appease and entertain the broad base of ticket buyers satisfied by such fare. These films did not feature helpless heroes, tergiversating dames, or extreme measures in visual style; they didn't traffic in doubt, mistrust, shadow-sliced *mise-en-scène*, or compositional tension, or ironic mirroring—all keynotes of *film noir*. A new cycle of cop films, corresponding to the half-decade of screens riddled by lawman firepower in the 1930s, worked a tough half-decade in the 1950s trying to instill a recoverable sense of purpose and moral values that *noir* had impressively discredited. Some very good films resulted (*The Big Heat, The Big Combo, Tight*

Spot, The Narrow Margin, Where the Sidewalk Ends, etc.), but *noir* despair and dissonance had penetrated too deeply to be ground away. It had become part of our national identity and, for the filmmaker, a resource ready to be tapped. From the late 1950s up to the present, it has hovered over or emitted deep-grained static from within all the films that could conceivably belong to this accommodating genre. A little bit of *noir* goes a long way, too; it doesn't take much to imply that one is unlikely to get anything accomplished, especially if one is deserving. Characters with reasonable goals become pawns in exhibitions of futility. It's not any stacked deck in particular that's important; it's the unfair advantage existence has over you and your desires. Narratives of crime and gangsters stress not so much the exhilaration of such a life but its fundamental desperation.

The genre has gone bleak since *The Godfather* films. It has always been bleak but now is bleaker. It has diminished in star power and verbal wit. It is determinedly ugly. The iconic sweep of the New York City skyline, or of downtown Manhattan, was often employed and had a kind of corrupt majesty. We don't see it much anymore (except in generally dopey comedies). The common icon of New York City, indeed any city now, is "XXX, Live Sex," and so forth. That is the identifying sign of a metropolis, large or small. And we are soon treated to a prolonged wallow in seedy and diseased environments and an earful of inner-city dialects (most flavorfully transmitted by rhythmic repetitions of "fuck," "fucking," "motherfucking," and their host of variants). Top to bottom, the genre's conventions, major or minor, have been more or less toward the downbeat. Productions of the 1930s and 1940s, especially, had a likable blend of innocence and depravity. They didn't mind jolting you, but they also wanted to win you over. Today's films like to grind your face in all kinds of unpleasantness. Why? Because they can, and that's the easiest, most visible arena where innovation can be displayed. The appeal of the illicit is strong, and this genre specializes in the creation of illicit worlds, or demonstrates how our world of barbecues and bus stops is one and the same. Moreover, points of view are prone to sudden shifts, and a favorable response toward someone making progress in difficult circumstances may have us pulling for the arsonist about to burn down the local orphanage to get his match lit in the gusting wind. Nor are we immune to the exhilaration that accompanies accounts of upward mobility or the sight of the extravagant creature comforts of home and office that illustrate it. It's never, of course, as simple as that—a single, clear response. Something like an atonal bouncing ball is set in motion, pinging erratically from the Fear of Success key to the Fear of Cops key to the Fear of Payback or Rival Mobster key to the Fear of Guilty Pleasures key. For most viewers, such quick peeks into one's own soul are absorbing and instructive. There's always an unstated moral outlook that will show or imply an apt punishment for your midnight rides, usually a self-applied remorse or shame, but occasionally one may find support, as well, for one's sick or foolish fantasies. In any case, those characters who draw forth your criminal allegiance are, in the movies, apprehended or killed (unlike in "real" life, which often shows top-level criminals taking a post-trial stroll, draped by a crack lawyer or two). Besides, good filmmakers will let their legacy help them make the kind of crime films that need to be made. The inescapable self-consciousness of working in a genre with such a long history will be yet another creative challenge, another reworking of the genre's conventions to explore contemporary conflicts.

Second Thoughts: Recapping the Obvious

The blurbs for two recent books on the gangster/crime film, *Pump 'Em Full of Lead: A Look at the Gangster in Film* and *Hollywood and Gangland: The Movies' Love Affair with the Mob* (see the Bibliography), boil it right down: the urge to excel, to exhibit prowess lesser mortals cannot, or will not; to be a star, *the* star—star gangster, star quarterback, star porn star, star clerk, star bag lady, star nerd—the best at whatever it is one does. This is the goal: distinction, and the power that travels with it. The history of our typical ineptitude stands in high but compassionately chastised relief against the virile triumphs of these paragons of performance, and our psyches seem to demand that periodic vicarious fantasies be nurtured to make us want to keep rolling these particular dice. There is an uneasy alliance between lawlessness and superiority, as though the latter somehow entailed the former. To excel is to transgress, to star is to leave others in your wake. Hence, also, the *satisfaction* of seeing over-reachers and overachievers fall and fail—first rise, and then fall, a two-fold pleasure. The input of the director certainly makes a difference in the creation of "better" or "worse" films, but it is star power that rivets our attention. Imagine *Little Caesar*, *The Public Enemy*, or *Scarface* without Eddie G., Cagney, or Muni. Such a request should elicit an involuntary wince, perhaps even a shudder. Unthinkable. Sacrilege. Imagine the same films without LeRoy, Wellman, and Hawks. No big deal. All three happened to be very good choices for their assignments, not easily bettered, but one could entertain, without much strain, acceptable substitutes.

Having survived the millennium, we may note that this purgative process seems to have vanished by the 1940s, as a kind of effluvial slough of underworld lingo and paraphernalia; the crucial "outfitting" (the gangster as sartorial dandy) gone, there is, at best, an intermittent urban daring in congenial environments: nightclubs, poolrooms, parking lots, warehouses, even a castle, perhaps, with moat and dungeon, instruments of torture, dustless and well cared

Dreams &
Dead Ends

22

for, and a palpable air of sadomasochism.[5] Where there was once a harnessing of energies, there is now a scattering. Even with *noir* heroes as scaled down as the self-satisfied Frank Bigelow in *D.O.A.*, or the dense Joe Sullivan in *Raw Deal*, or the plaintive Al Roberts in *Detour*, the films seem to be reflections of their psyches, the worlds depicted subject to their warped wills and stricken fate. But by the time we get to the neurotic inarticulateness of Corman's *Machine-Gun Kelly* or Dancer's tight-lipped, professional plunge to destruction from his frequent-flyer business trip demeanor to the choreographed bounce his body takes down the freeway ramps until it crashes to the streets with a sickening dull thump in Don Siegel's *The Line-Up*, that precarious comradeship between criminal and ticket-holding customer has shattered. In both these films, moreover, it is women who gum up the works—women representing the uneducable counter to the gangster's "owning" of the world—his natural adversary.

Yet from a slightly different bird's-eye perch, that spiky mountain range of gangster films from 1930 to 1932 (fifty-plus) gains in bite and stature and by smooth gradations eases onto hilly rural settings for adventurous car chases after bank robbers and villainous urban bloodsuckers, until these settings dissolve to the fog-saturated, mist-imprisoned California valleys and alleys and farms. From this angle one might say (incautiously) that the gangster film, strictly speaking, peaked in 1932 and then was subjected to a series of adjustments, after which urban law-and-order films became a more upbeat entertainment of a similar kind by shrewdly retaining its star performers and their urge for (now righteous) action. The gangster turns to bank robbing, roaring and clanking down back roads in stolen cars, and lying low in farms and barns and roadside businesses and girlfriends' apartments. No romanticized Bonnies or Clydes here, however. The gangster becomes a charmless bully, a bundle of negative traits that merits annihilation. Hollywood probably thought it best to make him a really rotten bastard, perhaps to pacify Hoover, whose job was being made more difficult by the public's sympathy for real-life, just-folks desperadoes like Dillinger and others, more worth backing than Hoover's much ballyhooed but ineptly performing FBI. There is no place for Rico's dumbfounded awe of his own mortality (you need to have developed some pretty funny notions of yourself for that), a moment which clearly privileges his defiantly foolish but admirably persistent effort to challenge both society and Fate (his threatening bark the outward sign of his deep need to make something of himself) despite the film's prevailing ironies. The 1930s gangster was doing much better in real life, much better than at the movies. We are secure participants of the hopeful ambience created by lawmen who now go after the often overfed, sniveling, woman-abusing, psychotic—he will usually shoot *somebody*, often his own gang member, for some less-than-called-for reason—

unfeeling social cancer (think "Barton MacLane" and you've pretty much got it) and rid the world of this menace, dead or alive. Gangster mannerisms become suddenly something to chuckle at, now that the movies have captured and/or reformed him, most notably in a series of smart, laugh-out-loud comedies with Edward G. Robinson (*Smart Money*, 1931; *Little Giant*, 1933; *A Slight Case of Murder*, 1938; *Brother Orchid*, 1940; *Larceny, Inc.*,1942) in which the former menace becomes lovably naïve and tenderhearted. Humphrey Bogart spent most of the 1930s in the shadow of Cagney and Robinson, playing a succession of scowlingly unregenerate, smirking, sadistic rats until he agreed to take the lead role, a gangster just released from prison with a soft spot for Okies, cripples, orphans, small dogs, and mountain air, in *High Sierra*, and woke up the next morning a star. (It was perhaps that backlog of accumulated nastiness that permitted a martyrdom the right side of mawkish.) But the gangster's transformation is complete. You cannot watch *High Sierra* (1941) and not like Roy Earle. We kiss him goodbye through the blur of involuntarily activated waterworks, the gangster having now become a royal figure with whom we went through a difficult period of national crisis, sharing in a kind of necessary rampage, who we can now honorably enshrine. The gangster continues to be an unassimilated figure, however, the near-retarded, amoral exuberance of Paul Muni's *Scarface* (1932) as *sui generis* as Roy Earle's majestic loneliness.

It remains for him to be socialized by the war effort before he disappears for good (discounting retrospectives), slipping chameleon-like into the profiteering nightclub ambience of *noir* and, eventually, the business suits and Swiss bank accounts of corporate bigwigs. The gangster's tough-guy tactics would prove useful against the Japs and Krauts. The war films he takes part in tend to stretch credulity to a shredding point, suggesting that we could not be winning, or have finally won, the war without the likes of Cagney, Robinson, and Bogart jumping in to help the upright guys like John Wayne, Errol Flynn, and Dana Andrews. The gangster was so good at annihilating the enemy that we had to think we were damned lucky to have bred him.

These absurdities give way to the starker visions of *film noir*, that postwar efflorescence of Hollywood product that has remarkably survived its purely contemporary appositeness. Its portrait of a complex national mood of guilt, corruption, economic and social change, and domestic instability within often dimly lighted passageways of despair makes a continuing kind of sense in the 1990s (after having survived both a reversal of heart and being knocked out of bounds within its own camp, and the 1950s open challenge of moral fixity and biding its time through the satiric 1960s until it slowly seizes the opportunity to rebuild the solid if disparate—that is, stylistically disunified—community of filmmakers, aficionados, teachers, critics, sympathetic sensibilities, and assorted defectors from optimism). *Noir* is, if nothing else, cynical and downbeat (at surfaces and depths) and most often partial to a reality-transforming style. It works the medium vigorously to its own purpose, with a usually consistent succession of visual choices. Yet, sometimes bafflingly, style is not the true index of its attitude or statement. Thus the almost mystically photographed and dreamily narrated *Raw Deal* has a quirky sheen of romance (doomed, of course) at odds with its rock-bottom pessimism. So the degree to which a *noir* message is being put forth cannot be discerned through lighting and camera work per se. Rather, it is in the combination of the least tangible aspect (direction) with the most (script/story) that the degree to which the film gives in to despair, or survives its influence, can be measured. Tricky business, though. Some films give no trouble at all. *Detour* offers a perfect match: its minimalist bleakness of style mirrors its hopeless outlook perfectly. And while in *Ride the Pink Horse* (1947) the *noir*ish elements are relegated to disturbingly hellish journeys, these are brief and the mood of a border carnival town, vital and brightly lit, asserts itself throughout (dark and light in a kind of battle). The conclusion stresses the number of important things—moral, racial, political, sexual—that have been confronted and somewhat conservatively resolved. It's easy to spot *Ride the Pink Horse* as a film inclined, from the start, to arrive at upbeat ends.

But what of *The Big Combo*, whose dark-drenched interiors belie Lieutenant Leonard Diamond's moral victory, placing the film squarely in the 1950s moral spectrum? Here the style belies the statement being made. It's hard to know how to proceed. This is a *noir* that wants to transcend its own eloquently presented evidence, and it does so by a few choice moves: certain shots of Susan Lowell's *radiance* (Lt. Diamond's infatuated point of view); a carefully orchestrated and never ignored emphasis on Diamond's lonely chivalric quest, which he does not abandon; the abruptness with which the powerful Mr. Brown crumples and whines under the light of truth and is carted off, a loser in the battle over Susan; and in the larger struggle of cynicism over moral vision. Finally, there's the scene we are given of the break in Mr. Brown's emotions when he inadvertently authors his buried guilt in his unconscious scrawl of Alicia's name on the moist windowpane; even Brown, the film insists, is vulnerable, having harbored, against his own self-interest, feelings for the wife he had institutionalized many years ago to advance his career, a turning point that let him rise to be Mr. Brown. Brown has chosen evil, Diamond good. Bragging, Brown taunts Diamond by asking whether he has any notion of why he's who he is, a nobody, and Brown a big shot with expensive suits, and Diamond answers: "Guess I'm just lucky," and he means it. This even though Brown rubs it in by reminding him that the woman he is obsessively in love with is his mistress. *The Big Combo* has to be, shot for shot, one of *noir*'s blackest works. But it's a 1950s film, defeating what Brown stands for and relieving us by showing Diamond's steadfast integrity paying off.

The postwar gangster, then, a la Mr. Brown, is (except for often being older) a war-profiteer, a gold digger's dream, a nightclub owner with first dibs on the knockout thrush he has hired for his club, a thoroughly corrupt and venal individual, whose extensive criminal background has been carefully kept secret or perhaps hidden in some vault inside incriminating, tampered-with "books." He is a "legitimate" operator and has some cops on his payroll. He keeps, unlike his predecessors, a businessman's front, never invites pathos, is sadistic, and is dependent on the often psychopathic contributions of loyal or resentful gunsels. He can be aloof and contemptuous, like underworld boss Mike Lagana in *The Big Heat* (1953), or loud and socially boisterous, like mob leader Rico Angelo in *Party Girl* (1958). He is the boss, the big guy, but rendered small-time by the filmmaker's scorn, a man often undone by a careless mistake or underestimation. But he is the stepping stone to his corporate incarnations in the 1950s who represent entrenched and invulnerable evil, screened by trigger-happy employees and shielded by a cynical core so acquisitive and nasty that only a nothing-to-lose, invulnerable, and angry adversary (usually a disenchanted ex-cop) can wish, or be asked to, destroy it. The vigilante cop thus joins the vigilante Westerner, in a very busy decade of mopping up the mobs. He's had some sleepy periods but has been a particular project of Clint Eastwood, who has kept the Western (*Coogan's Bluff*, 1968) and the Eastern versions (*Dirty Harry*, 1972) alive. Well, more than alive, as a similar figure seems to be all over the place, tilting hats, drinking week-old coffee, and sharing cat food. There must be dozens of "lone wolf" cop and gumshoe movies made every couple of years. Mistrust and fear of cops will guarantee they'll keep coming for a long, long time.

Cops and gangsters. Some films give them equal time, but they have their own cycles too, which rarely appear at the same time and are therefore not really in competition. A spate of one tends to provoke a spate of the other, as if to correct the imbalance. Some hit a nerve and stay around, others go straight to television. I'd say the cop cycle has been more in evidence partly because the gangster has been, of late, ethnically specialized and thereby easily scapegoated, but also because of his business in drugs, expanding and highly profitable but out of favor as fomenting violence and spreading a dangerous social plague that puts everyone at risk.

Since gangsters could now freely be named and were safely ensconced in history books, it was time to invite them all back to our screens and make new sense of them. Where they actually begin as the major figure in their films is hard to say, but their main calling card was a biographical emphasis, and if *Baby Face Nelson* (1957) is the first to boldly name him as its subject, maybe that's where this new cycle begins (though *I Died a Thousand Times*, Stuart Heisler's remake of *High Sierra*, predates it by two years). A fascinating batch of low-budget films showing the gangster as out of control (the only other group of crime films outside the cop and cop-oriented destroy-the-syndicate films) are the heist/caper suspense thrillers that display the criminal as surviving through a kind of professional specialization. These gangster biographies hark back to the 1945 *Dillinger*, who was not at all like his screen predecessors of the 1930s but an unmistakably *noir* Dillinger, vicious, psychopathic, not too bright, woman-betrayed, and still, with all that going for him, unsympathetic. It stands alone, filling a large gap between the Code's prohibition against the gangster as the central figure and the mid-1950s to early 1960s cycle we are currently discussing. The view of this cycle sees the gangster as mentally disturbed. He exhibits this condition the whole film, until his social demonstration of it leads to his demise. This links up eerily to the 1973 *Dillinger*, but there, outside a *noir* perception of things, his helplessness arouses sympathy. He is like a retarded child who knows no other way to be. Cheaply made by budget-shaving studios and independents, such films glutted drive-ins with the requisite action and sex, and dared to make the people and doings attractively defiant, unsettlingly unpredictable, and, gratefully, with no evident sign of the actors having spent much time with a voice coach. *Machine-Gun Kelly* (1958), *Al Capone* (1959), and *The Rise and Fall of Legs Diamond* (1960) all fit the bill.

The problems of these characters (and their fictional brethren, like Roger Corman's *I, Mobster* [1958]) seem to emanate from whatever it is they're immediately dealing with. There is no Big Picture for them, or for their creators, to see. No gloss, no frills, no insights to help mold a perspective, and sometimes, as films, no really good reason to go on watching them, they nonetheless attest to the gangster's survival in a limited-field mental terrain. He seems to keep filling a need, here perhaps the criminalization of nonconformity, seen as mental disease. This arrested, disturbed, neurotic phase, for all the modesty of its productions, exerts the most influence on the next forty years of gangster and criminal characterizations, although one shouldn't underestimate the impact of the gangster's companion low-budget 1950s corollary, the professional killer. Both need to have gangland or mob connections to qualify for this genre's already spacious dimensions. The inundation of serial killers of the 1990s (occasionally female), on the strength of numbers alone, deserves a genre of its own; it's as though the two-bit psychopaths of films *noir* were flipped out of the criminal context of their films to play out their terrifying idiosyncrasies to independent conclusions. That such characters now occupy center stage bespeaks a lack of faith in our ability to contain their crimes or fathom their causes. Brainy psychos (the two terms go together in a socially convenient anti-intellectualism) have long been on call for *noir* duty (Nick Bianco, terrorized by giggling killer Tommy Udo in *Kiss of Death*, complains to Assistant D.A. Di Angelo: "He's nuts and he's smarter than you are!"), but their instabilities did not derail the entire film from its dramatized schedule of threatening incidents and nick-of-time arrests. This is in part because the character is connected with a criminal network and is destined for capture by agencies we need to have faith in, despite the ease with which we may entertain contrary conclusions. The technology-savvy diabolism of the modern, murdering-by-blueprint lunatic probably derives from *noir* nonmobster, noncop thrillers featuring educated, sexually perverse masterminds of murder—murder meticulously planned by a superior intelligence of the kind whose elegant command of manners and attire makes people defer to his suggestions and judgments (*Gaslight* [1944], *The Spiral Staircase* [1946], *Laura* [1944], *So Evil My Love* [1948]). The fastidious decors in such films have an almost decadent excess about them, as though they were the coping mechanism of repression, the aesthetic overstatement disallowing any observer to stop the urge to pause at taste, compelled to fly past that to pathology. This is a kind of disorder, or differentness, not so unlike the phantasmagoric environments elaborately constructed out of a troubled psyche in later films like *Silence of the Lambs* (1991), *Kiss the Girls* (1998), and many others. These sinister "smart" guys belong in categories like "Horror" and "Fiends."

The crossover patterns are there, nonetheless, most notably their proneness to a Jekyll-Hyde vacillation, which they seem to have no choice but to play out. They can appear relaxed and gentle then turn hyperactive and killcrazy. Frequently they are sympathetic by default; the others, inured to whatever a day may bring, are uninterested in imagining their own situation and continue untouched by the conflicts their peculiar cohort or acquaintance has let cage his good humor. On the whole, although the killings are more tied in with psychological problems than with social or environmental influence, the figures gain sympathy by being sensitive enough to *know* there's a black cloud hanging over their heads, a life burden the others have yet to assume. With a bit of cheating, one could see this cycle being played out between the years separating two Roger Corman quickies: the poor, inevitably sympathetic soul that's Charles Bronson's *Machine-Gun Kelly* (1958) and the scathing grotesquerie Corman makes out of Shelley Winters's *Bloody Mama* (1970), two Freudian treasure troves which still remain critically unperturbed.

The Golden Age:
The "Classic" Gangster Film

The gangster-crime film took root as long ago as Griffith's *The Musketeers of Pig Alley* (1912) and then struggled in unfertilized soil through to the end of the twenties. It took a combination of the sound film, Capone's Chicago, Prohibition, and the mood of the depression to inaugurate the first distinct phase of the genre. It begins with *Little Caesar* (1930) and ends with *Scarface* (1932), and it is the source and example of all the phases that follow.

In general, the dynamics of gangster films of the thirties are simplistic, relying on the public's fascination with actual criminals and their exciting, if alarming, exploits, and in tune with the rhythms of an industry approaching high gear. The gangster's fizzy spirits, classy lifestyle, and amoral daring were something like an Alka-Seltzer for the headaches of the depression. In the ruined hopes of that period, the gangster's grand designs were part of a dialectic of the audience's fantasies and dreams and a rote Christian morality. Characters like Edward G. Robinson's Rico, James Cagney's Tom Powers, and Paul Muni's Tony Camonte succumb to a combination of hubris, social fate, and moral reckoning in plots resembling those of classical tragedy. The films they appear in establish a tradition of popular tragedy in film. Strong figures cursed by their nature, their environment, their heritage find their desires and goals overwhelmed by an immutable and often unpredictable concatenation of forces. The power they held over audiences is directly related to their show of strength within the disintegration of the depression. The depression created some desperate fantasies—a film like Gregory La Cava's *Gabriel Over the White House* (1933), with its protofascist abandonment of democratic procedures, suggests just how desperate some of them were—and the gangster, as the self-made man who has, like us, no fear of pain and death, who behaves amorally and as though oblivious of his mortality until the world's weight crushes down on him, is one of them. If the films insist that one can't win, under that given it's how you lose that counts. In a maze of dead ends, the immensity of the gangster's will and the size of his passions give him heroic status. (This view of the gangster persists as late as *Bonnie and Clyde* [1967], with the important difference that he is placed in a dead, empty past, not a densely actualized near-present.)

As the genre evolves, and refines itself through time, it becomes increasingly self-conscious and sophisticated. Its beginnings, as we might expect, are innocent of later complexities. *Little Caesar*, *The Public Enemy*, and *Scarface* present their material with classic straightforwardness. Their wish is to record the reality of the gangster's world and his character, to convey, with non-metaphoric immediacy, the particulars of his behavior. The interest is in what he might really be like, the ways in which he is an actual menace. He is a character who exists as the film reports him to exist. These are essentially traditional, mimetic works—imitative, illusionistic, persuasively real. Conflict is used literally and transparently. The camera's presence is hidden, its processes concealed. The "reality" of any shot dominates our awareness of the camera's movement or position. Even very noticeable rhetorical conceits like the machine-gunning away of calendar pages in *Scarface* are in the service of either supplying essential information or become part of the movement of a straight-ahead narrative. They are incorporated into an illusionistic mode. Ambivalence is well-defined, explicit. On the one hand there is society and its system of laws, on the other the tragic, often appealing, hero who breaks its laws, and by his actions activates both our need to hang onto moral and social laws and our wish to get outside them. What is seen is understood as real, permitting undeflected involvement and suspension of disbelief. We believe what we see and, for the moment, care. The issues are defined and definite. We feel the clash of two opposing and distinctly delineated forces. We watch and listen to a story that contains the possibility of tragedy.

The films occupy time present: there are no flashbacks. The narrative sequence is undistorted. The story takes place over a period of time and unfolds sequentially. It is implicit that a straightforward unraveling is adequate, that the gangster's story is appropriately told that way—a tale that has a beginning, middle, and end, rising and falling action, denouement, resolution. The gangster's aggression and vitality are honored; the films imply that there is a purpose in his acting out his will. He is simple, innocent, and vital; the expression of these qualities is engaging. In combination and in excess, however, these qualities are dangerous to the status quo. They cause upheaval and must be quelled. It is the aim of the early gangster films to *show* the hero act and be stopped without attaching corresponding values to his actions or their violent termination, other than the applying of utterly conventional moral homilies. Grounded in literalness, physicality, and emotion, these films are not enlightened or enlightening. They are not interested in the implications of the world they so vividly create.

If the world is a real world, it is nonetheless not our world but the gangster's. On those occasions, relatively few, when the gangster steps into a world more recognizably ours, he stamps it as his. Icons that represent *us* seem somewhat out of place and extraneous or blank and characterless. In one sense, the films are travelogues and documentaries. The people we see—tough guys and their women, tough cops—are stylized by speech, behavior, gesture, and expression to a point that sharply distinguishes them from us. Our identification is an external one. The gangster remains outside us. We can never be, or completely want to be, him. He is placed above us or below us. We are awed onlookers of the atypical intensity of both his life and death. He is a *version* of a human being, sufficiently deviant from the norm for us to observe him as separate and apart. His role is fixed.

The gangster's character and identity are not only well defined, they are also magnified. The early films are primarily actors' vehicles. Robinson, Cagney, Muni project a quality of *being* that dominates *meaning*. Their respective contexts serve as platforms they use to assert their personalities. Their characters are larger than life, and their environments—typically fashioned for verisimilitude—heighten, amplify, and extend their presence. The films are controlled by the power of the actor's performance. He determines our degree of involvement and detachment. What we feel toward the character is cued by the character's candid revelations of his feelings, which the actor's talent establishes between the lines of an often perfunctory script. Our attention is not directed to abstract, thematic levels but to the character's experience. If, for example, there is a question about loyalty, it does not take thematic definition, as it usually does in later films of the genre. Our interest remains exclusively on the level of the character's response to the situation We are interested, in *Little Caesar*, in what Joe's disloyalty means to Rico, how it affects his feelings. Its importance is grounded in the character; it is not an intellectual concern of the film.

The early gangster films remain fresh and vivid because we feel them not as pale and awkward instances of what the genre keeps on doing better and better but as a genuine achievement, something unique that the genre did not attempt again. They are direct, unreflective, naively representational—and as such, their excellence has not been surpassed. *Scarface* was the ultimate expression of the genre's early phase. The gangster film, left with only the potential of its structure, one possibility of which had been exhausted, had to seek a new direction. Throughout the thirties it led a somewhat dormant and desultory life. The gangster became a domesticated creature, an industry pet, an anachronism (*Little Giant* [1933]): the films he appeared in lacked narrative bite, social thrust and intensity of characterization. Major productions were few and far between, and they grew lyrical and romantic or portrayed the gangster as a victim of social conditions (*Dead End* [1937]), *Angels with Dirty Faces* [1938], *The Roaring Twenties* [1939]). The gangster had become the stuff of legend more than fact. His qualities, partially mourned, were emblematic of a period put behind. Or he became an object of parody, humor, and sentimentality. Lloyd Bacon's *Brother Orchid* (1940) is representative. All the genre's serious matter is turned into a joke. Notwithstanding the vivacity of the performances—the direction is anonymous—the film is just a time waster, something concocted for momentary pleasure and diversion. A spirit of affectionate ridicule prevails, a far cry from the gloom and viciousness of the early sound period.

The flurry of early thirties gangster films laid down the bases for future developments. They established a milieu and an iconography. They posed an opposition between insider and outsider, society and its outcasts, and conventionalized that opposition. They dealt with crime as a social issue. They implied that in American society, intense life is only possible in the underworld and created characters whose function was to resonate that implication. The fate of those characters told us that the dreams they had were not possible, but it was something we had to learn, and live through, during the course of the films (subsequent gangster films incorporate it as absolute knowledge — they either shift the nature of the dream or predicate its impossibility).

The early phase of the genre was a process of discovery by doing. The films seem innocent of complex intentions and are locked into the immediacy of their contexts. Thematic implications, and the extension of material to larger contexts of understanding, are incidental and inadvertent. It was left to succeeding films to recognize the implications of matters the genre pointed to and that the early films dealt with concretely and nonconceptually. What was deliberate about the early films was the attempt to capture the flavor of the gangster's life. The critic who has sampled the whole range of the genre and is instructed by its development may of course discern and perceive the bases upon which successive stages of sophistication rest. Frank Hamer in *Bonnie and Clyde* is certainly not the same as Flaherty in *Little Caesar*, although their function in the narrative is quite similar. We *feel* them differently. They are embedded in the consciousness of their respective films. The critic cannot pretend to an innocence the genre itself unceremoniously sheds. Our experience of the genre's progress increases our ability to understand it at any given stage. We understand Flaherty better than the filmmakers of *Little Caesar* did. (We can speak of "themes" in *Little Caesar* and at the same time claim that it is innocent of them.) As pioneers, director Mervyn LeRoy and company were preoccupied with making certain things visible and establishing their germaneness as points of focus in dealing with a world inhabited by specific types who engage in specific conflicts. It was the prerogative of the films that followed, and their audiences, to determine what was meaningful about it.

The whopping impact of *Little Caesar* in its day is somewhat difficult to account for by the evidence the film itself provides, especially from a distance of over sixty years. However, in the economic strife and demoralized psychology of the depression, Rico's personal initiative was highly compelling in a context of general paralysis. Life's actual inhumanities and injustices made Rico's end run around morality and law a logical, and not entirely unjustified, choice. His ability to take defiant action overwhelmed whatever else the film might have been trying to show. From our perspective, the film regains the balance it must have originally hoped to maintain, but contemporary reaction implies that the character broke loose from his aesthetic fetters and assumed somewhat troubling extra-artistic dimensions. The film did not have to explain who Rico was. The gangster is a creature born of the historical moment, the conditions of his world creating a special field of opportunity for an enterprising person of his kind. Capone, the first and greatest gangster—the man whose name is synonymous with "gangster"—was the model, and everyone knew it. Capone was a dangerous criminal, but he was a hero too, and this seems to have significantly colored how the film was received. Critics have pointed admonishingly at *Little Caesar* as glorifying the gangster, and while it is true that Edward G. Robinson's memorable performance could possibly subvert the moralistic bias of the script and Mervyn LeRoy's dry, precise direction, it seems less in the service of that goal today than it must have to its contemporaries. The public must have been ready to respond to Rico in a predetermined way that biased out contrary elements. (It must be remembered, too, that Prohibition created a nation of criminals—the films of the period suggest that whatever else Americans were doing, they were drinking. It was easy to admire disproportionately those whose business it was to provide citizens with liquor, however debased in quality.)

Little Caesar was a phenomenal success and gave rise to a rash of imitations. The addition of sound gave the gangster film a true potency. Compared to many silent films, *Little Caesar* is visually staid, but the sounds of gunfire and slang, and especially Robinson's snarling delivery of his lines, are vivid compensations. The film was so timely and thrilling that LeRoy's attitude toward Rico must have gotten overlooked. Viewing the film now, it is possible to have a more reasonable relationship with it. Rico, as LeRoy and Robinson give him to us, is, in addition to his good (read: strong) qualities, vain, dumb, ugly, brutal, foolish, a bully, and basically insecure. It is a clinical and decidedly antiromantic portrait. Small in most respects, Rico is made an amusing spectacle through irony. We do not like him, and we are not (in the main) moved by him. Yet Robinson makes him so imposing, so important, so malignantly mesmerizing, that we cannot be indifferent to his fate. The world of the film belongs to Rico; we eavesdrop on it as fascinated spectators. The death of a man whose presence defines the world he lives in is always awesome. The classic pattern of the rise and fall of special individuals existed, of course, long before the gangster film, but for the American public, its transposition into the immediate historical present and the close connection between its "fictional" figure and his true-to-life counterpart within a new medium of astonishing and widespread impact made it once again a pattern by which to grip the human soul. This is not the least of *Little Caesar's* contributions.

It is also the major narrative convention of the early gangster film. *Little*

Caesar focuses on a strong central figure who dominates the action and dwarfs the other characters. The plot is determined by this choice, and the criteria governing the selection of scenes obey the single-minded expediency of bringing a sharp attention and a rich cluster of ideas to bear upon the figure. This proved to be an influential pattern. *Little Caesar* provides a "poetics" of the gangster film. It is to the gangster film what *Oedipus Rex*, in Aristotle's analysis, is to Greek tragedy. Like tragic characters, Rico is presented as acting by choice; he creates his own destiny.

The gangster genre supplied a need for a tragic character we didn't have, a character whose top-dog status and plumage (however sweatily earned) carried correspondingly magnified (and undemocratic) drives, deeds, and feelings. Our mixed attitude toward Rico, who violates (indirectly) universal laws and (directly) social laws, reflects our ambivalence toward the man who thinks and acts big. The film is conceived on this level of ambivalence. America invents the gangster as tragic hero against the grain of its democratic ideals — rapidly souring in the socioeconomic conditions of the depression. Ethical matters related to success are diverted by the positive, ambitious actions of powerful men who, though powerful, die and thus express, fatalistically, an inversion of the American dream.[1] *Little Caesar* pulls us both ways. Rico is a character we both admire and scorn, a hero and a fool, a character we need and a character we need to reject. From the beginning then, the culture's attitude toward the gangster seems split down the middle.

By the time *The Public Enemy* was made (1931) the gangster film was a thriving genre. The groundbreaking severities of *Little Caesar* had given way to an impetuous flair. Prodded by the public's enthusiasm and its own momentum, the gangster film had become an exciting, and to some minds a disturbingly violent, fixture of existence. The succession of charismatic, antisocial heroes obviously fulfilled a public need. Film aggression took on new extremes not incompatible with entertainment.

The steady flow of gangster films not only kept a curious public informed about some unpalatable aspects of American life, it also, by insistent repetition, intensified the genre's concerns and its subject matter. The gangster film was only a fictional mode, but unpleasantly exact about some rather touchy matters. It impinged closely on actualities. The problems it dealt with were neither historically remote nor fantastical. The gangster's anarchic lawlessness and criminal success had its analogues in real life, and there was no reason to assume that the films' balance between make-believe and fact could be indefinitely sustained. Add to this the moral backlash of a middle class worrying about young minds being warped, and the un-Americanism of so sordid a view of life, and the disappearance of the gangster film by the end of 1932 comes as no surprise.

If *Little Caesar* can be said to have pioneered the gangster film, *The Public Enemy* is the classic representative of what it was like in its heyday. It works its conventions and icons with a deep-rooted authority. The stiff, stark quality of *Little Caesar* is gone. The plot is similar to *Little Caesar's*, but the sequence of scenes has a different feel altogether, seems more organic and less pontifical. The sadistic charm of Cagney's Tom Powers gives the film a high velocity and a seductive tone that the morality of the script cannot overtake. *The Public Enemy* is more fluid and less angular than *Little Caesar*, the edges of its thesis constantly blurred by the humanity of its characters. In its editing and staging, *Little Caesar* resembles a slide show about a rare species in foul bloom. LeRoy's attitude keeps trying to make us detached and curious. His disengaged, objective approach produces a mechanistic continuity that, I find, makes us in part want to resist it. *Little Caesar* has the inexorability of a theorem. The repeating and contrasting of scenes take on the quality of a demonstration. *The Public Enemy* is no less organized a film, but its patterns seem more spontaneous and evolving, less predetermined than *Little Caesar's*. *Little Caesar* is served up in oddly seasoned chunks: *The Public Enemy* is more like a stew to which this and that ingredient is added as the film progresses. *Little Caesar* is like an echo chamber: scenes are played off against each other with a pointed artifice (Rico's defiance of Flaherty over the telephone is the pendant to his opening speech in the diner; Joe's "intimate" scenes with Olga are versions of his later ones with Rico; Rico's dismissal of San Vettori is echoed by his dismissal of Little Arnie Lorch; Joe called to Rico is like Rico called to the Big Boy; Tony's Good Mother who sends him to church, is contrasted with Rico's Terrible Mother, Ma Magdalena, who keeps him in a dark hell.) In *The Public Enemy* the continuity is strictly progressive and building, each new scene incorporating what has preceded to make a new synthesis within a steady narrative current bolstered by an undercurrent of recollection. And where *Little Caesar* is content simply to shift locales and emphasize milieu by juxtaposition, *The Public Enemy* is a loving re-creation of people and places, visually dense and richly atmospheric.

The difference is that Wellman is closer to his world than LeRoy, more interested in a lifelike marshaling of detail, and more open-minded in attitude. LeRoy gives the impression of having made up his mind in advance about how to see and present this subject. Wellman appears to be more the accurate observer of first impressions, transcribing the feeling tone of his world as it passes by his camera. Wellman is not hostile, nor mocking, nor admiring. He seems, above all, to have a nonjudgmental curiosity. He presents, but he does not insist. The viewer thinks and feels in a region of possibility, and to a large extent is left to construct his own attitude and interpretation.

Little Caesar (1930)

Contemporary audiences tend to indulge the scissors-and-paste primitivism of *Little Caesar,* its grinding obviousness. Many gangster films have come and gone and what might have seemed fresh and provocative in 1930 now seems antiquated. Edward G. Robinson's integrated performance of Rico nonetheless makes the film go. Such an assessment of *Little Caesar* is not at all surprising. Films are things of the moment, and one's primary response to retrieved cultural ephemera[2] is a diverted curiosity about their period markings. Robinson's grunting dominance does carry us through some technical creakiness and behavioral inaptitude. The film is not most profitably discussed, however, as a colliding series of adequacies and inadequacies as determined by the progress of time. It is a cannily constructed whole whose parts do not conflict but exist in firm, if somewhat stiff, aesthetic relation. Much referred to, and occasionally discussed, *Little Caesar* has never been looked at as a whole. At best, it has been seen as a reservoir of generic, iconographic motifs and situations.[3] In part because it established the tradition, it has gotten somewhat lost in the cross fire of here's-where-it-all-started commentary. Its confident craftsmanship and alternation of tones,. its blending of the tragic and comic-sardonic, its almost pedantic (but oddly satisfying) direction, its narrative austerity and gestural recalcitrance work together in impressive unity.

Unlike *The Public Enemy*, the film it is most often matched and associated with as a "classic,"[4] *Little Caesar* has no interest in exploring the causes of crime. Everything functions to reflect Rico's character. The audience, as is common, occupies a privileged position, understanding Rico the way he himself and others around him cannot. The terror, the grandeur, and the foolishness of his inflexibility are inextricably conjoined. His czar complex and his inferiority complex, his success and his failure, his iron will and his vulnerability keep Rico's characterization in a precarious balance. Any social emphasis is fleeting at best.

The "emotional" scenes in *Little Caesar* are not very effective. Whether the fault lies in the inadequacies of the script or in the way the performers detonate their dialogue, or both, the agonies of the young lovers (Joe and Olga) caught between obligations to the mob and the promise of a free future and Tony's religious conversion under his mother's guidance manage only to convey, often acutely, Rico's momentary absence. LeRoy's dispassionate approach simply kills these scenes, but it allows the audience to supply its own emotion into Rico's. The implicit, unobtrusive scorn lurking behind LeRoy's objectivity prevents any scene from being directorially overworked, and the rigid progression of incidents seems to obey a predetermined rhythm. Compared to the rich chiaroscuro and throbbing animalism of *Scarface*, *Little Caesar* appears drained of pictorial superfluity and human gestures of any but the bluntest and most obvious kind. Its stripped-to-the-bone minimalism gives *Little Caesar* an obduracy of pace and style that is unique. It is a film that doesn't budge. The bare, lineal narrative—a model of tightness—the clarity of the characters' relationships, the economy and simplicity with which atmosphere is evoked, the unstrenuous echoing, paralleling, and repeating of scenes and images—these may be seen as virtues by a critic kindly disposed. *Little Caesar* is not a classic simply because it is a prototype, but be-

Little Caesar. Knife in hand, Rico lets Joe (and us) know that he plans to "be somebody."

cause it is so firm and so compact. The most restrained of gangster films, its Spartan efficiency is opportunely functional in defining and displaying its perversely animated central figure.

Following the brief martial fanfare over the credits, *Little Caesar* begins with what must be the quickest holdup in film history. (Events are not made much of, the stress is on revelation of character through key incidents.) In long shot, in the gloom of night, we see a gas station. Three shots are fired, and two figures scurry out to their car. The next scene shows us who they are—Rico and Joe. (Rico has committed, we infer, a cold-blooded murder, and although it is presented almost as an abstraction, it is an irrevocable, consequential act that separates Rico from the codes of society and makes him an outsider.) They order spaghetti and coffee in a diner. Rico has turned back the diner clock to give himself an alibi. Joe thinks Rico is real smart. Rico vociferously insists that he wants to "be somebody," and that they should go East, where big opportunities for fame and fortune lie. Joe says that if he could make it as a dancer, he'd "quit." Rico is incredulous. The scene establishes that although Rico dominates Joe, Joe has let him know from the beginning that he is pursuing a different goal. Rico cannot take him seriously. It becomes apparent, later, that for Rico to admit to himself that Joe wants something that doesn't involve him would be unendurable. Rico's self-assurance is dependent on Joe's allegiance. In retrospect, some envy also seems to color this conversation. Rico is psychologically forced to deny Joe's choice because it is one closed to him.

We learn much about Rico through his friendship with Joe Massara (Douglas Fairbanks, Jr.—laboring in his role as a hood. Joe's presence works against any facile explanation of criminality as being socially or environmentally induced. Joe comes from the same ethnic background and social class as Rico. **The Golden Age**

Little Caesar. Rico Bandello, about to sweep Sam Vettori and Otero off the desk as he makes his bid to become the gang's CEO, or, more informally, Little Caesar. The world belongs to whoever's got what it takes to conquer it and hold on. (Museum of Modern Art)

He is faced with the same options and temptations, yet he chooses an alternate path. His larger function, however, is to act as Rico's foil, providing, by contrast, an index of his cohort's aberrations. Joe's relationship to Rico is also integral to Rico's downfall. By leaving Rico, Joe inflicts an ill-understood distress that finally nags Rico into inaugurating a disastrous series of actions.

When they hit the big city, Joe gets work as a dancer and falls in love with Olga (gap-toothed Glenda Farrell, who looks the part, but her stiff line-readings and squeaky tones show her not quite the actress of physical ease and speedy articulation she'd become only a year later), his dancing partner. Meanwhile Rico powers his way up the criminal ladder. He assures his boys of Joe's loyalty, but Joe is obviously entranced with Olga and his own success. Rico chides him and finally threatens Joe into helping the gang rob the nightclub where he works. The robbery is enacted and Rico shoots the police commissioner. Joe vows to Olga to break free, despite the lack of precedent. On the strength of this heist, Rico takes over as boss of the gang. Maintaining his new position is a time-consuming job. There are banquets to attend, rivals to worry about, stoolies to bump off, the law to deal with. Joe is lost track of. Rico has to be reminded at the banquet that Joe has failed to appear to do him honor. Rico seems disturbed but defends Joe. Basking in his new success, Rico has not particularly felt Joe's absence. After all, his whole world is paying him homage. He is the celebrity he always wanted to be, a man everybody fears and looks up to. He has also found a new admirer-confidant in Otero, a nervous, homely member of the gang whose genuine devotion to Rico fills the gap left by Joe.

The homosexual nature of the Rico-Joe relationship has often been remarked, and I suppose it is true, although it is not explicit. The closeness of Rico to Joe is the closeness of an emotional tie based on needs only remotely erotic (although a tinge of abnormality is present in the usually ignored Rico-Otero relationship). That Rico "loves" Joe is beyond doubt. That Rico is ugly and charmless and wants to keep his "beautiful" friend to himself for private needs and public display is also beyond doubt. But Joe's crime, in Rico's eyes, is a betrayal of male solidarity and friendship. Joe's remaining outside his influence is also troubling to Rico as a sign of the limitations of his power. Rico has Otero's loyalty, but that does not suffice. He and Joe have been through things together, and his desire is partly governed by an emotional nostalgia. Rico's suffering gains the viewer's sympathy. To love and need and be ignored is a serious and painful condition.

None of this is given overt emphasis, but the film cannot be understood without pursuing the implications of the Rico-Joe relationship. When Rico discovers that it was Joe who telephoned to warn him of Little Arnie's attempt on his life, he says to Otero, "I didn't think he cared enough." The whole of what not having Joe means suddenly hits him hard. Now that he has made it to the top—the Big Boy has promised him total control of his territory—he sends for Joe, ostensibly to reward him for his loyalty but also to check on his reliability and feel out the state of the relationship. Rico offers him a share of the North Side, a generous offer of partnership he cannot imagine Joe refusing. When Joe reiterates his passion for dancing and refuses, Rico has a tantrum. With a lover's acuity, he fastens on Olga, his rival, as the cause of all the trouble; it is she, a woman, who has warped Joe's mind. (Fear, mistrust, and misunderstanding of women is a staple of the genre.) He promises to kill them both if Joe doesn't abandon her, gesticulating wildly with his phallic cigar and blistering with a hatred born of hurt. LeRoy's sudden close-ups of Rico's face convey a rage and pain and disgust new to the character. The scene is played out in Rico's recently acquired, ultraposh apartment. Rico possesses everything he ever wanted—luxury, status, and power—everything but Joe. His hysterical attempt to regain Joe does not so much reflect on the monstrousness of his will but rather points to the irony of his ambition. He says to Joe, "I need you" (echoing Joe's earlier appeal to Olga). He is referring to the business of running the territory, but his immoderate anger at Joe's refusal reveals the true nature of his need (to us, not Rico, who does not understand his feelings). The scene is interrupted by a phone call from the Big Boy, who proposes a candidate to help Rico run things. Rico says no, assuring the Big Boy that his handpicked man, Joe Massara, is the best choice. When he returns from the phone, Joe is gone. This device makes clear the ascendency of emotion over reason in Rico. All Rico has to do is stop and think and it would be crystal clear that Joe is the worst choice possible, that he is not only not interested but is incompetent to fill that role and, in the eyes of most people, is not to be trusted. Yet Rico insists upon Joe. This is folly.

Rico cannot live with the fact that Joe prefers another to himself. He can't just forget Joe and tend to his duties as King of the North Side. When Joe runs away, Rico goes to Olga's apartment to make good his promise. By the time he and Otero get there Olga has already called the police. Rico busts in, fulminating. Joe stands tall against his gun. Rico, suddenly overwhelmed and paralyzed by emotions he cannot comprehend, does not shoot and backs off. Otero has no compunctions (he knows who *his* rival is), but Rico averts his aim. They both run. Otero is shot by cops. Rico escapes, but he is now alone and must go into hiding. Joe's betrayal marks the beginning of the end. Olga and (implied) Joe finger Rico for the murder of Commissioner McClure. This series of events alters our involvement with Rico. First his suffering and then the humiliation he undergoes bring us closer to the character. Our pity also makes us his superior. All that Rico does have that we cannot does not add up in human importance to what it is possible for all, or most of us, to have—love, friends, supportive relationships.

One of the engaging aspects of many gangster figures is their appetite for life, their freedom in expressing their desires. The gangster enjoys the rewards of success: liquor, women, fancy clothes, money to burn: his zest for action and his plunge into forbidden pleasures serve to put our own drab existences into perspective. But Rico is not engaging. He is just formidable. He doesn't enjoy life. He is not a happy man, except during those moments when his vanity is being catered to. He doesn't drink, and he forsakes the company of women. There is little to admire or envy. The nakedness of his power drive and his stubborn purity are forceful, to be sure, but not pleasurable, and offer little impetus for emulation. He leads a compulsive, joyless existence. Purity is a difficult quality to warm to; very few people have it. The pure man is unnatural, a freak, a pervert. He does not cooperate with life on a give-and-take basis. Purity is perhaps the most heroic of endeavors and the most foolish; it is the greatest assault on the way things are. Rico, who cannot yield, cracks, and that is how it should be. Purity nonetheless is abstractly, something admirable, and its destruction involves a sense of loss. The pure man is also a relative of the clown. The comic aspects of *Little Caesar* follow naturally from these (apparent) contradictions.

Rico can be seen as the most ridiculous of a group of ridiculous people. His mechanical egotism is certainly presented in a comic light, as a quality that a man less naive and less stupid might control to his advantage, especially when it seems to endanger his very survival. Rico has no self-control or self-awareness. His pretensions are continually undercut by irony. *He* thinks he's a big shot; *we* know he isn't. A man who has to brag so much about his own importance must be insecure. The only person who takes Rico totally seriously is Otero, a runtish, admiring secretary/valet/gun who feeds Rico's self-delusion by his solicitous loyalty. Rico's awkwardness is also connected to the film's class fatalism. Rico's clumsiness, once on top, suggests he has no business being there, that it takes more than a gun to rule smoothly and convincingly. Rico's fate is an object lesson for upwardly mobile minorities, one supported by the facts. Rico could never aspire to the Big Boy's WASP invulnerability. He could never possess the respectable facade that taste and culture and (presumably) inherited wealth provide. The Big Boy is above the law; he not only never dies, he never gets caught. He is protected by his veneer and (implicitly) by powerful friends who could always get him off the hook if the going got rough. Rico's fate, as an upstart Italian, is to get riddled by an Irish cop's bullets. Italian and Irish seem to have been designated to kill each other off. Their access to the upper echelons of power in legitimate businesses and professions is blocked. When Rico, heady with power, asserts that even the "Big Boy is through," we know that his grasp of reality is feeble indeed. As the audience intimates its limits, the grotesquerie of Rico's ambition becomes manifest.

Rico's gang is shown as a bunch of comic puppets. Rico's dominance thus becomes less of an achievement. LeRoy can't take them seriously, but Rico does. Tall, bulky Sam Vettori is just a blockhead, but for Rico he is the figure he has to discredit and topple (poor Sam spends his time sitting at his desk and playing endless games of solitaire, badly). The swiftness of Rico's rise is a tribute to his daring, but he can claim credit to little else. Episode after episode is arranged to keep the figure reduced, to remind us that Rico is nothing without his gun. Noisy, crude, and unrelaxed, Rico's vigor among a band of robots is rather comic. His concentrated energy and self-discipline, and even his obvious guts, are given semiludicrous definition.

Even in the early portions of the film, where we cannot help admiring Rico's pluck in cutting his way through the competition, his cockiness has a comic edge. LeRoy's framing emphasizes Rico's smallness within groups of standing figures. His acceptance of Vettori's tag of "Little Caesar" indicates an oversized vanity. His trigger-happy solution to any and all difficulties suggests a comic pathology. As he rises in position, his vanity becomes more absurd. At the banquet, his lack of poise is apparent in his halting, empty acceptance speech. His guests clap on cue, not out of genuine regard. Rico insists on having his picture taken with Diamond Pete Montana and cannot fathom why Pete refuses. Who wouldn't want his picture in the paper (a childish urge to be noticed)? He gets a gold watch on the occasion, but it turns out to be stolen. Having bought ten copies of the newspaper with his picture on the front page, and feeling like a million in his new, expensive coat, he struts openly and foolishly down the street. An easy target, he is wounded by machine-gun fire from a passing milk van as he admires his watch. During the funeral procession for Tony (whom he has killed), he sits and fidgets in the car and complains. "Gee, we're moving slow." The derby he adopts as appropriate to his new-won leadership rests uncomfortably on his head. There is a peculiar shot of him in bed, his back against the bedpost, looking like an overstuffed midget as he discourses to Otero (fawning at his feet) about a successful future. Anticipating an important meeting with the Big Boy, Rico dons a tux under Otero's sartorial

Little Caesar. The Big Boy himself invites Rico over for a taste of high living. Rico, pleased with the idea of himself existing within such a splendor of gold frames and gaudy furniture, nonetheless thinks nothing of flicking his cigar ashes onto the Big Boy's rug. The gesture nicely undoes his own ridiculous pretensions and assures us that his stay in high society will be brief. Rico is a stupid but honest enough brute. His childishly emotional vitality is an answer of sorts to the corruption, indolence, betrayal, and cowardice of others. Gunned down like an urban rat, his famous and eloquent disbelief of his own demise is enormously more impressive than lawman Flaherty's long-distance take-no-chances, hail-of-machine-gun-fire execution.

(Museum of Modern Art)

supervision. The shot has him standing on a table looking into a mirror. He wonders if he cuts the right figure. Otero, beaming assurance from below, tells him he looks grand. From that height he is easily convinced.

The most complex scene of Rico as a comic figure is the meeting with the Big Boy. Rico's unease in the Big Boy's affluent quarters points to both his vulgar virtues and his pathetic delusions in the context of the proprieties of the Big Boy's ostentatious lifestyle. Rico cuts a hapless figure, but one we can identify with. His behavior is, of course, keyed to *his* particular limitations, but they are limitations common to most of us. Rico is quite Chaplinesque in this scene, his naiveté triumphing over the situation by its obliviousness to decorum. In this environment, his vulgarity is welcome. His fumbling with the butler, his misconception about the gold frame costing fifteen thousand dollars, his comical perching on the edge of an expensive chair are errors and discomforts we easily recognize. When he spits off the tip of his cigar and flicks ashes on the Big Boy's rug, he speaks a language we can all understand.

But the scene cuts both ways. Rico's timidity is not admirable. He is moronically sucked in by all the glitter. He receives the Big Boy's flattery with ingratiating excess, unaware that he is being expertly manipulated. The Big Boy sits on his desk and looks down on Rico as he explains the logistics of the new regime. Made to appear unnaturally small, Rico becomes a disappointing yes-man. (The image recalls earlier ones in which Rico sits on top of a desk or lounges comfortably while delivering ultimatums to Sam Vettori and Little Arnie.) Not unexpectedly, the next scene shows us Rico clumsily assuming the Big Boy's mannerisms, parroting his language and his gestures in quarters modeled directly on his superior's.

Rico's dialogue is also frequently comic and characterized by reductive ironies. The implications of his wooing of Joe go by unrecognized. When he tells Otero, "The bigger they come, the harder they fall," he fails to consider himself a possibility. When he corners Sam and publicly humiliates him in front of his gang with, "You can dish it out, but you're getting so that you can't take it," the new-minted epigram is a sign of Rico's incisiveness. When he repeats it to Arnie Lorch, however, it suggests a mental stolidity and loses all its force (on us, anyway; Arnie, who hasn't heard it before, seems impressed). Yet Rico is capable of supreme gestures of contempt. "Fine shots you are," he yells from the sidewalk where he lies wounded by Arnie's machine gunners. His final defiance of Flaherty has a savage power that rescues the character from decline and reinstates him in the viewer's eyes as a man of strength and backbone. LeRoy seems to have arranged the film so that one distinct impression gives way to another. We are given pieces of Rico that we have to force into a whole. The pieces, taken singly, are varied, but they fit together. Rico is a whole whose parts are brought under separate and often ruthless scrutiny. That he retains an integrity and a coherence bespeaks how strongly he has been conceived by Robinson and LeRoy.

The audience, then, is kept at a distance from Rico by comments on his vanity (obsession with apparel, the reflex combing of his hair), his lack of self-awareness, and his bungled personal relationships—all signs of internal malfunctioning. Rico's attempt to bend reality to his will is also pitted against strong external forces that affirm by their inexorable nature, the outrageousness of his assumptions. Rico tries to control and outwit time.[5] For a while, through planning and energy, he stays on top of time. He's always where he has to be at just the right moment. But staying on top of time, synchronizing opportunity and desire, is the best one can ever hope for. One cannot do more. Time never slips, but humans do. Rico's successes and failures are both connected to time. He turns time back by adjusting the clock in the diner. He times the holdup of The Bronze Peacock at exactly midnight, New Year's Eve, when everyone will be distracted. He dashes from his dinner to kill Tony just as Tony is climbing the steps of Father McNeill's church (emphasizing how swiftly and ferociously he can act). Once he reaches the top, however, when there is little left to achieve and the pace of life slackens in accordance with his kingly functions, his neurotic momentum overtakes the rational balance required of his position. His restlessness rushes things. He cannot sit still and clock along in a well-regulated fashion. He complains that the funeral cortege is moving too slow (from this point on, all Rico's haste can do is quicken his inevitable fall). He anticipates the Big Boy's demise far too quickly. Taken off guard admiring his gold watch, he is machine-gunned in the street. His prolonged rant at Flaherty over the phone gives the police enough time to trace his call. Time, which once appeared as an ally, ultimately fails Rico.

Rico's desire to stay one step ahead is a disruption of the natural process of time that time itself readjusts to redress the balance upset by Rico's precipitousness. It is another of the character's violations that can only be brought into line by his death. The cop Flaherty, in contrast, is seen as time's loyal subject. He stands for the law, another force Rico has to deal with, but he is a far weightier figure than his function as society's answer to criminals suggests. His portrait matches Rico's in severity. Flaherty plays a waiting game. Occasionally frustrated by some of Rico's minor triumphs, he knows, deep down, that he holds all the cards and that Rico is a sap. A rigid, fearless character, Flaherty's contempt and ridicule of Rico indicate he is an agent of forces stronger than Rico that will eventually triumph.

Flaherty is Rico's nemesis. Thin, haggard, his face a pallid mask, his vulturous presence (Rico calls him a "buzzard") is a constant reminder of the fate awaiting Rico. Flaherty literally haunts Rico, appearing with spooky precision at every turn of fortune Rico undergoes. Rico can't shake loose of him; he is the devil coming for his due. Flaherty's uncanny stillness and patience tell us that Rico's drive and hurry are so much useless energy. Flaherty never wastes a move, never rushes, merely appears and stands and seems to mock. His deathly figure intrudes upon Rico's highest moments—the robbery of The Bronze Peacock, the funeral for Tony, the banquet—as if to remind Rico that he is there and will always be there, waiting for the right moment to close in or for Rico to play into his hands. His caustic gallows humor is in character.

The film does a good job of keeping Flaherty's specific and emblematic aspects in equilibrium. As a cop, he would prefer to put the cuffs on Rico so that the society he endangers (and Flaherty serves) can administer the proper punishment, this despite a personal grudge ("If I weren't on the force, I'd do the job cheap"). But the cuffs, and Rico's insistence against them, are used to suggest how determined Rico is to be free. For Flaherty to control and shame Rico would be a greater victory than to kill him. Rico is victorious in forcing his own death. His freedom and defiance are qualities that stay intact. If Flaherty wants him so badly, he can have his dead body, but nothing more, and that's what Rico gives him. One excellent moment that juxtaposes the personal and impersonal qualities of Flaherty occurs when he is standing in the street reading the society page entry devised by Rico's gang to announce Arnie Lorch's departure from town. Flaherty cracks a smile, showing us he's human. Then, instantly, his face hardens into its typical determined scowl.

The inevitability of what Flaherty represents creates sympathy for Rico. Flaherty's cold wisecracks at the end seem unnecessarily brutal. His calm satisfaction at trapping Rico makes us turn, with a mixture of awe and pity, toward the figure who emerges from the lowest squalor, deranged by drink and degradation, to take his last stand in the bleak, desolate city streets. The memorable long shot of Rico prowling aimlessly through the streets at night may make his smallness conspicuous, but the resolve of his gait tells all. Flaherty massacres him at long range through a billboard, with a machine gun. The shot is framed so that the audience, but not Flaherty, sees the choreography of Rico's fall. The vain jerk has a touch of nobility after all. "Little," yes, but "Caesar" too. Flaherty as executioner is a mean, cheap figure in comparison, but knowing enough to wait it out, he prevails.

The city becomes another force, like time and the law, that doesn't "give" under the pressure of Rico's aggression. Rico comes to the city and makes it his home. His home becomes a prison, a place of no exit. He rides high for a while but soon meets his doom in the dark, deserted streets of the city he once briefly ruled. The film also alludes to Rico's violation of the social order, which the order itself invites. The state of the society provides the temptation for men like Rico. His hardness is a product of his time, his callousness a response to life's demands. The conversation in the diner implies the thwarting of legitimate channels of activity. Joe and Rico are a pair of desperate characters both trying to make a living and also wanting something special out of life. Joe hears some of Rico's big talk, but then asks, "What's that got to do with the price of eggs?" Rico's got it all figured out. "Shoot first and argue afterwards." He says, twice, that he wants to "be somebody." Robbing gas stations is beneath his dignity. His contempt for Joe's dancing is based on an ideal of personal accomplishment. (He forces Joe into the gang because he resents Joe's success as a dancer. Success achieved independently of his personal philosophy becomes a threat to his self-esteem.) Joe's eventual success does seem fantastic and unreal; it is certainly more difficult to accept than Rico s failure. The truth of experience is embodied in Rico's corpse. The world is cruel and harsh, and Rico, trying to get ahead the best way he knows how, is destroyed, victimized by two interconnected forces—the either or choice offered by socioeconomic realities and his low, immigrant status.

Rico dismisses Joe's dream of "money" with contempt. For him it's a matter of pride. Ostensibly, Rico s career illustrates that "those who live by the sword perish by the sword," but it is also his ambition to rise from a lower to a higher level that is edifyingly halted. The taboos of the underworld microcosm are not startlingly different from those of the legitimate macrocosm. The acceptance of violence as the means to reconstitute vertical hierarchies is a naked version of more discreet uses of power practiced outside its boundaries. Rico's struggle for executive supremacy is not professional enough. He causes chaos in the underworld, which is running smoothly and peacefully until his arrival and is planning some strategy of coexistence even under McClure's incorruptible reign. Rico, advised to go steady and take it easy with his cannon, promptly shoots McClure. It is made clear that he doesn't have to; he does it to get noticed. Shooting McClure is a rash, risky act, but it puts a feather in his cap and makes it evident that he means business. The result, however, is that everyone's neck is on the line. Diamond Pete is too swiftly deposed. Rico's fast takeover creates havoc, and he is too unstable to handle his new power well. Pressures from within and without eventually crush the unreasonably ambitious man. If hard times lead to vice, one should indulge in vices safer than ambition—especially if the form it takes is gangsterism. Dancing, a legitimate (if odd) route, pays off. And what of the others?—the film is mum. The exploitative, sanctioned businessman, the corrupt politician are lost to sight beneath the tragic, expressive layers of the gangster.

The film's visual scheme is built around depression extremes—seedy diner and vile flophouse at one end and the contemporary pleasure dome, the Bronze Peacock, at the other. (The Club Palermo occupies a neither-here-nor-there midpoint, a place where plans are laid that lead to either the flophouse or the haunts of the idle rich.) The screaming inanity at the Bronze Peacock, the profligate boozing and flamboyant wealth, justify Rico's holdup—he's just redistributing the wealth. The denizens of the flophouse project the other great reality—poverty. Rico goes through both. He can't legitimately attain the one, and he won't settle for the other. Since there is nothing else, he must die.

Little Caesar is a visually exact and cohesive film. It uses the camera limitations of the early sound film to its advantage. In place of camera dazzle, we get camera aptness. Its lighting strategy is uncomplicated but sound. The two-thirds of the film devoted to Rico's rise are brighter in mood and look than the last third, which takes place completely at night and is more ominously lit. The sobriety of its visual style, reflected in the prevalence of talky exchanges between characters photographed by a stationary camera, prohibits the meddlesome nuances that might endanger the stark, unadorned tale the film wants to tell. That sounds like a specious excuse for impoverished filmic imagination, and I'm not sure I can defend myself in any other way than running the film. Everything LeRoy does seems right. Camera distance is astutely judged to correspond with purpose and import. Midrange, eye-level framing records a stylized unity of behavior, speech, and interior mise-en-scène. On those few occasions when something more is demanded, LeRoy's camera is up to the task. The excitement of the Bronze Peacock robbery is captured by a montage sequence of unexpectedly disordered rhythm. While the point of view is objective, the danger, daring, and precision of the execution (as suggested by the simultaneous-action dissolves) mirror Rico's subjectivity. Up to that point, the film's rhythms have been quite regular, have established a progression of evenly spaced and articulated scenes, and minus a few point-of-view shots, the camera has been objective. This visual intrusion is a device to break the tempo and suddenly to envelop the viewer with a feeling of Rico's recklessness. The overhead shot of the roulette wheel establishing Arnie Lorch's gambling house is perhaps mere window dressing, but it does reveal a concern for effective transitions.

When Rico is introduced to the gang, the camera dollies in, pans around, and dips and rises, without cutting, to pick out each individual character and also to describe how they are connected by membership in the gang. The camera lumbers rather gracelessly, but the technically awkward maneuver fits the occasion. The camera becomes Rico's eyes. Rico, as a new member, must take in the group as a whole and also each individual as he is introduced. The camera movement imitates Rico's struggle to size up the situation properly and take it in. LeRoy's control is evident also in his judicious use of close-ups. There aren't many, but when they come their impact justifies LeRoy's choice and his selectivity. The close-ups in the first half of the film are only of objects—clock, diamond stickpin, invitation card, newspaper column, all of which represent extensions of Rico's attitudes and feelings, their importance, and isolation through close-up, determined by Rico's perception of them. The characters in the first half of the film are never shown in close-up. Group and medium two-shots dominate, emphasizing Rico's influence and control over others. In the second half of the film the importance of objects is diminished (the decor getting progressively barren), and close-ups of people replace those of objects. Rico's problems are now internal, not external, and the camera must examine his face to reveal the nature of his strife.

The first confrontation with Joe, in which Rico comes to a boil, contains several close-ups of Rico, bringing us close to his frustration, letting us feel the force of his emotions. The most extraordinary series of close-ups occurs when Rico is about to shoot Joe at Olga's apartment. LeRoy has held his most expressive close-ups in reserve so that justice may be done to the dramatic potential of this encounter. Joe makes his choice: "Shoot, Rico, get it over with." Rico is taken aback by a man who does not fear his gun. Joe's close-up shows him staring Rico down, Rico advances, then slowly backs away, completely disturbed, the rug pulled out from under him. As Rico retreats, his face, in close-up, goes out of focus. The bewildered look on his face and the gradual loss of focus convey the dazed state of a man buffeted by feelings he doesn't understand. It is the film's most intense moment.

The credit sequence of a film like *20,000 Years in Sing Sing* (1933) has more filmic flash than the whole of *Little Caesar*. By that time, the camera was free of the restrictions imposed on it by the early sound film. *Little Caesar* doesn't have a very big bag of tricks, but there's not a shot in it that betrays an insufficiency of means. It is to LeRoy's credit that the film never feels pinched but, on the contrary, is inventive, resourceful, and appropriate in its camera technique and visual style. The film establishes from the beginning its restrained approach, and the final shots, especially, have a solemn decorum that would have been ill matched to a more intemperate manner throughout. The shot of Rico falling—a slow-motion choreography done without camera manipulation—is held just the right amount of time for us to savor his imperial collapse, and the camera is back far enough to catch the complete roll of Rico's derby after it hits the ground. As we watch the hat roll far from Rico's bullet-riddled body, the symbolic and naturalistic qualities of the image fuse in ironic grandeur. LeRoy's reserve gives us a classical tableau of pointed linkage among person, object, and environment. To have cut into a close-up for emotional pull would have broken the impression of detached awe.

The concluding shots are complex without sacrificing directness of impact. A poetic conception of image and character discreetly heightens a climactic multiplicity of statement. The callous reality of the age and the dream of escaping it are evocatively synthesized.

Rico is the last to understand that he can die like any man. His farewell to the world—"Mother of mercy, is this the end of Rico?"—is singularly cruel in that his vanity continues to get the better of his understanding. It is not a conscious refusal to recognize his human limitation but a deep trait of character that allows his incomprehension to take precedence over the brute fact of his mortality. The line could be read with emphasis on "this" or "end," and it would make a difference. Robinson's stress on "Rico" suggests that the character is self-absorbed to the end, and his eyes are large with disbelief. Irony, pity, and sympathy converge.

The billboard Flaherty rips his bullets through advertises Joe and Olga's dance act—"Tipsy, Topsy, Turvy," a "laughing, singing, dancing success." The image points to the disparity between the gritty fact of Rico lying dead and the extravagant display of Joe and Olga's success. "Tipsy, Topsy, Turvy" undoubtedly comments on the ups and downs of Rico's fortunes, but the more generalized idea of life's unpredictability is also there and must have registered on contemporary audiences.

The billboard dominates the screen in both size and light. It radiates a glittering fantasy, an immoderate wish fulfillment. Joe's choice may conceivably lead to this, but the effect is that of a dream. Rico's lifeless body lies behind, not visible, but we know it is there. The image holds a sense of the vacillating parameters of the audience's imaginative life, a need for illusion fighting a basic disillusion. Reality is for an instant masked, but not convincingly. This was also the era of escapist musicals, to which the image alludes. Flaherty machine-guns the image, literally penetrating its facade. The attempt at a grim pulp poetry succeeds nicely.

The shot also works against a clear-cut moral point. Gerald Mast's opinion that *Little Caesar* "glorifies amoral brutality"[6] is too simplistic in the light of the feelings the ending provokes. The conclusion of *Little Caesar* reinforces the timely truth that in the world outside the theater one either flew very high or very low, and most viewers were flying low indeed. When the opening musical refrain returns to close the film, it takes on the character of a funeral march, an exit music of aggression stilled. And what lies dead is not just the gangster but his dream.

CREDITS	*Little Caesar*		
	(First National, 1930, 80 min.)		
Producer	Hal B. Wallis	Cast	Edward G. Robinson (Rico)
Director	Mervyn LeRoy		Douglas Fairbanks, Jr. (Joe Massara)
Screenplay	Francis Edward Faragoh		Thomas Jackson (Flaherty)
	(from the novel *Little Caesar*		Glenda Farrell (Olga)
	by W. R. Burnett)		Stanley Fields (Sam Vettori)
Photography	Tony Gaudio		Sidney Blackmer (Big Boy)
Editor	Ray Curtiss		George E. Stone (Otero)
Art Director	Anton Grot		Ralph Ince (Diamond Pete Montana)
Music	Erno Rapee		Maurice Black (Arnie Lorch)
			William Collier, Jr. (Tony)

The Public Enemy (1931)

Little Caesar is an articulation of Rico's dream to be on top. The dream motivates the character; it is explicitly announced as his ambition. *The Public Enemy*, less than half a year later, already treats this dream implicitly, uses it as a given, implants it in the character without directly referring to it. *The Public Enemy* transfers the dream to a level of behavior. The audience is not absorbed by a determined overreacher whose dream of power and personal success takes the form of actions unmistakably expository of that dream. In the case of *The Public Enemy*, it would be more accurate to say that the audience is absorbed by an embodied dream of vital behavior. The meaning and the outcome of both films are the same, but in *The Public Enemy* the gangster's goals are not so unrealistic and out of reach as they are in *Little Caesar*. Tom Powers's aspirations are located in his desire and his ability to be a certain way, to exist in a lively manner. Exercising that desire freely and to the full violates the same social and moral codes as Rico's enormous ambition and entails the same consequences. The outward signs of his success are offhandedly represented, not pointedly observed, as in *Little Caesar*. What matters, what is gripping, is Tom Powers's personal vitality in a context of inertia, stolidity, and hesitancy, and it can only have scope outside the boundaries of legitimate activity.

The Public Enemy introduced, in James Cagney, the most dynamic of screen gangsters. His portrayal of Tom Powers made him an instant star. His combination of childlike sensitivity, insolent grace, and gleeful viciousness proved irresistible. Director William Wellman recollects how Cagney got the part:

> I make a picture called "Public Enemy," and we hire a guy named Eddie Woods to play the lead. We get a relatively unknown guy named Jimmie Cagney who has a tough little way, and he is playing the second part. I didn't see the rushes for three days because I was working late and said, "Aw, to hell with them. I'll see them over the weekend." When I looked at the rushes, I said, "Keerist! Hasn't Zanuck seen them?" And he hadn't either, because he had been out of town. Now Zanuck was then working for Warner Bros., and he was doing half the pictures and Hal Wallis was doing the other half. I was working for Zanuck. I immediately got hold of him. I said, "Look, there is a horrible mistake. We have the wrong guy in here. Cagney should be the lead." Zanuck said "Well, you know who Eddie Woods is don't you?" And I said, "No, I don't. Who is he?" "He's engaged to marry Louella Parson's daughter." I said, "Well, for Christ's sake, are you going to let some *newspaper* woman run your business?" He said, "Change them." We changed them, and Cagney became a big star. . . .[7]

It was a momentous choice. Wellman's instinct about Cagney was right. His runaway performance almost throws the film off-balance, but it is Wellman's choice to give him that much rein. (By the time Raoul Walsh made *White Heat* [1949], Cagney's identity was so established—even after a decade of non-gangster parts—that Cody Jarrett's psychopathy seemed a condition appropriate to a figure we had known for a long time, something lurking finally made explicit.) Wellman, working with a talented unknown, wisely left him free to define as widely as possible his screen persona.

Wellman claims, in the same interview, that Zanuck let him do *The Public Enemy* because he promised to deliver "the most vicious picture ever made." One would expect *The Public Enemy*, therefore, to be tough and tawdry. In fact, it is elegant and mellow. Cagney's brutality is at times unnerving and repulsive, but Wellman allows us to understand it first and condemn it only later, if at all. Cagney's contribution, moreover, gives the film a verve not seriously compromised by the gross ironies of the final scene. The "crime-does-not-pay" lesson fades far sooner than Cagney's gaiety. Taken by itself, the script of *The Public Enemy* shows its hero to be a failure in all things, but Cagney's dancing shuffle of joy on a public street after "scoring" Jean Harlow is one of the enduring moments of happiness in the history of art. No one can ever claim to have been happier, nor has anyone ever deserved to be. Moralists had good cause to be alarmed.

*T*he Public Enemy opens with a series of images reconstructing the pre-Prohibition period of 1909. The pans and dissolves that alternate with cutaways to stockyard, factory, brewery, and urban congestion evoke the living conditions of the lower classes and define the boundaries of their world of work, play, and relaxation. Wellman's street scenes have a documentary neutrality. The sidewalks, lined with bars, crawl with life. Exteriors and interiors are crowded with hard-drinking people. The noisy march of a Salvation Army band becomes part of the general din and then fades as the musicians exit from the frame. The old, the young, the sober, and the drunk mix together in the teeming street. The effect is Zolaesque, the vivid overlay of details creating a naturalistic clutter rich in statement. Here, indeed, is an environment in which crime can "breed." Wellman doesn't hurry his images, they come at a measured pace and casually construct a comprehensive sense of a time and place. (Nothing in *Little Caesar* resembles Wellman's devotion to authenticity in the opening of *The Public Enemy*.) The pictorial beauty of this sequence and its period charm are rare in the genre. Much care has been taken by producer and director alike. *The Public Enemy* is a project Wellman is clearly interested in. His involvement shows in the acuteness of his mise-en-scène and in the presence of shots savored for their own sake, in addition to conveying meaning and information.

The opening of *The Public Enemy* deftly combines period flavor, narrative, and social awareness. Wellman is not being critical but exact. He coolly works in points as he describes. The brewery, an imposing structure, has a dominant influence on social life. Wellman pans along the path the beer takes from the bar (in pails dangling from a long plank) across the width of the street, while a Salvation Army band cuts across the street lengthwise, contrasting two extremes and establishing a direct link between drinking and community life. Prohibition will surely upset a society so dependent on booze. In the tavern, the overflow of froth down the sides of beer mugs evokes both a nostalgia for less restrictive days and an aura of excess. A modified use of Soviet intellectual montage makes an implicit analogy between human congestion and stockyards, and the blast of a factory whistle is a shorthand indication of proletarian milieu and routine.

Tom Powers, born in this environment, is its victim. As a child, he exercises opportunities for delinquency. Pampered by an indulgent mother and beaten by a harsh father, he quickly adopts a thorough disrespect for authority. After his father dies, the task of controlling him falls to his mother, who is not up to the job. His favored elder brother gobbles up legitimate priorities, leaving Tom to fend for himself in the urban jungle. His brother Mike (pulling virtue on top of rank) becomes, for Tom, a focus of contempt and a target of implicitly envious hatred. (There is surely irony in Mike's saying to Tom, "I wish you'd try and stay home a little more" — this from a character who has just enlisted, who works days on a streetcar and spends evenings at school.) His brother lectures him and slugs him, but Tom doesn't hit back. He learns to take punishment, control himself, endure humiliation. When his father cracks the leather belt across his bottom, he holds back cries and tears. His upbringing toughens him. The gangster's advantage over most men is, often enough, his contempt of pain and death. *The Public Enemy* explores, with a sociological awareness, where and how such hardness and invulnerability originate.

John Gabree writes, "Nowhere, not even in the scenes in *The Public Enemy* where Tom and Matt graduate from petty to grand larceny, is there any statement that social conditions breed crime.[8] Actually, the film's logic seems based on just that assumption. Any clearer cause-and-effect relationship would amount to overt didacticism. Tom's brother succeeds in resisting the pull of crime partly by accident and partly by a strong will. He is not a pleasant character. Wellman suggests that his choice of night school and drudge work in place of the possible fast buck is conditioned by his place in the family: as the elder brother, he must, in the absence of the father, assume the role of the family's masthead of respectability. His anger at Tom is motivated by jealousy as well as moral principle. The film does not whitewash him. Tom accuses Mike of pinching nickels from the streetcar he operates, and when he returns from the war, his mental health impaired, Tom says, "Your hand ain't so clean. You killed and liked it. You didn't get them medals by holding hands with them Germans." Neither charge is denied or confirmed, but his brother's hysterical reaction to both charges implies at least a partial truth. Mike goes to war with an air of nobility, enlisting out of the blue. In effect, he is abandoning family for personal glory. Tom gets stuck with making do at home in a difficult period. Mike escapes to fight legitimate battles in a foreign land for abstract principles. Tom stays to fight less prestigious battles at home in the interests of economic survival. Both brothers want to achieve, and the world they live in shatters them both. Mike's psyche is damaged in the war and Tom dies young from bullets. The mother suffers passively through it all. If, in *Little Caesar*, a relation is made between the gangster's activity and business, in *The Public Enemy*, the relation is between the gangster's activity and war. The relation, to some degree, undermines the surface distinctions between legitimacy and illegitimacy.

If social conditions do not *force* people into crime, the film implies that if you follow the natural drift of things you end up a crook. Conditions certainly do not favor virtue. The film is not a rabid tract. Tom's environment, class, and upbringing do not compel, but they hinder rather than help a calm, law-abiding existence. *The Public Enemy* is also concerned with the breakdown of the family, that archaically utilitarian, deeply emotional structure doomed to crumble in the advance of progress and industry and their broader, less personal units of loyalty. Tom moves from home to the Washington Arms Hotel: he chases a rich dame from Texas. Mike goes to war in Europe. A policeman's catalog of Tom's sins is capped by "he lies to his mother." A world on the go disrupts community and family life, breaks apart its traditional patterns. The society is in flux: one takes one's chances or vegetates and gets left behind. The film is morally conservative in charting the disaster of dislocated activity, but no acceptable alternatives exist. The old, lethargic ways are being pressured by quick social change. Mike's route at home is a slow crawl to anonymity. Maybe Tom could have become a cop and gone on the take, but making him a gangster was probably less disillusioning.

The film also indicates how entrenched and deadening a lower-middle-class environment can be and that Tom's move for easy money is inspired by a sense of the inhibiting structures he was born into. The unambitious stand still as they grow older and get nowhere. In the 1909 section, Tom and Matt, as kids, are seen entering a neighborhood "boys' club" run by Putty Nose, a period Fagin of low morals (he sings dirty songs to the kids) and even lower ethics. Tom and Matt cross through a tableau of school-age kids picturesquely arranged in a vaguely animated pursuit of various activities and nonactivities. The 1915 section opens with Tom and Matt cutting across essentially the same

The Public Enemy. A bunch of two-bit punks listen to their venal mentor. One, Tom Powers, looks especially intent, and is headed for bigger things.

image with essentially the same cast of background characters engaged in young-adult and more sodden versions of their former interests. The little fat kid who was sprawled vacantly in an armchair is now numbly gambling in a small-stake card game, and so forth. The impression is of an anonymous group of people whose station in life is fixed. In this context, we can see how Tom, like Rico, wants to "be somebody," to bust out of this deprived, depressing limbo of aimless loafing. It beats school and a nickel-dime job, but to slouch around sulky and morose in the dead air of Putty Nose's club is to make a poor settlement indeed. (It is preferable, though, to being "good." Tom's alternate education—lots of fieldwork—is better than a "straight" one. The ambience of Putty Nose's club is not one of depravity but [relative] vitality.) The club is packed with surly ne'er-do-wells, too demoralized to work and too gutless to strike out for big things (the comic image of Matt, Tom, and three other fledgling thugs crunched awkwardly on Putty Nose's bed—Tom's feet don't touch the ground—sums up the cheap, small-time flavor of this life). Cagney's entrance announces him as a man to reckon with—the walk, the smart mouth, the tipped hat, the expressive body language. When Putty Nose gives him a gun, one can be sure he'll know what to do with it. On his first job, Tom panics from inexperience, but not even Putty Nose's treachery (he refuses to harbor him), his own failure, or the sight of his buddy's corpse (shot in the act by a cop) dent his resolve to make plenty of dough the fast and easy way and lead a stylish life. It is still the best choice of any available.

Little Caesar was an unusually ascetic gangster hero. Tom Powers is the prototype of the high-living gangster, synonymous in the public mind with fast, fancy cars, easy money, loose women, boozing, swank nightclubs, and reckless, uninhibited activity. Wellman doesn't soft-pedal Tom's relish of these things. Tom knows how to live, and we admire him for that. We respond to his amoral enjoyment of a full array of life's pleasures. We lose sight of the cost to others his living so high and free exacts. The gangster's defects become virtues, the surface manifestations of his success obscuring his more important failings. Wellman doesn't gloss, nor does he suppress, Tom's weaknesses. He lets

Cagney's momentum, though, sweep the viewer away. We are so caught up in Tom's urge to live that we do not take full advantage of several opportunities to back away from him. The values he carries are too attractive. Long after the film has made it clear that he's a lost cause not worth backing, the shock of his mortality registers.

Matt, the more cautious, less intense character, acts as a foil (like Joe Massara in *Little Caesar*) to Tom, reminding us of his abnormalities. Tom feeds his self-esteem by bullying and lording it over Matt, however inoffensively. We laugh at Tom's belittling remarks and lose sight of the insecurity that dictates his behavior. Tom's contempt for Matt's relationship with Mamie (shown as a satisfying combination of sexual lust and human feeling) is implicitly connected to his own irritating affair with Kitty. (Pushing the half grapefruit in her face elevated Cagney to a status of folk hero. The gesture, underneath its entertaining sadism, bespeaks a crude solution to sexual dissatisfactions.) Tom interprets Mamie's influence over Matt as a sign of Matt's weakness. Matt and Mamie's dallying in bed causes Tom to order him to hurry up for the next job. Tom wrests Matt from his wedding celebration to help him finish off Putty Nose. Matt leaves, despite Mamie's concern. Marriage would naturally sever the two men's close relationship, and Tom's insistence is his means of not losing hold on Matt. (Matt tells us that Tom "ain't the marrying kind." In gangster films, the hero rarely attains a well-regulated sexual life. It would blunt his other duties, compromise his existential independence, and make for a degree of social integration he was born, it seems, never to experience.)

The cold-blooded murder of Putty Nose is the first scene in which Tom's brutality makes us question our identification with him. Tom's cruel cat-and-mouse preliminary, with Putty Nose pleading for his life, is given a divided emphasis. Matt's disturbance is the visual point of convergence of our own. The killing takes place offscreen, the camera observing Matt's helpless, sickened reaction. The nastiness of Tom's line of work, which Tom enjoys, provides a potential turning point in our attitude, one cued by the silent, dismayed figure of Matt. Tom reminds us that Putty Nose nurtured their career in crime, and when the heat was on abandoned them to fend for themselves. His death, then, is proper on grounds of vileness, and for the violation of both human and gangland codes.[9] But Tom's motive is not primarily one of social, human, or professional justice. He has been egged on by Nails Nathan; the killing of Putty Nose would confirm Nails's faith in his toughness. Besides, Putty Nose's "bad" influence is twisted into a backhanded compliment: if it weren't for Putty Nose, "We might have been ding-dings on a streetcar." It boils down to a personal grudge carried to excessive lengths. Putty Nose's punishment does not fit his crime, and Matt's presence tells us so.

Tom's relationships with women are complete failures. It is partly the women's fault but mainly his. His love for his mother is genuine, but he gives her nothing but grief and some occasional guilt-money. As a child, he prefers the streets to home. As a youth, home is a place to drop in on once in a while. Finally, after a tiff with Mike, he moves to a hotel. Throughout, he is the lost child, denying his need for mother and experiencing difficulties with other women because of his divided, immature self. The three women he comes in contact with want to mother him and, secondarily, domesticate him. We are semigratified to see Tom resist, but the women's protective gestures and verbal comforts (echoing his mother's "my baby") attest to the character's sexual immaturity. The scenes with women define the pathetic aspects of his character. Matt warms to Mamie, but Tom tires of Kitty, giving her his opinion of a cozy, domestic breakfast by administering a grapefruit facial. He wants something else without knowing what it is. He thinks he finds it in Gwen (Jean Harlow), but that turns out a bust.

The scenes with Harlow have a strange flavor all their own, as if Wellman doesn't know quite what to do with her. Maybe it's the dialogue (combined with Harlow's unconvincing upper-class delivery) that's responsible: "From Chicago?" "Not exactly. I came from Texas." Wellman certainly doesn't *help* his players through their lines. On the other hand, the stiffness of their scenes does convey a sense of Tom's discomfort at being out of his element, and being dominated to boot.

Gwen is given to us as a woman who exists to move from one sexual conquest to another and who looks like she was born for no other purpose but to wear expensive clothes and move with a statuesque imperturbability. She breathes "class" (the double entendre of her staying at The *Congress* Hotel is apt). Tom wants her but is confused about how to get her. She is mysterious and, if attainable, not by any route known to him. Her cool eroticism baffles his lower-class flamboyance. He seems destined never to have her. Ironically, just as he decides out of frustration to leave her, she makes her pitch. As they are about to cross class lines, effect a merger of proletarian vitality and sensuous culture, Matt intrudes to announce Nails Nathan's death (his head kicked in by his horse). Since Gwen represents Tom's social aspirations, it is a significant interruption. Tom leaves to shoot Nails's horse (a symbol of the aristocracy of wealth—analogous to Gwen—who kills the imposter Nails) and begin his descent to the gutter from which he came. Gwen, robbed of her pleasure, deliberately, and without losing poise, shatters a glass in the fireplace. Each figure adheres to his or her social destiny.

Gwen's seduction of Tom, however unsuccessful, rests on her ability to mother him. "You're not running away from me," she says and, holding him to her breast, calls him "my bashful boy." Responding to this need, Tom becomes sexually manageable. The third of Tom's women, Jane, again mothers him as a setup to intercourse, and succeeds, but without his knowledge or help. Upon the scattering of Nails's mob, Paddy has told his boys to lie low. He has taken away their money and their guns and has left them in the charge of an aging whore who feeds them food and drinks and provides them bedding in her apartment. All the boys but Tom adapt well to this enforced retirement. He gets restless and drinks himself silly. Jane loosens his clothes and puts him to bed in solicitous, motherly tones ("Be a good boy and sit down." "Let me help you." "I'll take your shoes off, too." "Just a goodnight kiss for a fine boy.") Tom resists verbally but allows himself to be kissed and handled, his basic need for a real mother making the best of a substitute one. At breakfast, Jane alludes to their night together; in his groggy state she has managed to seduce him. Feeling betrayed and violated, he gets furious and slaps her. Disgusted and full of hate (he believed, after all, that he was merely being tucked into bed), he storms out of the apartment in defiance of Paddy's orders, fleeing the deceitful presence of woman and rushing to whatever fate awaits him. Matt, the sexually normal, follows him to the streets and gets gunned down.

From here on to the end, the character becomes a figure of death. He stands in heavy rain, his face a revenger's mask, and single-handedly walks into Schemer Burns's headquarters and wipes out most of his men (the revenge motif is not present in *Little Caesar*). It is difficult to decide what meaning to ascribe to this action. Tom is a man whose world has fallen apart. His brother hates him, his mother cannot claim him, his best friend, sticking by him, has been murdered, his "love" has proven unattainable. The gesture may therefore be suicidal. He cannot hope to survive as one against so many. Part of the gangster's "lesson," though, is to understand that he is mortal, and Tom may well believe himself invincible. Wellman has him slop down a gutter's edge toward the audience, clutching his wounds, the low angle rhetorically magniloquent. The tragic rain pours down ceaselessly. Tom, falling, utters his epitaph: "I ain't so tough." These words are not addressed to himself, or to us, but to the cosmos: it is a tragic utterance worthy to reverberate in the vastness of space and time. The water, glittering in the light of the streetlight, is a kind of baptism streaking a truth across his brightly lit face, a point of revelation surrounded by his otherwise rigid, black, impenetrable frame.

The film could end here, the moral lesson completed, a measure of self-understanding achieved. We get, instead, a double coda, anticlimactic and sobering. The film does not want to end on so heroic a note. Tom survives to be bandaged up on a hospital bed, barely able to move. The driving force behind the film is harnessed. The reunion with his family brings to completion the sentimental motif of the lost child. Tom wants to come home, to make

The Golden Age

57

peace with his brother. He is penitent about the grief he has caused and seems on the verge of a virtuous regeneration. The sentimentality, however, is turned around by Cagney's sublimely individualistic gesture of giving a soft fist tap to his mother's lowered, tearful head. This stubborn self-assertion makes the whole of his previous self come alive and blots out any hope (fear?) that the character has undergone a change. Wellman attempts to dispel the glory of his moment of high humor by later dumping Tom's trussed-up carcass through the doorway of his home. It is a shocking image, suggesting the true end of criminals like Tom—the crowning indignity—but the dull thud of his drop has a brutal, chordal finality, and his mummified appearance the ghastly grandiloquence of myth.

The "heavy" conclusion, with its thick ironies (the song "I'm Forever Blowing Bubbles" plays throughout; shots of Ma humming happily upstairs as she prepares Tom's bed are intercut with Tom's delivery; the slow, steady tread of Mike's feet [from ground level] walking toward the interior of the house, presumably to burst Ma's bubble of expectation; the parody of a homecoming; the record that keeps revolving—its stuck needle making a sound like a heartbeat), is a justifiable attempt to bring the film to a more somber point. Much of *The Public Enemy* is lighthearted, and its humor helps to increase our involvement with the characters (unlike *Little Caesar,* where the humor typically works against the characters). The humor, as Wellman directs it, seems to issue naturally from the vitality of the characters' response to life. Wellman, as an authentic recorder, must capture that facet as well. In *Little Caesar* scenes are tagged as ridiculous; the humor is "arranged." In *The Public Enemy* humor crops up unexpectedly; it is a quality that Cagney, especially, seems to carry with him and can at a given moment exercise. His spontaneous comic invention in the first nightclub scene, his high-spirited cruise down city avenues in his new convertible, the robbery of the gun, and the wonderful moment in the hospital are "good times" Wellman captures with a breezy insouciance.

*T*he Public Enemy is intelligently organized, its slice-of-life approach shored up by methodical layers of meaning in continuity. Dress is carefully matched to rises in status, and the characters' very movements seem to respond to their change in attire (speech idioms, however, remain unchanged and are played off against alterations of dress). The musical score is integrated with the characters' materialist advance. At Putty Nose's, a lone honky-tonk piano crashes away; at the nightclub where Tom and Matt pick up Mamie and Kitty, a brass-dominated orchestra plays "Toot Toot Tootsie"; in the more elegant nightspot where Matt and Mamie's wedding celebration takes place, the entrance of the nattily attired guests is accompanied by a smoother, more genteel orchestra, string-dominated. The grayish tones of Dev Jennings's photography imply a neutrality of outlook, and it is only toward the end, when a sense of mounting drama permits it, that the images become more expressive and sinister—a shot of a moving car taken from underneath, Cagney at a curtain-blackened window peering through a narrow, illuminated slit, the low angle of his stumbling in the rain, a pair of unattended machine guns in a window with the curtains gently blowing in the breeze. In the absence of a Flaherty figure, with its built-in social morality, there are few one-to-one confrontations. Group scenes are the norm, and personal inclinations assume morally ambiguous values in context; for example, the scene with Lehman, the brewery owner which establishes a direct connection between business and crime and in which Leh-

The Public Enemy. "You mean like this?" Tom, about to go the limit against Schemer Burns's mob, still sports a twinkling eye, as he here enjoys playing the "How to get a free handgun" special at a neighborhood gun shop. This illustration could also be called "Gulling the Jew," as resentment of minorities, especially successful ones, was more openly tolerated than in our present day, where even a hint of such prejudice could prompt an invitation to your local courtroom. (Museum of Modern Art)

man's ongoing hypocrisy is seen to be a worse evil than Nails Nathan's exploding of it. The gangster film's most dangerous probe was that the system was corrupt all the way to the top. The presence of Lehman and the scarcity of police hint at that condition.

Where Leroy comes across as a caustic moralist ("Wild Bill"), Wellman's less stolid sensibility can be discerned in his treatment of three representative scenes:

1. **Prohibition eve.** People are seen frantically stocking up on liquor. Some are drunk already, and guzzling. They stagger around singly, in pairs, in groups. They converge on and away from the liquor store from all sides of the frame, on foot, in cars, wheeling baby carriages full of booze. A flower truck stops, opens its rear doors wide, dumps all the flowers in the street, and loads up with liquor. A bottle falls out of a car window, smashing onto the sidewalk; a woman gets out to inspect the damage. Liquor runs down the gutters; people crisscross each other, slightly dazed and crazed. The sequence tells us all we need to know about the folly of Prohibition, but Wellman eschews the moralist's scorn and the satirist's guffaw. His tolerant view embraces more complex possibilities. It is a funny sequence. The public's reaction may be too hysterical, but Wellman implies they have a right to some hysteria. They are silly and excessive, but not enough to scorn. The brevity of the sequence (55 seconds) reinforces its comedy; everything is rushed, one outlandish shot is juxtaposed

The Public Enemy. Mike towers in clenched-fist rage over casually smirking brother Tom, whose "blood-money" feast looks less than midway to a finish. Ma, uselessly torn (she respects Mike but enjoys Tom more), is in retreat off-frame. She could no more stop socioeconomic forces from creating such crisis moments than she could take her own Catholic life. Shown early as "weak" in being powerless to stop her drunken husband's belt buckle thrashing of their son Tom, she has no authority to dredge up to prevent this kind of hostility from arising. She can only plead for peace and get maybe a few mealtimes free of skirmishes. The Powers, as a family unit, are history. (Museum of Modern Art)

rapidly with another. But the rapidity also suggests something dangerously obsessional. There is a sense of menace—the blind staggering, the smashed bottle, the violence of movement, some incongruous, bizarre imagery. Wellman implicitly connects the noisy madness of this moment to the coming gangland violence Prohibition in fact spawned. A more priggish and pretentious mind, a coarser and more assertive directorial style, would have not been able to maintain the delicate balance of this sequence.

2. The welcome home dinner for Mike. Here a simple but effective comic device modifies our reception of the scene's serious tensions. Mike, his mind somewhat damaged by the war, has come home with his purity of outlook even more pronounced. Tom and Matt, without giving it a second thought, have contributed a huge keg of beer for the occasion. The keg is placed on the dinner table, its large bulk controlling the visual field for viewer and characters alike. The serious emotional conflicts that ensue are hazed by absurdity. Wellman gets a lot of mileage out of this inert, gross, ridiculous object. Mike's violent breakdown is, in part, brought about by having to deal with the keg's inescapable presence. The comedy of the characters having to talk to each other through and around the keg, however, puts Mike's anger into perspective (and even Ma's having a beer). The keg stands for moral and family divisions, but its obstreperous thereness lets Wellman direct for complexity of tone. With the characters blocked from each other by the symbol of their moral-ethical differences, their conflicting points of view are both reduced in importance and fanned to extremes by the looming keg, which parodies the surface decorum of this family reunion. When the emotions reach their peak, Wellman frames first Mike and then Tom without the keg in view. The keg, of course, *does* nothing. It is there, like the director is there, detached but guiding the outcome. When we first see it, it is certainly noticeable but not noteworthy. As the scene goes on, its presence becomes funny; a while later, it becomes less funny. When the conflict erupts at last to serious consequences, Mike hurls the keg into a corner. It has done its (and Wellman's) job.

3. The potato chip scene. Paddy's bar. Paddy discourses to Tom and Matt about the financial rewards of going into the liquor business. Wellman's entry is deceptively casual, as if the camera just dropped in to observe a typical but unimportant moment in the characters' lives. Matt and Tom lean, their figures framed in full, against the counter, Paddy on the other side. Tom, facing toward the camera, is chewing food and having some coffee. Paddy is snacking on potato chips. From this wordless *temps mort* opening, Wellman moves, with a quickened tempo, to the grotesque close-up of Paddy shoving handfuls of chips into his mouth, scraps falling down his chin. The image conveys his gluttonous greed, but again, the context prohibits a severely critical attitude. The chips, unobtrusively part of the scene, suddenly emerge as a comic prop. Wellman narrows his focus to isolate them; issues and feelings within the scene are linked to how the chips are used. The seriousness of the issues, however, are undercut by the comic inappropriateness of the means used to articulate them. Tom and Matt's passivity—Tom calmly goes on eating without a word—suggests, as well, how they are subject to the powerful forces working through Paddy, who is not their cause but their agent (Paddy's eating as the comedy of mechanical motion).

Wellman's direction of these scenes has a contoured precision, a readiness and confidence, and an alertness for discreet intensification of "realistic" frameworks that transforms the potentially bland into the vivid. The sensibility governing these scenes is unique in the genre. *The Public Enemy* is perhaps the most "balanced" film in the genre, mixing equally horror and hilarity, gruesomeness and gaiety. Wellman shows himself a director who is relaxed but never lazy, his reflexes primed to catch the provocatively ambiguous gesture, action, and expression on the wing.

CREDITS *The Public Enemy*		
	(Warner Bros., 1931, 83 min.)	
Producer	Darryl F. Zanuck	Cast James Cagney (Tom Powers)
Director	William A. Wellman	Edward Woods (Matt Doyle)
Screenplay	Harvey Thew (from a story by	Jean Harlow (Gwen Allen)
	Kubec Glasmon and	Joan Blondell (Mamie)
	John Bright)	Mae Clarke (Kitty)
Photography	Dev Jennings	Beryl Mercer (Mrs. Powers)
Editor	Edward M. McDermott	Donald Cook (Mike Powers)
Art Director	Max Parker	Leslie Fenton (Nails Nathan)
Music	Vitaphone Orchestra, conducted	Robert Emmett O'Connor (Paddy Ryan)
	by David Mendoza	Murray Kinnell (Putty Nose)

Dark Transformations
The Descent into *Noir*

2

The thirties was a period in which tragedy, and its pleasures, could prosper. Audiences needed to encounter the truth of hard times, but also needed psychological support, to be reminded of the value of human endeavor. Tragedy, a harsh but not hopeless mode, was a suitable approach for the genre. Tragedy is not truly disturbing, because human error is justified and ennobled, because feelings are focused on and honored, and because it drains us of our difficulties instead of clarifying them by analysis or repleting them by further complications. The appearance of tragedy is a sign of the culture's faith, innocence, and idealism. Early gangster narratives, whether they related specifically to the rapacity of American capitalism or not, were resonant myths of defeat that echoed with heroic, positive reverberations. The gangster was uplifting, awe-inspiring, and grand, even in death. Movies created dreams and fantasies that made a hard life bearable. By 1939, the depression was over and Raoul Walsh's *The Roaring Twenties* put the turmoil of the recent past into an ambiguously elegiac perspective. It felt like the gangster's swan song, but it wasn't. In 1941, during a period when America was energetically involved in the war, *High Sierra* (also Walsh) was released. The gangster had the first of many new roles to play, and the genre was imbued with a new purpose. From this point on the genre becomes extremely flexible and the gangster's role less fixed. His character and identity are no longer well defined, something we can expect. *The Killers* appeared in 1946, after the war. In both films views of freedom and possibility narrow. America had beat the depression and won the war, but all it had accomplished was to create new and more complex problems in place of old, problems the structure of the genre was ready to handle.

The intervention of the war and its effect on industry product perhaps accounts for the thematic continuity between the two films despite their five-year separation in time (it may be said that *The Killers* assumes the world of *High Sierra*, takes what is essentially an attitude and consolidates it into a vision). That Mark Hellinger produced both films and John Huston worked on both their scripts might, however, point to a more concrete explanation. Each may also be seen as a metamorphosed version of earlier films. What was Rico in *Little Caesar* is now Roy Earle in *High Sierra*. The underworld milieu of *The Public Enemy* is now the milieu of *The Killers*. The reasons, however, for telling the story of a gangster like Earle or like Swede are now completely different, and the emphases have shifted as well. In *The Killers* Swede dies early in the film and a new kind of hero, Reardon, assumes the prerogative for action. In *High Sierra* the final shots do not focus on the gangster's death but rather on Marie, the survivor, who has understood his qualities and whose life will be informed by them. Both films imply that the premises governing the early gangster films have outlived their usefulness. The genre assumes a new and more conscious vision of America's limitations and flaws.

In *High Sierra* gangsterism as such appears not to be a concern. The genre is used self-consciously, as a vehicle for ideas. Symbol, metaphor, and allusion are more evident. From *High Sierra* on, the genre's interest in revealing and exposing the realities of crime and criminals seems minimal; what is revealed, exposed, and examined by means of the genre's structure and iconography is society itself and the kind of life its people lead. The opposition between legal and illegal forces is not anchored to a literal dimension and goes even beyond its relevance to larger social issues to an existential plane. In both *High Sierra* and *The Killers* the gangster's death is not a necessity but a release. Neither film makes a critique of the gangster; it is the society, not the gangster, that is bad.

High Sierra is the gangster's romantic apotheosis, and an irresistible, often moving film, despite its heavy-handed script, racism, sexism, a cloying subplot, and gallery of stereotypes. Walsh's warmth toward his players brings out the deep feelings beneath their tough exterior; their humanity is at the forefront of attention. *The Killers* is the locus classicus of *film noir*. It has the true *noir* acidity, unpleasantness, and ill will. It manipulates its actors' movements and feelings instead of giving them scope, as in *High Sierra*. Its melancholic undercurrents struggle in vain against an icy pessimism. *High Sierra* is a film of serene, unnoticeably virtuosic, noncoercive visuals, spacious and in the main, brightly lit. *The Killers* is a showcase of dark, tightly framed, unstable compositions. Roy Earle achieves a triumphant transcendence; the characters in *The Killers* are mired in a morbid metaphysics. The credits of *High Sierra* rise up over the mountains into the sky, announcing its theme; the credits of *The Killers* unfold in the black of night following a shot taken through the front window of a speeding car, its headlights garishly illuminating the surface of the road. The two films seem very far apart, but the former extends into the latter in important ways.

Both the nominal hero of *The Killers* (the one who gets top billing—Burt Lancaster's Swede) and Humphrey Bogart's Roy Earle are anachronistic dreamers with a desire to have things be what they are clearly not. Parallel scenes of stargazing indicate the distance traveled between the two films. In *High Sierra* the gangster Earle and Velma (the crippled farm girl he has fallen in love with) look rapturously upward at a star-filled sky. Earle's yearning for the stars complements his yearning for Velma—for something good, pure, and beautiful. He misreads and distorts them both by poeticizing them. He conceives of both as attainable in terms that render both unattainable. They cannot be attained because they do not exist on the level he conceives of them. The stars, of course, feel nothing, and Velma does not feel toward him the way he feels toward her, the way she makes *him* feel. The scene comes early in the film, however, and there is nothing specific within it that points to the folly of his poetic and spiritual misconceptions. The character does not know he is mistaken, and the viewer, although curious about certain oddities in content, design, and execution, is not entirely disengaged from the possibilities the character envisions for himself. The difference in *The Killers* is that Charleston, the character who discourses to Swede about the stars, knows that they are unattainable symbols and deceptive lures and that men dream in vain. (The scene takes place in a prison cell.) He points the brightest of them out to Swede and explains how it doesn't seem to be the brightest because it is so far away. It is the film's philosophical premise, which the viewer unequivocally understands. While Charleston, the choric pessimist talks on, Swede plays distractedly with Kitty's scarf, the old man's wisdom lost on him. In an early flashback, however, he has already muttered, out of a delirium of pain, that "Charleston was right." The pessimism *High Sierra* documents, in a progressive shedding of all hope for life on earth, is a given in *The Killers*. The film does not have to arrive at it. It uses hopelessness as a point of departure and gives it precise definition.

Observing where *High Sierra* starts and finally ends, one can see it as taking one giant step toward what film historians now refer to as *film noir;* it establishes the conditions of *noir.* With *The Killers, noir* is in full swing. It must be understood, however, that although *noir* films are partial to gangsters and criminals, they are not their exclusive domain. *Noir* becomes the gangster's new home, but one he shares communally with other urban action heroes and antiheroes—cops, private eyes, murderers, John Does displaced from their daylight world into nightmares of criminal violence, psychopaths, and other lone-wolf variants. *Noir* was an attitude that could be applied to most any kind of film, and was. It hardened and nastied up a soaper like *Mildred Pierce* (1945), existentialized a Western like *Yellow Sky* (1948), and confounded a culture piece like the normally imperturbable George Cukor's *A Double Life* (1947). Although the gangster and his milieu were ideal subjects for *noir* expressivity, the very assumptions of *noir* prohibited large-scale characterizations that took control of a film, and so the gangster, instead of standing out from his world, was made to blend in with it. The less operatic private eye is the prototypical *noir* hero.[1] (Reardon, the insurance investigator of *The Killers*, is but one of many versions.) The private eye literally investigates the conditions of life via foul-play plot metaphors. The pressing problem is to make sense of a world that either is introduced as chaotic or is soon made chaotic. The tendency is to pull things together, to discover and uncover, if only in disenchantment, how the networks of social and personal life now function, and by the process of decipherment—which involves both reason and force—effect a coming to terms with the world. The ambiguous morality of the private eye testifies to new confusions that beset the hero. His efforts to unravel the knotted and/or slithering flux of values and actions in a world yet to regain its balance or purpose is a paradigm of the average citizen's loose psychological footing. The bewildering adjustments of returning soldiers are mirrored in *film noir*'s tortuous plots, treacherous relationships, unpredictable events, dark frames, and refinements of pain. For those who remained at home, *noir* expressed through the civilian hero visited by sudden catastrophe a version of the war experience he had been spared. Whether the audience identified with or merely observed (a matter relative to the film's technique) a protagonist not unlike itself pounded by (apparently) undeserved circumstances, a ritual purging of guilt was made possible (Arthur Lubin's *Impact* [1949] is a model film).

Noir cinema is about people who live in the night and make their fearful way through darkness. The gangster is only one of those people: he is joined by others who must adopt his ways and means to survive in a world of terror and confusion. In *The Killers* no one character is allowed to be the center of attention. It is interesting to note, too, that the gangster's criminal activity in both *High Sierra* and *The Killers*, takes the form of a caper—a crime not against a person but an institution (the sleek, moneyed world of Tropico Springs in *High Sierra*, the anonymous, impersonal Prentiss Hat Factory in *The Killers*).[2]

Roy Earle and Swede are prisoners of their dreams and of life. The gangster as dreamer, and his fate, makes us understand that life is a prison, that surviving and adapting means imprisonment. *High Sierra*, by creating a warm, sympathetic character, asserts the validity of the dream that vanishes with him. The film allows Earle to choose where he will die. *The Killers* is much darker. Swede has no choice; all his intensity is undermined by the utter futility that surrounds him. In *High Sierra* the vibrancy of the characterization modifies the hopelessness the film arrives at. *The Killers* postulates the absurdity of desire, thus inhibiting from the start the character's potency. It takes as a matter of course what *High Sierra* is at pains to advance—that men act and want in vain, given what the world has become. When Roy Earle tells Marie what being in prison felt like, she understands completely what he's talking about. She has never been in prison but from her own life knows what it is. That life itself is a prison is an explicit theme the characters talk about implicitly. In *The Killers* it is the gestalt that governs every detail, large and small. It would be superfluous to allude to it directly.

The early gangster was a man of the city; his soul was urban. Not a single blade of grass appears in either *Little Caesar* or *The Public Enemy* (except perhaps in the 1909 section of the latter). Rural urban, East West exist in strict opposition and carry specific values. Rico heads East; Earle heads West. Usually, a choice has been made, and the polarities are evoked in passing, not put into conflict. (There are exceptions. In Rouben Mamoulian's *City Streets* [1931] the issue is whether the Kid [Gary Cooper] can shake off the city's corruption, quit racketeering, and take his Coney Island sweetie [Sylvia Sidney] off to God's country.) In *High Sierra* the distinctions blur. Earle starts moving west from Indiana, reaches California, and finding life there inhospitable, plans to head back East. He doesn't make it out of California. What so many succeeding crime films take for granted—California as the end of the line—is given initial cognizance in *High Sierra*.

Roy Earle is a man of nature. When released from prison, he goes immediately to a nearby park to savor its green world. He drives West at a slow, leisurely pace, appreciating the countryside. When he stops for gas at the Last Chance (foreshadowing, none too subtly, his fate), he gazes at the mountains, mesmerized. At the end he is chased up into the mountains, the environment he has identified with, where, the radio informs us, "natural rock formations shelter him." But not for long, for man has conquered nature, and Slim makes his way over the mountain's other side to shoot Earle in the back. To be one with nature, a man has to die. The road is closed, and Earle is cut off from the top of the mountain as well as from the human throng below. It is the human condition of 1941 that Roy chooses not to accept. The environment he flees through appears open and free, but man has mapped it out, controls it. As the spaciousness of nature is evoked, a cop, pleased by how expertly the lines of his map are containing Earle's escape, mutters excitedly, "We'll have him bottled up." The film closes off all possibilities. Moving West is no option. Earle races along the edge of the California coast and is forced inward. Seeking nature is no option. The film's definition of a no-exit condition and its causes is considerably different from its predecessors in the genre. Options become meaningless when there are no human beings left—or when humanity, taken as a whole, has become hard, materialist, cynical, greedy, and mechanical. One asserts one's value by dying, by refusing to live on the world's terms.

In retrospect, *High Sierra* seems to use the gangster as a means to explore America's wartime uncertainties about itself. It almost seems incapable of taking a position on the state of things, until it finally leans grudgingly toward a gloomy vision. *The Killers*, five years later, has its mind made up about what the genre can be used to expose. Its tricky time sequence mirrors the complications of postwar life and abandons as useless the straightforward chronology characteristic of the early rise-and-fall phase of the genre. Its perplexing orchestration of past, present, and future is integral to its theme and method. Its framework designedly shows that the prewar illusion of possibilities has, in a few quick years, been closed off by a mechanical society and that present placidity and progress are based on a lie. This requires that the past be dredged up. Colfax's killing of Swede is an absurdity, a meaningless act. Colfax doesn't hate Swede—he has no feelings toward him at all—and Swede doesn't have the money. Swede's not after anything anymore, he's given up. He kills Swede to keep up appearances, to maintain the illusion of his respectability, which there is an outside chance might be threatened. Killing Swede backfires on him, and he never had to do it. The accident of running into Swede again explodes his life, and Reardon takes advantage of the accident. The gangster does not die for the old reasons.

Colfax may be seen as representative of the society that has accepted him. He is a present that's coping with the past as though it held a future. The future, though, belongs to Reardon, who has no past. We know, though, that one cannot treat American history as though it did not exist, and Reardon cannot purge it by exposing one of its minor episodes. He is an antihero who gets nothing done and, at the very end, seems vaguely aware of it, passing his achievement off lightly. The man who could have been a hero in the past is placed in an impossible situation. Swede is a goner from the beginning. After losing the boxing match, his last, he says to Lubinsky, with a defiant, proud earnestness, "I stayed the limit." The statement, the stance, has the potential of assuming a Hemingwayesque affirmation within a hostile universe, but the film as a whole seems to respond, "So what?" In contrast to *High Sierra*, one does not assert any value by dying; one just dies. At the end of a film that has mostly taken place in darkness, the lights are turned on in Colfax's house to expose the final gestures of the characters and let us see the meaning behind what has occurred. The house lights go on, the jig is up. Reality and the fate of those who oppose it, or try to master it, are illuminated. What we see is unbearable—a stage tableau of dying illusions and the tired cynicism of those instrumental to their demise. The exposure is uniformly devastating. To illumine reality is to show that it is horrible.

High Sierra (1941)

High Sierra assumes we know what gangsters and gangster films are about. It tells an old story in a way that suggests that a pure mimetic narrative of a gangster's life can no longer be the basis for a serious film. Its narrative is symbolic, playing meaning off against form. What used to be an end in itself—showing the kind of man the gangster was and how and where he lived—is now a means to an end. High Sierra is interested in exposing the mediocrity of the culture and in showing the death of the American dream, and it uses the outsider, the gangster ex-con, who knew America another way once and has to face what it has now become. The hero's being out of sync is a device by which the film produces its statement.

At one point in the film Roy Earle visits Tropico Springs to case out the hotel he will be robbing for Big Mac. A series of dissolves takes us quickly through the rich resort environment and scenes of young, smooth bodies at leisured play. Although Earle carries (awkwardly) a tennis racket and has taken his black suit jacket off, he still looks out of place in this bright, hedonistic world. In the hotel, he stops to buy a pack of cigarettes. He takes a pack from the counter, throws down some change, and turns to go. He is stopped short by the counter girl's brittle, "Twenty-five cents, please." He turns around and disgustedly obliges. Later, during the robbery, there is an echo of this scene. Earle is pacing the lobby waiting for Red and Babe to finish cracking the safe. He walks over to the counter, looks down at some cigarettes enclosed in a glass case, nonchalantly shatters the glass, and takes a pack.

The second scene completes the first, after a long wait, and illustrates something about the character and his relationship to his world. The smashing of the glass is satisfying because it is the act of a free man. It appeals more to *our* memory of the earlier scene, not the character's. Earle's gesture is precise, unfrustrated, unvengeful. He's not mad, or vicious, and he takes one pack, what he needs, and no more. It is a reflex of the days when the world used to be his, a gesture of independence that is modified by what we already know from the previous scene, that he has been in prison a long time, that cigarettes are now a quarter, and he must pay exactly that to get them like any other person. The method of the film is here seen in miniature. If the world boxes Earle in it is still possible, even to the end, for Earle to act in positive opposition to it. Earle is not conscious of the meaning of what he does, but the audience is. Through the gangster Earle, High Sierra examines the issue of freedom in a country that supposedly stands for freedom. As the last of the old gangsters, he puts into perspective what his predecessors might actually have been up to. He establishes a subtext for preceding gangster films.

Very loosely based on the (debatable) personal qualities of John Dillinger, *High Sierra*, made seven years after Dillinger's death, becomes a meditation on a vanished world. From the tense and energetic perspective of 1941, the Dillinger era of folk-hero bank robbers is nostalgized. Life used to be lived with poetry, loyalty, codes of honor. Earle, as a vestige of that era, is consciously made into an aristocrat. His name is significant. Roy (king), Earle (nobility). He is royalty, a prince among men. He dies near the top of a mountain, shot in the back by a small-town hick, and falls from a great height with emphatic momentousness, a scapegoat and a spectacle for the gaping crowd below. In an increasingly institutionalized society, one that is, moreover, unified by a moral purpose (arming for war), there is no room for the likes of Earle. As the weave of plot-subplot (the Goodhues) demonstrates, the film is interested in the transition from one world (the depression) to another (postdepression). In all respects, the present is shown to be a lesser world, a world that has sacrificed human values. The strict code that the gangster must die because Crime Does Not Pay is so played down it almost doesn't enter the mind. In this film he must die because he is too good, too selfless, too generous, a natural aristocrat trapped by a dragnet of middle-class values.

High Sierra opens with an Earle well past his prime, having just completed an eight-year stretch in prison. Big Mac has pulled strings to get him released. The condition is that he lead a final heist. Earle has no compunctions about this last job; it's part of the deal, and Big Mac is a good friend. It would be disloyal not to go through with it. Besides, it will put him on easy street. He handles his end with decorum and dignity, but he is saddled with Babe and Red, two foolish, would-be big-timers who, in contrast, panic, crash their getaway car, and die. The cowardly inside man, Mendoza, survives to finger Earle.

We are given nothing of Earle's background, nothing about why or how he became a criminal. We know only that his parents worked a farm in Indiana (he's "just folks" down deep). He is a commoner who has had distinction (notoriety) thrust upon him, and a public figure who has lost (if he indeed ever had) his public. (The headline announcing his release from prison is accompanied by a smaller one, "Citizens' Protests are Ignored.") His tough exterior is exceptionally vulnerable to penetration by the plight of the insulted and the injured. One by one they come to him for help, for recognition—Pa Goodhue; Velma, his crippled granddaughter; Algernon, the daffy black; Marie; Pard, the dog carrying a curse; Big Mac with his bum ticker—and Earle accepts them and wants to help them, out of goodness and because he identifies with their needs. In taking on this bundle of woes and responsibilities (partly self-created), he reduces his chances for survival. The demands of dealing with them all finally box him into a mountain, where he confronts his fate.

High Sierra. Woman knits, while men plot the caper. A group shot, conveying relative positions of power, later rigidly conventionalized.

Earle is disturbed by his isolation from the normal processes of life. He has no home, no family, no wife. When he meets the Goodhues, his desire to help them issues from his need to be accepted by normal people from whom he is estranged by his profession but with whom he feels a root kinship (Pa calls him "son"). The Goodhues, having left their farm, are journeying to Los Angeles—Joad-family style, in a broken-down jalopy—to start a new life.[3] Earle believes he can alter his destiny by becoming a part of the family (his dream of returning to his boyhood farm is a yearning for lost innocence). He falls in love with Velma because she is beautiful and decent, but also because she is a cripple—her condition tugs at his kindness and sympathy. The irony is that Roy *has* a family, the adopted one of Marie and Pard, which he mistakenly slights as unworthy. Moreover, as pleasant, friendly, and "decent" as the Goodhues might be, they are shown progressing toward a level of lower-middle-class mediocrity that is wrong for Earle. It is a situation in which the audience does not want what the character wants and knows better than the character what is best for him. Earle's idealization of Velma reflects his longing for a life that's not possible for him, his pursuit of her is masochistic. Velma betrays him, but with the pain comes also relief and release from a destructive pipe dream. Earle is set free to discover the love and loyalty of Marie. Along with Pard, they become the kind of family the gangster often has to settle for—a pickup family, tired, wounded, on the run, the car doubling as a house, occasionally holing up in a cheap motel, the feelings quickened by danger and shrinking time.

High Sierra would be easier to fathom, and far less interesting, were it not for the unshakable presence of the Goodhues, who not only clutter up Earle's life but, for most audiences, clutter up a good film. Whatever we might wish, they are not incidental to the film. It is only through the Goodhues, in fact, that the true nature of the film as a parable of America becomes apparent. Earle's confrontation with them allows for a near-Jamesian plane of concern with issues revolving around old and new, guilt and innocence. It is no accident that they are given so much space.

On the surface it may appear simply that Earle's courting of Velma verges on the ridiculous and that Velma's sweetness is insufferable. All the scenes with the Goodhues, in this light, can be passed off as aesthetic sore spots or mere period sentimentality. Nothing can be further off the mark from the finesse with which these scenes are managed and the wealth of meaning they contain. We must remember that Velma is a cripple, and not only to create an erotic perversity or to generate a certain kind of action. Her condition is symbolic.

The Goodhues, far from being an idealized version of honest, good folk evilly driven off their land, are seen as weak, corruptible opportunists. Only Pa is real and shrewd (Ma is appealing too, but she is not well developed). He is the oldest and therefore has his roots laid deep in the expansive past his family is in the process of disremembering. They are, it is true, pitted against the filthy rich like Pfeiffer who come to live it up in towns like Tropico Springs, and their struggle to survive merits sympathy. All the scenes with the Goodhues, though, are ambivalent in tone and approach. Both Roy's vision of them and their true nature have to be registered. The scenes can't be too moving and convincing, the family can't be too attractive, because the viewer must sense Roy's mistake in admiring them out of all proportion.[4] Yet since Roy wants so much to become part of this family (moved by sympathy and the misery of his own homelessness), the Goodhues can't be handled brutally or cynically. It is only the last scene with the Goodhues that is marked by Roy's bitter realization of how misdirected his love and dreams have been, and it is the only time Marie and Pard appear with the Goodhues.

Pa tells Earle that Velma's "just as sweet as she's pretty," and Joan Leslie certainly fulfills everyone's fantasy of a healthy, virginal farm girl (with a touch of Hollywood radiance)—everything is in keeping but the clubfoot. Because he has arranged for curing her foot, Earle expects an automatic loyalty of her emotions, especially since he considers her so "decent." (It is frustrating to see Earle [Bogart], so awkward in front of this bland, empty-headed, frivolous teenager). But Pa also mentions that the family is traveling West to avoid a possible scandal around the crippled Velma's dating a divorced insurance man back home. (Roy Earle quickly asserts that *his* Velma could never have done anything wrong.) Velma is being brought to her mother, who has remarried, for safekeeping. She is not as innocent as Pa and Roy believe her to be, and her final, selfish attack on Roy marks her as none too sweet either. One can understand her hunger to be normal, but once cured, her cruelty to Roy is unforgivable. She deserves her choice, the pasty Lon Preiser, destined no doubt to achieve dubious accolades in the insurance world. Pa and Roy, as oldtimers, are being crowded out by the selfishness of youth, at home in the brave new world of California. Roy is too old, too knowing, too grand for Velma; nor can he ever join the Goodhues in dull contentment behind a new white picket fence. Free of her deformity, Velma reveals her grasping, vacuous nature. She illustrates, perhaps, what young America, America the land of the second chance, wants. That she should prefer Lon to Roy is enough to disgrace her in anyone's eyes. One feels sorry for Pa that he should live out the rest of his days in the witless company of Velma, Lon, and their "modern" friends.

Walsh's patience with this subplot is exemplary. He just waits it out and lets it go sour. Then, at its most unpleasant point, he stages the thrilling moment when Earle tells Lon, "Get your hand off me." The wait is well worth it, and the satisfaction would not have been so keen without an extensive groundwork having been laid. Walsh's balanced viewpoint on all the characters has kept the viewer's attitude flexible. We do not dislike the Goodhues, but we wonder about them since we side with Roy, and Roy keeps going after them and it doesn't seem to do him any good. All our pent-up annoyance is channeled into the hatred Roy finally unleashes toward Lon. We want to kick those people out of the film, and Walsh lets us do it.[5]

Our pleasure at bidding good riddance to the Goodhues notwithstanding, they have served their purpose, and it is necessary to come to terms with what they are in the film. King Roy Earle represents the old world, Velma the new, and despite the passion of the former and the curiosity of the latter toward each other, no connection between them is possible. In *High Sierra*, the old world either dies (Earle, Big Mac) or is corrupted (Doc Banton) or exists uselessly (Pa). Old Pa calls Earle "old-timer"; Big Mac calls Earle "old-timer"; Doc Banton calls him "old boy"; Kranmer baits him about losing his touch, Babe says he's getting gray. Roy, the guilty man, the ex-con who has been illegitimately "pardoned," is looking for something decent and thinks he's found it in Velma. He is a corrupt man struggling for purity. The film says it doesn't exist, that no one who is civilized can be free of corruption. Velma may look innocent, but there is no such thing, outside nature, as innocence. Americans like to think otherwise. The myth of America as a land of new possibility where one could start afresh dies hard. But die it must, as must Earle's love for Velma.

Earle's tragic flaw is one of sentiment, of idealism. His sentiment traps him, leads to his death. Because he is good, he wants something good, and is blinded by Velma. He creates in her that good that does not exist, except as an ideal. That he wants to fix Velma's foot is of course a sign of his generosity and humaneness, but it is also a sign of his folly. Velma is impure, flawed; without her clubfoot she would appear to be perfection itself. Earle wants her pure, unflawed; he needs to have her so. Her cripplement is the one thing that undermines his illusion, and so he tries to cure her. He refuses to accept her as flawed. He can't see her shallowness and keeps going back to woo her. But Velma is not like Earle; she wants for herself. Ironically, it is her clubfoot that has kept her pure. Once free of it she enters the corrupt flow of life from which she has, by her condition, been removed—although her affair with Lon Preiser tells us of her urge and her desire. It seems that Preiser has perhaps used her, then let her go. Once she's cured, he comes to California to claim her as a bride. *High Sierra* is quite ruthless in exposing Earle's illusions, and it is possible, too, that the audience's own flaw of sentiment is being indicted as well.

While it is true that Earle comes to transfer his love of Velma to Marie—starts loving a person instead of an idea—it is doubtful that he understands the nature of the shift. Marie, however, does understand the situation, and this is perhaps one reason why she is given the most attention at the close of the film.

High Sierra. Roy Earle settles the bill, while Velma, fascinated by his presence, looks on.

Earle does not write the note at the end out of knowledge but out of instinct and feeling. Earle is not illuminated. Marie is left to ask the question, "What does it mean to crash out?" Her choices throughout are intelligent ones. She sees Earle's value, knows he is good. She chooses to place herself with him, no matter what the consequences, and it is not blind love that decides her, but a mature assessment of values. She knows what's going on and what it is best for her to do with her life. In contrast, Earle is a victim of his feelings, not understanding what is pulling him toward Velma nor the futility of it. He keeps Marie because he's sorry for her. When she first declares her love and loyalty, he looks confused. Distracted by Velma, he does not understand what it represents. Earle is maybe too simple to be tragic, but his simplicity is his value, a quality that others do not have. Compared to others, he wants just simple, decent things. When that proves impossible, he accepts the "used," soiled Marie. His love for her is naive, touching, but careless and unrealistic. His instinct makes him give her all his money; his instinct tells him to refuse Preiser's money (which Marie gripes about later). As a result, he is forced to hold up a store and is spotted. If the film is a tragedy at all, it is Marie's; she suffers the burden of knowledge before, during, and after the film. Marie makes a choice not to call Earle down: of the two alternatives, that one is better, and she conquers her feeling in order to be able to make that choice. Earle, knowing she is below, forsakes his shelter and, calling out her name, becomes an open target. A creature of pure feeling to the end, he dies unenlightened.

The world Earle reenters after his stay in prison is a closed-off one, peopled by a new breed who do not share his values or his needs. Earle wants only to start life anew, and everywhere he turns he finds nothing available for a man of his past deeds and future dreams. From the beginning, the world is shown as a reduced place, spiritually dead, motivated mainly by a dry, meaningless appetite for newfangled ways and an itchy disillusion with the status quo. Earle's bad luck is not mere accident but the world's means of rejecting his sensibility. Even his dreams and fantasies are outmoded. The disturbed babble of his nightmare of crashing out and reaching his childhood farm is placed in a context of farms being taken over by banks. The sequence of dead ends is consistent from beginning to end.

Roy visits his old farm and muses that the pond must be "fished out." The farmer, terrified, identifies him as Roy Earle, and Roy leaves, feeling stigmatized even on his own turf. Before this incident, he has had to deal with Kranmer, a shifty ex-cop who has replaced the trustworthy types that used to work the rackets. Earle clearly dislikes him and shows it by slapping him in the face (he can't do more since he still has to work with him). But Kranmer's kind is here to stay, and it is Kranmer's bullet, later, that slows Earle down. En route to California, his straightforward goal gets snagged by his meeting up with the Goodhues, who ultimately devour precious time and botch his plans. The sight of Velma infects him with unattainable hopes. His cohorts turn out to be a sorry bunch—a frightened inside man, a pair of punks uncool enough to steam and bicker over a woman, the homeless, clinging Marie, and a bad-luck dog named Pard whose three previous owners have bizarrely died. His run-in with Pfeiffer is a sweeping shorthand comment on economic injustice. Big Mac turns out to be dying from a variety of causes, dreaming in vain of a last caper that would yield a batch of gleaming stones (his longing seems to be for the jewelry itself, and not the money). Doc Banton has sold out, playing it safe in the faddish health racket by catering to the vain needs of well-to-do women; he is timid about risking his neck for Mac and Earle. He tells Earle that Earle is "rushing toward death." Velma throws him over for a divorced insurance man. Mendoza lives to squeal about the caper. Mac dies in his sleep (perhaps helped by Kranmer—it is left unclear), throwing well-laid plans awry. A cop interferes during the robbery. The newspapers opportunistically call him "Mad Dog" Earle. Pard insists on adopting Earle and later indirectly causes his death. Some world, some run of luck. Earle's black suit labels him a doomed man, sets him apart from the rippling, white luxuriousness of the denizens of Tropico Springs and the prole-to-bourgeois change in garb of the Goodhues. Earle must face and accept the ultimate obscenity—Velma's engagement to Lon. His love for Marie is short-lived, but is the only thing of value he manages to wrest from life before dying. At last, the pressures of the world drive him up the mountain, where he barricades himself heroically and hurls defiance at those gathered below with the mettle of a warrior.

Walsh's visuals reinforce the hell envisioned by the script. The radio announcer informs his listeners:

The road up the mountain is a jam of traffic. Spectators are coming from all over.

It's infernally cold up there. . . . The rock above where Earle is hiding looks like a huge iceberg. Whenever the flares are lit, the faces of the crowd gathered around here look like white masks of snow. They look dead, all but their eyes.

The blow-by-blow description continues, in the flat, excitable tones of a sportscaster:

There've been more rumors flying around. One is that Earle's about to give himself up. Another is that they've sent to March Field near Riverside for a squadron of armored bombing planes to blast Earle out. While all this is going on, the sheriff and his men hold conference after conference. Nerves of everyone are getting more taut. As a matter of fact, the crowd is getting very restless. Huge spotlights are trained on Earle's rocky fortress. . . .

. . . the coldest place in the world tonight, cold and unreal. One is awestricken by the gruesomeness of this rendezvous with death. The morbidly curious onlookers standing by as if they watched a game, the tall pine trees clustered around like a silent jury, the stern-faced officers of the law waiting for the kill . . .

When it is all over, Marie weeps, and the cynical reporter cuts in with "Big Shot Earle." But he doesn't have the last word. Tears of grief turn imperceptibly to tears of joy as Marie thinks of Roy's freedom. The final shots are transcendent. What Earle has meant, his dignity, is imprinted on Marie's face and the viewer's soul as she walks toward the camera, eyes glowing, head high; rising in the frame, she disappears from view. The camera then isolates the majesty of the mountain, and the film ends. Yet the irony remains that she's happy for *him*. The film implies she'd be better off dead.

All this takes place in California, a "land of milk and honey," as Doc Banton says. But it is a place where everything of value dies, including Doc Banton's old self. The American dream dies in California, at the edge of the ocean where civilization must confront its corruptions. Big Mac's fate is illustrative. Confined to bed, he drinks and smokes himself to death while entertaining fantasies of one more big heist. The film says it can't be done anymore, and deep down Big Mac seems to know it. He too, in disobeying Doc's orders, is "rushing toward death"; it is as if he wants to die. Finally, his heart stops. Pa's fate is similar. In California he becomes irrelevant, defunct, aimless. In getting there he shows savvy and will; having gotten there, he has nothing to do. An honest, hardworking Ohio farmer, and a man of feeling possessed of small, but

High Sierra. Star Lupino closes the film for us, after making the most of opportunities to emote, as above. (Museum of Modern Art)

valuable, wisdom, is reduced to total ineffectuality. We are shown what his life amounts to on those occasions when Earle comes to visit. On the first, he is mowing his tiny lawn; on the second, he is sitting in his chair, half asleep, reading a newspaper; on the third, he is admonishing Velma and her friends to ease up on the volume of their partying. All he can say to Earle is a weak, "I'm sorry." There's nothing for him to do except sit around the house. Mabel, Velma's distasteful mother, is reported "gadding around uptown," in the swing of things. And Pa must face the truth about Velma, too. We have been told of his uncertainty about Velma's affair back home; he would like to believe that Velma did nothing wrong. He loves Velma, but his response to the drinking and smoking and raucousness that characterize her life at the end leaves it doubtful whether he likes her anymore. Big Mac is a clear case. Earle explains to the fence. "There he was dead, with a half a million bucks beside him." But a character like Pa, who the film shows us has nothing to do, might as easily be described as dead.

The three figures who respond to Earle, who like him, can communicate with him, and enjoy being with him, are the classic outcasts of the society: a black, a woman, and a mongrel dog. All are shown as vital, feeling creatures. Algernon has no designs of "crashing out." As a black, he knows that's impossible. But he makes the most of his situation. He catches fish by an ingenious fishing device (Babe and Red go out every day but come back empty-handed). When he plays with Pard, his face lights up with genuine delight. He knows his place, but within it, there is scope to be human. Pard and Marie both want to "crash out." Pard does it literally, by escaping from the cabin. Marie by joining her life with Earle's. All three, in their own way, understand Earle, much to Earle's indifference, since he wants to be understood by the Goodhues, who represent the norm of an emerging postdepression middle class. Mabel is dumbfounded by Earle's wanting to help Velma. She's suspicious of his generosity. Velma repays him by betraying him. Even Pa scratches his head over Earle's constant help to the family, muttering absently, "Durndest fella . . . durndest fella." (To highlight the incongruity between Earle's profession and his deeds, the scene moves immediately to Doc and Earle driving away from the Goodhues with Doc asserting vigorously, "It's criminal that nothing's ever been done with that girl before." The word "criminal" is stressed, and it is the only time it appears in the film.) We may infer that society is mechanical and inhuman (the emphasis on the technology used to corner and destroy Earle supports this) and that only those outside it can remain human.

High Sierra uses the gangster as a value center, a man of honor, integrity, and feeling in a world shown as mean and humanly defective. The gangster, whose violent ways set him apart, is a fit vehicle for themes about the rejection of the world. He functions well, by virtue of his existential alienation, as a yardstick of the society's and the culture's deficiencies. It helps that Walsh is not a moralist of the rote kind. He does not distort the world to scourge it as the script sometimes invites him to (Earle says to Big Mac, "Sometimes I feel that I don't know what it's all about anymore") but records with equanimity its impervious, obdurate presence. Also, there is not the slightest touch of hammy saintliness in either Earle or Marie. They are very much of this world and rightfully gain every drop of viewer affection by their stubborn unpretentious humanity, their delight in things, their warmth, their courage. No

High Sierra. The average poor but morally grounded American family —as a bad joke? Aren't the plain, jes' folks Goodhues this film's family? No. When push comes to shove, they show Earle the door. Suspicious, insensitive, middle-class wanna-bes. The interim model shown above is characterized by warmth, fellow-feeling, generosity. No pretensions here: hunted criminal, freelance drifter, black cabin-sweeper, and a wet mutt dog who enjoys being with nice people. They look like they're from separate worlds but under these circumstances can be responsive to each other. Roy Earle (Humphrey Bogart) stares distractedly at something off-screen, moody and pensive. Ida Lupino, more down-to-earth (though flatteringly photographed), has a moral/spiritual glow as well as a physical one. Centered, and in full light, she is about to make herself useful when Algernon sociably hand-delivers a telegram for Roy. Alone and maligned, he is welcomed to stay (though conceived racially as lazy and dumb). Finally, there's Pard, Algernon's dog, who everybody comes to love. Lupino's dominance in the shot points to her actual top billing over Bogart, who became a big star only after *High Sierra*. (Museum of Modern Art)

director surpasses Walsh in getting down the difficult stuff of people simply living, doing, and being—getting in and out of cars, picking things up, eating, sitting, walking, looking at each other. If *High Sierra* succeeds in achieving a spiritual emotion, its exaltation nonetheless proceeds unforced from credible flesh and blood occupying ground space with a convincing human flexibility.

Walsh's sangfroid amid the conceptual extravagances of the film does not cramp his handling of the bread-and-butter elements of the genre—the shootouts, chases, and so on, which are filmed with the drive for which he is renowned. Walsh was a perfect choice for this film because his flair for violent action has always been free of morbidity. (Can one imagine, too, someone as tic-y as Buñuel being given his head with the Goodhues?) The generally high-key lighting fits the spacious environments of this outdoors gangster film. Interiors are generally well lit, with everyone's expressions visible. The concluding daylight chase is a generic tour de force of geometrical editing, terrain-dominated long shots alternating with close-ups of Earle and cops driving. Tony Gaudio's camera is always effortlessly at the right place for the viewer to gauge distances, road conditions, the precise contours of space traveled through time. Immensity is coordinated with intensity. There have been more spectacular chases since, but this one's tire-squealing excitement stands up well.

High Sierra is forceful and casual. When the action is rapid, it never seems abrupt, just economical. Expository material (like Earle's release from prison) is eased through in a series of quick, informative dissolves and a few pertinent gestures. Prior to the chase, dissolves of simultaneous action, rapid cutting, and a profusion of dolly shots convey the speed, intensity, and inevitability of the manhunt. The camera moves in close to the hard, harsh faces of the police, who seem to converge from all directions. *High Sierra* does not have the buoyant snap of Walsh's *The Roaring Twenties* (1939), but it is more of a character study and alternates portions of terse narrative with perceptive, measured illuminations of character and behavior. It has, though, the true Walshian flavor, the bittersweet tang of crudity and delicacy combined, and the Walshian legerdemain of flat, plastery forms and shapes infused by crackerjack intuitions. When Walsh has the right performers, as in *High Sierra*, he subtly plays them off against each other as carriers of emotions and values he either loathes or admires. The complexities of a Walsh film reside in the jiggly lines of characters' feelings in conflict, with tones boldly driven sometimes along, sometimes against the grain of these feelings.[6] Sentiment and sentimentality are punctured by a broad, black humor. Earle tells Marie of an inmate's suicide off the top tier making "quite a splash" while buttering a mound of pancakes. Marie winces, but remains composed. The humor is an index to both characters' stoicism. Marie passes Earle's "test" and they move on to a serious, empathetic discussion. Earle's last visit to the Goodhues has Velma, the operation on her clubfoot a success, dancing around with a lot of "hep" footwork. This is, technically, the heartwarming conclusion of the sentimental subplot, but the song she's whirling to is "I Get a Kick Out of You"(!). Sure enough, the scene later lapses into nastiness. Walsh's movies establish the implicit premise that anything can be made to fit, and this keeps them not only surprising but honest. Many of the fine moments in *High Sierra* are, in fact, quiet and underplayed, the sense of time clicking away scissored pleasantly by loose, throwaway details: Earle's piqued ripping of an evergreen leaf upon first spotting Marie; Marie sitting outside the cabin idly poking the ground with a stick, knees tight, feet splayed; Earle coolly sipping a drink in the hotel lobby while Red and Babe work on the safe. These are the shots one wants to see again and again, not least because they seem to have disappeared from movies altogether, in their unaffected form.

The Roaring Twenties (1939) was an attempt at an old-style gangster film. It had an almost apologetic foreword by Mark Hellinger, as though there were some need to explain why one would bother making a gangster film about the old days at this late date and differently troubled hour. Hellinger shrewdly tied it in with the approach of the war, but the film had the air of a one-shot. *High Sierra* appeared a year and a half later, and again looked backward. Neither film seemed at all interested in reviving the genre but rather in making a specialized use of it, and in reflecting about the past. Films about modern crime were being made, mostly B programmers (Paramount's Lloyd Nolan quickies the best of the lot). *The Roaring Twenties* and *High Sierra* did, as major productions, keep the gangster film visible during a period of meager output, and both films showed the genre was useful in presenting a disgruntled view of the world. Both films, however, reworked past models and dealt with a bygone era, in traditional style to boot. They represent not so much an advance but a synthesis. During the war, combat films, musicals, comedies, and women's pictures held sway. When the gangster wasn't, on occasion, shifting his energies to the war effort, he had little relevance indeed. The postwar gangster film is absorbed into a new means and a new sensibility: *film noir*.

High Sierra is the culmination of the first phase of the gangster film, and it was made by the studio that pioneered the genre a decade before. Its basic structure sticks close to the classic pattern—the rise and fall of a big shot—with this difference: the pattern is inverted. Here it is no rise and all fall, but by falling the hero rises. He does not die squalidly, in a gutter, but nobly, at the foot of a mountain, and his death is equated with freedom. Having transcended the world and the judgments of morality, the classic gangster has achieved the best he could have hoped for. In what was to come, he had no place.

CREDITS	*High Sierra*		
	(Warner Bros., 1941, 100 min.)		
Executive		Cast	Humphrey Bogart (Roy Earle)
Producer	Hal B. Wallis		Ida Lupino (Marie Garson)
Associate			Joan Leslie (Velma)
Producer	Mark Hellinger		Henry Travers (Pa)
Director	Raoul Walsh		Arthur Kennedy (Red)
Screenplay	John Huston and		Alan Curtis (Babe)
	W. R. Burnett (from Burnett's		Barton MacLane (Jake Kranmer)
	novel)		Henry Hull (Doc Banton),
Photography	Tony Gaudio		Willie Best (Algernon)
Editor	Jack Killifer		Cornel Wilde (Louis Mendoza)
Art Director	Ted Smith		Jerome Cowan (Healy)
Music	Alfred Deutsch		Donald MacBride (Big Mac)
			Elizabeth Risdon (Ma)
			Minna Gombell (Velma's mother)
			Zero (Pard)

The Killers (1946)

*T*he *Killers* begins where *High Sierra* leaves off. In *High Sierra* the gangster, having run out of time and space, makes a spiritual escape. His death is a release from human society. In *The Killers* the hero is shot dead after the film has barely gotten under way. His death, as well, is meaningless as are aspects of the past, present, and future that determine it. *The Killers* is an unusually complicated film, and all its complications are meaningless, a busy masquerade of life beneath which lies a limitless despair. When Nick Adams asks one of the killers, "What's the idea?", the killer replies with an absolute and coldly frightening metaphysical certainty, "There isn't any idea," rendering further conversation on the subject superfluous.

The *noir* attitude, linked by several commentators to a feeling of postwar guilt and uncertainty, infected practically every "dramatic" genre, including the gangster film. The gangster can no longer exert his will: his activity gets throttled and circumscribed at every turn. He gives way to less imposing, more ambiguous figures, like insurance investigators and private eyes. Crime becomes a less kingly and aristocratic enterprise and turns into something seedy, unpredictable, and sad. The crime film accumulates a gallery of grotesques and oddballs, not rigidly accounted for as in the past. Bit players crowd the corners of the frame with sinister or melancholy finesse. Unlikely candidates get cast in heroic molds, clumsily risking all for nothing or fighting their way to a meaningless stalemate. Those we look kindly on are either impotent or naively obsessed: they give way to insensitive high-gear hustlers cutting cynical trail maps through a landscape of foiled dreams and human relationships.

The Killers takes Hemingway's museum piece and uses it, with a kind of insolent nonchalance, as a symbolic introductory gesture, an absurdist framework for its more ambitious concerns, including a tortuously contrived explication of why Swede came to die as he did. Unlike Hemingway's story, there is no point of illumination for a young Nick Adams. In the film, Nick's gesture of help is just futile, and he's left to squander his young manhood in the unprepossessing environs of Brentwood (the film forsakes the subtle-as-a-thumb "Summit" of the story, preferring the unpointed, nondescript Brentwood instead). There is no place in the film for Hemingway's sentimentality or for the tonic purism of his dialogue with its inadvert-by-design beauty. Director Robert Siodmak's film is too steadily gouged and perforated by a cynicism that will not admit of revelation of any kind but the most despairing.

*P*aul Schrader's contention that *film noir* represents a triumph of style over content[7] was never more amply demonstrated. Perhaps the first place to show

how manner subverts matter or, at the least, colors it to its desired hue, is at the level of narrative structure.

The Killers has affinities with *Citizen Kane*'s (1941) influential attempt to justify, explain, and account for a particular human life. The film lets us know why Swede (Burt Lancaster) didn't run or fight back and just let himself be killed. Pieced together, in a jumbled way, is the whole of Swede's mature career. Through Reardon (Edmond O'Brien) the film is also interested in the Oedipal imperative to uncover the truth and face the worst knowledge as a cleansing mechanism. Why did Swede die? The film says he died for nothing. The narrative structure, by its very nature, enacts a pattern of irrelevance. Swede is dead, nothing will bring him back to life. Every time we see him in the film we know he's dead.

In case Burt Lancaster's magnetic presence distracts us into thinking more positive thoughts, the film reminds us again and again that Swede is dead, and not only of his actual death, but that he was dead while he was alive. The boxing match establishes that Swede is dead. A spectator tells Lubinsky that Swede is "getting murdered," that "he can't last," that "they're killing him." When he gets knocked out he *looks* dead (for a moment, despite what we know to the contrary, we imagine he might be). More to the point is that he is treated as though he were dead. For his manager and trainer, he no longer exists as a person. They ignore him. Lubinsky tells him, "There isn't going to be a next time." Swede is incredulous. For Swede it means he's through, that his life is nothing. Death is not simply a biological matter. Swede's being KO'd is metaphorical. His manager departs with, "I never did like wakes," leaving Swede to mutter to himself under the shower. Siodmak's framing is significant. Swede showers in the background, centered between the conversation going on between his manager and trainer in the foreground. We see him clearly in the frame, but they talk about him as though he were not there. In other flashbacks we watch his attempted suicide and are present at his funeral.

Reardon's amateur-detective enthusiasm is thus seen in ironic perspective. Not only can't he be of use to Swede, his meddling causes the death of all the others. A sense of irrelevance is further obtained by the confusing chronology of the flashbacks. They follow no discernible order at all. Presumably they solve a "mystery"; what in fact they do is expose a chaotic world in which people are doomed to exist at cross-purposes, a world that throws unpredictable and implausible monkey wrenches into one's desires and aspirations. To venture forth, to act, to dream, to plan, to reason, to feel is to place yourself at the mercy of a universe that obeys no laws but that manages to close in on you fatally. Swede finally gives up, and he can't even do that. Colfax finds him quite by chance.

The flashback structure is continually at odds with Reardon's forward momentum. The more Reardon discovers, the more we are plunged into the past

Dark Transformations

81

as an irretrievable given. Nothing can be undone or averted—not even what's to come. His inspirational detection is discredited by the ugly facts and realities he unearths. The narrative maintains a contradictory pull. It's a puzzle we don't very much want to finish because we know it's not a pretty picture. Worse, when the pieces are all in, we see that the puzzle, or what we have of it, is beside the point. Nobody cares, not even Reardon. Detection films normally let the audience share a sense of triumph in the outcome, activating a playful, rational virtuosity. If you didn't get it, well, you *almost* got it, and the fun was in going for it anyway. *The Killers* sets up the pattern but undermines any such pleasure.

Indeed, one is never finally sure of very much except that a lot of double crossing has resulted in a lot of corpses. *The Killers* plays on viewer confusion to a borderline limit. The viewer is invited to read the situation but is left frustrated by withheld information. Let us pursue just one example. Reardon's trail has led to Kitty. Under a threat, he's flushed her out and arranges to meet her. He wants to get her to implicate Colfax and force her to come up with the stolen money, but he tells *her* he wants to make a deal. Kitty suggests The Green Cat nightclub, but Reardon refuses. He says he will send a man to The Adelphi Theater to take her to him. We do not know yet that he plans to be this man. He hangs up the phone after making the arrangements with Kitty and, very pleased with himself, smiles to Lubinsky. The scene ends. When Reardon tells Kitty in the cab that *he's* Reardon, he gives her the impression that he's safe from her henchmen, who he has anticipated would have been waiting for him at The Green Cat. She replies, "I should have known," implying that she didn't. It turns out that she has and has set up a tail, who in turn will be followed by the killers in Colfax's employ (the ones who murdered Swede). While they ride in the cab and try to read each other, there is no way we can know exactly what is going on or decide who is outthinking the other. Reardon tells the cabbie to go to The Green Cat. Kitty says, "I thought you didn't like The Green Cat." Reardon: "Only when I'm not expected." (A cryptic remark.) It is only afterward that one can figure out, or come close to figuring out, what has happened. Kitty has figured that Reardon would come and has set up the killers. Reardon has figured that she would have figured and has set up Lubinsky at The Green Cat. We don't know this, though, until the killers make their move, which is after a long scene with Kitty and Reardon that includes Kitty's flashback. And we are never certain whether Reardon has set up Lubinsky, or whether he has bought Kitty's "I should have known." Did Lubinsky take it upon himself, as a canny cop somewhat ironic about Reardon's abilities, to come to The Green Cat, where he imagined Kitty would maneuver him to go? The movie could have told us, but it doesn't. His appearance comes as a surprise, however he got there. Kitty takes her signal for the killers to act and improvises a trip to the powder room, leaving Reardon a sitting duck. Reardon apparently falls for it. But he has said to Kitty that he thinks he's being "expected" at The Green Cat. Yet why does he let Kitty escape? In any case, isn't he living a mite too dangerously? (The scene is also complicated by the possibility that Reardon is taken by Kitty, finds her provocative.) Kitty has told Reardon that she took the first plane for Pittsburgh when she heard he was looking for her. Yet she turns out to be Colfax's wife. Is she lying? Are they separated? When Kitty gets picked up, is she heading for the house or fleeing? She arrives long after Reardon and Lubinsky, although she has a head start. The unraveling is worked out in an atmosphere of deliberate confusion, partly to undermine any notion that things have been settled. You know there is more to it than Reardon knows, but you're also pretty sure it doesn't matter. Scenes are played in such a way as to provide the feeling that the plot is not totally accounted for. Reardon's quest is ironic because nothing can ever be made to come out right in an absurd universe.

The characters in *The Killers* are as problematic as the narrative. Vintage gangster films had arresting heroes easy to identify with. In *The Killers* no character emerges as clearly central or has the indisputable blend of qualities that would ensure audience identification. A viewer looking for someone to latch onto, to function as a value center, is left bewildered. In Reardon, the viewer is left with a choice by default, but one so unsatisfactory and unsympathetic that detachment is necessary. The character we would like to get behind, Swede, is shot dead early in the film.

Reardon has a compulsive desire to solve the mystery of Swede's death. But Reardon is no Oedipus. He is an insurance man from Newark, New Jersey, a city both geographically and spiritually distant from Thebes. As in Greek drama, we know the result at the outset and have to sit it through, but the parallels to a hero who must discover the roots of a sick society and purge it of evil are deflating ones. *The Killers* does not demonstrate an implacable universal justice; it does not demonstrate anything. It *rests* on a grim view of no possibilities. Reardon suffers no agonies; he is simply an agent who makes the implicit explicit. He is motivated by an abstract curiosity. What he uncovers has no ultimate effect on him whatever. His activity is an extension, as well as a violation, of his job. He learns nothing, feels nothing, beyond his own excitement. He is a hero without heroic credentials, he has no past, he has no future. He inhabits merely an unappealing present that he cannot escape and that is the only thing he can express or reflect for us. He is the prototype of the true *noir* hero, coming from left field to replace his larger-than-life forerunners. He does not truly represent himself (or perhaps he does so only momentarily) but the insurance firm. His personal goals stop short of infringing on institutional needs. His gains are deflected back into the firm. His identity and his drive to

Dark

Transformations

83

succeed are compatible with the firm's legitimized profit ideology. He survives, leaving a string of corpses in his wake, people whose rootlessness and disaffection made them social outcasts and life's casualties. The only winner in this film is the insurance firm (the net result of Reardon's escapade is that the "basic rate at The Atlantic Casualty Company, as of 1947, will probably drop one tenth of a cent"). If Reardon wants to run a risk it's his affair (though it requires special pleading) but he is ultimately protected by his firm. A bleaker heroics can scarcely be imagined.

But Reardon is a dreamer too, albeit of a different stripe. *The Killers* extends the notion implicit in previous films that life is in the underworld. There is no dream possible for a man like Reardon unless he acts like a gangster, exists in his milieu. Reardon wants to have a dream like the others, which is why he pursues the case. He fills his emptiness with a vicarious dream. The irony is that all dreams are used up. The charade of charging up his life, though, is preferable to continuing in its mechanical mediocrity. Practically, it is senseless for him to be drawn in. It is established early that the money doesn't matter to the firm. The only possible reason is to experience emotions he cannot in following the normal pattern of his job. In contrast to Lubinsky, who has no real passions, who is older, more socialized, and more impersonal, Reardon takes the bait like a greedy fish. As a cop, Lubinsky is too duty-bound to be an active force. He continues to investigate when things fall into his lap. Reardon takes on a creative, aggressive role. Where Lubinsky is mildly engaged, Reardon is absorbed. Where Lubinsky has accepted his limits, Reardon wants to test his. When developments in the case occur, Lubinsky follows them up as part of his job. Reardon becomes elated. The activity of both suggests a premise that can be stated in either of two ways. Either legitimate life takes the vitality out of people, or there is nothing in legitimate life *for* vital people.

Reardon's passions are the same as those of the criminals he hunts. He wants excitement. As he gets in deeper, life becomes dangerous. Reardon is scared, but he loves it (after Dum-Dum kicks him in the head he even shows his battle scar to Lubinsky with a barely effaced boyish pride). His association with Swede is made explicit: he carries Swede's scarf, the symbol of Swede's dreams, with him throughout the film, and he must finally deal with Kitty as Swede had to. He says candidly to Kitty, "I wish I'd known the old Kitty Collins." The statement is gratuitous on any level but the personal. The difference between Reardon and the criminals—a very real one—is that he doesn't care, and they do. Reardon playacts at what others do for real: he's *in on it* rather than *of* it. He's susceptible to being drawn in, to wanting in, but he is not one of them and does not have to face the consequences of those whose entire lives have been given over to the illusion that the world may accommodate their hopes. Through Reardon, however, the film makes it clear that an active, intelligent man, with plenty of opportunity for advancement in his legitimate line of work, would rather be a gangster. The scene in which Reardon, gun in hand, waits behind the door to surprise Dum-Dum is an entirely private scene, bringing us close to the character's emotions of fear and excitement in a challenging situation. Nothing in the normal operations of the insurance business provides kicks like that.[8]

Burt Lancaster's Swede is the exact opposite of Reardon—slow, dumb, sensitive, vulnerable, a born loser despite his physical attractiveness. (It was Lancaster's first role, and while his virility is unquestionable, his youthfulness is used for pathos. Siodmak controls him perfectly, integrating him into his vision of things so that Lancaster works for the film and not the film for Lancaster, as is so common in Lancaster's films throughout the fifties and sixties.) Victimized by the wiles of a beautiful woman, Kitty Collins (Ava Gardner), he awaits his death as a welcome end. What the film says about Swede is best discussed in the context of the choices available to him. For a man like Swede, what possibilities are there for a meaningful life? Again, the persistent implication within the gangster film is that people turn to crime because there's nothing else worthwhile to do. The desire to be a criminal is an ancient one, but the nature of legitimate life, as *The Killers* gives it to us, only gives it further inducement. The film enacts so strong a pattern of futility, however, that even the life of crime is presented as disheartening and hopeless.

The Killers puts into motion a good many people most of us do not know; it acknowledges their presence among us, it acquaints us with their drives, needs, and frustrations, most of which differ from those of the settled and complacent who have bought into the society and its institutions. Swede grew up in a Philadelphia slum. His close childhood friend, Sam Lubinsky (Sam Levene), went on to become a cop. Swede opted for a crack at the big time in the ring. He had a nice girl who came every night to watch him fight. Swede busts his hand and has to quit. Drifting into the numbers racket, he loses his girl to his respectable friend and becomes sexually enslaved by Kitty Collins, a woman after big money whose double-dealing leads him to an early grave. He pulls a big heist but never gets to enjoy the money. Apart from his fatal passion for Kitty, he is alone, friendless (but for Charleston), incommunicative, emotionally dead. When the killers catch up with him he is pumping gas in Brentwood and spending his nights in a rented room, a man with nothing to live for.

Such is Swede's history, told in the film without a trace of moralizing. Swede's desire for dignity makes him want to be a boxer. He doesn't like the idea of being a cop like his friend Sam, and it promises a life of mediocrity anyway. Swede thinks of boxing as an honorable calling, and he follows it honorably as an alternative to the bureaucratic life.[9] After he breaks his hand, Sam tries to convince him that "there's always the Department . . . not a bad life, Ole, twenty years and you've got a pension, $2,200 a year, to start." Swede rejects this ("some months I made that much in one month") for a life of crime. Sam pinches him and sends him up, even though he knows he's covering for Kitty. Once out of jail, he joins the big caper—the ultimate metaphor of the dreams and ambitions of Swede's kind. Kitty, now Colfax's woman, becomes for Swede the crystallization of his aspiration—to go as high as her is to go as high as one can. The caper will release him, win her. He takes his chance and loses. Sam and Lily (his former girl) survive to lead a life of domestic contentment.

There is a temptation to see Sam Lubinsky as the person who has it all together. Good-humored, relaxed, concerned, and happily married, he is what Swede might have become if he had played his cards right. Both were dealt a weak hand, but Sam managed to ride his to a reasonably comfortable life and a socially useful occupation. If Reardon, in the final analysis, is an obnoxious busybody, maybe it is Sam, tough and forceful when he has to be, but human and gentle too, who is an acceptable model—the good man as hero. Maybe, but the evidence says not likely.

We first see Lubinsky on the roof of his home (a kind of slum penthouse) painting some chairs. (Reardon has come to pump information out of him, and Sam soon complies with a flashback.) The sequence is complex. Lubinsky is up high, comparatively, but it is as high as he can go, and his contentment indicates that he has accepted this limitation. Perhaps it is not intended, but the set is a glaringly obvious one, extremely distracting. Its falseness fairly mocks Lubinsky's achievement. In a film that is most concerned with capturing what goes on in the depths below conformist levels, this excursion into the commonplace takes on an unreal quality, as if to undermine the basis of Lubinsky's choice. Lieutenant Lubinsky is a man in charge of his own rooftop, which is echoed in the receding line of houses pictured in the painted backdrop.

Is he happy? His flashback recounts the turning point in Swede's life, his last fight. It focuses on Lily's commitment to Swede, Sam's attraction to Lily, Lily's friendly recognition of Sam as a third party, Sam's feeling for Swede, and Swede's departure into an unknown future. Reardon asks, "And you put the pinch on him?" Lubinsky shrugs, "When you're a copper, you're a copper." No question of where one's loyalty lies. The tone of regret cannot hide a basic guilt—he *has* sent Swede up and is in part responsible for his fate. And although Swede ignored and abandoned Lily, Sam has married the woman who might indeed have been a loyal, loving influence in Swede's life.

Lily interrupts to serve lemonade. Sam comments on how she always loved Swede and how he (Sam) always loved her. Lily chastises him. Sam says to Reardon, "It worked out fine for me, anyway." Lily chimes in with, "I haven't been too unhappy myself." There is no element of a grand passion, and a certain regret mixes with the predominant tone that these ancient matters have been laid to rest. Siodmak makes the most of a lovebird in a birdcage dangling conspicuously in the frame. The device comments on Sam and Lily's domesticity; it is a trap, after all, and it may be a lesser existence to live on as they do than to die as Swede. Kitty and Swede's large failure is in contrast to Sam and Lily's tepid success. But they too carry with them the past, their old commitments, the former days of possibility when Swede was part of their lives. (Reardon is the only figure who has no past, the only one safe from both its glory and contamination. He is the unquestioning agent of a dynamic, forward-looking historical prosperity. In contrast, all the other characters' sense of self is based on what they once were, in the prewar years: for them the present has a tired and bitter edge.)

Beginning her own flashback, Lilly euphemizes, "He was a good boy. Swede and I . . . well . . . stopped seeing each other." Both Sam and Lily try to minimize the importance of Swede. They are people of feeling, but their remarks are also condescending, as if the past involving Swede was a period of foolishness they have long left behind. But Lily and Sam protest too much. "I seem like a good deal of a heel, don't I?" Sam asks Reardon. "First I marry Ole's girl, then I send him up for three years." Lily breaks in to protest that she was not "Ole's girl." They are both, within a context of mutual love and understanding, protecting themselves, justifying the choices they have made. They cannot undo what they have done, and their lives are touched by guilt. Sam knows he was second choice, that Lily saw qualities in Ole that he did not possess, and that she took him as a leftover.

The flashbacks visually reinforce the authenticity of their former selves. Lily is quite attractive, and also spunky and vibrant. Sam is likable and humorous, with a lively lower-class proficiency of speech and movement, and what he lacks in muscle and good looks he makes up for in fellowship and human concern, a true decency. The scenes in which they appear in the present project an altered image. Lily looks weary, asexual; Sam appears smug and rather bored. Their relationship is warm and trusting but bland. The "love" of Sam and Lily, seen as an alternative to Swede's passion for Kitty, is not particularly favored. The film's view of love is as gloomy as its view of everything else. Sexual bondage or humdrum marriage, take your pick. These are *noir's* rigid alternatives.

The sequence ends with Reardon being informed that Sam and Lily are just at the point of going to Swede's funeral. They have sent for the body to give it a proper burial. At the funeral, Sam says to Reardon, "If you ever find out who killed Ole, let me in on it." This is of course a sign of loyal feeling for a lost friend, but it is also Sam's means of assuaging his guilt. What he does later is not for Ole, who can scarcely be said to benefit, but for himself. Lubinsky must, like all the rest, come to terms with his past. He fits the pattern of the film. His doing is a matter of undoing; it goes nowhere, it proves nothing. The hunt for Swede's killers acts as a bridge between his pre- and postwar life.

If both Reardon and Lubinsky gain our interest as their lives get revitalized by the process of investigation, they are still in contrast to a more sympathetic underworld. The film mitigates their success partly by creating sympathy for the gang members, partly by showing how foolhardy their involvement is (neither has anything to gain), partly by underlining their cynical carelessness about human life, and partly by showing them assume the airs of tough-cop and tough private investigator with less than stylish results. An aura of professional coldness hangs over them. They are two-bit heroes who go back to their two-bit jobs, having learned nothing, their moral-emotional natures undisturbed. Their experience provides no new horizons. They achieve no self-awareness; their assumptions remain unquestioned. Where one might reasonably expect, given the discoveries they make, some sign of regret at how awful some human lives might be, some sympathy and understanding of it, some interest in the why as well as the what—none occurs. If the nature of the hero can be said to determine the nature of the film, *The Killers* is a dark film indeed.

An article by J. A. Place and L. S. Peterson contains a still from *The Killers* of Edmond O'Brien and his shadow.[10] The caption reads, "Edmond O'Brien's shadow in *The Killers* suggests an alter ego, a darker self who cohabits the frame's space." The authors see this, intriguingly, as a two-shot of one character. The viewer is asked to entertain two different aspects of the character. What they fail to mention is that O'Brien's head is turned away from his shadow. His eyes peer suspiciously at some sensed external menace. Reardon's "darker self" may be apparent to a viewer, but it is lost to him. He is unaware of the potentially troubling aspects of his personality and nature that are coming increasingly into play. He knows that he argues sound insurance to his boss merely to win him over, that he is basically interested in something else. He never faces, however, how deeply he is implicated by the course of action he takes. His secretary calls him "dream boy," and she is not far from the truth. Reardon actualizes a level of infantile nightmare in which he confronts the fears and anxieties his daylight self represses. His "darker self" and capabilities emerge; he assumes, temporarily, a new identity. He cannot, however, see beyond its external dimensions.

The film even raises the possibility that Reardon's new role goes to his head, that he loses track of his accountability to the firm and begins to act like a figure of the underworld he now inhabits. This is a complicated issue the film leaves unresolved. He both is and isn't of that world. He partakes of it and holds his own within its dangers and temptations, but he is also insulated from its fundamental realities. By sheer persistence, he fulfills his goal; his audacities hurl him into near-fatal encounters, but they also pull him through. Yet he is clumsy and incompetent. The moves that any Bogart character would make effortlessly, with authoritative composure, he is awkward at and bungles. Reardon is, understandably, insecure in his role of weekend detective. He gets the drop on Dum-Dum, one of the gang, and begins a movie kind of interrogation, sneery tough talk backed up by a gun. Dum-Dum, as his name implies, is none too bright, but even he sees through Reardon's pose and tries the old mind-if-I-smoke routine on him. Reardon falls for it. Dum-Dum pushes him over, gets the gun, and instead of killing Reardon, with a look of genuine contempt, kicks him in the head and leaves. Later, at The Green Cat, Reardon gets outsmarted again when Kitty asks if she can visit the powder room. He agrees, and she promptly takes a powder.

The context governing both these scenes is important. Before surprising Dum-Dum, Reardon waits for him behind a closed door in a dark room. He is nervous, unsure of himself. It is implied that he has never held a gun before. He takes the gun in hand and seems concerned with how he should be holding it. He toys with an unlit cigarette butt. Hearing Dum-Dum arrive, he presses himself against the door, and only after what seems like an interminable time (Siodmak just lets the camera run) finally throws the door open and catches Dum-Dum off guard. The tension of the scene is not in the usual coordination of action and suspense (what will happen when) but in the drama of the character undergoing a trial. If Reardon's thoughts could be heard they would go something like "What am I doing here anyway? How do I use this thing? When should I open the door?" They stop short, though, of "Who am I?" and "Why am I doing this?"

By the time Reardon meets Kitty, he is an old hand at this sort of thing. He's in it up to the hilt, and, as I suggested before, one even wonders in what direction he is going. As his grilling of Kitty at The Green Cat intensifies, Siodmak's wide-angle lens distorts Reardon's face. Mean, ugly, unflattering, he's shot like a typical *noir* heavy. Is Reardon so cocky and confident that he's after the money for himself? Kitty plays her trump card, suggesting to Reardon that they go up to her place to discuss it further, an open sexual invitation. The film's ambiguities reach a climax here. The viewer now must wonder whether Reardon has been fooled, whether Kitty's lying, whether he *should* be fooled. Men fall instantly for Kitty. For Reardon not to fall would make him less of a man or would make him the kind of man who is insensitive to beauty and sex and dulled to passion. He is what we suspected he was. Impervious to Kitty's allure, he remains unchanged—not a real dreamer, he, but a company man.[11]

Reardon also takes some mild lumps from Lubinsky who, as an experienced man with guns, is amused by Reardon's newly acquired habit of playing with them. When Reardon meets Lubinsky after being disarmed by Dum-Dum, he asks, "By the way, did you bring along that extra 45?" Lubinsky: "Yeah, what happened to yours?" "Oh, it got lost, or stolen . . . or. . . .," ". . . or something." The subject is brought up again when Lubinsky and Reardon are driving to Colfax's house for the final showdown. Lubinsky needles, "Got your gun handy?" "Sure, why?" "Just thought I'd ask." He settles back with a pleased smile. Reardon is simply too compromised a hero to carry much individual appeal or ethical force. His cynicism is too thorough, and the film's cynicism about him is quite destructive.

Lubinsky's tweaking is, in turn, compromised by Reardon's achievement. Lubinsky doesn't discover anything. If it weren't for Reardon, nothing would have been investigated. Lubinsky's ineffectiveness is made apparent in the scene where he and Reardon wait for Kitty's call. Lubinsky says that his long experience on the force suggests they are just wasting their time, that Kitty won't call. His remark—"I know more about women"—is interrupted by Kitty's call. At the end, when they ride in the police car to Colfax's house, the shot juxtaposes Reardon's anticipation and Lubinsky's boredom.

The Killers is far too cynical to shed tears over Swede's fate. As the film progresses, the sadness of Swede's plight gives way to Reardon's slick success. En route, we meet a selection of the doomed and dying that make up Swede's world, and of whom Swede, with his youth and honesty, and Kitty, with her malignant beauty, are the most notable examples of wasted qualities. Swede's suicidal passivity and Reardon's energetic positivism, when aligned with what is revealed about their respective characters, make up the film's double-edged critique. Swede's character is consistent throughout the many flashbacks. He is a simple, open man, with nothing to hide. He deals with people with a vulnerable honesty and trustfulness. His early death is crucial in defining a world that goes on in the absence of his qualities, a world destined to be molded by the prerogative of arch-calculators like Reardon, whose efficient connections reduce Swede to a set of statistics.

> Real name Ole Anderson. Born Philadelphia, June 23, 1908. Mother died 1909. Father employed by Philadelphia Transit Company, died 1916. Started fighting professionally in 1928. Weight, 173. Last fight Philadelphia Sports Arena, 1935. Three years later, October 1938, arrested in Philadelphia for robbery. Sentenced to three years of hard labor by Justice Regan. Released for good behavior in May of '40.

The script merits a separate commentary that does justice to the economy with which it reveals the essence of the minor characters. Blinky, Dum-Dum, Colfax, Charleston, and Kitty, especially, are not just a collection of sufficient lines of dialogue or merely representative types *(The Killers,* like many *noir* films, takes to near-mannerist extremes the exploitation of the actors' physical properties to convey meaning). They are people the film makes us understand, people with lives to manage, decisions to make, and self-defined goals. Their private difficulties are played out in a subterranean world that has its own labyrinths and borders. It is a world difficult to live in, a world unrecognized by those who live apart from it and do not have to meet its grim demands. When Reardon tells his boss there might be an interesting story in what he's investigating, the boss replies, "I don't care," and goes on to make a speech about the firm as a public benefactor. It's a sure thing that neither Dum-Dum, Blinky, nor Charleston have any life insurance. The insurance firm and, by extension, those it serves are aloof from the squalor of the life the film invites us to participate in and to feel. The insurance firm alone survives and thrives. It is the defining image of postwar prosperity, protecting its legion of policyholders and oblivious to the ulcerous truths that exist beneath its skyscraping offices. Reardon, who moves between both worlds, relies on the firm's stability and also "serves the public" by ridding the world of a pack of worthless criminals.

There is the aptly named Blinky (Jeff Corey), thin, nervous, eager to please, afraid of rain, a former junkie. He is found in a "depot washroom, lying in a pool of blood." He survives long enough for the viewer to hear the raving deathbed recollections of his failed hopes. His flashback is prefaced by remarks from Reardon, Lubinsky, and the hospital doctor: "What are his chances?" "Nil." "How long has he got?" "He's beyond schedule now." Blinky, exhausted, stops talking. "Will he be able to talk anymore?" "He's dead now, except he's breathing." Lubinsky worries about whether his delirious remarks can be accepted as testimony. Blinky dies, muttering "a quarter of a million." During the war years he had been a sailor. Serving his country did him a lot of good. He comes home to get shot in a washroom and be the butt of black humor.

There is Big Jim Colfax (Albert Dekker), a "thief with a touch of class," who by virtue of being a "leader" and exhibiting a superiority of poise and intelligence that naturally entitles him to the biggest cut, gains Kitty.[12] Colfax has also gone legit during the war, finding his niche in the booming economy as a successful contractor. He and Kitty, having double-crossed the rest, have used the money to set themselves up as properly married, respectable citizens. The showdown takes place in his ritzy suburban home. The police and Reardon arrive to hear the shots. Dum-Dum falls down two flights of elegant stairs, dead. Colfax follows, fatally shot by Dum-Dum.[13] Kitty arrives to beg Colfax to swear her innocent. Colfax, dying, must endure Reardon's self-congratulatory comments. "I wanted you alive." Colfax asks for a cigarette. Lubinsky lights a match on his shoe. Reardon leans smugly against the wall, smoking, as he watches Colfax die and Kitty go to pieces. Big Jim's recognition and accept-

The Killers. Interesting moment. Big stories and little stories. Axiom: girls go for the guys with big dough. But . . . youth, vigor, sexual allure may compensate for indigence, limit-governed behavior, lack of ambition, even infidelity. Sex as woman's means for "advancement," something not possible without it. Men just have to flash the greenery. And there's some of it on the table (lower left)—"the stuff that dreams are made on," and the results of having scrambled for it. Killing time and lying low. The tactile surfaces of up-angled bills, strangely devalued by the company they keep. Cheap tasseled tablecloth, glassware, furniture, pack of Luckies—a still life of complementary frozen gestures and stalled movement. Hierarchized characters of tableau iconicity. Blinky, the weakest character, is pondering a Colfax bet or raise that has put him in a quandary. Blinky's rags have touches of refinement (cuff links and quality suspenders), but he is no match for the aggressively striped and sharply pressed look Colfax insists on maintaining in the same atmosphere. It will be a quiet evening. Blinky has seen fit to loosen his collar and carelessly drape his tie. His vaguely "Jewish" nose suggests that by the time of *The Killers*, the embarrassing precision of the ethnic stereotyping of the early 30s (like the gun merchant in *The Public Enemy*) has given way to a more guarded, working-by-implication approach. (Nonetheless, in Curtiz's *Bright Leaf* [1950], another Jeff Corey Jewish "turn" character seems steeped in a pretty briny anti-Semitism. I don't find that it caused any comment). A blood-debased creature, eerily controlled by the Wasp big-shot Colfax. Colfax, imposing even while sitting, is clearly upset by what's going on just above and behind him with Swede and Kitty, who share wary but fascinated looks while feigning other interests and business. Colfax, neutralized by Kitty's neck rub, can only seethe patiently while Swede has that "I'm-safe-if-I-stick-by-that-harmless-Blinky" look on his face. Colfax's return to the film via the accidental meeting with Swede has reignited jealousy and suspicion. Swede and Kitty's casual sensuality points offhandedly to Colfax's vain, big-bankroll pursuit of Kitty. Swede and Kitty dress somewhat indiscriminately, as if they know they'd look good in anything, and, indeed, their country and "thrift shop" attire, however nondescript, suits them just fine. Colfax's vanity is his Achilles' heel. His passion for Kitty persists, despite his dismay at her venality and infidelity. (They all die, of course, but that's *noir* [now you see 'em, now you don't].) It is a tense moment, one not conducive to harmony among thieves. People are both separated and realigned by astute framing, various geometries of composition, a just proxemics of "acquired" space, with the stone-rigid head of Colfax given a worrisome centrality. He looks fit to kill (the young, cocky Swede will do for starters, with Kitty as a deserving encore). It's not the money, it's not the power, it's not suffering sweaty weasels like Blinky, but Kitty who is the seat of unfathomable evil. *Noir* is always looking for explanations of human fear and misery and error. *The Killers* is another "Put the Blame on Mame" nocturnal saga, only done with the highest expertise. (Museum of Modern Art)

ance of his fate, sputtered out amid the coughs and gurgles of his final words, gain him a measure of sympathy. In a scene in which everyone adopts a conclusively cynical style, Big Jim's stands out.

Of the two remaining figures, Charleston and Kitty, Charleston (Vince Barnett) poses less difficulty. As his name implies, he is a relic, his better days (such as they were) behind him. His function is predominantly choric. He is a man who has nothing to show for his life except a limited wisdom that is destined to go unheeded. He is the warmest character of all, and a sad reminder of what it means to go on living in his world past a certain age. Of all the minor characters, he's the most nicely realized, and the "tone" he brings to his scenes gives the film a welcome depth of feeling.

Charleston is seen as one of the permanent fixtures of his world, to which he remains, in his own opportunistic way, loyal. A realist, he plays the game of survival for what it's worth. He tells us that he has spent twenty years of his life in jail, on and off. He opts out of the caper because it's too risky, and he doesn't want to spend any more time in jail if he can avoid it. He's only out for "easy pickings." He knows himself as a creature marginal to the already marginal world he lives in. His looks, his nature, his temperament have forced him to be an observer, not a participant, a thinker, not a doer. In jail, he tells Swede about the stars (a memory he is fond of), which he has read about in the prison library. Gazing on them through the bars of his cell window, he knows that they are not there for him to reach. He can only contemplate, abstractly and remotely, their beauty and meaning. He tells Swede he has "studied up" on girls, and that they are not to be trusted. He likes Swede and wants him to understand some important things. It is with a mentor's pain that he leaves the hotel room and walks out of Swede's life, knowing that his advice has come to naught, that Swede's destiny is to love and be betrayed.

Charleston comes to Swede's funeral to mourn, and Reardon spots him. The scene prior to Charleston's flashback is beautifully written and directed. Reardon feeds him drinks, expecting Charleston to spill all he knows, but Charleston takes his "easy pickings," gets drunk, and tells Reardon a shrewd bare minimum. The scene expertly balances Reardon's manipulation of Charleston and Charleston's refusal to be specific. They both get more or less what they want out of each other. Reardon is happy to get information, enough to keep him going, cheap. Charleston is happy to get enough booze to keep himself going, also cheap. Neither wins nor loses; the scene is played to a comic stalemate.

After the interview with Reardon, Charleston drops out of the film. The war years have not been kind. He's a lush, a human wreck, a sad, lonely old man with a dead-end poolroom job that keeps him in liquor. But he has his moment, sticking by his kind. The sequence dissolves from the poetry of

Dark Transformations

93

The Killers. Charleston lushes during Reardon's cocky questioning. A seedy poolroom provides the backdrop.

Charleston's exit line ("Me and Swede, we sure had some wonderful talks about the stars") to Reardon's office and the mechanical clack-clacking sound of his secretary's typewriter.

Kitty Collins resembles many manipulative women of the period, women who seem cursed by their beauty, who cannot do anything but use it destructively. She is more a symbol than a character. *Film noir* is full of appallingly seductive women of deceitfully angelic appearance. The men always buy them a drink, and life suddenly becomes a nightmare. These women are signs of a collective male desperation about the world as something that can be understood and put to right. They appear out of nowhere and wreak instant or eventual havoc. They are destroyed like vampires or vanish like apparitions. They are society's misogynist fantasy— woman as an object to be feared, woman as scapegoat for the world's ills. *Noir* films both celebrate these women as icons of idealist fantasy and loathe them as incarnations of an insatiable and debilitating sexuality. They are also, like most extended characterizations of women in the genre, indexes to male simplicity.

Kitty is a modern Circe. When Swede meets her at Jake the Rake's party, it is as much her siren song as her looks that transports him. Kitty has no feelings; her game is power, and power alone. She dominates her men with mere glances, and when circumstances force her to be verbal, she can be quite vicious: "You touch me and you won't live till morning." When she breaks down at the end, we are glad that Colfax, the last and biggest fall guy, cannot bring himself to lie to the police by protesting her innocence. Yet she crumples so completely that the effect is not mere gratification of a moment long overdue. Kitty, too, as a *character*, is one of the film's many failures. She is, after all, not the *cause* of Swede's obsessional love but merely the handy object ready to receive the glow of Swede's sexual idealism. (If she did not exist, Swede would have had to invent her. It may be noted that she is at her most striking in her first appearance, when Swede gets hooked. Her later scenes present her as less unreal, more flesh and blood.) Her gift is to rule men cruelly, but she seems to be beyond rational or practical motive. She does seem aware of what she is doing, but there is no conflict in her character. It is as if she has no mind or will but is rather a vessel through which a force operates. It is possible to see her as sick and disturbed, someone who hates men with an inexplicable compulsion, but that doesn't quite explain her. As a symbol of male fears and desires, she withholds, lures, inflames but also validates the passion of love—makes it deep, crazy, intense, worthwhile. She is the risky alternative to a homogenized or indifferent love relationship, a big question mark in the erotic imagination of an era.

If we see Kitty purely as a symbol, she makes more sense. It is not necessary for her to be explained, because she's just *there*, a tool of the film. She is the lure that drives human beings. She needs no motives, and cannot be shown to care for anyone. Her whole purpose is to preserve her alluring presence to others, which she does until she meets Reardon, whose mind cannot receive her because he is a new order of man. She makes a good attempt to reach him, through means that she imagines are in accord with his sensibility, but fails. It is the imagination of men like Swede and Colfax that gives her life. She entreats the dead Colfax, "Come back! Come back!" We don't know what happens to her—the shot dissolves to other characters as she is imploring Colfax. We do not see her dead or incarcerated. When the dreams of the men who created her die, she ceases to exist. Her claims to innocence, are, in one sense, true.

Kitty and the money are used as symbols and metaphors for objects of human passions. Without such lures, people would just *settle*. Living in the mainstream is a trap, but dreams are also traps. Yet men are compelled to reach for the stars, for Kitty—to want what they cannot have and abandon what they can have (Swede leaves Lily). *The Killers* says this is a delusion. There is no knowing what the dream is or how far away it is (Charleston's explanation of Betelgeuse). Kitty is an untouchable and is referred to as "dynamite." She warns Colfax not to touch her or he'll be dead. Swede, after enormous self-control, touches Kitty, kisses her, gives himself completely over (in Kitty's flashback), and ensures his death. That Kitty is unattainable does not prevent men from wanting her. On the contrary, people do things even though they know there is no point to it because they must do *something*. Film noir implies that there is no purpose to asserting one's will, that the society is too vast, that one can't make it (unlike the early, heroic phase of the genre). Yet, as conditions get more hopeless, motives vaguer and vaguer, and goals more illusory, the desire to assert oneself gets stronger and stronger. *The Killers* shows that this is fundamental to the American psyche, labels it as criminal, and makes it succumb to the realities of experience. It exposes human illusions in a context that suggests that certain people will never relinquish them, and whether they do or not, what will happen will happen anyway.[14]

Noir visuals offer a highly subjective interpretation of events and settings. A viewer feels, from the very first shot of *The Killers*, that he is being worked upon, that verisimilitude is not an issue, that the world will be distorted by framing, lighting, and composition to specific ends. Woody Bredell's photography realizes a sophisticated conception of meaning residing in contrasts of black and white, light and shadow. Hollywood photography has always been highly skilled; when matched, as here, with directorial imagination of a high order, the results are most impressive. It is not the least of *film noir*'s contribution that it called for a great deal of technical expertise and visual invention to get its vision of the world down right. *The Killers* achieves the quintessential *noir* look right away and sustains it throughout. What it has to say demands an intensification of visual means not required of the gangster films preceding it.

One notices immediately how the image is comprised of imbalanced masses of light and dark, and how the characters and what they do are dominated by a lighting scheme that minimizes their importance and creates meanings independent of language and action. A car races through the night, the camera angle taken from the back seat. Its headlights glare along the asphalt surface of the road, bordered by a total blackness. The killers approach the diner, visible only as two black shapes that cast long shadows, ominous silhouettes of death. The light, often coming from a single source, burns holes through the darkness, as if to compensate by intensity for its meager allocation of space. Nick Adams, running through the darkness to warn Ole, darts through a vertical rectangle of light, the high angle emphasizing the uselessness of his energy. The eye is led by light, and a viewer expects that what is lit is what is most important for him to see clearly in the shot. Siodmak's manipulation is unsettling in this respect. Light strikes unpredictably, where least expected, and with a blinding brilliance that rivets the attention. Nick throws open the door to Swede's room and light crashes onto the open door. Nick's face is in shadow, his expression not visible, and his body is framed off to the far right with the door centered. Swede lies in shadow, the wall above his bed daubed with harsh light. He speaks a monotoned despair from out of darkness. Reardon, Nick, and the Brentwood coroner, Plufner, chat over Swede's bullet-riddled corpse in a dark foreground; the wall in back is brightly lit. The contrasts are not merely stark but seem to invert the values typically carried by light and dark. The effect is one of a hellish environment against which the actors cannot compete.

There seems also to be a conscious attempt to dislocate the audience by subverting traditional associations, connected with light and darkness. Traditionally, light is positive, darkness negative; light is security, darkness insecurity. Dark is evil, stifling, terrifying, deadly; light signifies life, hope, and growth. Darkness is falsehood, light truth. In *The Killers* light hurts and terrifies. The eye is assaulted and the characters endangered by light. To move or rest in darkness is never to get anywhere, but *noir* choreography and framing imply there is nowhere to go anyway. Darkness meanwhile can be protective, comforting, a safe region in which to brood and endure. Reardon's investigation brings a lot of things into the light and results in many deaths. Colfax recognizes Swede in the Brentwood daylight and vice versa. As Swede cleans Colfax's windshield, the exchanged glances tell us that they both see clearly each other's identity. Swede hugs the shadows of his room as if his wish were to retreat even further into them, to withdraw completely into the solace invisibility would bring. He stares in the blackness of his room toward the closed door behind which lies the lighted hallway; a thin slit of light cuts down from hinge to hinge. Behind the door, the killers listen, intently. The door bursts open; Swede, startled, lifts his head into a streak of light. The killers fire and fire, their faces surreally illumined by each gun blast.

In crowded frames, a glut of people and objects creates a dense patchwork of hard blacks and whites. Shadows, in the main, are precisely sculpted—sometimes in odd, clawlike shapes. In uncluttered frames, darkness penetrated by a single light that isolates an object or a face is the norm, as in Swede's death, where the light hits his hand, in mid-frame close-up, sliding down the bedpost and knocking a glass off a nearby table. Variations of this pattern are matched closely to decor and meaning. In the insurance boss's office, for example, the lighting is high key, even, and of a neutral gray cast. The lens is not as extreme, the focus is softer, more "natural." This office is the region most remote from the milieu of the story. Siodmak is attentive enough to adjust the lighting as Reardon moves from the boss's office to the reception room occupied by the firm's secretary. In this room, from which one enters into one world and leaves for another, Siodmak admits some mildly expressionist touches, such as the diagonal of dark gray shadow over the secretary's desk and Reardon's shadow on the wall. In the total isolation of the boss's office, everything is uniform, untroubling.

Light is also an agent of deceit, of false hope or, at the least, an ambiguous promise of possibility. The stars shine for Charleston in his cell, their beckoning is a mockery of his and Swede's condition. Swede's enraptured admiration of Kitty's vocalizing is taken in a two-shot. Separating the figures is a large, decorative glass lamp, with the light in the form of a candle. Kitty stares away from Swede. Swede stares at Kitty, and we are made to stare at the candle, shining brightly, commenting on Swede's love for Kitty. When Swede leaves Lubinsky outside the sports arena, after rejecting Sam's suggestion that he join the force, we get a long shot with the framing of figures indicating the psychological distance that separates them. Lubinsky stares at Swede, walking farther and farther away toward what looks like a tunnel of light. Finally, his silhouette merges into a white mist. Swede, as we already know, is walking toward his doom.

The Killers. The Olympian viewpoint of the continuous crane shot and the busy lines haphazardly "closing" asymmetrical compositonal pockets imply the futility of this "successful" robbery.

The visual style of *The Killers* is characterized primarily by fixed camera setups and tightly composed images spatially manipulated by light and shadow. Siodmak's camera rarely moves and never ostentatiously. When it does, it is for a good reason. In the opening diner scene, the brisk, short dolly going from Nick's end of the counter up to the other, where the killers are questioning George, conveys, with a subtle economy, the tension that hangs within the enclosed space of the diner. A wonderful moment of camera mobility occurs when Lubinsky, spotting the hot jewelry Kitty has slipped into the soup, leaps from his table in the restaurant and catches up to the waiter returning the dishes to the kitchen. A long shot has previously shown us how crowded the room is, with people and tables, but when Lubinsky cuts through to intercept the waiter, traveling nearly the full length of the room, the camera dogs his heels at startling speed. The illusion is of rapid, agile motion through a congested area, a perfect execution of a difficult maneuver. The effect is exhilarating, and the movement also tells us something about Sam's skilled, quick-witted performance as a cop.

The one virtuoso sequence is the robbery of the hat company, and again the choice has tonal and thematic implications pertinent to the film as a whole. It is done in one long take, the high-angle crane shot keeping the viewer detached. Once we know a cast of characters, the normal emphasis would be to bring us in close to the robbery, create suspense about the mechanics of the heist and about the potential of imperfect performance on the part of members of the gang. Siodmak, however, eschews this for a more futile level of engagement. The scene as shot provides a triple perspective on the action. We see every aspect of the robbery. The gang, disguised, enters the main gate with the other workers. They climb the staircase to the payroll office. The camera looks in from a window as they take the money, pans to follow them down the stairs, pulls back and rises to catch their escape through the main gate, and then lifts to an extreme overhead shot of the whole locale—factory and street—to show the gun battle and eventual escape by automobile. Throughout all this, the camera never stops running and never comments. It imposes a godlike objectivity on the action and, as well, a sense of irreversibility. The viewer "participates" but is impotent to intervene. Any emotion invested would be worthless. The event must take its course. The film has brought us close to these characters, has made us understand how much the robbery means to all of them, and now the camera takes us as far away as possible, enforcing a detachment against our will. It becomes merely something that once happened—one among a whole series of hopeless ventures. Superimposed on the visuals is a voice-over. While we see the robbery being committed, Reardon's boss, Kenyon, reads a dry newspaper account of what transpired (the means of transition to this sequence). Naturally, it clashes with our own attitudes, representing a limited point of view about which we form our own opinion. The complexity of viewpoints intermixes and cancels out into a numb and frustrating acceptance. The whole episode seems evanescent, unreal, unimportant, a fragment of a dream.

Siodmak's mise-en-scène departs incisively from tradition. Objects loom menacingly in the foreground, disproportionate to any "natural" arrangement. Occupying odd positions in the frame, they make ferocious oblique thrusts at the viewer. The sharp diagonal of a thick staircase, the ropes of a boxing ring take on the consistency of steel and jut into jarring prominence, altering typical compositional balance. Objects separate characters or comment ironically on their words and deeds. Deep focus accentuates the shape and texture of most objects in the frame. Mirrors belie appearances. Ceilings hang low, pressing down upon the characters. Even simple shots, requiring one would think no special emphasis, like Reardon making a telephone call, are compositionally slanted. We watch him talk, in medium close-up, while the distorted composition works on us. A funeral becomes an ominously stylized tableau of stiff forms, odd angles, glowering skies. A film like *The Public Enemy* integrates foreground and background into a harmonious blend or strives, in its mise-en-scène, for a fullness appropriate to the action or event. Siodmak uses crisp focus throughout the frame to create a tension between foregrounds and backgrounds. He works the interior of the diner, for example, into a complex visual repletion. In the foreground, one of the killers and George are separated by the counter. Behind George is a long mirror, reflecting downward on George and the killer and also picking up stuff the camera could catch only if it were reversed. Waist-high to George is a partition to the kitchen that the second killer opens from behind to talk to George; behind *him* we know that Nick and the cook lie bound and gagged. The image contains a lot; the eye has no choice but to roll around, trying to see everything and also hold it in balance.[15]

The frequent high-angle shots do double duty. They provide a fatalistic perspective on the actions of the characters and, as establishing shots within tightly bordered locales, they create oppressive environments by aerially squeezing down the horizon line. Through both high-angle setups and wide-angle lenses, movement is agile but constricted within dense milieux. *The*

Killers takes us into numerous underworld settings. *Noir* films choose their settings in consideration of the lure of the seedy, the illicit, the provocatively dangerous. *The Killers* is rich with atmosphere, moving confidently through a variety of locales busy with movement and noise—sports arenas, poolrooms, diners, offices, cheap hotels, expensive nightclubs, loud restaurants, prison cells, hospitals, factories, suburban homes, city streets. Such is the force of its emphasis that even "neutral" or potentially pleasing environments become infected—a drab boarding house in Atlantic City, a scruffy, charmless rural landscape, a small town violated by gunfire. The film's quietest, most peaceful and lyrical moment occurs in prison, where Charleston and Swede strike a chord of friendship and feeling. One does not go to prison by choice, but in the world of this film it is a relatively pleasant environment.

*T*he Killers is one of many stylish, implausibly twisty melodramas that together define the first postwar phase of *film noir* and the gangster crime film. Some of its commentary is conscious, some of it comes automatically with the general implications of *noir* stylistics. Certain assumptions, of the kind I have been making, are more easily argued than others; some may seem less tenable when derived from a single source, an individual film. *The Killers* is representative, but *noir* films should be played off against each other to get a fuller sense of the *noir* vision. *The Killers* takes its place in a cycle of films whose nature is determined by the cast of mind of filmmakers working in phase with the realities surrounding them—social realities, historical realities, psychosexual realities, the realities of the motion picture industry. The more one acquaints oneself with the spectrum of *noir* cinema, the more one understands its individual products as unique wholes and also as works connected by a common ground of shared assumptions. *The Killers*, certainly, is a serious film, not at all lighthearted. As a gangster film, it brings a strong despair into the genre. In *The Public Enemy* it is a hoofer's grace that prevails, despite all. The callous cynicism of *The Killers* portends a psychological disturbance in the perception of the world it would be critically inaccurate to neglect. The film is also made with such care that criticism is obliged to tend to its details and account for their subtleties. This is not a task for one critic, but for many. One example of a near-imperceptible created meaning should suffice to indicate how close an investigation is called for. When Swede explains to Nick why the men have arrived to kill him, he says, "I did something wrong, once." There is a full pause after "wrong," and the "once" that follows it is tinged with regret and irony. Reardon, who has just heard Nick's account, remembers it as "Once I did something wrong." Different man, different tone, different attitude, different speed, different stress. It is unlikely that such minute detailing is accidental.

The early image of Swede getting cold-bloodedly massacred without lifting a finger to defend himself hangs over the rest of the film, invests it with an aura of foul absurdity. The world is not only sinister, but meaningless. The enigma that Reardon purports to solve is really a red herring, since the revelations that ensue fill in a picture of life for which there is no solution. The references to a new, grotesque violence attest to *noir*'s affinity to the repulsive.[16] The coroner says that the bullets "near tore him in half." Blinky is reported found "lying in a pool of blood." The hat company guard receives a "bullet in the groin." We get an ugly close-up of Swede's horribly disfigured hand. Reardon gets kicked in the head with a sickening thump. The excitement, the glamour, the tragic quality of violence belong to another period. *Noir* violence is mean, ugly, reductive, geared to an ambience evoked by "Newark" and "Pittsburgh" and to the nasty perplexities of human betrayal and brutality.

The film's critique extends outward to include everything. (The force of Hollywood typecasting is such that characters can exist both as individuals and as examples of their kind multiplied to infinity. Thus Blinky is the epitome of a legion of Blinky's, and so on.) Scenes of compassion get swallowed up by an overriding scorn. The rootless underworld figures are doomed, the settled society made contemptible by irony (its representative, Reardon, indirectly causes the death of a group of people who on occasion prey on their own kind but have long since stopped doing harm to anyone else). Crooked ways lead to a dead end, but the alternatives are either demeaning or insidious. To dream itself seems tantamount to performing an illegality, and dream and dreamer alike seem able to function only in the lower depths of the society. When they infringe upon the smoothly humming world of normalcy, that world rejects them, using one or another kind of protective mechanism. The police force, the insurance firm, and (implied) the newspapers form a unified circuitry of opposition to any but the most circumscribed aspirations. (Reardon tells his secretary, "Call up Reynolds on the *Ledger*. Give him the story. He's done good turns for us." It is Reardon's boss who reads the newspaper account of the robbery that reduces the drama of the event and disallows emotional engagement, the camera assuming a dry, documentary objectivity. There seems to be a similarity, if not a complicity, of attitude between the insurance firm and the newspapers.) There is also a casual glance at Colfax's successful postwar contracting business, alluding to the rising economy. Reardon finds him in his office, looking very legitimate, hunting cap on head, rifle in hand. In what way does the legitimate Colfax differ from the old Colfax? How many Colfaxes lurk behind the facades of legitimacy? In the interests of the general economy, such questions are ignored. The scene subtly puts into question the foundations of the new prosperity.

The Killers's depiction of small-town existence is equally dispiriting. Brentwood is drab and dull. Henry's diner is jokingly referred to as the town's center of life. Following Swede's murder, the police chief's only interest is in "protecting the lives and property of our citizens." He claims that Swede "lived here, that's all." He washes his hands of the whole affair: "It's up to the state police." (Throughout the entire scene, in the background, two men are seen in an adjoining room polishing what might be either the town's police or fire department vehicle.) Through his smug indifference and his moralistic insistence on his town's boundaries, the film offers an unflattering vision of isolationist, rural America cultivating its own dreary garden. When Dum-Dum gets wounded escaping from Mrs. Hirsch's boardinghouse, Reardon, the sophisticated Newarkian, amusedly tells Lubinsky, "Every cop in Brentwood's claiming credit for the shot." The film's attitude toward small towns is pretty caustic.

The ending of *The Killers*, not surprisingly, fails to provide the "relief" common to most films of all genres (through to the sixties, anyway). The scene dissolves from Kitty's hysteria to the insurance office, far removed from the fray. Reardon and his boss tidy up all the loose ends of the case. Masquerading as a "light" scene, a pablum envoi of sorts, this final sequence sustains the film's cynicism down to the last twist. Reardon's boss, bright and cheerful, his faith in the *principle* of life insurance justified and reinforced, commends a weary, yawning Reardon for a job well done:

> Kenyon: And just to think, none of this would ever have come to light if it hadn't been for a $2,500 death benefit.
> Reardon: Uh—(yawn)—huh.
> Kenyon: Well, I suppose you're waiting to be congratulated.
> Reardon: Ahh—it's the job.
> Kenyon: Owing to your splendid efforts, the basic rate at The Atlantic Casualty Company, as of 1947, will probably drop one tenth of a cent. Congratulations, Mr. Reardon.
> Reardon: I'd rather have a night's sleep.
> Kenyon: Why don't you take a good rest. I must say you've earned it. This is Friday. Don't come in till Monday.
> Reardon: Thanks!

Nothing has had any significance. After all the smoke has cleared, it's back to work on Monday.

The cynical humor of this scene is typical and recalls another moment in a lighter vein. Lubinsky enters Lou Tingle's café, an underworld hangout, and joins a man and woman sitting down at a table. A quick, nonchalant exchange follows:

Charlie: Hello, Sam!

Sam: Hiya, Charlie.

Charlie: Miss Bryson . . . Lieutenant Lubinsky.

Miss Bryson: How's tricks, Sam?

Sam: It's been a long time.

Miss Bryson: You're partly to blame for that.

Sam: Only ninety days' worth.

Miss Bryson: No hard feelings.

Since neither Charlie nor Miss Bryson appear again or have anything more to say, the conversation must be illustrative. Life is that kind of a game, with both sides sticking to a set of rules there is no way of changing. The game is often vicious and costly. Between moves, a resigned, defensive, disenchanted humor lets the players take it all in stride. Swede, alas, saw nothing funny in it; he couldn't curl his lip if his life depended on it, and it did. In the toughened-up world of *The Killers*, the hard-boiled style is one's survival kit. By showing that as the going mode of human interaction, and an unsafe and unreliable one to boot, *The Killers* hits rock bottom. There's nowhere to go but up.

CREDITS *The Killers*

(Universal, 1946, 105 min.)

Producer	Mark Hellinger	Cast	Burt Lancaster (Swede)
Director	Robert Siodmak		Edmond O'Brien (Jim Reardon)
Screenplay	Anthony Vellier and John		Ava Gardner (Kitty Collins)
	Huston (uncredited), based on		Sam Levene (Sam Lubinsky)
	the story by Ernest Hemingway		Albert Dekker (Big Jim Colfax)
Photography	Woody Bredell		Vince Barnett (Charleston)
Editor	Arthur Hilton		Jack Lambert (Dum-Dum)
Music	Miklos Rosza		Jeff Corey (Blinky)
Art Directors	Jack Otterson and		Virginia Christine (Lily)
	Martin Obzina		William Conrad (Max)
			Charles McGraw (Al)
			John Miljan (Jake the Rake)
			Phil Brown (Nick Adams)
			Harry Hayden (George)
			Donald MacBride (Kenyon)

The Genre's "Enlightenment"
The Stress and Strain for Affirmation

3

The futility of *The Killers* was exceptional, but its depressing outlook remained a keynote of *noir* cinema. *Noir* bile stains both *Kiss of Death* (1947) and *Force of Evil* (1948), but their narratives assert a desperate hope in the social activism and moral enlightenment of individuals. Both films say you can climb up out of the hole. But where is up? Both tax the viewer's faith and credulity in constructing hope out of despair. *Gun Crazy* (1949), which is built around the appeal of guns, cars, and sex in a sleepy, unvigorous world, exhibits criminal pathology as engaging, if destructive, energy.

The world of *The Killers* is like a fact that has to be worked with. The middle phase of the *noir* gangster crime film can be divided into those films that reiterate the hopeless vision of *The Killers* and those that attempt to create values in the face of it. The three films discussed in this section belong in the latter division, and each illustrates the difficulties involved in this period of saying something positive. The odds against establishing life as meaningful are just too strong.

These films are evidence that looking for a way out is in the American grain, that however logically persuasive the *noir* outlook might be, the culture is not going to accept it sitting down. *The Killers* closed off every avenue by either literal death or ironic contempt. If every avenue is closed, all there remains is the will itself. In these films, the question of where to go becomes a filmic, dramatic, social, and psychological question. The sense of desperation and strain that characterizes them is a legitimate reflection of the difficulties of providing an answer.

The old-style gangster is now completely useless: it is impossible to employ him meaningfully. Given the worldview of *The Killers*, there's no such creature—just losers. The classic gangster could oppose and lose, but these films understand at the outset that dreaming of being somebody and getting someplace is not even a possibility anymore. In *The Killers* a brief scene at Lou Tingle's café shows Swede flashily dressed in a camel coat, high-styling it with Sam and others—an echo of the old gangster. It ends immediately as something that is impossible to sustain for even a minute within a *noir* vision of things, and it is not present at all in *Kiss of Death*, *Force of Evil*, or *Gun Crazy*. The old categories of gangsterism are discarded and the kind of fantasies associated with them eliminated. Within the genre there are no more Toms, Ricos, or Earles. We are not shown the "gangster" getting anywhere as a gangster. What the films show in their ninety or so minutes is not the process by which the gangster gets to the top or to the bottom or both; they locate him *at* the bottom or *at* the top and examine what his life there is like. If these criminals—

Nick Bianco in *Kiss of Death*, Joe Morse in *Force of Evil*, Bart and Laurie in *Gun Crazy*—get somewhere, it is as people, not criminals. Crime and its activity have become fundamentally metaphoric.

Common to all three films are willed solutions to the problem of leading a meaningful life in a civilization that has gone awry. The films grope for sense, for purpose, and the only direction they find is one of faith. After *noir* and what *noir* suggests about a collective psyche, faith is the only possibility. The characters in *Gun Crazy* embrace action for action's sake until that leads toward and dissolves into the greater reality of mutual love. The heroes of *Kiss of Death* and *Force of Evil* are placed in Christian schemes and are reborn. The films' struggle to avoid despair parallels the characters' efforts. The appeal they make is conservative and traditional. Our problem is that we've lost our way in the world, that we need to turn to our roots and regain our capacity to love and believe. We must have faith in ourselves and must trust our brother. The triumph of the lovers in *Gun Crazy* is secular, but Nick and Joe undergo the Christian myth of death and rebirth. They must die to the ways of the world, go down to come up clean.

The films take on the difficult task of providing an answer, as it were, to *The Killers*, of working their way toward something of value from repulsive starting points (Nick, for example, is the lowest of characters—he's got to be a stoolie to survive). They lack, I believe, the coherence of *The Killers* and earlier genre films. The pointed stylization of *The Killers* proceeded from a philosophical confidence. If life is unalterably grim, there is the luxury of expressing it. The hideousness can have intellectual and aesthetic coherence. But *Kiss of Death* can't take a coherent view, even a grim one; its resolution requires an element that is literally a deus ex machina. It gets itself going, runs into contradictions, then cries help. (In different ways, the same is true of *Force of Evil* and *Gun Crazy*.) What may be seen as aesthetic breakdown may also imply a new maturity in the genre. The incoherence reflects the honesty of the struggle. The dreams of earlier gangster figures were perhaps adolescent, the romanticism of *High Sierra* a delusion. Roy Earle transcends a human, generic corruption and the contingencies of human nature and human institutions. The avenue of transcendence is now replaced by faith and the taking of action that forces an awareness and an acceptance of one's own part in the evil.

It is significant that this shift in emphasis is accompanied by a realistic mode of presentation. *Kiss of Death* moves out of the studio into real locations, struggles with "real" exigencies in a way that parallels its struggles with dramatic credibility (the ending, Nettie). The most powerful sequences in *Force of Evil* are shot on location. The "real" world in *Gun Crazy* operates as a context for our judgment of the characters' unconventional and frantic exploits. In all three films, women become *real* women (not symbols or metaphors or even "stars") that men can turn to for help and sustenance. They become centers of meaning, they pose an alternative to the way things are. If the problem is how one can remain human, they are an important part of the answer.

Gun Crazy puts less strain on our credibility because the breakthrough of its characters, however valid, is shown to be self-destructive. *Kiss of Death* and *Force of Evil* must contend with characters who survive, and they must set up the conditions for their survival. For Nick and Joe to get where they must involves, to some degree, the films appearing to float away from their real contradictions toward an ephemeral optimism. *Gun Crazy* is more acute, in that its conception rests on a set of contradictions that is maintained to the very end. Bart and Laurie succeed in ways that do not violate the film's larger context of reality.

Bart and Laurie choose a route that leads to sure death. "Living" becomes a form of self-destruction. This may seem like nothing new, but the distinction is between behavior that turns out to be self-destructive (the early gangsters) and behavior that is psychologically dictated by self-destructive impulses. In *High Sierra* Earle looks for possibilities and chooses death. In *Gun Crazy* Bart and Laurie instinctively choose death from the start. Their humanity is also their downfall. One can't exit like Earle anymore. Bart and Laurie know in their bones what it takes Earle the whole film to find out and that the best legitimacy can offer is a carnival act. Their masochism is not a romantic choice but a given of existence, a revelation of what the world has done to the psyche. By exercising an impulse to live, they destroy themselves. This would explain why there is no specific "enemy" in the film, just the society rather neutrally going about its ways.

The early gangster died in the city, a specific form of civilization in part responsible for his death. Roy Earle fell from a glorious mountain, in pure, clean air and clear weather. Bart and Laurie are destroyed in a mist where nobody knows for sure what is happening. There is little oxygen and it is difficult to breathe. One can't see or hear well. They're in a *swamp*. Transcendence and glory give way to fear, terror, and confusion. It is a very qualified romanticism. They are not killed by a world that has no place for dignity and humanity (Earle as more *human* than society): in their own humanity they carry the seeds of their own destruction. The aura of innocence (just kids) established around them creates pathos, but it is also ironic. They were never innocent. Both their pasts are contaminated, and Bart's innocence is clearly exposed as false by Bart himself when he acknowledges that he and Laurie go together "like guns and ammunition." Innocence is self-delusion (America was never innocent); it is synonymous with repression. Bart, as a child, is given to us as abnormal. When we see him first as an adult, he is uncomfortably normal.

Laurie gives him the opportunity to be himself; she directs his ambivalent salvation. If it weren't for Laurie, he would be nothing, a miserable, repressed man, denying life and its corruptions by a facade of respectability. In that the film saves him from a living death by plunging him into irresponsible and socially deviant excitements, it can be seen as an alternative to the utter defeatism of *The Killers*.

The choices made by classic gangsters like Rico were real choices that arose from distinct self-conceptions. They wanted to be big shots; they thought, with hubris, that they could be. Bart and Laurie, Nick, and to some extent Joe, never think of themselves in such terms. As the world and their psychology interact, they simply do what they must do, as opposed to choosing. They have but one choice, making it not a choice at all. They are cornered from the outset, stuck with their own human condition from beginning to end. Their problem is that they are human in a nonhuman world. They want to be alive, and that leads them straight toward death. *Gun Crazy* implies that purity does not exist and that a stance of superhumanity is passé. The gangster is becoming less remote from us. Living means corruption; corruption means living. That is the human condition. What is dead about the world around Bart and Laurie is its deluded effort toward mechanism, order, propriety, and life on the installment plan—a veneer that smothers emotional and physical realities. All three films pit simple, basic human needs in opposition to a world that denies them. In *Kiss of Death* it is the family as an emotional unit, in *Force of Evil* it is the need to rejoin the human community, to recognize that all men are brothers, despite the separateness that the drift of society induces. In *Gun Crazy* it is the power of sex. All three films are a prelude to the strongly humanistic bias and to the explorations of inverted categories (life is death, order is chaos, sanity and reason are madness, the real is an illusion, the nightmare is the reality) characteristic of the tail end of the forties through to the mid-fifties. And in contrast to the amorality, cynicism, and self-confident behavior of previous gangster heroes, there is a noticeable flavor of guilt and atonement.

Kiss of Death (1947)

Much of the tension in *Kiss of Death* resides in our strained identification with its stoolie hero. The film's problem is to construct a character and a situation that supports its action of playing ball with the cops without sacrificing the element of personal worth and heroism. It helps that Nick Bianco (Victor Mature) hates what he has to do, but it is still asking much of an audience to pull for a stoolie—it's just not done. We don't want Nick to cooperate with Di Angelo (Brian Donlevy), but he has to because of the anarchic presence of Tommy Udo (Richard Widmark)—a hysterical projection of the gangster as threat to any and all human life. The film finds a have-your-cake-and-eat-it solution by having the hero's unwillingness to fink frustrated by the police force's incompetence, which forces him to go it alone against Udo. Nick, however, is not entirely free of the taint of being an informer. At the end, in a spirit of belligerent martyrdom, he takes five of Udo's bullets. We are told he lives, but five in the belly is a properly painful comeuppance for betraying even a fiend like Udo, who trusted him. As one may already infer, the film takes a back seat to none in ambivalence.

The law is unpleasantly portrayed. Brian Donlevy's smug, severe, assistant DA undermines his schematic "goodness." His associate Max Schulte (Millard Mitchell) is a surly needler, prone to gratuitous verbal harassment. Di Angelo sits surrounded in his office by icons of his importance—official documents on the wall, a picture of George Washington, photographs of banquets and dinners, a fancy desk, the American flag. He behaves with the doggedness of an ambitious lower official (much is made of his being an *assistant* DA—convicting Nick is the stepping-stone to a series of convictions that could accelerate his career). Almost all the shots of Di Angelo show him behind his desk, making deals with a vulnerable party or dryly considering courses of action over the phone. He is both insulated and trapped by his position. He can talk tough because he holds all the cards. He is a cold, unlikable man and, but for his manipulation of Nick, ineffective.

Nick tells Di Angelo, "Your side of the fence is almost as dirty as mine," summing up what we have felt all along. The senselessness of Di Angelo's reply that "the law only hurts bad people" is obvious in that Nick, a good person, is being cruelly and unfeelingly used. Throughout this scene Nick repeats, with deep emotion, his wish to see his kids and relates the details of his wife's suicide with a controlled despair. The cops aren't interested in any of that and eagerly pounce on the eroded will that can supply them information. They squeeze Nick unmercifully and then taunt him about his squealing. At the orphanage, the nun can't tell the cop from the criminal. The warden at Sing Sing refers contemptuously to Nick's playing ball. After Nick squeals, gets an honest job, and changes his name to protect his kids, Di Angelo asks him to appear in court to give evidence against Udo. Nick says that would be taking a big risk. Di Angelo threatens him with loss of parole (Nick was promised that he'd be left alone). The DA's incompetence allows Udo to go free; justice is aborted. Di Angelo calls Nick to report that Udo has evaded the police's tail. Nick finally realizes that he has to take matters into his own hands, that to count on Di Angelo is useless. His family can't go on living terrorized by Udo, and both his peace and his dignity are compromised by being always at Di Angelo's mercy. When Di Angelo comes to take him into custody, Nick tells him off: "He's nuts and he's smarter than you are." Nick, though, is not a murderer; he

Kiss of Death. Assistant D.A. D'Angelo (Brian Donlevy) badgers self-disgusted stoolie Nick Bianco into naming names. Bulldog-rigid Donlevy uses bulk and bribes, threats and intimidation, moral leverage, and family photos to get Nick to sing. *Kiss of Death* is not a *noir* shoo-in but a seasonal (Christmas) offering featuring hard-nosed, grayish cops, stomach-sick stoolies, and one sensational psychopath. It seeks, through Nettie's feelingful narration, an affirmation one cannot easily agree to. Ya gotta have faith. (Museum of Modern Art)

would like to kill Udo but will not. He is forced to call on Di Angelo again. He finds Udo rather quickly (what the police are doing all this time is left unclear—Di Angelo is shown sitting behind his desk when he gets Nick's call) and sets a trap. The police are to appear in time to catch Udo armed. They show up, but five bullets too late. The audience receives little guarantee that it will be protected against crime by the likes of these incompetents. Indeed, it is advised that to be dependent on them in any way is to invite a ruthlessness the more insidious for being legitimized.

Both Di Angelo and Udo work on Nick through the family. Di Angelo shows Nick pictures of his kids (nicely framed) and asks to see Nick's wallet photos. Nick refuses but Di Angelo forces the issue, playing the sanctity-of-children angle for all it's worth. Nick sees through the tactic to make him talk and says "no deal." The pompous, slippery Di Angelo, though, has his way. Di Angelo has no personal concern for Nick's family; he is just doing his job, in which humiliation of the father through his children is an effective strategy. His values are official ones. He never, until (presumably) the very end, rises above his ingrained prejudice against the ex-con, and when he has Nick over a barrel acts like he is doing him a big favor by letting him see his kids. He wields his upper hand firmly but unkindly, making Nick sweat and plead, finally, for the privilege of squealing. When Nick spills the goods, Di Angelo's response runs from indifference to contempt. Brian Donlevy's large, neckless head, square frame, stolid

Kiss of Death. Stoolie Nick Bianco encircled by cops during a final croon.

expression, and deep radio voice combine nicely to pull the rug from under Di Angelo's uprightness. He is visually a "heavy." His stiff, stony, thin-mustached face is in contrast to Victor Mature's suffering "people's" mug, upon which toughness and dishonesty lie as alien qualities. Nonetheless, the exchange of pictures between these two fathers supplies a common human denominator that unites hood and cop. Their human bond, however, is superficially broken by the roles society has created for them to play.

In *Kiss of Death* our assessment of right and wrong is kept blurred. The characters can't be tagged in the old ways. The film constructs a trap in which we watch the hero squirm and from which there seems to be no escape. That a way out suddenly materializes is perhaps illogical but emotionally acceptable. What Nick wants is nothing big or threatening, just some room to breathe for him and his family, and this makes it possible for us to acquiesce in an ending that holds out hope by seeming to bypass its own evidence.

Noir is a cinema of suffering, and, like Swede, Nick is another case of the kid on the corner who gets shafted by life. Mature's visual presence is similar to Lancaster's in *The Killers:* large, ungainly, styleless, pathos-handsome, but with a more vulnerable fleshiness epitomized by the loose, soft mouth. He is not differentiated from the rest of humanity by any menacing or eccentric qualities. (His hostility toward the law is intense, but justifiably, not pathologically, so.) He is a human being who will settle for reasonable satisfactions. His wants are average and unexceptional. Yet he cannot attain them. *The Killers* could not simply tell the story of Swede; it needed Reardon's hustle to keep it going. In *Kiss of Death,* Nick is too corralled by decency to be exciting, so the psychopath Udo is brought in to liven things up.

Udo says he is arrested for "shovin' a guy's ears off his head . . . traffic-ticket stuff." When he takes a dislike to someone, in one case someone he doesn't even know, his desire is to "stick both thumbs right in his eyes, hang on till he drops dead." He shoves Rizzo's mother (in a wheelchair) down a long flight of stairs and cackles. At a boxing match, he vociferously requests that the boxer pursue his advantage over his opponent by tearing the other eye out of his head. Crazed by jazz and dope, he spends a sleepless life looking for kicks, his killings motivated as much by fun as pragmatic necessity. James Agee astutely observed, "It is clear that murder is one of the kindest things he's capable of."[1] And he gets the best lines: "I wouldn't give you the skin off a grape." Widmark makes this monster credible. With his colorful underworld lingo and magnetically evil countenance, Udo is hard to resist. He is terrifying, but he delivers an excitement the bland, conscience-stifled Nick cannot.

Udo is not explained, but it is implied that he is a product of postwar conditions. The world has these crazy people in it, and Udo, with his smooth face and blond hair, fits no previous category of gangster.[2] He can be seen as analogous to Kitty in *The Killers*, a force that the world must contend with, a presence that activates people, a concentrated symbol of what the world is, at its depth. Or perhaps more like an emblem full of significations, the postwar equivalent of

Kiss of Death. Richard Widmark as Tommy Udo, his spectacular screen debut. He dresses in black and has the heart to match. We see him here with "my friend Nick," entering an old-fashioned opium house (Nick: "What's that funny smell?" Udo: "That's perfume.") as a treat for his "pal" Nick, who he has met in stir. (Museum of Modern Art)

the plague in past cultures. His mania for being thought of as a "big man" perhaps reflects unfavorably on the principle of success so firmly anchored in the American psychology. It is of note that Bianco wants to enter the social mainstream. His ethnic stereotype is replaced by the baffling Udo, a strange, unpredictable, cunning creature. The name is puzzling. Udo. Who is he? What is he? The "criminal element" has not only gone off the deep end, it can't be easily defined. Nick can be (and is) explained by socioeconomic theories of the thirties, but Udo is a more mysterious product of the postwar world. The Udo figure is a fixture of *noir* cinema, and his lunatic successors have provided many a frightening moment through three decades of the crime film. *(Noir* gangsters, like Udo, are usually *killers*, rather than "gangsters.") In *Kiss of Death* somebody fiercer than Nick, a milk drinker, is necessary to define the brutality of his world.

The film is narrated by Nettie, Nick s wife. (They marry within the course of the film, a while after Nick's first wife commits suicide.) Her love for Nick puts an added strain on our response to him as a hero. Some say that her high, sweet voice is too cloying and that her narration should have been dispensed with, but the character's exaggerated sweetness is essential to motivate Nick. If she weren't there, as is, Nick would never go after Udo. She functions crucially to ease us back from the ugliness of the world, a palliative. She stands for goodness, decency, loyalty, the family, and by her youth, freshness and hope. *Kiss of Death* does not really offer a "happy" ending, although it tries to set one up, through Nettie. Nettie is a survivor, and she informs us of that in a composed, accepting tone. The vision of the film *includes* her (she is not tacked on), and there is no convincing argument as to how her inclusion damages the film, only automatic impatience with the character's goodness. It might be charged that the film backs off from its grimmest conclusion—Nick dead on the pavement and Nettie cast adrift in an inhuman world saddled with Nick's children. But Nettie's voice is the first we hear: its patience and gentleness guide us from the very beginning, alleviating our worst fears. Nettie may be "good" but she's not stupid. Her commentary is neither unrealistic nor free of critical edge. (One cannot ignore, as well, the sadness of her voice.) It is she who states the notion (previously sounded in the 1933 *20,000 Years in Sing Sing*) of prison as a place where there are "plenty of jobs and no prejudice." The ending, then, with Nettie telling us of Nick's survival, comes as no surprise. It has been implicit from the start. It is the point of her telling us the story. The film has made a choice. Through Nettie, it suggests past history as a purposeful series of events. The world may be terrible, but it can include individual triumphs, and people can change.

Kiss of Death, in any case, underplays its optimism. Nettie's voice-over is in competition with the visuals, which often conflict with and contradict her tone and her position. It has a detached, unreal quality; it is a murmur of possibility more than an assuring fact. At the end, we are virtually given a choice. If we prefer to hope and believe in *this* one family's survival, we can; if not, the visual evidence of Nick being placed in an ambulance with five slugs in him invites us to entertain less sanguine possibilities.

Nettie's presence is an antidote to the unrelieved nastiness of Nick's history—the only reassuring component of a life marked by misery and deprivation. As a child, Nick has seen his father gunned down in the street (Nick trusts the elderly lawyer, Howser, because of his fatherly manner—Howser calls him "son"). He turns to crime because of poverty. All his efforts to go straight are frustrated: no jobs for ex-cons. His "friend" Rizzo has an affair with his wife while Nick is in prison, then abandons her. She commits suicide, sticking her head in an oven, and leaves two orphaned children. Nick is a trapped man wherever he turns. In one direction is Udo; in the other Di Angelo, and both are ruthless. Nettie is his only solace, the new mother of his children, the only reason he has to go on living.

The relationship between Nettie and Nick, given the nature of both characters, is unerringly developed. The first scene between them, in the prison's visiting room, is an extraordinary evocation of love based on sympathy. Nick is only interested in Nettie as a messenger, though he does respond to her kindness. Director Henry Hathaway establishes the bare, depressing decor, then hangs in close to the characters, deleting the background, pairing, then isolating them in the frame, using the slight echo of their voices to supply an emotion the underplayed dialogue suppresses. Coleen Gray's "no no no no" captures perfectly both Nettie's strength and her fragility. Her love for Nick grows out of her desire to assuage his pain; his is in response to being cared about. The falling in love happens here but with a quiet, invisible depth. The silence is oppressive but also pregnant with the sense of something being born. The situation itself (the characters separated and made uncomfortable by prison regulations) requires a reticence that Hathaway exploits for dramatic and aesthetic gain.

We learn that Nettie, as Nick's former babysitter, has always had a crush on him. This accounts for the somewhat peculiar nature of their domestic scenes. Nettie being swept off her feet by Nick's kisses and embraces may appear faintly comic, but it is also apt.[3] Nettie's is a sexual infatuation that she does not lose upon assuming the responsibilities of a wife and mother. Nick, to her, is a fantasy come true. She is amazed suddenly to find herself his wife. Her behavior is consistent with the image of the child bride she is intended to be. In all, she is the right heroine for this film, possessing that combination of passion, frailty, and devotion that alone could inspire Nick to act on behalf of the many needs she fulfills for him. The film does not offer much in the way of reward for Nick's guts in facing up to Udo. Presumably, he earns the right to continue his work at the brickyard unharassed by the police and to enjoy the comforts of a lower-middle-class existence. The love, though, is glued in so many ways as to appear indestructible. This is where the film's true optimism lies.

Kiss of Death was shot entirely on location. The trend began in 1945 with producer Louis de Rochemont's The House on 92nd Street (also Hathaway) and was going strong by 1947. Taking the camera into the Tombs, the Chrysler Building, Sing Sing, and into actual restaurants, nightclubs, apartments, offices, and so on is not necessarily a filmic virtue, but it does alter our relationship to a film, makes a difference in our perception of the interplay of character and environment. Kiss of Death brings effective studio techniques to bear on natural-location shooting. The world seems to have been transformed into a sound stage. A subtle excitement exists, though, in our knowing for certain that it is the real world being photographed. All the conventions and characters seem less folkloric; the impression is that we are watching the actions and attitudes of real people. The opening robbery in the Chrysler Building could just as well have been shot in a studio, but the sense of the camera having to contend with the actual space of elevators, passageways, and lobbies crammed with people makes the sequence tighter and tenser than it might otherwise have been.

The mixture of authentic settings and melodramatic crime fiction is a potent one. This kind of film benefits from an increase of verisimilitude, and big cities are drably photogenic, too. So are prisons, and the views of Sing Sing are in and of themselves fascinating. Throughout, Hathaway's camera and composition are restrained and sober. Sing Sing is dispiriting (and dramatic) enough without it being necessary to dramatize it further (Michael Curtiz, in the earlier 20,000 *Years in Sing Sing,* in contrast, has a field day exploiting his set). The shot of the prison factory in which Nick learns of his wife's death (a motif repeated later in *White Heat*) is especially memorable. Hathaway's camera records the row upon row of busy, mechanically twisting machines and the high noise level without obvious commentary. It would be interesting to know what the response of the common workingman was to a scene that closely duplicated his own working conditions. If prison isn't better than a free life, as Nettie suggests it might be, it is at least not significantly different.

Most of the interior shots are cramped. Norbert Brodine's camera must often have had very little room to move. The film gains rather than suffers, however, from this inconvenience. The tight framing and stationary camera create an appropriate sense of confinement, and since the backgrounds, although controlled, are authentic, there is a threatening air to the constriction, as though something outside the frame may intrude. Hathaway also finds ways of using natural locations so that they seem as dramatically made to order as any studio jobs. Thus the interior architecture of the orphanage above Nick as he enters echoes the oval window in the warden's office at Sing Sing, a subtle parallel perhaps. Udo hurls Rizzo's mother down the staircase, and the following scene between Nick and Nettie is conducted on another staircase. The terror of the preceding scene discreetly carries over.

Kiss of Death is decisively plotted, the course of events sandwiched between two intricately suspenseful sequences that depend on exact manipulation of time. Between these hard outlines, there is a good deal of sprawl. Part of the illusion of documentary authenticity perhaps requires a muffling and relaxing of drama. The documentary style influences editing procedures. Hathaway uses a quiet, orderly, almost casual progression of scenes, unlike Siodmak's brusque and hard-edged method in *The Killers.* Where Siodmak punches, Hathaway slides. (This style reaches a climax with Hathaway's *Call Northside 777,* a "true" story in which scenes are connected so loosely and casually [and undramatically] that the rhythms of life itself seem to have been captured. Perhaps the presence of James Stewart, with his slow movement and even slower drawl, helped determine the tempo.) A more coercive editing, and more studied compositions, would have worked against the documentary feel.

Udo's murder of Rizzo's mother is illustrative of Hathaway's method. It occurs about halfway into the film and, hideous as it is, is handled as calmly as if it were no different from any other scene. The buildup is long without being tedious. We know Udo is crazy, but how crazy? Udo and Ma Rizzo talk and talk. Udo paces nervously. The sound of the elevator from outside adds to the tension. Udo puts his cigarette out on the floor. We can almost, after a while, smell the thrill of the viciousness he's contemplating, and the scene has gone on long enough for a sufficient characterization of Rizzo's mother (not particularly likable—a tough old bird—but surely deserving of a less horrendous fate). Finally, Udo makes his move, wheeling her down the hall to the staircase. Hathaway's long shot catches the complete, horribly clattering movement to death. The film then quietly shifts to the next scene as if what happened was nothing special. (Hathaway and writer Ben Hecht wisely resist the temptation to include more of the same. Now we know how crazy Udo is; he becomes identified with his gruesome act. That he is capable of such things is enough to intensify his characterization and mark the remainder of his appearances.)

Norbert Brodine's lighting is solidly *noir*. *Plein air* exteriors are harsh and gray, and most of the scenes are shot at night (after Nettie and the children leave for the country and disappear from the film, the screen goes almost completely black for the last half hour). The ending, with the blaze of handguns on dark city streets, is hard-core *noir*. *Noir* emphasis can also be seen in characteristic actions and situations. Nick waits for Udo in his darkened house, listening intently for any sound. In broad daylight, Nick and family wait for a train at the station. A black car pulls up. (It's nothing, but one never knows.) The children twice approach the track. Nick pulls them easily away, but the tension in the air colors the simplest actions with danger and unease. There are as well the settings dear to *noir*—boxing arena, dense, smoky nightclubs, city streets at night, telephone booths, elevators, the decor of offices. The accumulation of caustic details is also typical: the pictures of horses on the wall behind Howser's desk, Nick flipping through the newspaper to find where the obituaries are continued and seeing the notice of his wife's death toward the very bottom, Udo rattling on about his birthday.

Kiss of Death is not a pretty film. The world it depicts is sordid and violent. *Kiss of Death* is also virtually humorless—only the outrageousness of Udo permits some unhealthy laughter. Yet Nettie tells us at the end that everything worked out fine. It can be argued that her reassurance acts as a release and a relief for those who want to take her at her word. That Nick's heroism should be

Kiss of Death. Seedy, cynical veteran cop Millard Mitchell watches, waiting for Nick to play "Christ suffering the little children to come unto him." Ben Hecht, shame on you. (Museum of Modern Art)

totally in vain would also be unwarrantedly nasty. But the problem of the "happy" ending is not confined to Nettie's words; it is inherent to the depicted action itself. The conclusion of *Kiss of Death* raises the issue of convention and iconography operating alogically, violence "arranged" in such a way as to oppose credibility. Nick takes five bullets at close range and lives. Is this possible? If not, is it acceptable?

Lawrence Alloway has dealt with the nonrealism of movie violence intriguingly and persuasively.[4] Assuming that his idea of playful, choreographed violence that exceeds credibility but is ritualized as expected convention is partially to the point. Then the conclusion of *Kiss of Death* is deliberately managed to leave the possible/impossible choice open-ended. It is improbable that Nick survives but not impossible. First of all, Nick is a strong, healthy, oxlike man (you believe it when he floors Di Angelo with one punch). Second, Udo shoots (as he has promised to) for the belly, to see Nick squirm. There is, too, Nick's will to nail Udo. Nick has to stay on his feet, for if he should fall as dead Udo will leave before the police get there to catch him in the act. Nick has had to taunt Udo to begin with; it is one of Udo's men who first pulls a gun, and he has probably been instructed by Udo to finish Nick off, since Udo can't risk being found with a gun. Nick goads Udo into doing the job himself. Nick's will and endurance are extraordinary, but his personal fate, and the entire movement of the film, requires the immense effort. Nick's survival is therefore an act of enormous will on his part and requires a similar act of will on the audience's. The action is a metaphor for the film's idea that a meaningful life can be hammered out through determination. Martyrdom is the final test. One Nick dies so that another may be born. Nick has shed his former identity as a lawless, cop-hating mug. Whereas it is Nick who is shot in the leg by a cop while trying to escape early in the film, now it is Udo. The ending of *Kiss of Death* may violate the limits of realism, but it is best seen as an attempt to translate ideas into actions.

The act of will is an act of faith, and the film has been surreptitiously guiding us toward accepting Nick's victory by utilizing a specifically Christian framework. We are reminded throughout of the birth of Christ. The film opens on Christmas eve, Nick "shopping" for his kids by pulling a job. Bianco means "white." "Nettie" is not far from *netto* (clean) and *nettare* (to cleanse). At the orphanage, the nuns can't tell which of the three men (Di Angelo, Schulte, or Nick) is the criminal, and the new (squealer) Nick is graced with Christ-like images: a cross over his head at the entrance, a vast canvas of Christ suffering the little children to come unto him as a backdrop when he kneels, open armed, to receive his own children, who at first don't recognize him, then ecstatically embrace him. The accent seems to be on purification through pain and faith.

Kiss of Death. Kind-faced, cross-haloed Nick visits his daughters at the orphanage. The cops, in comparison, look like thugs.

"Nick," of course, reminds us of the saint associated with Christmas. Bianco is directed by Di Angelo to meet Udo at the St. Nicholas arena. Nick and Udo have a last supper at Luigi's, in which Udo fattens him up for the kill, then waits outside in his car to gun Nick down. As Nick leaves the restaurant, gunless, to face Udo, we see a mackerel in a store window. The assistant DA is named Di Angelo. After Nick martyrs himself, Di Angelo, kneeling over him, says, "Thanks." These signs function unobtrusively, but they supply a conceptual underpinning that unifies and corroborates the film's emphases and clarifies its aims.

Far-fetched? Consider: age (Nick is 29 when imprisoned. 32 when shot—Christ's ministry, crucifixion); the fish (sign for Christ, Good Friday, Easter—the film ends in Spring); Udo takes Nick to Club 66 (*Revelations,* 13—the number of the Anti-Christ is 666); Nick as bricklayer (a construction craft like carpentry); Nettie as Christ's bride, the Church (she takes care of Nick's kids—the Church as the refuge of the children of man); Udo is captured alive (in the Last Judgment the devil is locked in Hell); Di Angelo (God—"Nick! For the love of Heaven . . .") wants Nick to sacrifice himself (Christ must defeat the devil—and die—out of personal initiative). We may be dealing, too, with inversions compatible with a *noir* attitude: God as a somewhat inept and sinister *Assistant* DA—a discredited, out-of-order God who can't handle things anymore. Nick becomes Christ by becoming Judas. Nick's elevator ascent on Christmas Day as an inversion of the incarnation; the jewels as iconographic of the Gift of the Magi—which Nick here *robs*; the Flight into Egypt fails—Nick shot by the cops (Herod's soldiers); an existential Christianity that counters the despair of logic with faith and insists that man must not look to God but help himself. And Ben Hecht, after all, was an old hand at making more out of less and simply keeping himself amused within a system he held in contempt—*Scarface*, one recalls, was the Borgias in Chicago.

CREDITS **Kiss of Death**

(Twentieth-Century Fox, 1947, 98 min.)

Producer	Fred Kohlmar	Cast	Victor Mature (Nick Bianco)
Director	Henry Hathaway		Coleen Gray (Nettie)
Screenplay	Ben Hecht and Charles Lederer		Richard Widmark (Tommy Udo)
	(from a story by Eleazar Lipsky)		Brian Donlevy (Di Angelo)
Photography	Norbert Brodine		Taylor Holmes (Howser)
Editor	J. Watson Webb		Millard Mitchell (Max)
Art Directors	Lyle Wheeler and Leland Fuller		Mildred Dunnock (Ma Rizzo)
Music	David Buttolph		

Force of Evil (1948)

After making this film, his first, director Abraham Polonsky became a casualty of the blacklist, and he did not resume directing until 1969. The scarcity of his output and his sacrifice to the cause have combined to draw special attention to a small but ambitious film that, unusual though it may be, fits comfortably into the genre and works intelligently within its structure. The film picks up much power by bringing its concerns to the underworld for articulation. *Force of Evil* urges recognition of not only the utility but also the value of a film genre.

Polonsky's discussion of *Force of Evil* in two separate interviews indicates, should the film itself fail to, that he had a lot on his mind to crowd into a seventy-six-minute melodrama. The seriousness of his aim—an examination of the sick soul of modern man living within a capitalist system—is apparent. How successfully his themes are realized is debatable. Polonsky has gracefully admitted his failure:

> It was my first film, and I think there's a difference between what I really intended to do and what came off. I didn't know *how*. And then, despite good reviews, it wasn't a successful picture at the box-office. Of course it was a difficult picture, and, of course, it was experimental in a way, deliberately experimental. But, nevertheless, I thought that the general weight of it would be obvious, that people would feel it, but it wasn't felt except by very sophisticated audiences.[5]

A curious response. He underrates the film, but the artist is often his most severe critic since he alone knows what was in him trying to get out and how far the results may have fallen short (the audience sees only the results). It is also gratifying (and unexpected) for the "experimental" filmmaker to suggest that it might have been his own inadequacies of execution and strategy, and not the audience's dimness, that were responsible for failure (it would have been easy, as is common, to excoriate mass taste). The big issue here is whether movies ought to be made in disregard of their audience. Polonsky implies that they ought not to be, that an awareness of the public is part of the filmmaker's discipline, and that one measure of a movie's quality is how widely and discernibly it communicates. Perhaps he is right. Movies are part of a *popular* culture; they are not a private art, like poetry, designed for the individual connoisseur.[6] *Force of Evil*, with its thematic complexity and literate dialogue, miscalculates its level of intelligibility to a general audience (or did in its day, at any rate). The presence of John Garfield is its only surefire commercial asset, but he cannot dispel the privatistic nature of the "experiment." It is a dis-

Force of Evil. Leo's human concern for Bauer is disrupted visually by a receding line of cynical cops.

tinctive film with a genuine personal stamp, but that is maybe one of the reasons for its understandable lack of commercial success.

Polonsky was shrewd enough, however, to adapt his thoughts to a solid genre. It may be that the genre hinders him somewhat, obscuring his critique and forcing his themes into an awkward obliquity. My own view is that the icons and conventions of the genre give what might have been maudlin a hard, steely edge. The genre's inherent viciousness prevents an imbalance toward a soggy humanism. The austere, sober mood plays off nicely against the typical kinetics of this kind of film, making Polonsky's points more, not less, noticeable.

The story is about a group of unhappy, guilty people involved, in one way or another, with the numbers racket. John Garfield plays Joe Morse, a lawyer gone crooked in the hope of a cool million. His older brother Leo (Thomas Gomez) runs a small numbers bank that goes broke because of Joe's high ambitions. Joe also causes, indirectly, Leo's death. Upon discovering Leo's dead body, Joe experiences a change of heart and with the support of Doris Lowry (Beatrice Pearson), Leo's former secretary with whom he has fallen in love, decides to cooperate with the law.

Garfield was, at the time, at the tail end of his extraordinary popularity. He was the people's star. He had the true urban, ethnic vibes, a ghetto authenticity in manner and speech. He projected guilt better than anyone else on the screen, and nowhere so movingly as in *Force of Evil.*[7] The character of Joe Morse betrays his kind; he feels superior to Leo and his scraggly band of employees. Yet he is a sensitive man, with a conscience. His cynicism is a front. He is a man divided against himself who doesn't, deep down, believe in what he says, who is pained and hurt by what he is doing to others. His drive to succeed is based on a specious philosophy whose moral shabbiness he is at last made to confront. He knows he is not better than others (that his advantage is merely power), yet talks himself into thinking that he is. An unhappy man, his only moment of joy is at the end when, crushed by circumstances, he is released from his false self-conception.

What is unusual in Joe Morse's characterization is his self-awareness. He acknowledges his acquisition of power, his impulse of greed, with atypical (in a hero) candor. Introspection is anathema to most American films; characters normally do things without knowing why, or if they do, it is just implied. They don't stop to articulate or explain and slow the movie up. In *Force of Evil*, though, we become very interested in observing the rhetorical con job Joe Morse performs on himself and the modifications of it on the sensitive register of Garfield's face.

The central relationship is between Joe and Leo, a set of Cain-and-Abel variations smoothly joined to the superficial level of the action. After their mother's death, Leo has sacrificed himself to put Joe through college, and he resents Joe's success. The brothers are estranged, having not seen each other for years prior to their first meeting in the film. Joe is handsome, self-admiring, a smoothie. Leo is ugly, harried, and tyrannical. Both are corrupt, though Leo protests his morality, a morality the film progressively undermines. They love each other as brothers, and each insists that what he does or has done is for the other's welfare. They clash throughout, philosophically and emotionally. Joe tries to relieve his guilt by making his brother rich. Leo's intense refusals have a touch of perversity. He too is guilty, envious. Ultimately, he is blinder than Joe, and no more morally upright. After one confrontation, Joe tells Doris, "I pretended to make him [join Tucker] and he pretended to be forced," an insight Leo is incapable of. He continues to protest his "honesty," an old-world figure who cannot risk admitting to himself that his bitter, hardworking life has been in the service of corruption.

The nuances of their relationship revolve around the brother-versus-brother situation and its timeless, dramatic, biblical qualities. For all their superficial differences, Leo and Joe are the same: they are brothers. They cannot see that they do the same thing, are bound together by both love and corruption. And they cannot see because in following the ways of the world their natures, and their true knowledge of things, have been warped. Polonsky is getting at what living in the American economic system does to people, Leo and Joe and everyone else. Capitalism promotes greed and greed causes hatred, envy, guilt, and fear.

At the top of the moral muck heap created by the itch for money and success is Tucker, Joe's boss, a former gangster gone legit with Joe's lawyer know-how. (The first shot of Tucker is of his hand reaching out above his massive safe to take money from Joe.) He lives with his wife Edna in a cold and almost ludicrously ostentatious apartment filled with classical statuary. Tucker is all money; as a human being he is as unfeeling and meaningless as the decor surrounding him. He cannot, or does not, perform sexually. Edna, making a play for Joe, says her husband is like "a stone," reminding us of the statues. Edna herself is not more lifelike. Living with Tucker has made her remote to her

The Genre's

"Enlightenment"

121

own sexuality. She pursues Joe with a mechanical tenacity, playing seductress in a timbreless, soft monotone creepily lacking any inflection of true passion. Her conquest of Joe would mean a total enslavement; Tucker would own his soul and Edna his body. Joe reads her lust accurately as an exercise in power and refuses her advances, telling her that if she wants to break somebody to go break her husband. It is a sign of the hero's potential salvation.

Tucker and his wife are morally diseased; their cancer is incurable. The rest are involved in what seems to be a losing struggle with their moral natures. Polonsky shows us how people give up, get resigned, betray each other when they live in a society that says grab, succeed, and forces people into corruption to stay alive. Capitalism causes rifts in the human community. *Force of Evil* is a gangster crime film with Wall Street as its locale. (The opening shot is an extreme high angle showing people scurrying like insects along and across city streets.) The force of evil is American business, symbolized by Wall Street. "Business" is the recurrent theme. Wally, Ficco's henchman, tells the informer Bauer that his outfit is in "business." (Later, Ficco has both Bauer and Leo killed.) Leo protests he runs an honest "business." Joe runs Tucker's "business" and talks to Bauer about loyalty to the firm. Even Hall, the prosecutor after Tucker, falls into the category. Joe says, "Hall's in business, and Tucker's his stock in trade." Business is the American way of life, and because it is ingrained, legal, and philosophically supportable, its destructiveness remains unnoticed until an analysis is made of it. *Force of Evil* is such an analysis.

Polonsky claims that the ending—Joe deciding to help Hall (a figure never seen)—was a concession to get a seal and that what he really wanted was for Joe to face his own defeat. That would have been victory enough; the character's decision to reform did not need to be stressed. It provides a false note of social reform, as though one man's evidence might cure an entire city of corruption. Polonsky wants to have Joe morally reborn, but inwardly. There is much in the film, besides, that implies the humane reconstruction of society would be a long and perhaps impossible task. Joe's farewell to his posh law office foresees a repetition of his own career; the office is waiting for a "smart young lawyer trying to get ahead in the world." Joe says to Doris, with unsentimental accuracy, "I didn't have enough strength to resist corruption, but I was strong enough to fight for a piece of it." But it is Leo who hits the nail on the head in the following conversation with his wife, who is arguing against his giving in to Joe:

Sylvia: You're a businessman.
Leo: Yes, I've been a businessman all my life, and honest, I don't know what a business is.
Sylvia: Well, you had a garage, you had a real estate business.

Leo: A lot you know. Real estate business. Living from mortgage to mortgage, stealing credit like a thief. And the garage — that was a business. Three cents overcharge on every gallon of gas, two cents for the chauffeur and a penny for me. A penny for one thief, two cents for the other.

Business is all, and it is evil. Little guy or big guy, it makes no difference; the blight of profit is all-pervasive. Also, Joe's "I decided to help" is in a context of a brother dead, a love disrupted, and (presumably) an upcoming term in jail.

Edna tells Joe that he's "not strong or weak enough" a man to take her, and she is right. Joe's weakness, however, is his salvation; strength of the kind Edna demands would make him into another Tucker. He's the man in the middle, torn by good and bad. Instead of receiving Edna, he seeks out Doris, as fascinated by her image of innocence as she is by his image of corruption, and it is her faith in him that allows for his turnaround. Another choice is made for him by Leo's death. Leo has a weak heart and he is old. He tries to back out of the business, but it is too late; years of toil and anguish have done him in. As long as Leo lives, he and Joe will be at each others' throats, Leo bellyaching about Joe but really voicing his own frustration and Joe trying to clear his conscience by pushing Leo into an office on Wall Street, "up in the clouds." The battle between them would be prolonged forever, with no "discovery" possible. When Joe literally "sees" Leo's dead body, all that is finished. He has no excuse not to start afresh. He must stop thinking about his brother and attend to himself. Contemplating Leo's mangled corpse dumped on the rocks near the river under the bridge, he is released from his conflict and his former values. Leo's bodily annihilation liberates Joe by annihilating his morally gangrenous identity.

Doris is an important element in Joe's liberation. Indebted to Leo for giving her a job, she is prone to defend him against Joe, but Joe exerts a power over her — sexual, of course, but more than that. His confidence and success appeal to her shy, guarded temperament. Joe dallies with her, secure that his virility and charm will carry the day. But this seemingly frail girl is made of stronger stuff than he allowed for. Joe learns that Doris can't be treated as a toy, but it is partly her experience of him that strengthens her.

Joe is so impatient with her innocence that he tries his best to demean her, to make her low enough to satisfy the demands of his cynicism. What he thinks and says about her, though, is in part true (Doris accepts his roses *and* his hundred-dollar-a-week job). She does have the desires he says she does — human ones, corrupt ones — and he does her a service by bringing her out of her shell of propriety and sentimentality. She is forced by her love for him to face her-

"Enlightenment"

123

self, the truth behind her angelic mask. She undergoes the painful process of understanding what she is, as opposed to what she tries to be. She grows up, transformed from a child ignorant of the ways of the world to a woman who can love strongly enough to sustain a man suffering acute agonies of conscience. Her high, soft voice, almost annoyingly well mannered at first, eventually carries some of the best, most sensible dialogue ever written for a movie actress. The film does not allow her to remain sheltered and innocent. She must assume responsibility for herself and others.

Why the script of *Force of Evil* remains unpublished when many lesser scripts are readily available in paperback is a mystery, since it is among the most beautiful of the American cinema. Polonsky departs from the tough, predictable, snappy idiom of the gangster crime film. What he supplies, Andrew Sarris calls a "crypto-poetry."[8] Whatever it is, nothing quite like it has been heard on the screen in English since. The dialogue is full of verbal echoes; people speak a strange, incantatory language, with phrases repeated like musical notes. The wonder is that it works so well as dialogue—not as poeticized speech but as the poetry of speech. The performers have to be given much of the credit. Polonsky's dialogue is good, but it is above all splendidly *spoken*, with naturalness, spark, credibility, and beauty. Polonsky says he was trying for the "babble of the unconscious."[9] The first-person narration has some of that quality, the images shown evoking ideas and emotions in the speaker that get uttered in a fluid, uncensored form. (Where Joe's narration is coming from we never learn, but in time, it must obviously be after the events described. Perhaps we can assume it is from prison or some milieu that enforces meditation and recollection.) Polonsky's achievement, though, is much greater than imitation stream of consciousness. Lines like Doris's "I don't wish to die of loving you," spoken from within a grimy telephone booth, fuse the sordid and the tragic, the prosaic and the poetic. The line evokes a classicism seasoned by centuries, a theatrical language naturalized and humanized into an ordinary eloquence.

Polonsky's script is a model of how literary value can be put to use in the film medium, how images and ideas can be synthesized, blended, and made to reinforce each other. Most "literate" film dialogue is a pompous embarrassment to actors who have unlimited freedom of movement through space and time. Polonsky prevents his talk from being stilted and artificial by conceiving his film world as something in between dream and reality. *Force of Evil* does not so much record or analyze as evoke. It contemplates humanity. It has little, basically, to do with the numbers racket. Its focus is on how people live, and have been forced to live, for centuries, American capitalism being merely the latest and most stifling form of human misery, separating man from his world and from his fellow humans. The film has a specific locale, but it is given to us in a hazy, surreal way. The characters speak a language appropriate to their milieu but seem as well to be abstracted from the particulars of that world, as though the drama they are enacting has occurred many times before throughout human history. *Force of Evil* has a timeless, frozen quality, antithetical to realism. History is evoked through analogy and allusion—July 4, 1776, the classical decor, the Cain and Abel myth, the church music playing softly, then more insistently over the scene of Bauer's death and Leo's capture, the poetic diction. What is happening to Joe and everyone else is the same old story: there's nothing new under the sun. Polonsky integrates it into a modern setting and a gangster tale by counterpointing image, music, and dialogue and letting each add its separate dimension of meaning without breaking any of the requirements of a representational film. The genre itself provides a modest, unassuming but sturdy framework that prohibits deleterious lapses into pretension and ornateness.

The principle of repetition and contrast so apparent on the verbal level is also consciously employed in the visual scheme, but less obviously. One thinks immediately of the great Russian silent films, of montage as meaning, but Polonsky's method is more discreet, the exigencies of the commercial cinema necessitating a subtler approach to visual significance. The opening shot looks down from a great height upon Wall Street, and the theme of high and low, descent and ascent, is sustained to the very end. All the characters literally have their ups and downs, with Joe traversing the greatest distance. Joe's descent to Leo's body beneath the bridge is photographed and edited to make a climax of the motif. It takes him forever to get there. He works his way down in a lateral zigzag, moving up into and then across the frame. Time seems to stretch, and the symbolic overtones of dawn, rocks, river, and bridge supply a thematic gravity rarely attempted with such rhetorical abandon. Characters are linked by the motif. There is a startling dissolve from Bauer (the frightened accountant) being dragged down the stairs in a police raid to Joe going down a long flight of stairs to meet Tucker, who has symbolically pulled Joe down into the hell over which he presides. (An earlier scene has both men descending a long, curved staircase while hatching strategies about the upcoming fix on the number 776, "the old liberty number.") Ficco's thugs hoist Leo up the stairs of the restaurant in a grotesque but moving version of the calvary of Christ.

The telephone is also a recurring motif. We are not told it is significant, but so much that is important involves the telephone that it accumulates an inescapable weightiness.[10] Polonsky has this to say:

The telephone is a dangerous object. It represents dangerous kinds of things. I don't like instant communication. I like it to take a long time before I understand you and you understand me. In the film it forms the structure of the characters' relationships. I had a big telephone made so that it would loom very large in the foreground of those close-ups. I guess the telephone was an easy symbol for the connections between all the different worlds in the film. These worlds communicate with each other through telephones instead of feelings.[11]

Polonsky also uses his characters as repetitive signs. Leo—sweaty and turbulent; Doris—thin and shy; Joe—healthy and authoritative; Bauer—mousy and quaking; all are rigid enough in look and behavior for Polonsky to use them in the first half of the film as replicas from scene to scene. They appear and we think "that kind of woman, that kind of man," the way we might observe a style of furniture or a kind of plant. Not being strong enough to fight their condition, they take their place, in the beginning, among the other fixtures of their world. They seem mechanical and drugged, and oblivious of their condition. By a gradual process, Polonsky reveals them as individuals— hurt, in pain, and confused. Pressured by demanding events, they are unable to continue taking refuge in their roles. They come alive as people and modify their status as signs. Those whose moral nature has been crushed entirely and who have no capacity for change—Tucker, Edna, Wally, Ficco—remain serviceably stiff icons throughout.

The dark look of *noir*, though not as intense as in *The Killers*, dominates. Interior decor is stark, arid, and grim. Shadows abound, and what light there is is usually harsh and uneven. Several scenes take place in near-total darkness. The shoot-out between Joe, Ficco, and Tucker has them all crawling around in the dark, hunting each other like animals. Framing is always careful, pointed. Long shots isolate people as either the clumsiest or most vulnerable points in the frame (Joe walking down a deserted Wall Street, Doris left sitting on top of a lobby mantelpiece, Bauer's nervous entry into an office suddenly full of outsiders), while close-ups are used not so much for intimacy but to convey terror and alarm (Joe's eyes peering over the transom of his office door, Bauer shot in the face). One interestingly framed shot is in the restaurant scene between Leo and Bauer. Leo has always been solicitous of Bauer, touching him, protecting him, leading him home. Now, though, they are separated by a table, indicating the gulf between the two caused by Bauer's decision to betray Leo. Polonsky frames so that Leo is at one side of the table and Bauer at the other—to the far left and the far right of the frame, respectively. Between them, directly in the middle at a background table is Wally, who has worked on Bauer to set Leo up. Prior to Leo's entrance, Polonsky also conducts a shadow game between Wally and Bauer. Wally has been, almost literally,

Bauer's shadow. As they wait for Leo (Bauer in foreground, Wally in background), Bauer lifts his arm to drink and the shadow Wally makes on the wall raising *his* arm to drink is perfectly timed to Bauer's gesture. Bauer and Wally are joined against Leo.

The exteriors are something else. *Force of Evil* is one of the few gangster crime films interested in the beauty of the city. Normally, the city is either "there," as in *Kiss of Death*—an authentic backdrop to what is going on with no particular attitude attached to it—or is seen negatively *(The Public Enemy, An-*

Force of Evil. Man and telephone, in a shot that communicates our anxieties about the relationship.

gels with Dirty Faces, a good percentage of gangster films). George Barnes gets marvelous shots of city streets and buildings that we sense are different without knowing quite why, because we do not expect the city to be beautiful. But a feeling for the magnificence of the city is the only explanation for the unsettling effect of these shots. Cities, in and of themselves, are clearly not the cause of misery or crime. A deserted Wall Street at dawn seems as pure as any travelogue waterfall. The film's conclusion is the climax of its odd pictorial beauty, a series of breathtaking long shots of Joe completing his downward quest to be reborn. Here, at the city's edge, the dawn casts a splendor on everything. Joe begins his descent accompanied by a solo wind instrument moaning in high register. The river breeze blows foliage into motion while a string orchestra soars into melody. Joe strides by a lighthouse symbolic of his moral awakening and finally reaches Leo's broken body sprawled on the rocks. Even this image, however, is more awesome than horrible, conveying truth, not terror. Depending on one's taste, the effect of this finale is either bombastic or stirring. The voice-over narration is actually understated, but the music and visuals are rhetorically ponderous. But there's beauty and poetry, too, in both the sound and image track and that finally touches on the sublime. The chromatic climb of the music matched to Doris and Joe's resolute upward movement—the last shot—completes the attempt at sublimity.

As in *Kiss of Death*, a Christian framework appears to be operating although exactly how is even less clear than in the former film. The upshot of all the betrayals—Bauer betrays Joe through Leo; Joe betrays Leo through Tucker—seems to be that Leo dies for everyone's sins. The biblical drift of Joe and Leo's relationship is confirmed when Leo specifically alludes to the Cain and Abel

Force of Evil. Hotshot mob mouthpiece Joe Morse on the way to discovering his brother's dead body dumped on the rocks beneath the George Washington Bridge. Images of ascent and descent, confusion and purpose, energy and stasis, come together in the above still, in which the heroic and the insignificant aspects of human endeavor and commitment commingle inseparably. Bridges at dawn, however, have a compelling beauty almost irrelevant as function, and Joe's gesture toward redeeming his soul and acknowledging his responsibility in his brother's murder partakes of some of the bridge's majesty.

(Museum of Modern Art)

myth in his anger toward Bauer. At the point of his lowest emotional state, his life crumbling about him, Joe, sleepless, walks dazedly down Wall Street at dawn toward a huge, centrally framed church, his small figure overwhelmed by the surrounding architecture. (The shot is framed so that the church has special emphasis among the equally imposing high-rise office buildings. The point seems to be that it is there, in the midst of greed and evil, but ignored.) Joe appears to be progressing toward it—the shot is held so we may ponder its importance—but it is far away, and it becomes apparent that he has not chosen it as his destination (he has still greater woes to suffer). Bauer's betrayal of Leo is infused with the symbolic overtones of bread and water, and the peculiarity of it is most evident to a viewer. In taking Bauer home, Leo pulls up at a bakery for Bauer to buy some rolls. In the background of the shop is a church entrance. After buying the rolls, Bauer flees from Leo and runs toward the church with the rolls. When Leo follows, Bauer ducks into the alley adjoining the church, the place where he is to meet Wally and set up Leo's betrayal, and cringes. Leo, more concerned with Bauer than himself, flings the rolls away and yells at Bauer, "You want to live to eat these rolls, don't you?" Later, Bauer awaits Leo in the restaurant and specifically orders and drinks water. When Leo arrives, he is, as his dialogue suggests, ready to die, but he does not expect it will be through Bauer or under these circumstances. After Wally kills Bauer, his hired thugs carry Leo up the stairs to choral music, each arm propped, Leo's expression and agony reminiscent of Christ's. It is through Leo's death that Joe is redeemed.

One accepts Polonsky's vision of change because of the sadness that has preceded it; a more cynical man could not have brought it off. Polonsky gets an unusual depth of feeling from his performers, and the sorrow of life is made quite eloquent. *Force of Evil* does not speed, clatter, or contort as much as other films in the genre—it has very little "action"—but it broods and reflects insightfully. And it is not only symbolic and metaphoric. It condemns, rather boldly, the connections among politics, business, and crime, and its images of the gangland boss and the corrupt lawyer have perhaps a greater veracity than more melodramatized versions. Its view of crime as business equates the two. Tucker's organization is seen as a huge corporation taking over the independent businessman (not that Polonsky has anything favorable to say about free enterprise—Leo is no answer, he's part of the problem). Hall's wiretapping is as underhanded as Tucker's policies. The cops are terrible—brutal, unfeeling, paid off. And the people are infected by the disease. The cycle of corruption is complete. Crime is now organized and legitimate, creating jobs for large numbers of workers who are either oblivious to what they are involved in or prefer not to think twice about it. What most gangster/crime films skim over, or treat indirectly, *Force of Evil* bluntly acknowledges.

Both *Kiss of Death* and *Force of Evil* maintain the social criticism associated with the genre but conduct it on different terms. The gangster/criminal in each is not exactly integrated into the society (shown as bad) but is permitted to work himself out of a personal trap. That the society benefits, or will benefit from the working out, is a side effect. Both films create a human being within inhuman conditions. It is apparent, though, that Nick and Joe discover the full range of their humanity only by finding themselves in conflict with their society. Their struggle, a privileged one, is unique to their being outsiders, but what constitutes their outsideness is different from the old films. They fight for the survival of their basic humanity, which is threatened. They are not our opposites but images of ourselves that we cannot mistake, or choose to see, as *other*, as we could the early gangster heroes. We share a common humanity. What here may be inferred becomes, in the fifties, a thematic staple of crime melodramas.

Neither film departs from an emphasis on individualism—but what American film does? The solution to a bleak view of life is provided by an individual willing to risk his neck in a violent showdown. One may rightly consider this a weak analysis of what really needs to be done. It may be ungenerous, though, to expect solutions to either crime or unhappiness. The anxieties both films speak to are still with us today, and our remedies seem no less desperate.

(Enterprise MGM, 1948, 76 min.)

Producer	Bob Roberts	
Director	Abraham Polonsky	
Screenplay	Abraham Polonsky (from the	
	novel *Tucker's People* by	
	Ira Wolfert)	
Photography	George Barnes	
Editor	Art Seid	
Art Director	Richard Day	
Music	David Raksin	

Cast   John Garfield (Joe Morse)
Beatrice Pearson (Doris Lowry)
Thomas Gomez (Leo Morse)
Roy Roberts (Ben Tucker)
Howland Chamberlain (Bauer)
Marie Windsor (Edna Tucker)

The conflict in *Gun Crazy* is between a man and a woman who have and act out a lust for experience, a violent feel for life, and a society whose obligation is to choke such urges off. The matter is complicated by locating the conflict primarily within the young man himself, who feels the guilt of his antisocial drives and is aware of the possible consequences. Bart and Laurie don't appear to be gangsters at all. They don't talk or dress or behave like gangsters. Yet by what they do, and what they feel about what they do, they are a new version of the old, by now outmoded, gangster.

Bart and Laurie do not have much of a grasp of what they are doing. They are young, intensely attracted to each other, and want the freedom to live an exciting life. Bart occasionally initiates some conversation about what they do and have become, but his confused reservations cannot alter the course of powerful, destructive emotions. Director Joseph H. Lewis seems to get behind the feelings of his young people. We feel that they have the right to make of the world what they want it to be. The film unapologetically conveys their urgency without pausing to explain it at any length.

When they meet, Bart, just released from the army, is doing nothing and has nothing to look forward to. Laurie is wasting her vitality by crack-shooting in a two-bit carnival. When they spot each other, they recognize a way out of their present deadness. Their high prowess and élan, spurred by the danger and thrill inherent to guns, takes on, as it inevitably must, a criminal form. The breaking of social, and interconnected moral, laws is a speedy (and metaphorically useful) way to announce not so much their defiance of society but their commitment to freedom of action. The commitment is instinctual, not rational. The film, curiously, seems to justify both the lover-criminals *and* the quiet society they disrupt.

Other characters are treated neutrally. Here and there they grumble, but to a normal degree. The cook in the hamburger joint, the violinist in the dance hall, Bart's sister and friends, the stern but sympathetic Judge, the police, the employees of the Armour plant are shown as no better or worse than they might reasonably be according to the duties they have to perform.[12] They represent no external threat. Bart and Laurie's problem is therefore seen as one of inner frustration, peculiar to them. They do not turn criminal because jobs are scarce; they get jobs and could continue holding them if they so wished. There is a place in the society for them if they choose to take it. It would be, for them, however, a joyless, invalid, restricting existence. Bart, upon learning of Laurie's murder of her supervisor during the Armour job, asks her in anguish why it is they must be killers "just so we don't have to work"—a hard line to bring off, but very much to the point.

Gun Crazy. Dark-bordered aftermath of early robbery. Bart astounded that he fired at all, even at a tire. Laurie, fighting off terror by grim determination, is on the verge of giving in to excitement over what they've just accomplished. Remorseless, she is clearly the more dangerous of the two. Lewis keeps close to their emotions throughout, making viewer intimacy with the daring duo a sure and touching thing. (Museum of Modern Art)

The social values Bart and Laurie violate are not shown as particularly fine or worthy of emulation. They are just subscribed to by the majority, who have a cautious investment to uphold. Bart and Laurie could, presumably, end up like Ruby (Bart's sister) and Ira Flagler (her husband). A life like that would come cheap and easy. One would get destroyed, worn down, in a piecemeal fashion, over a long period of time. Ruby's domesticity is portrayed as none too attractive. She receives Bart's homecoming phone call apron-clad, her hair in disarray, snapping at her noisy children and looking generally frazzled as she assures Bart that the kids are "wonderful." When Bart and Laurie return to Ruby's for refuge, Ira is away in San Francisco, having left Ruby the job of caring for home and kids. Laurie's radical gesture against home and family in grabbing the baby for hostage indicates how irreconcilable the two ways of being are. If it is a matter of wasting away like Ruby or risking a life of high adventure, *Gun Crazy* suggests that Bart and Laurie's alternative is preferable. A line must be drawn, however, at murder. Murder, however, may be just an excuse to destroy them. Otherwise, the film would be advocating killing anyone who is excessive, unreasonable, and undemocratic.

The apparent reason Bart and Laurie must be destroyed is that their robberies and Laurie's killings are serious threats to society and its laws and to human lives. Their real crime, however, is that they love too strongly, too intensely, and with too sexually direct a passion. This is as much a threat to the status quo as any damage they inflict upon people and banks. The existence of sexual passion in a sexless society is dangerous. Their love is perverse, because it has to be; it can't exist within a normal social arrangement. The hesitant Bart has to meet the demands of Laurie's consuming, undomesticated sex drive. (Both have signaled to each other, through their guns—and some choice double entendres—that that's what they're in it for and why they must perform together and not separately.) When Bart proposes to Laurie, she gives him a queer look but accepts; perhaps it will be a means to regulate herself, although the implication is that she had never figured on anything so "square." Laurie uses her sexuality to keep Bart going, to intervene between him and his conscience, which is always telling him to make a declaration of peace. Through passion one may gain a measure of nobility or at least of authenticity. Their mad love catapults Bart and Laurie out of any normal existence. The violence they enact sustains that love and, egged on and deranged by passion, they proceed to increasingly dangerous acts. Lewis does not moralize or criticize. He understands the value of such passions, and their cost. Those who love that strongly must suffer the consequences of isolation from other people and from society. (That Bart and Laurie are married is a fact that sort of fades away; they even pawn their ring—an invitation for us to consider them, in effect, not married.) The attractions of danger and crime are linked, perversely, to sex, but sex is nonetheless the inspiration to meaningful, if destructive, action. During the action sequences, Bart and Laurie rise to their highest level, their most thrilling, uninhibited behavior. Lewis implies that the world cannot tolerate such free impulses, but he does not condemn his characters for living them out, for asserting their only means of discovering what it's like to be alive.

John Dall is such an unlikely candidate for a gangster hero that it takes one a long time to accept him in that role. Peggy Cummins is odd, too. They are not screen personalities and must create who and what their characters are from scratch. They are present in these roles for the occasion of this film alone. There would be no point in having either repeat their role again, unlike, say, performers like Cagney or Bogart or Harlow or Ava Gardner. We identify with the characters not as "stars" but as people plucked out of a mass for their strange qualities, urges, and obsessions. That they project so vivid a presence here (as opposed to their other films) must be credited to Lewis, who seems inspired by their very inappropriateness and peculiarities. Dall's gangly boyishness, long, smooth face, and monotonous voice contrast with the actions he is called upon to perform. Cummins's oddity rests partly on her slight British accent (explained by her father's owning a shooting gallery in Brighton) delivering funky, overboiled dialogue, on the hard edge to her sexuality, and on her somewhat chunky carnality. She does not have the typically glamorous figure of a limned starlet. Her extra poundage is provocative in its common solidity. She exists on the screen as a tough-looking, meaty gal conscripted overnight into being an actress without undergoing the usual studio grooming. Both give excellent performances, performances of unpredictable freshness and a natural awkwardness under pressure that draw us toward them as versions of the desperadoes we might, under similar unfettered circumstances, become.

Gun Crazy has won praise for its set pieces—the carnival sequence, the Hampton and Armour robberies, the finale in the swamp—but as bizarrely beautiful as these parts are, they do not impede the flow of the film. *Gun Crazy* is not stylized but stylish. It races forward with an incredible vigor, the line of

Gun Crazy. The terror and exhilaration of do-it-yourself criminal life. Lewis found some great small towns to shoot in. This loosely framed image, which aims to "wrap us up" in the action, points directly to Lewis's concerns and achievements. Remarkable for the riveting immediacy with which it captures the spontaneous confused excitement of amateur lawbreakers, it also succinctly differentiates Bart and Laurie's gun-craziness. In the scene of Bart cleaning his guns in the hotel room, we see that his early fascination with guns as a means of being "somebody" has taken hold. He's a marksman and a connoisseur, and there's weirdness in a relationship of an identity so oddly bestowed. Laurie's seems more typically tough and sex-driven, the gun more unmistakably phallic, and a way to power. Bart cannot bring himself to fire it (a common *amour fou* emphasis). Strange passions require peculiar adjustments and careful monitoring (they're *fou* because of their unshakable grip and compulsive manifestations). These are two fierce urges above: Laurie's trigger-happy murder of any threat to her thrilling criminality, and Bart's equally intense need to restrain her. (Museum of Modern Art)

the story flawlessly developed into a building drama of connected incidents, culminating in a classic car chase. Lewis brings great polish, imagination, and energy to an action choreography that is always going somewhere. Even at its most crafted and designed (the Armour robbery), the film never loses its spontaneity or forward motion. It never stops dead in its tracks. It works on you physically, especially through its brilliant tracking shots of Bart and Laurie fleeing from one or another tight situation.[13] Its turbulence is a release from *noir*'s pessimistic stasis.

Lewis achieves a sharp sense of reality and a rough kinetic force by stressing the amateurism of his criminal pair and by having their dialogue, at important moments, assume a nervous, improvisatory air. Bart and Laurie's appearance and movement seem to lack a screen history in the genre—the witty changes in costume, the natural clumsiness of their mad, unprofessional scrambling, the rapid, breathless gutsiness of the robberies they pull. Nothing ever goes smoothly, which is often the case when desire outdistances know-how. One feels, however, that it is the very danger that goads them, that if the job were too easy they wouldn't bother. They have energy to burn, and they need something for it to work against. On the night before the Armour job their suppressed energy is indicated by the hurry and impatience with which they scribble the layout of their getaway on a sheet of newspaper. During this scene Lewis creates an intimacy with the characters. Laurie sits, smoking, and leans her head across the table to watch Bart go through the plans; her hair is disheveled and she seems totally comfortable. The dialogue is characterized by the broken-phrased, soft muttering of people tuned to the minutest nuances of personal speech habits and facial communication. The overhead shot makes the audience willing accomplices. When we see the Armour plant, it seems like just a big building we are determined to see robbed.

Dreams &

Dead Ends

Lewis's innovations and variations on traditional illusionistic style make it more vivid, give it fresh pertinence.[14] The surprise of *Gun Crazy* is not in the novelty of its technique nor in its visual modernity but in its ability to pull us in and make us care and believe in new ways. The technique is not used to break the illusion. Rather it discovers new and virtuosic ways of refining and intensifying it. What Ortega y Gasset once said of modern Europe, that it suffered from "the fatal divorce of culture from spontaneity," was still not true of movies in the "high forties." *Gun Crazy* is living proof. Upon a half-dozen viewings, it remains weirdly fresh and interesting; each change of scene, each camera setup, remains pleasurably surprising. None of its seams are evident.

Lewis's approach, one could say, is objective. His way of observing the world is not a judgment upon it but a description of it. Bart and Laurie do not throw the film off-balance; the world is not a projection of their psychology. The reality of what they are is inseparable from the reality of what *it* is. They are not seen in relief. The cars they drive, the streets they run through are as well defined as themselves and make their presence felt. Bart and Laurie are imagistically favored only in the sense that they are the people this story is about. They have to earn their prominence in shots that give the illusion of equal (natural) distribution of emphasis. In the scene where Bart and Laurie hastily rehearse the Armour robbery, the ashtray filled with cigarette butts and the lamp in the background become absolute participants of the scene: the characters and the decor are photographically integrated and interrelated. Bart and Laurie's faces and bodies are not obviously central to any image; they have to cut their importance out of a total pattern. The viewer has to weigh and judge the special validity of Bart and Laurie within a no less insistent mise-en-scène. Lewis's direction allows the characters the opportunity to earn that slight edge by which they may arrest our attention, and through the struggle they attain an especially powerful credibility.

In *Gun Crazy* one always feels the weight and density of the world they oppose. One need only recall the Armour plant itself, an imposing and exactly defined—externally and internally—structure, through which and against which Bart and Laurie must demonstrate their visual prominence. It is difficult to say, for example, what one notices most—the numerous, inertly hanging slabs of meat or the characters walking and running across the floor that separates them. By *surrounding* characters in motion with a still but visually striking environment, Lewis welds his desire for both accuracy and drama. And, of course, creates meaning, for those rows of dead carcasses are precisely what Bart and Laurie's instinct for life urges them to escape from and leave behind—an emblem of the employees at the Armour plant and all sodden adherents to a bourgeois homogeneity. One recalls, too, the characters facing their end in the mist that envelopes them, blurs their shapes, and through which their faces struggle to achieve definition. And, as well, the sharp, lethal angles of irregular vegetation that echo the violence and broken pattern of their lives.

The justice the world enacts, therefore, is not primarily moral but rather the inevitability that ensues from its being *there*, and felt by the viewer as there, throughout the film. In one sense, Bart and Laurie are the world they oppose, are never really disconnected from it. Therefore, they cannot be moralized. Bart's fascination with guns is not condemned; he's obsessed with them the way someone else might be with stamp collecting. It's just a bad break that his childhood compulsion happens to contain the potential of being socially dangerous (reform school later supplies the guidance that children who have not lost their parents might have gotten from the beginning). The judge accepts Bart's explanation that his skill with guns gives him a self-respect (everyone feels that it is important to be good or distinctly superior at *something*, it almost doesn't matter what). Laurie's slick shooting at the carnival speaks to Bart on the level of a shared interest and expertise, and the expertise is automatically transferred to a sexual level. Here is someone who might understand him, the outsider, who is cursed by his obsession and ostracized from the human community—and she is a female, a potential mate.

In all the shots of Bart as a kid, the framing implies his deviant status. The film opens in a typical *noir* style with a heavy night rain. Bart hurls a rock through a store window and steals a gun. He whirls around in fear, back to camera, and stretches out both arms (resembling a gesture of crucifixion) to hide the damage to the window. He runs and falls. The gun slides down a streaming gutter only to run up against a pair of shoes. The camera tilts upward in a point-of-view shot to show us the sheriff glaring down at Bart. He looks evil and ominous, as the child perceives him. Then there is a shot from above showing Bart looking up terrified, but framed oddly far to the left as though his shame and guilt were urging him literally to crawl out of the frame. In court, while people recount his past history, he is shown on the far right, hunched in a chair close by the window, spatially separated from everyone else. When his friend Clyde shoots at the mountain lion, we see in the foreground, far right, Bart's fist opening and closing hard with each shot. (Lewis later repeats this framing device to convey Bart's tension preceding his giving way to Laurie's sexual invitation in the hotel room. Her body pulls him, like a magnet, toward a commitment. We see his dangling hand open and close, and finally he gives in.)

From the beginning, then, Bart is seen as a victim of a special passion that denies him a normal life. He is sent to reform school and then joins the army, where he becomes a shooting instructor, further sharpening his skills. It is no surprise that he responds to Laurie, who not only shares his lonely gift but who admires him for it—it is a sign of the virility that can make its way in the world.

John Dall's Bart may look like just an ordinary small-town nonentity, but there must be something smoldering within. Packett, Laurie's boss at the carnival, says Bart and Laurie eye each other "like a couple of wild animals." We see less of this and more of the conscience-stricken side of Bart, but it's a safe bet that Laurie doesn't love him because of his conscience. Bart's character doesn't disintegrate, as the vein of male sentimentality running through the film might suggest. He does not come apart but emerges, stands revealed. Since he does not leave Laurie, she must be something that he wants. She rescues him from mediocrity. Her energy overcomes his scruples, makes him, in a way, worthy of her and of himself. Bart could never be normal anyway. He says he was bored in the army demonstrating how to shoot, and all he knows is guns. It causes him problems, but he lets Laurie dictate the course of his life. Out of love, to be sure, but that is another way of saying that his own gratifications enter into it.

For a while, it seems that Laurie is just using Bart, that he is interchangeable; maybe, if he gets too bothersome, she'd throw him over for someone more sexually enticing and less of a moral nuisance. But, driving away from Bart, her face is marked with distress, and she turns the car around, incapable of following out her own sensible plan of separation. She loves him, and the thought of living apart for several months is inconceivable. In yielding to love, she also yields her authority to Bart and simultaneously (in line with an ingrained cultural sexism) eliminates our response to her as a wicked female—although it must be stated that she remains a most powerful woman character even after she gives up most of her power. In any case, it is now Bart's turn to make decisions.

Trapped on his home ground, with every opportunity to revert to his old values, for his morality to assert itself, Bart's choice is to try to escape, and he knows there is little or no chance of getting away. It is he, not Laurie, who is now in charge. Bart has come home too late; he can never join the community he has always had a latent hunger for. What he has done has put him beyond the pale. It is ironic that all his know-how is now put toward escaping the environment that bred his respect for human life and social law. Laurie hears strange sounds, but Bart knows it's the dogs hunting them, and exactly how near they are. Laurie lags behind, tripping and falling, out of breath, amazed at the sudden curtailment of her energy. Bart knows it's the lack of oxygen in the mountains. There is an outside chance that Bart might make it through since he knows the region so well, but Laurie's failure to keep up erases that slim possibility. They lie down to rest in a swamp, awaiting dawn, and wake to a mist through which nothing can be seen.

The conclusion of *Gun Crazy* is remarkable. We hear the voices of Dave and Clyde, Bart's childhood friends, cutting through the mist, urging Bart to give himself up. Laurie, prior to their night's rest, has snuggled close to Bart, saying, "It's so good to be close with you." Now Bart tells her what we would like to hear—"I wouldn't have had it any other way"—and prepares to stick it out against his lifelong friends. Laurie, however, suddenly goes crazy, pointing her gun into the mist and shouting over and over again that she'll kill them if they come any closer. Bart, unable to permit the death of his friends, screams at Laurie to stop, and when she continues to shriek and is about to pull the trigger, shoots her dead. The police, thinking Laurie has shot at them, shoot and kill Bart. This takes place in a thick mist in which no one can clearly see what he is doing, and justice seems somehow the more profound for being so abrupt, chaotic, and contradictory.

It is a romantic ending. Bart is the only one worthy of shooting Laurie, and he shoots her partly out of love, dismayed at the sight of her gone out of her senses and unwilling to see her carted off in triumph by the agencies she has so high-spiritedly antagonized. It can also be said that Bart's killing of Laurie is Laurie's ultimate triumph: she forces him to adopt her own free measures, which include the taking of human life. Thus a poetic justice is enacted, for as soon as Bart kills her, he is shot. They fall together, touching, united in death near the top of a mountain, whose symbolic overtones are compromised by the swamp setting. They die in a timeless region, on an isolated island of mist far removed from the society they were born not to join, the fog of dawn commenting ironically on the error of their ways and acting also as a heavenly shroud, softening the brutality of their end and placing them in the company of others whose love was so great they had to die for it. Why, where, and how the early gangster dies is a relatively simple matter compared to this.

Bart and Laurie are young kids whose dreams are basically conventional, despite their unorthodox methods of attaining them. Bart's first impulse, upon securing Laurie from Packett, is to get married. Laurie, though more worldly, doesn't object. The proposal touches her, surprises her, makes her feel wanted and important, as her running away with Bart does for him. She says, too, that she wants to "be good." Bart wants to settle down on a ranch in Mexico and have children. In the cabin scene, Laurie earnestly voices the feeling that "we'll grow old together." Discounting their gun mania, and what it leads them to, Bart and Laurie are quite commonplace, even "respectable" people. They would be utterly conventional if they weren't vital. Previous gangster films may include, as a nuance, this suggestion, but here it is explicit. The gangster is distinct from the rest of us because of his inability to repress the urge to live vitally. Other than that, there is no conflict with the society. Wanting to live, though, destroys him.

Bart and Laurie become serious criminals by accident; their plans go haywire. They go on a conventional honeymoon—Yellowstone, etc.—smiling, happy, carefree, the pride of any set of law-abiding, morally irreproachable parents. Laurie loses their money in Las Vegas and they have to hock their ring. Faced with poverty and cheap hotels, Laurie proposes the route to easy money. Bart doesn't like it, but she lies down on the bed, naked under her robe, and he is convinced. (The next shot is of a gumball machine blasted by Bart's bullet—a metaphor for orgasm.) That becomes the pattern: sex gets them all excited so they go rob banks, robbing banks gets them sexually excited so they go to it again, and so on and so forth. It leads, however, to murder. Laurie shoots, out of what seems like spite, the supervisor at the Armour plant who has castigated her for wearing slacks. (She claims later that she kills through fear; a terror and desperation grip her that she can't control and to shoot is her only recourse. As she utters this important explanation, however, Laurie faces Bart but her back is to

Gun Crazy. The eye travels first, perhaps, to Laurie's broad expanse of white robe, but her gaze whips us immediately across the frame to where Bart sits, off-center, making sure his professional tools are in working order. Significantly, he is situated near the frame's edge—one of many such outsider/freak/warped shots of Bart in a kind of marginal position—and also at a distance from Laurie, whom he judges more dangerous to play with than his little arsenal. In a few moments Laurie, nostrils flaring, will win this particular altercation, convincing Bart that playing with Laurie on the bed beats playing with his guns on the table. But that divided, worried look stays with him the whole film. This "at home" moment (hotel room) holds most of *Gun Crazy's* themes and motifs and concern for texture, the sensual tactility of fabrics, underclothes and pillows in disarray, cheap curtains, metal, flesh, all sharp in moderately deep focus, a "compromise" that allows intimacy to surface even within the antithetical leanings of the long/medium shot that tends to let decor do its work. (Museum of Modern Art)

the camera and to the audience. Perhaps Lewis couldn't get what he wanted from his actress at this point, but it seems more likely that he wished to preserve the ambiguity of the characterization. Her apparent sincerity motivates Bart to take charge of both their fates.)

Bart and Laurie are kids at heart and in appearance. What stands out most in the early montage of robberies is the amazed look of those they victimize. What are this healthy, wholesome boy and girl doing pointing guns at them? Bart and Laurie want, in theory, what most "good" people want. They never get rich and they're not really in it for the money. They are not polished but awkward gangsters, getting by not on finesse but boldness. Their dialogue conveys a certain emptiness of mind, a stolid directness and simplicity. Laurie puts her values on the line bluntly: "I want action." Thinking he is about to part from Laurie for a long spell, Bart says simply, "Be good." Everything they do,

The Genre's

Enlightenment

139

they do rashly. Their purpose in life is to live high and have fun. They aren't cruel or cynical or unhappy; they don't give a damn about the image they cut in the eyes of the world. Bart and Laurie live in a prosperous society. Laurie wants the kicks that big dough can provide, but if getting the money weren't in itself a kick, she wouldn't bother. They exert a thoughtless enthusiasm for its own sake. What money they get they dribble away. The important thing is that they keep doing what they're doing, and together. Their daring is their spiritual lifeblood, and it is an accidental, fated quality that has grown from their early exposure to, and inexplicable curiosity for, guns.

In *Gun Crazy* interpersonal drama and conflict give way, finally, to the urgent outlawry that unites the characters. People who wield guns are dangerous and must be stopped, and even as Laurie concurs with Bart's dream of going away to Mexico and having children, we know it is an impossibility. It is Laurie's heedless suggestion that they have a last night out on the town. They pass hot money and are discovered. But what passes for the high life? Kid stuff: a roller coaster ride, popcorn, dancing softly in a fairground ballroom to the pathos of a run-of-the-mill vocalist's second-rate rendition of Tin Pan Alley heartbreak. They are a "normal" couple, unestranged from the people around them, unconcernedly having a good time, and *feeling* like a very normal couple. They tell each other, while dancing, that this moment is what they have been waiting for all their lives. Their orthodox dreams are more shocking than their violent acts. It is important, though, that what they do is still in the spirit of children looking for excitement. They rob banks and ride the roller coaster for much the same reasons.

Their normalcy is of course an illusion. They have been labeled freaks from the start. They think and behave as though normal because, apparently, they wish to be. They have seen what breaking loose was like, and their outing at the amusement park is the legitimization of their illegitimate urges—a symbolic farewell to their old way of life. Their dangerous desires take on the form of socialized play. But with this maturity and relaxation comes death—for them, a literal one, for others perhaps that death-in-life in which deep passions are made acceptably trivial. Bart and Laurie's situation is rich in pathos, but their death is necessary, dramatically, to keep them from being merely pathetic. We never feel sorry for them.

Gun Crazy is special to the genre, especially through to 1949, because Laurie, a female, seems to dominate the action, with Bart bringing up the rear. She kills, knocks people over the head, and talks tough while Bart wrestles with his conscience. This goes against the grain of what we expect should be happening and gives the film a unique, provocative clout. The movie doesn't explain how or why Laurie is up there on the screen doing those things; it just gives her to us in action. During and after the war, women in film (and in the society) secured stronger roles and showed that they could take care of business back home while the men were away (and, much to their chagrin, also after they had come back). A movie with a title like *Mildred Pierce*, though, tips one off that the character will carry the film. In *Gun Crazy* Laurie comes in out of nowhere, after a long introduction to Bart, and takes us completely by surprise. Her violence becomes a factor we have to deal with precisely because its degree is so unexpected. Her eroticism is equally strong and up front, not mysterious like a femme fatale's. She offers herself to Bart, conditionally: "I don't want to be afraid of life or anything else. I want a guy with spirit and guts." Her fearless will fuels the film.

Laurie can, and does love, and she applies, in her own way, a great effort toward living. She is incapable of Bart's introspection and anguish, but we can read her visually as neurotic and alienated. There is a stunning shot of her looking in on Bart's sister through the window and seeing the kids, the kitchen, the entire spectrum of a typical domesticity. How Lewis got that combination of fascination, incomprehension, revulsion, and confusion on her face is impossible to say, but it tells us in one second more about Laurie than she knows about herself. Later, inside, when she says, "Gee, what cute kids," it is with a mixture of polite compliment, personal longing, curiosity, and plain disbelief—as though children as a concept do not really exist for her and the mere sight of them both stirs and curdles her feminine sensibility. The film seems of two minds about the issue. If this is what she has been missing, it isn't much, but in one sense for a woman to accept internally that it can't be hers is what the culture defines as her tragedy. The scene is far from sentimentality and even sentiment; however, the emotion flickers for a second and fades. It is fitting that Laurie should die with a warrior's ferocity, teeth gritted in defiance and eyes blazing with the insanity that comes from following one's deepest urges to the limit.

That we are given a full history of the victimized male and only the vaguest account of Laurie is in line with the sense many melodramas of the period give of the male's inability to read and assess what women have become. Laurie's body may be unambiguous—her full figure, indeed, is given uncommonly distinct definition in motion and in long shot (compared to, say, Barbara Stanwyck's in *Thelma Jordan* or Lizabeth Scott's in *Too Late for Tears*, both made about the same time)—but her face, and what may be read there of her emotions and thoughts, varies from scene to scene. (Bart's expressions are both few in number and uncomplicated.) The film gives us a dozen Lauries, new face after new face, creating a tense and insecure relationship between viewer and character. It is clear that woman is something other than what men have assumed and counted on her to be, and what prewar Hollywood pictured her as.

Laurie is a much stronger character than Bart. Most of the time she's dressed in pants, and of the two she makes most of the decisions. Bart is compelled by her. She assumes the male role while Bart fusses, hesitates, and hangs back like a female. She is a psychopath, but so are a lot of male action heroes. Laurie stands at the crossroads of a muddled feminine identity, her behavior at explosive odds with the combined dictates of nature and nurture.

Her aggressiveness in the film is often so crazed and thoughtless, however, that it is possible to interpret her as one half of Bart's split personality. When Bart returns from the army, he is pictured as mild and well behaved. Reform school and the army seem to have knocked the passion and intensity of the child Bart clean away. He has been brainwashed. Laurie's biography is virtually suppressed, while Bart's is extensively supplied. Bart also assumes responsibility for Laurie's actions, saying that he has simply let her do his killings for him and that they go together like "guns and ammunition." He has no existence without her, nor she without him. She is the uncivilized part of his nature (appropriately designated as female—something strongly instinctual that he cannot understand—a theme common in American movies and given perhaps its finest showcase in John Cassavetes' A *Woman Under the Influence* [1975]) that goads him to live life according to the urgency of his true desires. Many of Lewis's close-ups at the end suggest by their framing the indissoluble unity of the two. We get a close-up of two heads instead of the expected one, or Lewis gets them both into a horizontal composition by eliminating half their heads, or their heads are arranged vertically so that although some of Bart's head on top or Laurie's below is eliminated, both faces remain in the frame, closely pushed together. When Bart shoots Laurie, the distance between them is erased by framing them separately, and *immediately* upon shooting Laurie, he is shot by what seems like no one; the bullets *follow*, but we do not see their source. (Laurie is also yelling "kill!" when Bart shoots.) As Bart falls, he bridges the distance between Laurie and himself by falling on top of her. The two lovers are one in perhaps more than the usual sense.

Most viewers may want to resist such an argument, since it undermines one of the movies' most vigorous female roles. It implies that Laurie, and everything valuable and interesting about her, is not, despite the evidence of our eyes, female. The argument, obviously, can't be strictly true. There are too many instances in the film where Laurie's emotion is hers and hers alone (driving away from Bart, shooting at the woman at the Armour plant, looking in on Ruby and the kids—although the argument can accommodate all these). She is a character in her own right. The film betrays a semiconscious cultural reluctance to go all the way with Laurie, especially since she is made to be active and Bart passive. There are ways and ways to modify a portrait of a woman that uncomfortably resembles a man and does violence to a culture's beliefs (and at the same time speaks to their need of being violated). The usual route is to show that the woman has been acting contrary to her nature. Laurie is too obdurate and extreme for that method to work, so she is instead seen as Bart's true nature displaced. Her entry into the film is shown as a materialization of Bart's fantasy. We see her appear from the point of view of the audience (Bart) watching the show. Her guns, firing away, rise from the bottom of the frame to the top as Laurie's face is gradually revealed. The passive Bart projects himself into an active alter ego. The visual device is inverted when Bart retreats toward the doorway of Ruby's house away from Clyde and Dave. Slowly, his head drops lower and lower in the frame until it is partially cut off and the shot terminated. It represents an irrevocable decision to stick with Laurie; he becomes their spokesman to Clyde and Dave. In the first instance, Bart conjures up an active Laurie to rise and overwhelm his passivity. In the second, he

Gun Crazy. Bart's boyhood pals, who now represent two large institutions (the police and newspapers), call on Bart's sister Ruby, at whose house he and Laurie have taken refuge, looking to cuff him quietly. Laurie holds Ruby's baby hostage, shocking Bart, who, as we see here, has intervened. Ruby's shack of a house represents exactly the kind of sodden domesticity Laurie will not settle for. Did Bart luck out or get shafted by running into, and then with, Laurie? What he says and ultimately does makes us believe he accepts their meeting as destiny and the rapture of her company more happiness than he could ever have hoped for. Given his generally troubled countenance, however, we may judge the message more mixed, guilt and anxiety close companions sometimes rivaling love and lawlessness for consideration. (Museum of Modern Art)

falls passively and cautiously into what he has accepted as the valid direction of his life, supplied by Laurie. That Laurie is not there to confront Dave and Clyde suggests that it has been Bart we have been dealing with all along, primarily, and not Laurie.

Gun Crazy brings a new sophistication to the genre's depiction of social and cultural conflict. While it seems almost too direct, and solidly imbued with a popular, lowbrow American mythology of guns and cars (that Laurie comes from the old world may suggest an imported source of corruption, but she is essentially as American as the greasy hamburger she wolfs down), it works through implication within a deft narrative continuity. (When one thinks what a preachy hash Lewis could have made of issues relating to gun and car obsessions, one is grateful indeed that he let the action ride without commentary and spared us the speeches.) By eschewing an explicit thematic focus it breezes through its contradictions and resolves them aesthetically through the beauty of its surfaces and its graceful, poetic, rhythmic movement. Lewis's balanced sensibility in a period of widespread psychological distress (1949) gives *Gun Crazy* a positive tone. Bart and Laurie's craziness is an integral, if repressed, part of the culture. Their unleashed energy is masochistic. It leads nowhere, but it is a sign of life. In the conception of the film, their death settles, without resolving, the conflict that flares to unmanageable proportions in *D.O.A.* and *White Heat*.

CREDITS *Gun Crazy*

(United Artists, 1949, 87 min.)

Producers	Frank and Maurice King	Cast	John Dall (Bart Tare)
Director	Joseph H. Lewis		Peggy Cummins (Annie Laurie Starr)
Screenplay	MacKinlay Kantor and		Berry Kroeger (Packett)
	Millard Kaufman (from		Annabel Shaw (Ruby)
	Kantor's story)		Morris Carnovsky (Judge)
Photography	Russel Harlan		Nedrick Young (Dave Allister)
Editor	Harry Gerstad		Harry Lewis (Clyde Boston)
Art Director	Gordon Wiles		Stanley Praeger (Bluey-Bluey)
Music	Victor Young		

Going Gray and Going Crazy
Disequilibrium and Change at Midcentury

4

Gun Crazy maintained its balance and a sense of seriousness within some bizarre premises but it was skating on conceptual and perceptual thin ice that was destined to break at any moment. The conventions and conflicts characteristic to the genre were strained, partly inverted, and put to strange tests. In D.O.A. they pretty thoroughly collapse, and in *White Heat* they are applied and thrown about with a whirlwind ferocity that blows them to pieces. If *D.O. A.* is the gangster's dissolution as a hero, *White Heat* is his last stand. Both films have a hard time keeping a straight face. The tensions and contradictions that infuse them can no longer be contained, and anxiety gets released as though involuntarily by a desperate, mocking comedy.[1]

The gangster crime genre, more than any other, is allied in spirit to the dark side of things, and it has always reflected contemporary tensions. It should come as no surprise, therefore, that it too starts disintegrating along with the national psyche in the year 1949. The quality of postwar life was profoundly changed by the dropping of the bomb in 1945. By 1949, fears, guilts, and anxieties had achieved over four years' time a psychologically ruinous density and momentum. Events at the turn of the decade merely exacerbated the prevailing mental and emotional distress.

> 1949 was proving the most nerve-wracking of all the disquieting periods
> the United States had known since V-J. Some years in a nation's history
> blur into a long-continuing story. Some mark a fateful turn. . . . The year
> 1949 was such a turning point. August, the concession of China to the
> Communists; September, the announcement of the Soviet atom bomb;
> August and September and the months before and after, the explosive
> questions raised by the Hiss case — 1949 was a year of shocks, shocks with
> enormous catalytic force.[2]

In the fifties the genre will examine the difficulties of remaining human in the new directions life takes after the impact of such events, but in 1949–1950 it too is reeling under the blows and groping to make itself a fit artistic instrument that can address the harried imaginations of its audience and still, of course, be compatible with entertainment.

1949–1950 was a banner year, and noticeably experimental, for the genre. A great number of crime/gangster *noir* police thriller movies were made. A sample: *Side Street, Criss-Cross, They Live by Night, The Asphalt Jungle, The Crooked Way, The Killer That Stalked New York, Panic in the Streets, Johnny Stool Pigeon, Manhandled, Mystery Street, Night and the City, No Way Out,*

One Way Street, Quicksand, Impact, Tension, Shakedown, The Sleeping City, Thieves Highway, Too Late for Tears, Under the Gun, Where the Sidewalk Ends. The very titles of these films suggest that the close of the forties experienced a kind of *fin-de-siècle* trauma. The list of leading figures—Farley Granger, Dan Duryea, Howard Duff, John Payne, Ricardo Montalban, Richard Conte, Richard Basehart, Dana Andrews—does not inspire a heroic certitude. These films are about every freakish calamity and human nastiness the mind can conjure short of the supernatural. *The Killer That Stalked New York* and *Panic in the Streets* are about plague carriers. *No Way Out* and *The Sleeping City* contain insane goings-on in hospitals; in *Johnny Stool Pigeon* a dude ranch is the scene of quirky violence; *Thieves Highway* depicts the brutality of the trucking industry; *D.O.A.*, though, is my choice for the time capsule.

In this unhappy psychological climate we find the genre beginning to examine its own assumptions. A film like *D.O.A.* opens up the problem of discrepancy between what is seen and shown and what is real, and shatters illusionistic assumptions about the relation between movies and reality. It questions the sustaining premise of the medium, that seeing is believing, that show and tell are valid. In *D.O.A.* seeing is disbelieving—in us and in the film. It reflects the culture's paranoia by incorporating the paradox that one can look and look and not see what is happening. It provides an answer to how one can make a movie about that condition. Its narrative and stylistic convolutions, within an imitative structure, imply that we can no longer treat film strictly as a representation. In concept and content, *D.O.A.* is the genre's modernist pivot. Film has reached by *D.O.A.* (between 1900 and 1950) its modern period, is doing what happened at the turn of the century to painting, music, and literature. It is doing it awkwardly, caught in the middle of a moment of transition.

   D.O.A., coming at the tail end of the *noir* period, makes filmically explicit the new feelings toward the world that preceding *noir* films registered but left filmically implicit. Thus a film as late as Robert Siodmak's *Criss Cross* (1949) builds to a climactic series of concluding images that are deliberately anticlimactic and point to the illusion of cinema conventions. *D.O.A.* just does what *Criss Cross* makes us recognize. In *Criss Cross* the camera drops in with Olympian irony on Steve and Anna declaring a surreptitious love in a parking lot. *D.O.A.* places us behind Bigelow as he gazes up at the lighted building where we will travel with him to witness his report of his own death. We are given a double vision that alters our reception of the whole film, even when the style becomes objective. We see a reality, we perceive it subjectively through the character, and we become the camera's eye, which has a selected perspective on both. The use of a subjective or expressive camera, or the creation of distorted environments, is time-honored in the cinema, but in conjunction with the theme of *D.O.A.* these effects take on special pertinence and become the tools of an aesthetic. It is not just that the camera cannot receive images passively but that what has always been assumed as objectively there to be recorded is not real. Reality is not what the eye can see. To get at the real—which is in fact not a visible matter at all—a filmic distortion that is analogous to, and complements, an upside-down metaphysic is necessary.

D.O.A. gives us a literal dead man walking around alive. Bigelow's death is his life, his only real life. One cannot take any comfort in that, as one can in the conception of life/freedom via death in *High Sierra*, *Force of Evil*, *Kiss of Death*, and *Gun Crazy*. Life and death, as terms, are rendered meaningless: they are meaningless as polarities and as distinct oppositions. Old categories and conventions become inoperative. They must crumble and fall away under the premise that nothing is what it seems to be, and that order and reason can no longer get at, or unravel, existence. *D.O.A.* cavalierly discards centuries of faith in rationalism, logical categories and mechanisms, objectivity, the possibility of reaching truth by definition, precision, and reason. Bigelow is forced to try to get at the bottom of things. He does, and it is of no consequence, because his story is too fantastical to be credible. The police aren't going to pursue Majak because nothing in Bigelow's story fits the categories. The cops are deader than Bigelow because everything they assume is totally illusory: we know that what they assume as real is not—the film has shown us that. They haven't seen what Bigelow has seen and therefore cannot be bothered. From their perspective their response is inevitable: they wearily hear him out and categorize him by a lie—Dead on Arrival. For Bigelow, unlike previous heroes, coming to awareness is useless.

The film is peculiar to watch because the presence of Bigelow in any situation makes it unreal: he baffles everybody, upsets their sense of their own identity. The inversion is apparent. People's normalcy is what is really crazy. Reality is insane. Only Bigelow is real—by virtue of seeing what things are really like—and he's berserk. If Bigelow's world—the underworld he must work within and which the genre typically sets up in opposition to a dead society—is unreal, Banning and Paula are really unreal, and the film makes us feel them as such. Paula's telephoning is simply at the extreme end of Chester's holding a gun to somebody's head and discovering it does not produce fear. Bigelow's tale tells us that life is more confusing, exhausting, and dangerous than we could imagine, and the film supports him visually by demonstrating that what we think of as real is not. With a brave irony, *D.O.A.* is shot on and in palpably real locations. It cannot, of course, have been otherwise, and the perversity of it is fully in keeping with a film that is almost gleeful in its pursuit of the intricacies of futility and ruin.

Within the premise of *D.O.A.*, the gangster cannot be set up as opposed to the society. Things are too mixed up for that. Bigelow has to play gangster, and he's just an accountant. Majak's gang can't handle the situation. Majak tries to reason with Bigelow and fails. He can't understand what Bigelow wants with him. All he can do—as the brains of the outfit—is play out his standard moves, which are absurd in context. He hands Bigelow, a dead man, over to Chester to kill. Chester uses gangster tactics of force to no avail and doesn't understand why Bigelow doesn't quake with fear. As icons of the smooth boss and the lethal psychopath, Majak and Chester verge on parody. The other two members of the gang are played for laughs—a big broad Mutt and a thin, little Jeff who lurk in the background with incongruous ominousness. The frustration that the gangster experiences in playing out his role, and the role's absolute irrelevance in this context, is pointedly shown when Chester, bewildered by Bigelow's staunchness, lashes out at a fellow gang member with his gun and smashes him in the nose. He whimpers away in pain and the matter ends.[3] What used to work for the gangster simply doesn't anymore.

The hero of the gangster crime film becomes progressively more aware of his humanity in relation to the world. *Little Caesar* ends with Rico stupefied. By *D.O.A.*, Bigelow's awareness places him on the brink of madness. The gangster in *White Heat* is literally crazy, a mental case. His wife says, "Cody ain't human." On the contrary, he is the only human in the film. In *White Heat* to be human is to be crazy. The film is philosophically romantic. It argues world and man as a unity. The world has been made crazy by man; in turn, it makes man crazy. The classic opposition between man (the gangster) and society now shifts to man (the gangster) and himself.

    D.O.A. and *White Heat* are two sides of one aesthetic coin. Both question film's traditional function of being a window to the world or of art as the world's mirror. *D.O.A.* breaks the glass. *White Heat* shows that the reality art must mirror is man's mind. It turns the mirror around to locate reality within man. To photograph the world is to photograph man since the world is his creation. This can only be made evident by the total context of the film. There would be no point in making the viewer look literally at a brain. It is something to be inferred from seeing Cody Jarrett's craziness in a series of episodes and environments. *D.O.A.* and *White Heat*, as commercial feature films, cannot risk, even if they wished to, a radical aesthetics. What they do is register a sense of the world that implies that the nature of the photographed image is an unreality. There is not a world "out there" to be recorded. The world is a reflection of the nature of man, not something divorced from man. *D.O.A.* is not occupied in calling attention to itself, but it uses interesting devices to scratch and crack the glass. In *White Heat* the world of the film, the external reality, becomes subtly, a mental landscape in the interest of the film's conception. In both, standard approaches are being interfered with. The fact that they use, for the most part, age-old and conventional techniques, is no matter. A shot of a chair in an Andy Warhol film is different from the shot of a chair in a Chaplin film, however exactly the technical means used to get the shot may correspond. Technique is always in the service of sensibility, and it is the sensibility of *D.O.A.* and *White Heat* that is new to the genre. A reflection in a window in an early gangster film is likely to be incidental; in *D.O.A.*, it is a conscious part of the aesthetic design. Even if it weren't, the context would insist that we receive it differently.

White Heat does not tell a story; it dramatizes a condition. Action and setting all refer finally to Cody Jarrett's being. The world is not mirrored but projected. The film articulates Cody's state of mind. The quality of the visuals (description as meaning) and the patterning of sequences resemble that of a romantic ode, where the form is organically a function of the mind and not the material of the external world. To show the world is to illuminate the character's psychology. Matter (inhuman) is infused with mind (human), and the mind is crazy. It is crazy because the world is ordered, rational, mechanistic and warps instinctual, emotional, primitive impulses. Cody's insanity is a reaction to what man has done to nature. He goes crazy because he hangs on to a primal connection with nature and feeling that is totally gone in the world he lives in. He is judged insane by those whose human instincts have been killed. Going crazy is the only way to *remain* human, and it is a suicidal stance against a world that is neither natural nor human. Cody is the human embodiment of man's destructive alteration of nature. As nature is awry so Cody is awry. His groan is nature's, his apocalypse prophetic. He destroys the world by destroying himself, its last human representative gone mad. (The explosions at the end are like what he explains happens in his head when he has a fit.) It is not just the conclusion that reflects fears about the bomb. Cody himself is a walking A-bomb. *High Sierra* adheres to the same outlines of the romantic hero, but Earle is treated classically and sentimentally. The storm and stress of *White Heat* are beyond sentiment, nor do they allow, as in *Gun Crazy*, the existence of opposing values—Bart and Laurie's versus the society's—to determine the death of the gangster. It is all internal. In *White Heat* the gangster represents humanity's last stand in a romantic rage of selfhood.

D.O.A. (1949)

Underlying many *noir* films is a lack of faith in anything but style, either personal style (the character[s] in the film) or filmic style (how the film is made). Style is seen as the only means by which imperiled and/or dislocated conditions can be met. The visual oddities of *D.O.A.* and its hero's desperate and spontaneous expertise make it one of the zaniest demonstrations of this faith. Within its black premise, its despairs are capriciously syncopated, its malevolence sportive. Strange people and absurd circumstances stretch credibility to the point where it either stops being a concern, or one must choose to accept or reject weird situations and their even weirder development. Life may be hard now, but it is instructive to confront what it was possible to imagine the world in 1949 could be like.

The possibilities of life are reduced to zero; life is a dark joke, nothing else. *D.O.A.* writhes in the ultimate throes of the *noir* attitude, as though several years of postwar trauma has shattered sense and structure alike. *Kiss Me Deadly*, five years later, has a perspective on *noir* that enables it to diagram its properties into solid patterns. It clamps into a vicious intellectual order the blundering chaos and experiential hazards *D.O.A.* freely and audaciously orchestrates. It is an art film, quite sure of its assumptions, and one that has obviously profited from years of the genre turning in on itself. going modern, *D.O.A.*, in contrast, knows that new means are necessary and makes a pioneering grope. Its unusual qualities in part reside in the struggle we can see it making.

D.O.A. is one of the most distraught films ever made. Its fatuous heroine, its wits-end hero, its inconsistent photographic and narrative style, its convoluted plot, its lack of faith in any course of action produces an almost Brechtian alienation from language, image, and character. It is a world breaking apart, and the presence of Frank Bigelow, the ordinary man, suggests it is our world. We can't indulge the fantasy that the gangster functions in a specialized milieu remote from us. Throughout the film it is impossible to tell who is a gangster and who isn't. The gangster is not part of a special society that performs bad deeds after normal folk retire for the night. Bigelow, understandably under the circumstances, must assume the role of gangster tough guy to discover why he has been killed. He becomes an impersonator, long (if strained) on style, short on substance. If there is an order to the universe, a meaning to life and death, he aims to find it out. Unfortunately, there isn't one. In *D.O.A.*, everybody's a loser. Bigelow tracks down who has killed him and finds out why, but, being dead, it does him little good. And the why involves no moral metaphysical justice; it's unthinkably ridiculous.

D.O.A. starts with a man reporting his own death. The police are suspicious, and Bigelow must insist that he be allowed to tell his story. They decide to listen. He is (was) an accountant in the hot, dull desert town of Banning, living a kind of nonlife that has sapped his juices. Life there is tedious, uneventful, but safe. He decides to take a vacation in San Francisco, absenting himself from the persistence of his secretary Paula (to whom he is unofficially engaged), but with her consent. You must go, she says, little knowing what's in store.

The film opens resoundingly, the bass drum pulsating in time to Frank Bigelow's measured footsteps as the camera follows smoothly behind him down hallways and long corridors, through doors and around corners, until he reaches Homicide. Then it sobers down, abruptly. The scenes in Banning are quiet but tense. Bigelow is itchy, fretting, dissatisfied. His male vanity wants life to offer something more than Paula's doting love. He is unhappy (an unsatisfactory past relationship is alluded to), and he is making Paula unhappy. Bigelow feels trapped; he must get away. He knows what he's turning from but not where he is going. It seems necessary to find out, however, what is going on in the world far from his desert town (in which being a success doesn't mean much). San Francisco is shown as a city on the make, and Bigelow drifts into a partying crowd of conventioneers—oafish salesmen and their lascivious women, one of whom shows an unwifely appreciation of Bigelow as a male novelty. (The disruptively loud whistle noise suggests both Bigelow's latent lechery and the loose, carnal world by which he is abruptly surrounded upon entering the St. Francis Hotel. The tone of the film is light, even humorous, until the Fisherman nightclub sequence.) Bigelow, now free, embarks on some harmless fun that by a quirk of fate leads to his death by luminous poisoning. *Noir* schemes are by nature irrational; people's civilized facades give way under stress; savagery breaks through the veil and runs its destructive course. Bigelow, in yielding to temptation, is a representative icon of this pessimistic premise. "Reality" is a sham; the "surreal" is the true universe, fantastical and deadly. D.O.A. may be a tawdry, overboiled treatment of this vision, but its picture of a deranged and derailed world has rarely been matched by even our most incorrigible absurdists.

Frank Bigelow is a businessman whose minor league pep gets absorbed by the more feverish pace of the big city and its shady, crooked operations. Most everybody in the film is connected to some business but not, as in most gangster/crime films, so that a parallel can be drawn between the criminal's ways and either normal business methods or law enforcement procedures. They are "gangsters" who'd vote a straight Republican ticket at the polls. Their respectability, like Bigelow's, is a veneer that reality, which becomes a veneer itself, sustains. In following up a routine business matter, Bigelow gets involved with a set of conniving people who give him a fatal dose of that decadence he thought would be a spicy change from Paula's smothering decency. Bigelow illustrates an object lesson not uncommon in the period: the values of conformity. Don't step out of line; be content. If you make one wrong move, something terrible may happen—you'll get arrested, lose all your money, die, whatever.[4] But in *D.O.A.*, the damage is done *before* Bigelow leaves his desert town, since he has already notarized Phillips's bill of sale. In the incredible consequences that result from that insignificant act, there is a lunatic justice. Bigelow wants to get out of Banning, and not just physically; he is granted his wish. What is staggering is the lack of proportion between cause and effect. *D.O.A.* is pop Kafka. No act, no person, is ever what it (he) seems, is in fact the very opposite—or *could* be, one never knows. Bigelow is forced into a tough-detective role, but the detective genre assumes that rational means exist by which to unravel what is happening. All the film says about life outside of Banning is that it is worse—crazy and thrilling but also sick, corrupt, cynical, depraved, and menacing. Proceed at your own risk.

Bigelow, however, can't stay in Banning. Banning, on the edge of the desert, is outside reality. Nothing can be discovered there. It is a place, simply, of heat and boredom. It is obvious why Bigelow cannot commit himself to Paula; life with her, in Banning, would be unreal. Nothing can be discovered through Paula, whose bourgeois romantic dreams reveal her as insulated from reality. Paula and Bigelow go to Eddie's bar for a drink; the place is lifeless. Eddie is listening to the races on the radio. The only other person there is a cop reading the paper—nothing else for him to do. Eddie has no business, the cop has no business, the jukebox has old romantic tunes (in specific contrast to the smart dance music at Haskell's party and the jazz at the Fisherman's Club). For someone like Bigelow, who wants excitement and experience, living in Banning is like living in a stuffy tomb.

Existing moral social metaphysical guidelines are inadequate. Bigelow wants to escape from what he has. Paula's love, however sincere, is shown as both possessively insecure and inanely earnest: She keeps calling Bigelow, to check up on him and out of real concern and loneliness, but what is Bigelow to tell her? She is out of it and could never understand the what and the why of Banning's most eligible bachelor's fatal predicament. Bigelow can't just say, "Paula, I'm dead" and hope to be understood. Under Chester's gun, he admits to her over the phone that he loves her and orders her to take all their money and buy that mink coat she's always wanted. He realizes the value of what he has had in Paula, but it is (a) too late, and (b) modified by context. Normality looks great when Chester's holding a gun to his head and when he knows that through an absurd accident he has been poisoned. The early Banning scenes, though, have shown us Bigelow's dissatisfaction, one that would have worsened without the exploratory move away from Banning and Paula. Paula at last hangs up the phone for good and, unasked, shows up at the Allison Hotel to wait for Bigelow. Her presence is superfluous and simply increases Bigelow's agony. The film makes her, too, leave Banning; she too is stifled by the quality of her life and, in particular, her ignorance of the present situation—a symptomatic ignorance. She says, "I tried to hold back, but I couldn't." Paula is Bigelow's only connection with the normal world, and he can reach her only by phone. She is brought, finally, into his world, but to no avail. The film sees her as just another casualty. The last we see of her she is standing in front of the hotel weeping ignorant tears.

Bigelow knew the world of Banning, its small collection of streets and shops. Once outside its familiar, lifeless environs, he encounters a series of forbidding but tempting settings. He's drawn into an unexpected, disorienting milieu, places he has never been and in which his footing is none too sure. That he manages, in the short time he has to live, to understand, to *use* his new environment is to his credit. His personal triumph, though, is, in the last analysis, meaningless. He's dead before the film begins, an unalterable state of affairs for Bigelow and for the viewer watching him alike. The doctor's pathological analysis is: "There is nothing anyone can do." This is the thesis of D.O.A., and it is unflinchingly supported by events and narrative structure (the flashback that brings us closer and closer to Bigelow's inevitable death). The police, who it is assumed routinely carry out their duties, are unconcerned and ineffectual. They patrol a world with no borders. What Bigelow tells them is going on out there, they can't comprehend. It fits nothing in their book. Even if they wanted to do something about it (and they don't), they couldn't. They can't afford to believe Bigelow, as it would rob them of their function. There is no protection possible for what has happened to Bigelow. There are no preventive measures.[5] After Bigelow's long, complicated tale is over, there is a shot of him in a chair, exhausted, with the rest of the cops hanging around. One of them is asleep, the others seem bored, as if what he had to say was interesting for a while but then, unlike a good, clean mystery novel, got bogged down in unnecessarily perplexing nuances. Bigelow solves the mystery, but in D.O.A. the "mystery" is on the level of paranoid fantasy—not teasing, but exposing. The cops take it all in, but it is not indicated that they have the slightest inclination of pursuing the culprits Bigelow has named. Their basically "so what" reaction to his story increases the paranoia of the film. The cops aren't corrupt or nasty; they just don't care. Their function is choral, the indifferent look on their faces serves as an icon for the despair underlying the film.

D.O.A.'s punchline is a kick in the head. The poison overcomes Bigelow;

he falls off the chair, trying to call for Paula, and dies. The police decently arrange for Paula to be contacted (she can't confirm his story, because he never told her). They mark Bigelow's file D.O.A. Dead on Arrival. What Bigelow has told them never happened, they never heard it, and there will never be a record of it. The implications of a world so mad are too frightening to admit. If they hadn't chosen to "mark it D.O.A." they'd have had to throw away the book and all assumptions of an ordered, rational civilization. But we are all potential Bigelows, and his story shows us that if there ever was a book, its pages now are blank.

As in his Reardon character in *The Killers*, Edmond O'Brien's Bigelow is a man devoid of conspicuous graces. The opposite of a poised, charismatic figure, he is again puffing, sweaty, ordinary. Bigelow has no finesse, but his determination and his ghastly fate secure him a fascinated attention. One cannot remain unconcerned by the disasters that befall him, but his ungainliness keeps us at a distance. One certainly doesn't *like* him, and what happens to him is in a sense justified. Smug and anxious, Bigelow is ripe for testing. His poisoned body is a metaphor of his soul. By the horrendous visitation of an unexpected death, his own, he is forced to toughen himself and achieve his finest hour, if in vain.

The only positive aspect of *D.O.A.* is Bigelow's strengthening of character and purpose as he nears death. Once poisoned, he becomes a man with a mission, and his effort is remarkable. In an alien, complex city, with the tiniest of leads, he finds his killer and disentangles an insidious network of evil. His energy gets directed into one channel; he becomes tough, remorseless, fearless, and sadistic. People threaten to kill him and he doesn't bat an eyelid, since he's dead and nothing worse can happen to him. In a way, he is in an enviable position, able to tear, bully, and pound his way through the world in a manner we, who fear death, humiliation, and defeat, cannot. He acts out the fantasies of the common man whose frustrations must remain bottled up—outwitting double-crossing dames, hunting instead of being hunted, bluntly accusing hypocrisy, venting cynicism, staring down a psychopathic killer, murdering his own murderer in a guiltless fury. Time is his enemy, in short supply, but it gives him drive. Bigelow discovers a style and an identity that surprises himself; the experience, the violence of it is cathartic. His despair and rage are provided outlets that might otherwise have never materialized. His guilt, his fear of experience are transformed into decisive action. He can no longer retreat from life. So little of it is left, he must face the consequences of what he has been and what it is possible, in the short time remaining, for him to become. His final advice to Paula is: Don't ever be frightened of anything again. There is no reason to suppose that Paula, pictured as she is, will benefit from this advice, but one can infer for Bigelow a resolution of his complacent unease.

Director Rudolph Maté, a great photographer in his own right (Dreyer's *The Passion of Joan of Arc* [1928], Charles Vidor's *Gilda* [1946], and so on), had Ernest Laszlo on the difficult job of supplying a "look" that would match the asymmetrical rhythm, disjointed narrative, strikingly contrasted settings, and swerving tone of *D.O.A.* Much (perhaps all) of *D.O.A.* is filmed on actual locations and (the exteriors) in natural light—difficult shooting conditions—and Laszlo also has to control his lighting to make evident the differences between the *noir* world of nocturnal frenzy and the flat, de-energized world of Banning and Paula. Light and dark must be adjusted for symbolic function as well and to the dichotomies of a world whose undemonstrative exterior belies its interior turbulence. At first, the photographic style seems careless and disorganized, but it is actually an inventive pattern of transformations that catches the unstable nature of experience that sprawls inconclusively in a zone between nightmare and reality. The emphasis shifts constantly according to the degree of deceptive play of what seems and what is. Certain effects and sequences are surprisingly bold and hallucinatory.

The photography actualizes Bigelow's internal state, the perception of a man bewildered by his own death, to whom the world seems both distorted and eerily precise and intense. Even long shots in which the character would normally take his place within the fullness of the environment seem to be dream images of the world now lost to him, distorted by his abruptly abnormal relationship to its commonplaceness. Bigelow, like many modern heroes, is a man trying to make sense out of a world that seems senseless. The dichotomy of Bigelow's outside, inside behavior is consistently reflected and analogized, as the camera shows us places and situations whose facades belie their true nature (like Bigelow, who is dead but seems alive): the businessmen's convention, the photographer's studio, the poison glowing in the dark (but not visible in the light), the Halliday character, Phillips's wife, Halliday's office building by day and by night, the fight in the drugstore (where the customers' and workers' initial obliviousness to the violence becomes comic). Maté and Laszlo achieve a quality of disbelief and hallucination antithetical to dramatic realism. Bigelow is typically dwarfed by the environment, but what the images capture is the *feeling* of what being a victim of circumstance and setting is like. The great shots of Bigelow running madly through the crowded streets and traffic, done in a series of wipes, are unforgettably nightmarish. His run is the expression of what he feels, but he runs through an actual environment, not a phantasmagorical one. The setting vibrates with an unscoured fidelity; people stop and stare at this man running at top speed, pushing them aside, heedlessly

D.O.A. Bigelow—confused and overwhelmed by a typical *noir* setting—gazes forward, but the eye is led by depth of field to the labyrinths behind him.

plunging into traffic—and then go on their way. Why is he running? Why not? The world is mad as he has just discovered. So he runs and runs and runs, as if there might be somewhere to run to. Finally he stops, breathless, and leans against a newsstand. *Life* magazine is visibly displayed (!). He looks up at the sky (for a sign? for help? for a reason?), and the sun glares down at him in a brutally overexposed image. God has departed, nature is dumb.

The shots of Frank Bigelow running full steam through the streets of San Francisco are a magnificent culmination of exacerbated *noir* tone, theme, and imagery, the sign of an attitude in extremis. The basic rhythm is of the "chase," but nobody's chasing him. He is running from intangibles, and in public view. The wipes are arranged in a disordered rhythm, come from unexpected angles, compositions, timing; their blurred edges seem to be pushing the image away—a classical technique utilized with expressive excess. The effect is an emotional chaos of terrifying force. The device of man running amok has been used since for similar meaning and effect but never as purely or as powerfully as in *D.O.A.* A crazed, agonized rage is no longer the property of the oddball estranged from the mainstream. The sight of Frank Bigelow, an ordinary, fully socialized man, going berserk in broad daylight on crowded, downtown streets depicts a loss of control and a wild desperation that may be *noir*'s greatest single achievement. Bigelow can't be ignored; his state of mind, physically expressed, impinges on the environment. The difficulties of existence may cause breakdowns as severe in any one of us, the need to express our inner reality outweighing the disgrace of becoming a public spectacle.

By running, Bigelow releases his fury. When he begins to move again, after accepting his awful fate, it is with a firm, determined step, but the glass windows of the shops he passes with increasing speed reflect a distorted environment of buses, streets, and buildings. Maté's perceptive shot eloquently expresses the emotional anarchy of Bigelow's transition from victim to angry sleuth.

Film noir often pictures mazelike environments, architectural labyrinths that work together with complicated narratives and plots as correlatives of insecure psychological states—the Armour plant in *Gun Crazy*, the bowels of the docked ship in *T-Men*, the nightclub in *Criss Cross*, the storm drains in *He Walked by Night*. *D.O.A.* metaphorizes Bigelow's internal confusion and fear by placing him in settings that provide visual echoes of his state and produce equivalent feelings in the audience. The St. Francis Hotel swarming with conventioneers; the noisy, smoky, congested Fisherman Club full of drunks and jive freaks (the editing of the musical sequence is emotionally taxing and breaks narrative and temporal expectation); the empty warehouse through whose intestinal complexity (exaggerated by deep focus) Bigelow scrambles after an unseen assailant; the striking shot of Bigelow racing from Chester's car on a black night shockingly ablaze with the glare of LA's "neon wilderness"; the endless corridors Bigelow paces through to get to Homicide (the impression given is that the police are too remote in the world of the film to help anyone); the confusing Orientalism of Majak's quarters, where the disoriented Bigelow tries to escape through a closet door and where in a rear room pregnant with the aura of arcane ritual, Rakubian's ashes rest in an urn; the drugstore in which Chester chases Bigelow through and across an abundance of brightly lit merchandise; Halliday's death against a receding, compositionally ornate backdrop of staircases seen from high angle—these settings create and sustain a disequilibrium germane to the film's view of life.

D.O.A. Doctors like this only pop up in *noir*'s aberrant psychological climates. This doc seems more thrilled by his confirmed hunch diagnosis ("uridium poisoning") than he is concerned with Bigelow's terrified reaction. "You've been murdered," he offers, flashing the evidence. This shot, which shows the irreversible acceleration of Bigelow's demise, may serve as a paradigm of *noir*'s arbitrary and lethal invasion of normalcy. It takes darkness to reveal your true self, the "poisoned" you who glows in the dark. Bigelow lurches through the rest of *D.O.A.* crazed—what a glimpse of the truth might do to any of us. When he finally shoots Halliday, it is while in the grip of an insane fury. One of the more audaciously extreme moments in black-and-white cinematography. (Museum of Modern Art)

The poisoning is the central generative metaphor. Bigelow looks normal, but inside he is sick unto death. The world, too, looks the way it always has, but it is also poisoned to the core. We have come a long way from the violent directness of early gangster deaths. Death is not a clean, quick matter. It is tasteless, odorless, something that rots the body. And it is invisible. In a shot that may stand for what the film says about reality and our ability to see it, the doctor demonstrates to Bigelow that he is dead, despite what he may think to the contrary. He turns off the lights of his office, plunging it into darkness. He holds up the vial containing the specimen from Bigelow's body and the poison glows in the blackness. This darkly witty device is the boldest example of the lengths to which *D.O.A.* is willing to go to articulate its theme. The truth is there to see,

Going Gray

and Going Crazy

but only under conditions of total darkness. The way we normally perceive the world prevents us from penetrating its reality.

The sliminess of Bigelow's death fits well with the neurotic conception of the film and the degree of asserted impotence: Chester's impotence in killing Bigelow; Majak's impotence in getting to Bigelow before Bigelow gets to the police; the impotence of the police; the impotence of Halliday in poisoning Bigelow to ensure gaining Phillips's wife; the impotence of Phillips's wife's ruse of the grieving widow; the impotence of Paula in coming to see Bigelow; Bigelow's understanding that it would be impossible to explain to Paula what has happened; the doctor's inability to administer an antidote; the sublimated anger of the jazz musicians at the Fisherman, shrieking insanely through their instruments to a jive-crazy crowd; the mink-coated red herring (whose classy beauty engages Bigelow long enough for Halliday to switch his drink) spending her life going from one jazz joint to another; Halliday's secretary's cover-up failing to prevent Stanley's poisoning; the elderly couple whose ice cream sodas are interrupted by Chester trying to kill Bigelow. All society is impotent or unaware. People behave as if the world was sane and rational, when it is in fact senseless. We knew Rico, Tom Powers, Roy Earle, Tommy Udo, Bart and Laurie would get it, that the forces of society would enact a just retribution. In D.O.A. there are no inevitable social forces of overwhelming power. The master criminal Majak is neither caught nor seen as much different or more imposing than any other figure. Although he's technically the equivalent of the old Big Boy, he is similar to Bigelow, careless about other people's lives because (getting old) he hasn't much time to live himself. When he hands Bigelow over to Chester, it is with an air of civilized apology.

What happens to Bigelow is no accident but what was bound to happen given the society's tendencies. The society may be calm on the surface, but it boils with evil and confusion and greed underneath and is ready to erupt at any moment. The detective plot dovetailing is a mask for the chaos that is at the heart of things. The Fisherman is like a purgatory of lost souls, presided over by a satanic house band—Laszlo's blistering close-ups of (especially) the sweating, gyrating saxophonist suggest a ritual for getting rid of pain. It is there, in the Fisherman, that Bigelow is poisoned, distracted by the beauty of the mysterious blonde. Everyone Bigelow meets seems crazy. When the doctors announce their respective verdicts he calls them crazy, and they *are* unlike any doctors we have ever visited. (The second flatly informs him, "You've been murdered," in the same tones he would point out the presence of a plantar wart.) The nurse gives him a queer look, as though Bigelow had no business getting poisoned. Frank Bigelow is a modern Everyman who assumes the burden of confronting a true knowledge of the world and its people; he pays for the knowledge with his life.

As a view of what goes on in America beneath its legitimate facades, *D.O.A.* is most unsettling. The cultured front of the photographer's studio is provided by an articulate foreigner (German?) who, nonetheless, in conference with his workman Angelo, decides to cooperate with Bigelow only when he comes across with enough dough (Angelo as the second-generation cynic who knows how the game is played). The man behind the uridium deal is the dead Rakubian, an Armenian who, masquerading as George Reynolds, frames the hapless, unsuspecting Phillips. His

D.O.A. An iconic "America"—several minutes long—shines caustically over Bigelow and Paula's hopeless declaration of love.

ally in the frame-up, Majak (his uncle), lives in an elegant retreat of Mideastern exotica and bosses a small gang. It is the American way of life, though, that extends them opportunity; they are shrewd manipulators of the country's money mania. *D.O.A.* is savagely satiric of the Sinclair Lewis boosterism of the forties and of the myth of metropolitan dazzle—the salesmen's convention, the advertising signs in the night, the glittery city-world that beckons with marquees like *Black Magic*, the drugstore with its bogus 4 for 69¢ come-ons, the "[Bank] of America" sign shining brightly on top of the frame during the final meeting of Paula and Frank Bigelow, hovering over their ruined love as a background deity of evil. Bigelow himself is a slick tax accountant. The stolen uridium is the route to big money in a world in which a paranoia about science, drugs, and chemicals reigns supreme.

Within an omnipresent itch of greed and a senescent materialism, there is nothing human left. Bigelow, who has seen "the horror," is just in the way, a pest, and it has taken a disaster to make him act, vitally and courageously. Chester is vital enough (Neville Brand repeating the Tommy Udo role), but he is an infant and, as Majak explains, is psychopathic. He is happy only when he gives pain. He likes to see blood. (He too, manipulated by Majak, is a victim, enmeshed in a world of pain, fear, and confusion.) The jazz band at the Fisherman is vital but crazy, flipped out, and, being black, they don't matter. Their freneticism, however, is seen as a response to life—and they carry a good many of their audience with them to a sphere of pure sensation.

D.O.A., through its rare, eccentric conception, tears away the facades of a leprous world. Scenarist Russell Rouse's ideas (and their implications) are unkind and discomforting. Life is a proliferation of blind alleys. Even the hardboiled dialogue and gunplay, especially Bigelow's, lacks the polish typical of a

**Going Gray
and Going Crazy**

159

slick entertainment; it points to the hollowness of the roles being played and seems a deliberate perversion of silver-screen escapism. Maté's attitude and Laszlo's virtuosity complicate the overall effect by imposing their own values on top of Rouse's. The density and exaggeration of the images create a neurotic environment that is an inspired contribution to *noir* visual style. Maté seems to direct his actors and build his sequences in the loosest way—no grotesque happenstance or spontaneous effect is ironed out. *D.O.A.* runs the gamut of bathos/pathos, the harrowing and the farcical, the developing-disintegrating narrative. Anything goes. Whether by design or chance, there is a fusion of theme, attitude, and style. The loose-endedness of many plot elements is appropriate to the demented progress of the narrative. The whirlpool dissolves that frame Bigelow's flashback give the effect of a delirium. The time of the film is a somewhat frantic amalgamation of real time and fantasy time. In the Fisherman, the songs take their actual clock time; the plotting of the film can stop when it wishes to, take as long as things take in reality. But this is not always the case. Time is contingent, unreliable; the clock is a machine with a slipping, jerking clutch. *D.O.A.*, like many modern works, is aware of the meaninglessness of clock (mechanical) time—that it has nothing to do with real time, the experience of time. Fantasy time becomes real time. Bigelow's urgency annihilates both clock time and conventional narrative temporality. We experience time through his heartbeat and his pain. When the film takes us back to the homicide office, we have lost all track of how much time has actually expired. In all, one suspects that care was taken to make the method of the film imitate its theme.

The modernity of *D.O.A.* lies in the freedom with which it handles its material. The film's energy seems to be directed to its material as such. The outlandish story pushes it toward a consideration of how it may possibly be told and filmed. Late *noir* in general is preoccupied with refinements in technique and visual approach. The result is the creation of a tradition in American film in which a passion for articulating the medium replaces the old obligation of illusionistic illustration and rhetoric. Works like Fritz Lang's *The Big Heat*, Joseph H. Lewis's *The Big Combo*, Robert Aldrich's *Kiss Me Deadly*, Robert Siodmak's *Criss Cross*. Samuel Fuller's films are still "gripping," but on a different level than even, say, the blatant technical schemes of an Eisenstein, whose filmic rhetoric urges us to accept, however it is offered, the reality of the image. His montage draws us into the film. His attention is not toward an abstract engagement with the medium but in using the medium to grab hold of our imaginations and bind them to the intense reality of what is on the screen. Late *noir* films do not abandon the illusionistic mode; they make it coexist with an interest in playing with and arranging the look of a film that is not kept hidden on the screen and that we are forced to respond to as something distinct from the reality of any image.

Thus *D.O.A.*'s strategy is to make us observers of illusion distancing us from Bigelow by making us watch how he behaves and by treating him as an actor in the movie of his own life surrounded by people who playact. The reality of what is being presented is periodically undermined by deliberately filmic intrusions—the poison glowing in the dark, the repeated whistle noise, the expanding iris that serves as a transition from the St. Francis Hotel to the Fisherman Club, the wipes that hurry us through Bigelow's mad run through the streets, the use of signs, the drawing of the saxophonist upon which the shadow of the saxophonist intrudes, and eventually the saxophonist himself, creating a triple image of likeness, shadow, and reality, the picture of Reynolds that turns out to be Rakubian, and so on. The film is insolent toward the established conventions of the genre and toward conventional procedures and assumptions of moviemaking. In accord with its theme and its sensibility, the seams of realism and naturalism begin to crack to let more than a touch of modernist chaos and aesthetic retooling drift in. *D.O.A.*'s transitional awkwardness—or, perhaps, its understandable lack of confidence in exploring new means of filmic expressivity—prevents it from having the unified impact of succeeding works more certain of their modernist assumptions, but it also makes it fresh and infinitely diverting in comparison to its more soberly assured successors. Its playful self-indulgence within its baleful premises delivers a satisfying black humor. No viewer can "settle" into *D.O.A.* Its grimmest moments are embroidered with a disconcerting humor. It is funny like Kafka is funny, or Thelonious Monk playing "These Foolish Things," or Nero fiddling. Its impertinences leave it wide open for abuse, but the joke would be on the viewer (and the critic) who fails to taste the film's peculiar seasoning and add his or her own grain of salt. When Bigelow signs in at the desk of the St. Francis Hotel, the register includes the names of Ernest Laszlo and Russell Rouse, the film's director of photography and writer, respectively. The in-joke is a tip-off that *D.O.A.* is willing to laugh at its own absurdities. It's deadly stuff but also a game—like Russian roulette with blanks. And, like many late forties crime melodramas, it is beautiful to look at.

The gangster, as previous films have defined him, would be out of place in *D.O.A.* Questions of morality, of social opposition, of degrees of authority, of achievement are all irrelevant. Yet we are given the gangster's night world, his hard idiom, guns, killings, and a man who is forced to behave like a gangster. Ultimately, it does not matter in this world whether one is a gangster or not. However, it is only by turning into a gangster, by adopting his tactics, that Bigelow achieves what little he does, and he is confronted by an obdurate situation that he must bend to his will. Bigelow is part of the society that he exposes. The opposition in the film is between what he thinks he is and what he

Going Gray
and Going Crazy

161

D.O.A. The childlike Chester, unable to scare Bigelow, turns to Majak for an explanation.

becomes and, analogously, between the society's respectable facades and its cancerous depths. Bigelow is not an actual gangster, but he assumes the functions of one. He battles a false reality/society to make it yield its truths beneath its layers of civilization. He gets a gun and penetrates to the depth of the underworld, where he meets its anarchic representative, the savage Chester (significantly *ruled* by the respectable Majak) and finds he is his match. Bigelow becomes what he opposes, and in a blind rage pumps his gun into Halliday, his poisoner and the embodiment of the world's deceit. Civilization is merely a front for our savagery. Bigelow cuts a path from the outside to the inside, from above to below, from nonawareness to awareness, and in the process enacts his own illegitimate desires. Presumably, he wants to find Halliday, his murderer, and exact revenge. More importantly, he discovers an outlet for his rage and anxiety, a means by which (having nothing to lose) he can assert his superiority and power without fear of guilt or consequence. He dies because he is a gangster, one who wants more than what life will yield. This is the reality at our depths, and the reality of the world we have created. *D.O.A.* implies that waking to that reality doesn't make a difference; *White Heat* destroys it.

CREDITS **D.O.A.**

(United Artists, 1949, 83 min.)

Producer	Leo C. Popkin	Cast	Edmond O'Brien (Frank Bigelow)
Executive			Pamela Britton (Paula Gibson)
Producer	Harry M. Popkin		Luther Adler (Majak)
Director	Rudolph Maté		Beverly Campbell (Miss Forster)
Screenplay	Russell Rouse (based on the		Lynn Baggett (Mrs. Phillips)
	German film *Der Mann,*		William Ching (Halliday)
	Der Seinen Morder Socht)		Henry Hart (Stanley Phillips)
Photography	Ernest Laszlo		Neville Brand (Chester)
Editor	Arthur H. Nadel		Laurette Luez (Marla Rakubian),
Art Director	Duncan Cramer		Cay Forrester (Sue)
Music	Dimitri Tomkin		

White Heat (1949)

If *D.O.A.* is the ugly duckling of the genre, *White Heat* is its master film. Its aggressive contemporary rhythms, its reverberating echoes of the past, and its prophetic properties place it squarely at the crossroads of the gangster film. After the tantalizing muddle of *D.O.A.*, *White Heat* stands solid, a monumental point of convergence for all aspects of the genre. It is a superbly executed film. Raoul Walsh's unruffled direction, with its iron grip on whole sequences linked unyieldingly together, makes *White Heat* the strongest gangster film to date. Its hard, clear outlines bang along with sledgehammer force and the tenacity of a power drill.

The title promises brutality, and contemporary critics were upset over the generous supply of pain, death, injury, and destruction. *White Heat* consolidated a new level of violence (pioneered by the 1947 *Brute Force*) that the fifties was quick to sustain and intensify. Its influence there is unquestionable. The nerve-jangling soundtrack also represents the beginnings of modern assaults upon the ear. The genre is a noisy one to begin with, but *White Heat* gives the ear its biggest workout yet.

Paul Schrader's attempt to unify the period of *noir* by style runs into trouble when he matches films like *White Heat*, *Gun Crazy*, and *D.O.A.*[6] On the level of content—what he calls "psychotic action and suicidal impulse"— there is a trim fit. A world of difference, though, separates the visual look of *The Killers* and *White Heat*. *White Heat* lacks the *noir* photographic style, its intense, ominous shadow world, brilliant contrasts, low-key effects, and splintered, confined, and pressured compositions. Its lighting is less extreme, and the gangster Jarrett's dynamism rushes the film along (he is in contrast to most hampered and unauthoritative *noir* heroes). Max Steiner's score does not brood, rarely quiets down, and forsakes subtlety altogether. It propels us through the film, picking up on the positive charge of the character and keeping the film in high gear. Cutting is matched to the characters' movements and dialogue, and the characters, far too animated for *noir*, are always doing something interesting or delivering bouncy lines. *Noir* is commonly slow and reflective, the camera kept running in a fixed position, the action framed tightly and in an unusual composition. The rhythms of a *noir* film often grind to a halt for the close observation of human pain. *White Heat* is characterized by the tracking shot, in which the characters speak, move, and behave expansively, creating the impression that there is plenty of space around and by editing that forces the movie forward. What we see of the world seems incidental to the characters' purposive placement of themselves within it. The feel of the movie reflects the irrepressible temperaments of director Walsh and star Cagney.

White Heat is the last big gangster film until *Bonnie and Clyde* (1967).

Going Gray
and Going Crazy

163

Much interesting activity was going on in the genre during the fifties and six-ties, but *White Heat* and *Bonnie and Clyde* stand out as the two major films of their respective periods. *White Heat* was entrusted to Raoul Walsh, responsible for the only two powerhouse gangster films since *Scarface* (excepting perhaps Michael Curtiz's *Angels with Dirty Faces*) — *The Roaring Twenties* and *High Sierra* — a director who had developed his style and approach before the advent of *noir* and who could be relied upon to keep the action moving without dis-tracting, fussy interludes. An old-style director for an (on the surface) old-style film — all meat and drive, no filigree, very broad strokes, and no complex mo-tivation to perplex the groundlings. The exactitude, force, and spontaneity of his direction almost make something affirmative out of psychological torment and apocalyptic narrative.

   White Heat gives the sense of being a one-man show — Cagney's Cody Jar-rett is surely one of his (or anyone's) most astonishing performances, but the power and effectiveness of the movie as a whole do not depend on so solitary a virtue. Where the film goes and how it goes, what it feels like, and what it means (or "expresses") are controlled by the talent, sensibility, and working methods of Raoul Walsh, perhaps the most underrated of American directors. The tone, the rhythms are his, and he provides the context within which the dynamic interpretation of the Jarrett character can have a far-reaching reso-nance and the crudities of the script be brought within the bounds of credibility. (Virginia Kellogg's original story was a tribute to the organizational efficiency of *T-men*. Only the pitiful remains of that conception survive, subverted by Walsh's [and his screenwriters'] contrary predilections.)[7]

   Walsh is exceptional in his control over long sequences, holding viewer in-terest by functional cutting and surprising detail and incident. He is not the only director partial to extended sequences, but he calls the least attention to the fact, setting up his camera and matching his shots in the interest not of vir-tuosity but of a natural, unbroken flow. His cutting almost never isolates ma-terial into special prominence. When he tracks, it is because his characters have to get from one place to another for a specific reason, and they are usually saying something pertinent and necessary that would be tedious to listen to in a more static scene. There are few "magnificent" shots in Walsh's films; no elaborate tableaux, no "business" that doesn't seem entirely in line with a char-acter's personality or the needs of the moment. Walsh offers a casual, not an acute, presentation of the world. His environments have a firm neutrality against and through which his figures move with overcharged emotions and fearlessly bold dialogue. They dominate their environment, but the environ-ment doesn't buckle over, like, say, Penn's in *Bonnie and Clyde*, whenever human life is present. Backgrounds are not arranged or photographed for conceptual or commenting purposes. They take definition and register meaning from the humanity and physicality of the characters—a quality very crucial to *White Heat*. Walsh's long shots are establishing shots, and there are virtually no close-ups. Middle distance is heavily favored. Walsh's people move and they move vigorously through a world that gives way because of their strength and not its infirmity. Walsh has a respect for things and places; he doesn't alter them or give them more than their due. If the characters can stand up to the world, it is a measure of their force and desire. Also, in any given shot, the mise-en-scène is not, as it is with some directors, detached from a character's presence in it but is rather to be read as signifying the meaning of the character's presence.

The opening holdup of the train is admirable in its precision and economy— not a wasted shot, nor one held too long. We know exactly how the robbery is to take place with hardly a word being said. We know Jarrett is nuts by the first shot of him sitting in the car, casually gnawing his lip. He kills two men in cold blood. One of his gang is abruptly scalded. They grab the loot and run. The incessant brutality, coming so fast, glues one to the screen. We are hit with so much so quickly that we can scarcely catch our breath before the cabin sequence—perhaps Walsh's greatest triumph—begins.

It is Jarrett's fit that Walsh works up to—and his sitting on his mother's lap—but so much goes on before it that when it comes we take it in stride as part of a sequence whose logic and drama are airtight. The radio report, the tracking shot that brings Ed and Cotton indoors, the arousal of the snoring Verna, the carefully graded revelation of Ma's importance, the odd effect of Jarrett drinking out of a delicate teacup, the sudden lurch signaling the presence of an as yet strange pain, the drifting around of the gang members doing one thing or another, the sardonic rivalry between Jarrett and Big Ed, the exploding gun when Jarrett hits the floor, the move to the back room where the unusual scene takes place, the eventual reemergence of Jarrett, back to normal—this is a wide context indeed. We are curious about and distracted by so much prior activity that the startling sight of Jarrett on his mother's lap becomes a disturbing but expertly managed revelation as part of a large, particularized, and modifying context. It is Walsh's tact in leading us to this moment that makes it work.

The moment itself is also perfectly framed and timed. It is only after an amount of agonized time that Jarrett allows himself to approach his mother for comfort. We are given time to respond to his endurance and his pride and are finally touched by his need. Walsh shows his body moving down toward her lap, in medium shot. A close-up would have been too sentimental for this

White Heat. Cody, his migraine subsiding, rises from his mother's lap. After a rough, fraying opening, this moving scene, much remarked on, takes us by surprise.

tough pair, would have emphasized the dependence that both would rather keep discreet in the interest of their separately effective functioning. A long shot might well have reduced the hero into something pathetic—a cheap tableau of Freudian explicitness that most directors would probably have settled for or approved as a "moving" touch. Walsh lets us know what is happening without showing us the full view of the action—the character's legs dangling, the mother's arms encircling—thus leaving the power of his characters undiminished and honoring their feelings. Walsh has shot it perfectly, without letting in elements of bathos and perversity that would be fatal to the sorrowful beauty of this mutual display of feeling.

The mess hall scene is also remarkable for its combination of conceptual daring and directorial tact. An extreme long shot of the mess hall, the guards patrolling the upper tier, quickly defines the boundaries of the milieu, the orderliness of the meal, the grim rigidity of the décor, the forbidding, ugly staunchness of the architecture. Then Walsh's camera tracks down from Jarrett's seat at the table and back as we wait in suspense for his reaction to his mother's death. He rises, moaning, his head in pain, and Walsh retreats with his camera to give Jarrett room to express his blind rage and terror. The camera pulls further back to let the character hurtle madly from one end of the mess hall to the other, trying to escape and at least release his fury. The opening shot, however, has shown us the inexorability of the environment; it is impossible io escape, to break it down. It is guarded, bolted, impregnable. Yet it is the perfect means to express the character's indomitable, insane will. Jarrett throws a punch and a cop falls. Jarrett races from one closed corner to another, knocking out whoever comes in his way. The camera finally stops following him and recedes to its original high-angle overview to show us Jarrett being dragged off, kicking and screaming. The vastness and solidity of the environment reassert themselves. The eating continues as before; the guards resume patroling.[8]

The power of this scene resides in Walsh establishing a strong environment and then allowing the character room, motive, and energy to try to combat it. That he will lose is given, but the attempt defines the dangerous, heroic, and tragic dimensions of the character. Walsh is not usually classified with the masters of mise-en-scène, but this scene is what using one's decor is all about.

The episode risks being ludicrous, overstated, and damaging to its hero, but Walsh encounters these risks by a judicious self-control and a proper reserve against "cinematic" temptation. Sequence after sequence in *White Heat* has a similar unmannered authority.

White Heat is echo, update, and a sign of what's to come all rolled in one. It is shot in thirties style and tempo, using the thirties' most consistent actor icon; it has the forties obsession with craziness and collapse; its brutality has the crunching continuousness of fifties gangster crime films. *D.O.A.* floats rootlessly in its nightmare world. *White Heat* is molded in the reinforced concrete of gangster dialogue, action, and conviction. Cody Jarrett is the most vicious gangster hero to date, but also the most tortured and suffering. He dominates the film visually and with his energy (it is hard to keep still in one's seat when Cagney starts moving), but he is controlled by his mother. At one point, Cody's face dissolves into his mother's. They are one and the same, he being the instrument of her vengeful will. Previous figures made choices, right ones and wrong ones, but they were their own. Jarrett's goals are not set *by* him but *for* him. He acts because of and on behalf of his mother, and the course she sets is ruinous. He is canny enough to fake control but never really has it (emotionally, at any rate). His actions are set forth with an ironic lucidity but also a deep compassion. Jarrett is a monster with a touch of the sublime. Something like a medical document, *White Heat* has, as well, a tragic tone and beauty; Jarrett's Oedipal fixation makes him both cursed and poetic.

The film is also very funny in a callous way. Walsh remains unfazed by the character's abnormalities, looping many a madcap moment into the drama (Verna spitting out her gum before kissing Cody, Cody chewing on a chicken leg while giving Parker "some air," Ma recommending Evans try *Task Force* at the drive-in—a film Warner Bros. released a few weeks later, Cody advising the prison doctor to "make like a doctor or you'll need a doctor," and dozens of other instances of a crude, lively humor). Walsh's carefree attitude and the absence of a moral context create an unusual mix of brutality and fun more disturbing in the long run than a heavy seriousness.

White Heat again shows us an outsider who has no place in the society and must define himself as an individual by antisocial aggression. Now, though, the society is armed to the hilt with technical apparatus and skill that no single person could dare hope to challenge successfully. Our sympathies should lie with those whose job it is to protect us from menaces like Jarrett. They don't. The film gives us every opportunity to back away from the character; he is an insane, amoral killer. We can and we can't. Jarrett poses a dilemma that the ending perfectly resolves.

Jarrett's derangement is explained. There is no mystery about it; it is a factor we take into account in judging him. Everybody in the film thinks he's crazy—except his mother—and for good reason. Jarrett faked headaches as a kid to get his mother's attention. They worked, but later became the real thing. His father and brother died insane, and mother devoted herself to her sick son. In the film he is a child to his mother, but a grown man with a screw loose to everyone else. Ma Jarrett (modeled no doubt on Ma Barker, but surely the toughest of mothers, on or offscreen—until Aldrich's Ma Grissom in 1971) has taken the place of her husband and is using her son as an instrument to wreak vengeance on the world that has destroyed her family. Cody, in fighting for the family's survival, beccmes a hideous version of the breadwinner. Where others may triumph in the Ivy League to honor their mothers, the unstable, deprived Cody turns criminal, all A's.

The family, though Verna is technically Cody's wife, is reduced to two—its radical limit. Ma and Cody illustrate the fate of the nuclear family. The family is not central to society, is not its sentimental cornerstone; it is not even peripheral. It is solitary and crazed. An old woman (we see her gnarled hands in close-up, stroking Cody) and her psychotic middle-aged son fight an immense network of law enforcement and treachery within the gang. Fallon as the substitute mother and Verna as the betraying wife are signs of the family as a shattered unit. Cody and Ma share deep family feeling, but everyone else is either out for himself or displays an unswerving devotion to the job society has given him to perform.[9]

The Jarretts and society are irreconcilable. The Jarretts are terrifying guerrillas who would blow the world up if they could—and Cody does. We are far from the sentiment of *High Sierra* or even the hard pathos of *Gun Crazy*. Nor is there a confusion of issues, as in *D.O.A.*'s tunnely, quicksand world. Jarrett is far more dangerous than any previous gangster, and he must be defeated. *White Heat* reflects the paranoia about the bomb. Cody is energy itself, a force unleashed upon the world. It takes an army and tons of specialized equipment to get him cornered. When trapped, he takes the initiative and mushroom-clouds the chemical plant by firing into the gas tanks—the climax of his latent suicidal motives but a final act of antagonism as well.

Jarrett's methods are straightforward, his goal single-minded. While in prison, he plots his next job. When out, he attacks, retreats, attacks. His directness is admirable in comparison to the law's duplicitous and bumbling routines. One comes to hate Fallon (Edmond O'Brien), the infiltrator. Jarrett confides in Fallon/Pardo, and one wonders if Fallon begins to understand anything about the agonized compulsions of this demented man. Cody regards him as his mother, is willing to split fifty-fifty, revealing the hurt soul that needs soothing. Fallon has no soul, he doesn't suffer, nor can he understand the man who does. He admittedly dislikes his job, yet risks his life to get Cody by joining his gang, and only his resourcefulness and Cody's trust allow for some very narrow escapes. Fallon is brainwashed. Cody at least gets the satisfaction of pulling daring capers. Fallon is an automaton, a machine (Cody's big mistake is in thinking he's a person), too cynical to feel and blindly loyal to his job. He is, like Reardon in *The Killers*, a true company man—in this case. a kamikaze member of the Justice League of America. Presumably, we owe him our thanks, but the betrayal of Cody, of personal feeling and contact (it is no exaggeration to say that Cody "loves" Fallon), is irreparably befouling. Fallon's code is institutional, neuter, sexless. Cody's is personal, virile, based on feelings. When Verna reports that Ma got it in the back, Cody shoots Big Ed in the back and takes Verna as the "prize," offering her his arm that they may progress together down the stairs—an ironic gesture of ironic gallantry, a sophistication on beating one's fists on the chest and dragging off one's mate. Parker tries to kill Cody, so Cody justifiably (by *his* standards) ventilates the car trunk. Fallon, on the contrary, lies and lies loathsomely. In wriggling out of one ticklish situation he says to Cody, "I'm human, you know . . . ," a statement that is part of his lie, and one the film does not bear out. Fallon is a payroll Judas.

Cody is associated with nature, mother love, personal integrity, and loyalty. (Even his brutal decision to have the scalded Zookie shot is, it turns out, humane, in comparison to his eventual fate. Cotton, by not shooting Zookie, allows him to freeze to death in the cabin and also provides the fingerprint lead that links Cody with the tunnel job.) When he learns that Big Ed wants to move in as boss and take Verna too, he is angered (and fears for his mother) but understands that it was "in the cards for Big Ed to make his try." Cody seeks the quiet of the woods to speak to his dead mother, knowing she is dead but keeping her alive in his heart the way a poet might nurture a conception, an image. His favorite fruit, mentioned twice, is the strawberry—a positive association connecting Jarrett with nature, freshness, sweetness. He envisions the final caper as a reenactment of the legend of the wooden horse (the character's naiveté is important here in eliciting our sympathy). Fallon rigs a buzzer system onto the truck. Jarret has no worthy adversary. He gets by all that Evans, Fallon, and the others try to snag him with. At the end, he cheats the police out of their satisfaction. Fallon hits him three times with a high-powered rifle and Cody doesn't fall. Exercising his last option, he blows *himself* up, lunatic-proud that he has at last made it to the "top o' the world." Fallon's last line— "He finally got to the top of the world and it blew up right in his face"—is just Hollywood's obligatory look-at-the-big-shot-now moral cliché, the inadequacy of which is now felt more keenly than ever before. Fallon has a right to utter the epitaph since he has risked his life battling Cody, but gunning him down like a sitting duck is no big feat, and he doesn't even manage it. Surrounded by

Evans and a mob of cops, Fallon becomes the spokesman for *their* values, having none of his own.

There is a long, rugged tracking shot that starts with Cody and Fallon walking from a porch across a driveway over to a truck. They come out of a house, talking, and Cody, as he walks by a spring shrub starting to bud, tears off a piece, and while they walk and talk, sniffs it, rips its buds and leaves and branches in quick, nervous gestures. Just "business," and similar to Earle's when he first spots Marie in *High Sierra*. The device, though, has a totally different impact here. Jarrett's worrying of that piece of bush shows both his instinctive connection with nature *and* his destructive potential, the pent-up viciousness that cannot help but destroy what it touches. It is the neurotic's response to life — in Jarrett's case, the thoughtless, tortured response of instinct warped.

The "natural" Jarrett is indicated in yet other ways. He departs the cabin in a storm, using it for cover, but the storm arrives at a point that matches his impatience to get moving, as if his own urges summoned it. When Jarrett escapes from prison, he heads straight for Ed and Verna. The wind whips ominously through the trees and shrubs as the camera creeps, in Gothic style, toward their house. The atmosphere of terror complements Ed and Verna's fear, but it is also nature itself responding to Cody Jarrett once again on the loose. When Cody sees the gas truck, he transforms it into a wooden horse, echoing the Homeric story and linking him to a heroic past. And Jarrett, as a primitive natural man, knows his enemy. He blows up a chemical plant; he parodies the psychiatrists; his idiomatic order to Verna to turn off the drive-in loudspeaker is, significantly, "kill it."

In *White Heat* the meaning of content and form is inextricable. Nature and man are a whole. In destroying nature man destroys himself. Industrial landscapes and objects are phallicized and appear to be biologically connected to the protagonist. They embody man's defilement of nature. *White Heat* suggests that the problem is not in man's institutions but in man himself and gives us a towering example of a violated psyche in Cody Jarrett. Cody spends a lot of time in prison, but neither the film nor he sees prison as the source of any problem at all. (Jarrett, in fact, regards his stay as something of a vacation from life and seems to have a pretty good time there until he learns of his mother's death.) The world is electronically wired and wants to add Cody to its circuits, but Cody's human instincts can't be combined with an inhuman, mechanical, chemical-electrical world. Not giving in to a world that has turned its humanity upside down makes him crazy. He is a life force that man-made bullets can't kill and man-made institutions can't contain. He cannot be killed, and yet he cannot continue living a life of madness and torment, so he blows himself up.

Evans and Fallon, while presumably alarmed at the danger Cody poses for human life, seem mostly concerned about the missing three hundred thousand dollars. What looks at one point like a spell of Cody's insanity disturbs them only because it thwarts their plan of using Cody to discover the money. His mental condition is the last thing they care about; his going nuts is just a bad break tor them. Evans is first seen with a cigarette holder. Smug and foppish (as played by John Archer), his image is unfavorable. Ernie, his associate, is a good, clean, American kid with a bent for electronics, a cipher in essence, all his value contained in the service he provides. *White Heat* seems in part intended as a warning to anyone in the audience contemplating lawless activity. A formidable, sophisticated machinery is set in opposition to Jarrett. The law has spectographs for dust particles; it can remove prints intact from the cellophane of a cigarette package; it can distinguish steam burns from flame burns; it has oscillators and psychiatrists, a whole battery of weapons for detection and submission. We get a prized A-B-C system of following suspicious vehicles, are informed of contact ranges. The establishing shot of the immense Halls of Justice is a signal for Max Steiner's music to swell into a pompous, official anthem. Yet while the law diddles with its equipment, Jarrett blows up the chemical plant. All the bullets and machine guns and tear gas (on top of the fancy technology and the vast network of national interagency cooperation) can't keep Jarrett from having his way. As the tanks explode, the frame shakes as though the apocalypse had come.

Contemporary audiences may possibly have gasped in awe at the new technology at the law's disposal, but the A-B-C system, especially, seems a little silly nowadays and may well have been intended as such then. The police do get roughly equal time and the film appears rather uncommittedly concerned with allaying the audience's fear of rampant crime by demonstrating surefire methods of dealing with it. The ticket taker at the drive-in, when the cop car, sirening, races by, claims that it "happens every night" (and ruins the movie). Fallon, when informed of the new intricacy of fencing operations, says, "in step with the times." Police diligence is apparently called for.

The cops are cooler, more controlled and self-satisfied than ever before, and the gangster is crazier than ever before. Evans is as cocky as they come. He assures Fallon of the good food in the pen: "Wonderful chef, arrested him myself." We smile, but recognize the character beneath the joke. At the end, Cody says to his hostage Fallon, "They won't shoot one of their own," assuming this as a basic principle, a universal code. Fallon advises him that they will. And they do shoot in, with Fallon there. (Fallon, who leads an amazingly charmed life, escapes.) Cody shoots Riley, but Riley is about to defect. Lucky (Evans stumbles onto Jarrett's motel after losing Ma's car; Fallon uses up a cat's nine lives), cynical, persistent to the point of willing to sacrifice Fallon, relying on informers and infiltrators, eager-beaverish in shifty ways, the police are pictured as a gadget-happy, inhuman lot. Cody's doing it all for Ma; the cops seem mostly interested in recovering the stolen money and showing off their equipment.

The film is equally unkind to a pair of professional psychiatrists who come to escort Cody to a mental institution. Walsh seems to regard them as saps and dolts. It is obvious that these two are incapable of helping Jarrett. Psychiatry has nothing to do with what disturbs Cody. He is not going to be helped by how a mechanical society defines a brain that isn't normal (that is, mechanical) and labels the abnormality by jargon x, y, or z. The viewer receives no evidence, either, that there is anything wrong with Jarrett's brain. He thinks quickly, acutely, and clearly. He wants to get out to revenge the death of his mother, and his sarcastic treatment of the psychiatrists—inverting the roles to have *them* appear crazy—makes it clear that he knows where they are at and that it has nothing to do with him. He uses them cleverly to escape, then junks them as part of civilization's refuse.

One puts a pipe in his mouth and leans back to voice a platitude. The other echoes his partner in dress and manner. It is as a *pair* that they are funny. The scene is comic, Cody making his craziness work for him until the opportunity arises to force this professionally supercilious pair to do his bidding (he orders the pipe man to "make like a loony"). It is tragic that Jarrett is incurable, but it is surely folly for anyone to have supposed that his passions could be contained by the theories of this textbook pair. (One offers, with ludicrous earnestness, that "hunger is a hopeful sign.") They join the ranks of other ineffectual tacticians. They don't care about Cody, only about how smart they appear in the new paradise of science. They don't go at Jarrett man to man, but through devices, signals, and theories. Jarrett expresses for the audience a resistance to these methods. While his adversaries trace and prattle, and maneuver their technology, he narrates of the wooden horse around his gathered tribe and kills like a savage.

Jarrett is not impotent—his animal appreciation of Verna's beauty in an early scene tells us so. The first shot of Verna shows her stretched out on a bed in a slip, snoring—no actress was ever introduced in so vulgarly comic a fashion. The ambience is erotic. As she drowsily lets herself off the bed one can almost smell a tired, lusty aroma. Her legs swing up and then around toward the floor, exposing her thighs. She and Cody are "making it" all right, but while Ma is there the relationship can never be satisfactory. She is a wedge between their animal passions. Ma hates Verna as the object that comes between her and her son, and she sees to it that Verna is kept insultingly in her place—an occasional toy for Jarrett's lust but of no other value or comfort. Cody trusts his mother and not only permits her jealousy to go unchecked but adds further abuse upon his wife. (Ma has sized Verna up right; she is a two-timing, promiscuous woman.) Only when Ma dies does Jarrett relax toward Verna, drop his guard. Ignorant of the fact that Verna has murdered Ma, he is kinder to Verna and seemingly more appreciative of her as a person. His mother is no longer around to advise him about how he should direct his passions. In a bold (for its period) scene, Verna hops on Jarrett's shoulders, and, both drunk, he piggybacks her up the stairs for an evening of carnal diversion. Cody's relaxation undoes him. While he is having sex with Verna, Fallon is transforming her broken radio into an oscillator that he will attach to the gas truck.

In *White Heat*, the classic gangster figure—associated with Cagney—takes on disturbing dimensions. Nothing like the emphasis of the old gangster films is possible in 1949, even with Cagney and Walsh, two artists who honed their style in that period, joining forces. The gangster has to be offered on a different set of

White Heat. Jarrett understandably likes the likes of a Virginia Mayo waiting for him as he alternates pulling jobs and doing time. Occasionally, he thinks it's advisable to re-establish authority within the gang, so he orders her about. She looks a bit frightened, as well she might, as she and "Big Ed" have been fooling around during his absences. (Museum of Modern Art)

terms. There is no specific location of conflict anymore. His adversary is the world and everything in it, including himself. There is no longer any question of wanting something, of directing himself to a specific task or goal. All he can do is exhibit an irreparably damaged psyche, an archaic, direct, human loyalty. His aim is instinctively to protect the remnants of his humanity—his mother and his attachment to her—by getting on *top* of the world, by wiping it out before it wipes him out. The conflict has never assumed such proportions before. Jarrett illustrates the strain and agony of self-definition. One must explode into violence to assert one's human presence in the world.

Fallon is amazed that Cody doesn't succumb to the impact of his bullets. "What's holding him up?" he asks. *White Heat* is a precursor of the monster movies of the fifties. A vindictive creature trashes civilization until, trapped, he is "scientifically" eliminated, destroys himself, or eludes the forces that threaten his lone, unique existence, leaving behind the fearful notion that he may return. *White Heat* is in this pattern. Jarrett, in a period of nuclear paranoia, destroys a chemical plant above which an American flag is flying—no close-up, but the eye picks it out in long shot. A frenzied avenger like Jarrett shows how wide a rift exists between the apparent acceptance of the course of

Going Gray and Going Crazy

White Heat. Cody's insanity linked to the environment that triggers his final act of suicidal aggression.

civilization and the urge for its deserved destruction. The gangster has always been the actual, as opposed to the sci-fi, monster of our society. He has been its threat, its predator, its existential deviant—incapable of conforming to a work-force mentality and refusing to reform or even quietly gripe out his stay in prison. (*White Heat* takes an anticonformist position. The Trader speaks with disdain of the "deserving employees" at the plant whose payroll he plans, with Cody, to rob. Cody could never hold such a job. Even Bo Creel, when released from prison, immediately reverts to criminality. On his second day on the job at the plant, he agrees to go in on the caper as an inside man.)

Our rooting interest in monsters suggests our insecurity about how society functions. The monster invariably comes from sea, desert, swamp, or jungle, and heads straight for Wall Street, the hub of the economy, and starts to topple the foundations of the socioeconomic structure. (Aliens, more sinister, head for Washington to administer a political lesson or issue governmental ultimatums.) Just as invariably, the army is called out first as the ablest means to ward off the threat; it goes about trying to bomb and bazooka the creature to oblivion. It always fails, and its personnel are usually presented as foolhardy boobs. More enlightened procedures are suggested but ignored. It makes for exciting movies, but such combat is seen as futile. The monster's visitation has a *meaning* that the army never takes into account. The old professor becomes a scapegoat for the advance of general knowledge, human knowledge, passing his wisdom onto his young assistant, who becomes the leading lady's choice over the more conventionally handsome but thick-skulled army man. Our advanced weaponry is not only frightening but senseless. Some tricky bit of lab work usually suffices to destroy the monster or make him retreat, precluding horrendous consequences for humanity and implying that a cautious, responsible use of knowledge can yield benevolent results, a truce between the primitive powers of destruction and the voraciously complex network of human progress. Brute force, on the other hand, can only increase hostilities. There are always some monsters in reserve that will appear on those occasions when human folly oversteps its bounds. *White Heat* balances didactic spectacle with tragic grandeur. Its monster is decidedly human; the gangster's fate is parallel to our lost humanity. The orgasmic splendor of his demise celebrates the life of instinct at its moment of destruction.

White Heat ends astoundingly. Cody, torn from the natural habitat of his mother's love, goes insane. He is a less fantastical King Kong who responds with insensate fury upon being deprived of what sustains him, and he is converged upon, like Kong, by a throng of enemies, some of whom take an active part in his destruction while others assume the gaping function. It is a perfectly devised ending, combining all the urges we've had toward the character. The wish to see him succeed and also be destroyed occurs simultaneously. By implying an analogy to the nuclear holocaust, which neither the law's inconsequential technological tinkering nor formal show of force can prevent, *White Heat* can be read as a film expressing profound reservations about the workings of its society and its potential fate. In the late forties the genre was raising the issue of what living in the shadow of the bomb, and within an increasingly conformist, mechanical society, was doing to our humanity. *D.O.A.* and *White Heat* announce that the threat to human values and feelings is serious. The nature of the genre in the fifties reveals it as prophetic. The fifties crime film explores the condition of a lost humanity—armored, warped, or gone underground in response to civilization's fallout—and the means by which it may be regained. *Noir* was a response to the initial shock of it. The fifties crime film shows that we have numbly accepted it as a way of life (that, at any rate, is the truth of the situation when the films begin). The fifties is also the first decade in which the gangster crime film attacks the society like a scourge, making explicit what was always implicit. The boldress of its brutality and its conscious attempt to alert America to its problems relegated it to the B feature. *White Heat*, in which the old gangster reached his culmination, was its stepping-stone. In his place came the syndicate and all its worrisome variants—including communists.

CREDITS *White Heat*

(Warner Bros., 1949, 114 min.)

Producer	Louis F. Edelman	Cast	James Cagney (Cody Jarrett)
Director	Raoul Walsh		Virginia Mayo (Verna Jarrett)
Screenplay	Ivan Goff and Ben Roberts		Edmond O'Brien (Hank Fallon,
	(suggested by Virginia Kellogg's		alias Vic Pardo)
	story)		Margaret Wycherly (Ma Jarrett)
Photography	Sid Hickox		Steve Cochran (Big Ed)
Editor	Owen Marks		John Archer (Philip Evans)
Art Director	Edward Carrere		Wally Cassell (Cotton Valetti)
Music	Max Steiner		Ian MacDonald (Bo Creel)
			Fred Clark (Daniel Winston,
			the Trader)
			Robert Osterloh (Tommy Riley)
			Paul Guilfoyle (Parker)

Going Gray and Going Crazy

Focus on Feeling
"Seeing" through the Fifties

On the surface the genre's treatment of crime and gangsters in the fifties is relatively simple when compared to the complicated views induced by *noir*'s psychological malaise. The genre assumed some new and fairly consistent characteristics. A quick review, heedless for the time being of implications, may isolate the following:

For much of the fifties criminal heroes are few and far between. The cop or citizen, moved by obsessive personal reasons, takes over as hero in films of criminal action. They become the agents by which public paranoia about organized crime can be momentarily dissipated. Crime becomes disgusting; it is pictured as powerful, settled, cool, on a comfortable plateau of semirespectability. While the criminal is restrained and businesslike, the hero who opposes him gets overheated and frustrated. He has played by the rules and gotten nowhere for too long, and so, like the gangster before him, he now takes out *his* aggression, not only against crime but against the world. If the forties was full of characters who were deluded into thinking that action was meaningful, the fifties action hero, fighting for the "right side" and getting somewhere, reveals the ugliness of his distress and his envy, hatred, and blindness. Fifties gangsters seem simply to want money and power, and when they have it, more. They're following the drift of the world, of competitive industries and corporations. The gangster is no longer explained. The reasons behind his ruthlessness are obvious—it is only the most ruthless who get to the top. Getting to the top means having the big money, having big money means having power over others, and the gangster wants that money and the power it brings, at any human cost.

In the fifties the tensions of the cold war are evident. Crime, like communism, is against the American way of life. The evils of these poisonous systems are analogous. Americans must stick together and support whatever measures, however extreme or unsavory, that a courageous individual adopts to penetrate syndicate operations and hierarchies. The gangster has run out of excuses and, with them, sympathy. In a period of prosperity, his motives are reduced to selfish greed. He no longer acts in response to a problem; he *is* the problem. Crime is corruption that exacts from the public good a daily price. It must be annihilated at its source. A major motif of the fifties crime film is the difficulty of threading one's way to the top, of tearing away the masks of crime and discovering where, how, and by whom the immense criminal empire is ruled. The underworld czar retains a grandeur, but of a diabolical, perverse, and often hateful kind. His vileness justifies the hero's savagery, but the crime-busting hero is part of the corruption. He exhibits the characteristics of the old gangster. In the exchange of roles, however, there is a difference. The fifties hero is generally humorless and morose, is less likable, and often more brutal.

If *noir*'s assessment of crime and its attitudes toward experience suddenly become archaic within a moral dynamism of "cleansing" action, *noir* lighting is, if anything, intensified in a certain subgroup of fifties crime films, reaching its apogee in the eye-piercing boldness of the Alton-Lewis *The Big Combo*, the Laszlo-Aldrich *Kiss Me Deadly*, and the Joe MacDonald–Samuel Fuller *Pickup on South Street*. *Kiss Me Deadly* (1955) in particular seems to exhaust the extremes of black and white photography. Late fifties gangster crime films have looser compositions, less dramatic use of black and white, flatter visuals, and a cooler, brighter, more neutral look—a prelude, perhaps, to the moral neutrality automatic to the loss of drama in the more even distribution of light and emphasis in the color film but also in keeping with a sinister assumption about the invisibility of crime and its efficient fusion into the mainstream of modern life.

The late fifties initiated a pocket of films evoking the exploits of notorious gangsters of the thirties, an explicitly neurotic gangster cycle that extends fitfully up to the present. From the perspective of the late fifties, the old gangster appears as a psychological misfit, his life a prolonged seizure of uncontrolled acts. He lacks the confidence of his thirties counterpart and also the stylish panache of innumerable *noir* hoodlums. His awkward, traumatized, alienated behavior invites a psychological understanding, not a moral judgment. *Machine-Gun Kelly* (1958) is a representative film. In a period interested in psychology and mental aberration, especially in a climate in which the issue of conformity looms large, the gangster is again useful as a vehicle to carry matters of concern to the society. In this case, being a gangster means, exclusively, being mentally disturbed, and therefore in conflict with the norm of sanity. The genre also responded to the Kefauver investigations into organized crime by producing many smash-the-syndicate and sin-city exposé films.[1]

These represent distinct shifts and real concerns, but the genre's major theme in the fifties is its unrelenting view of the world as a hideous machine in violation of human realities. If *noir* scrambled the terms of the opposition, the fifties inverts them. The gangster represents the society; society *is* the gangster. For human values to survive, it (he) must be opposed. Civilization has caused a greater chaos than it cured. The Western tells us how we got here—by combating evil savagery. The gangster crime genre shows us where we got to—the evil of civilization, which can be combated only by reverting to primitivity and savagery, by feeling and acting on emotions triggered by instinct. For the fifties hero, it is necessary for his whole being to be reconstituted by the charge of a powerful human emotion that connects him to other people. At the beginning of the films, he is undifferentiated. He is situated the same as everyone else—

locked into the ways of the world and living mechanically. By the end of the film, he undergoes an internal change that necessitates the external destruction of that which made him what he was.

The hero is always, however, implicated in his world; man and the world are fused. What *he* is makes the world what *it* is. By action or inaction, he is its cause. The early gangster films rested on the assumption that the gangster could be separated from the society (and the people who live in it) and placed in opposition to it. They also killed the gangster off, again and again, as though the ritual itself, devotedly observed, could make him dead and gone for real. But it was only a fiction about a reality that continued and changed in nature, requiring new fictions to grasp, engage, and exorcise it. The genre in the fifties suggests that the gangster never died but submerged himself in us. His place is ours; he lives where we do. We can no longer use plots that locate him above us or below us. We cannot identify with him as something external. He does not challenge civilization but is synonymous with it. He looks like us and acts like us. (In *The Big Combo* [1955] he is called "Mr. Brown".) We accept him and do nothing about him in the same way we accept and do nothing about the mechanical, inhuman nature of our lives.

The fifties demythologizes the differences between us (and the screen representatives who act on our behalf) and the gangster. Conflict does not revolve around Good versus Bad, Right versus Wrong. Both exist everywhere and in everyone. We are all part of the same corrupt "order" and hide behind the same facades and rationalizations. We all have the same potential for violence. What is special about the gangster in this period, what his success amounts to, is that he has gone the farthest in achieving control, reason, logic, and precision and has consequently lost contact with his real self more than others. He can be stopped only by the power of a human being restored to his fundamental drives, his basic instincts. The gangster is no longer on the outside but deep inside. In effect, there is no outside and inside—only society in the grip of its machinery. In *The Killers* Reardon was on the inside wanting to get out for a taste of life. The underworld as a place of dangerous, if futile, dreams no longer exists. There is no life. Everyone is walking in step.

D.O.A. implied that to see what things are like is to go crazy. *White Heat* gave us a madman and showed that his mind was not defective but disordered. The note struck in *White Heat*, that nature is all of a piece, is struck *socially* in the fifties, and as nature was shown to be perverted, now society is. Its mechanism has to be disrupted, and going crazy and violent is the only way. The attack is on reason, the force that has removed man from himself. People are separated and disconnected, and it takes something or someone overwhelmingly horrible to activate people toward their humanity. The nature of violence changes. It is now a necessary force, not seen as bad but as the only remedy. It is purgative when humanly motivated, and seen in contrast to the violence of a machine-run society whose violence is done to the soul and impersonally. In film after film, the hero loses control, goes into a violent rage, goes crazy, when his basic human needs are threatened. He does not act morally or out of understanding but from a primitive urge. Usually, this saves him. In *Kiss Me Deadly*, however, Hammer is so far gone he can't get back. Even going crazy won't help anymore.

Elia Kazan's *Panic in the Streets* (1950) uses the plague as a symbol for the human condition. We are warned that it is something that can spread like the common cold. The doctor who sees the severity of the situation and is bewildered by the human inertia and self-interest in the face of it, at one point states, "We're all in a community, the same one." This concept underlies the fifties crime film. Since we are all contaminated, we cannot keep separate. We must accept our corruption and help each other. We cannot perpetuate the situation of being in the same house but in separate, locked rooms. Thoreau's statement that "the civilized man has the habits of the house. His house is his prison" is apropos. The fifties gangster lives in places similar to ours, only fancier. It used to be that he was homeless, or the city was his house, or he left home for a state of urban transiency. In the fifties much attention is given to where the gangster lives. The sterile affluence of the decor reflects his dead emotions. Often, too, the hero's domesticity is invaded by catastrophe, as though it were a false reality that has to be annihilated. Home is everyone's prison, and the gangster now lives not just in the city but in the world we all inhabit. The policeman hero of *The Big Heat*, Dave Bannion, bursts into the gangster Lagana's home, destroying its facade. After the murder of his wife, he abandons his house and moves to a hotel room whose look Debbie ironically admires as "early nothing." It is only by being stripped clean of the civilization that keeps him a machine that he can get anything done.

The process, though, is twofold. Becoming a savage is not the answer; anger and hate are merely destructive. The hero can't do it alone; he needs help, and that help is provided by society's perennial outcasts—women—who direct, or effect, or cause the action and its resolution from the wings of the stage. In *The Big Heat* only Debbie stands between Bannion and savagery (the film makes clear that he has the same emotions as the killer, Vince Stone), and she becomes a sacrifice. Her death prevents an anarchy of totally unchecked emotions and instincts. Bannion lives out his emotions but is finally restrained by his human, civilized (in the good and necessary sense of being something more than animal), Christian, moral nature. He cannot become Vince Stone because he has known what it is to need and love another human being. It is significant, though, that the gangster very often lives. He is weakened, cornered, reviled, battered by fists, humiliated, but left alive, partly to prevent the hero from becoming a murderer but also because he is shown as the hero's other half.

Police and gangsters are equated. They may technically oppose each other, but they are essentially part of the same system and their organizations are run on similar attitudes and by similar tactics. To stay within the system is to perpetuate it. The outsider becomes, in the fifties, the only one the genre can use to represent a human being. The hero is frequently not a gangster or a policeman, and the cop, to follow through on his feelings, must either resign from the force or act independently of its machinery. In fifties films, unlike those of the thirties and forties, however, there are no outsiders to start with. No one has contact with his real self, his instinctual humanity. Everyone is divorced from himself and his fellow human beings. It is only within the progress of the film, under the impact of violence, that people turn against the course of their lives and gain access to their humanity. This makes them outsiders, people the system cannot accommodate or who cannot accommodate to the system. When the gangster as such becomes that which he used to oppose, the genre finds his substitute, one who can assume his former function. The situation, though, is far more precarious, since all depends on the hero's tenuous hold on his humanity. Naturally, the nature of the hero's alienation, the choices open to him, the view of gangsters—all the elements of the genre—must be newly defined and presented, since the climate of cold war America differs considerably from that of depression America.

In the past the genre achieved a temporary resolution of its conflicts by the gangster's death. In the fifties the hero survives in a world that continues as before but is slightly altered by his having taken forceful action. The "happy" endings of many of these films, however credible and to the point, are never entirely convincing and contain a level of ambivalence. The return to feeling and a genuine inner life does not abolish a system that is too vast to crumble overnight. The hero makes only a small, but consequential, dent. What is achieved feels like, and is, a drop in the bucket, but the hope these films extend at their close is necessary to their vision. That we find it easy to accept as integral to the films' meaning but difficult to believe as something that can seriously alter the quality of life (within and without the film) is an ambivalence the films themselves seem to recognize. The world restored to human feeling is *seen* as an answer and *felt* as virtually impossible. The hero's mechanisms are so ingrained that it often takes the whole movie, and a succession of painful, lethal occurrences, to have him act unhesitatingly at all. The strain of maintaining the impossible reaches a peak in a late film like *The Brothers Rico* (1957), where the abruptly optimistic resolution springs uncomfortably from structure, dialogue, and visuals that either state or imply that not only is it too late for effective action but that it was always too late—a view so pessimistic that one is hard put to think of its equal.

The genre in the fifties has an almost fanatical tightness. The films are extended statements of rigidly interlocked parts. No one can speak a line without it echoing with significance. Every shot is calculated; nothing is inadvertent. Dialogue is heavy, weighted, thematically resonant by design. Visuals are blatant, assaulting, undisguisedly filmic, as if to declare openly that verisimilitude reveals nothing anymore, that people must be made to see what in looking at reality or its illusion they cannot see. Realism and illusionism, for all their seductive pleasures, have numbed our eyes and minds, have made us immune to the real, and so they either must be intensified to a point where they can be noticed as functional modes—as one or another deliberate choice out of many —or abandoned as useless to the task of jolting the eye out of its idly gratified torpor.

It is impossible not to notice Fuller's camera in *Pickup on South Street* or that its movement and placement are aggressively leading us to see things in specific ways. *The Big Heat* uses sets to keep the action deliberately unreal and pointedly symbolic. Phil Karlson, in *The Phenix City Story*, closes the division between firm and actuality by using a real story as his base and by framing his fiction with real footage at the beginning and end. Illusionism gives way to emotions in the viewer that do not end with the film. The gap between our actual realities and the emotions undergone in the theater are bridged. We go out to meet a world that is an extension of the one we have just seen. The film does not allow us to expend the feelings it has created but leaves us full of them, giving pertinence to their vicariousness. *The Big Combo*'s stylized lighting puts us in the dark throughout the whole film as a fresh test to our vision. *Kiss Me Deadly*, from beginning to end, is an utter abstraction of reality. The visual scheme of *99 River Street* is in close conjunction with the problem of seeing that the film and its characters are occupied with. The "realism" of *The Brothers Rico* is kept deliberately "unquestioned" to make gradually evident the breadth and insidiousness of the veneer that must be sloughed off to get at the horror of reality.

In retrospect, and seen as a whole, the fifties films are a sentimental phase of the genre, not least because what they with great difficulty will into being as a possibility has since been proved false. The films have a very hard surface but are infused with a last-ditch spirit of humanism that films near the end of the decade have already given up on. It is the Dickens phase of the genre, just prior to the major overhauls of modernism.

There are frequent contrasts between the old ways and new ways, and old-style gangsterism is made nostalgic in a manner profoundly different from that of *Bonnie and Clyde*. Christina's "remember me," which initiates Hammer's quest in *Kiss Me Deadly*, bespeaks not nostalgia but the loss of the old world, of humanity. In *The Brothers Rico* old values and loyalties have vanished from the syndicate. In *The Big Heat* the anal Lagana evokes the reckless Lucky Luciano and assures Vince Stone that *his* methods will prevent, for them, a similar fate. In *Pickup on South Street*, the styleless, ruthless, impersonal Communists are contrasted with the longstanding underworld traditions and mutual give-and-take of Moe and Skip. The gangsters in *The Big Combo* are divorced from their own realities; they can't even see what they have made of themselves. Brown's methods don't leave any mark. McClure, the gangster from the old days, stripped of his hearing aid, watches Brown's technologically sophisticated torture of Lieutenant Diamond with a look of befuddlement.

While the genre's brutality toward women reaches shocking proportions in the fifties, women are nonetheless shown to function more decisively than ever before and are treated with a great deal of sentiment. They must be killed because what they know and feel threatens the whole system. They are cast as stereotypes, but highly valued ones. The handy old distinction between male reason and female intuition is rampant. The male must accept the female as his redeemer. Women can no longer be dismissed or underestimated. They are the only ones who see clearly, and they have to provoke the male out of his blind misogyny and his one-dimensional vision. (Ernie Driscoll tells Linda in *99 River Street*, "Don't mix me up. Women aren't like that.") As outsiders, they have a perspective on things. Men fear what women know, and the condition worsens when male/female roles are sharply defined and socially divided, as they were in the fifties—the era of the "feminine mystique." Women's loyalty, compassion, and erotic honesty baffle and dislodge the fifties hero but also call him back to fundamental realities—even if the effort means going crazy (Christina) and getting beaten up or killed (Christina, Debbie in *The Big Heat*, Moe and Candy in *Pickup on South Street*).

Beneath the surface cruelty, severity, and brutality of the gangster/crime film in the fifties, then, lies both a core of sentiment and rather simplistic, idealistic solutions to social (human) problems. But the genre did not lose its integrity; it remained honest. The fifties was a period in which material comfort and social progress gave a false sense of accomplishment, purpose, and well-being. Guilts, fears, and disturbances were hidden beneath social rituals that desensitized personal feeling and paralyzed individual wills. The genre exposed these dangers and attacked the bogus psychological panaceas of conformity and economic security by confronting its audience with not only the uncompromising facts of crime and violence but with a catalog of deadened souls. Its films blistered the placid surface of the Eisenhower era, their evidence running contrary to the illusion of calm and the rewards of prosperity. It was a brave but futile attempt to reach a humanity that had gone underground, and it required a new stylistic ferocity and a new viciousness of content. As if recognizing the failure of its biggest lost cause, the genre has since cooled down and gone in the direction of aesthetic spectacle.

The genre in the fifties was a reaction to the wit, cynicism, futility, and stylistic preciosity of *noir*. *Noir* knew something was wrong, but it couldn't be confidently (or ponderously) critical because it didn't know exactly what to attack. In the fifties the evil that seeped through *noir* takes solid shape. The films are not cryptic. They take aim at well-defined targets. They are less detached and more morally outraged than films of the period 1945–1950. They are looking to punch their way out of what *noir* sank defeatedly back into. *Noir* gouged around with a sharp knife, making little cuts and wounds that left a collection of scars. The gangster crime film of the fifties comes at you like a meat cleaver, ready to decapitate. The metaphor is not inapt. The insistence on the resurgence of instinct and feeling involves in particular the bludgeoning of heads—seats of reason and abstraction (99 *River Street*, *Pickup on South Street*, *The Brothers Rico*)—and direct violence with fists and hands. People in Karlson's films bleed as they have never done before. *Noir* distress did not intrude upon its aesthetics in a way that made the films ugly. In the fifties the films are beautiful and ugly at the same time. In the half-decade immediately following the war the genre reflected, and gave a scattered, ironic, and despairing analysis of, emerging psychosocial patterns. By the fifties the traumas were deeply internalized and life had settled into an unexamined, destructive groove. In battling so settled a condition the genre had no choice but to knock heads. B programmers were of course habitually degraded by reviewers, and the public was busy chasing after innocuous top-billed features and new-fangled wide-screen and 3-D processes. It is reasonable to assume that few people were listening to what these films had to say or even taking them seriously. The *Times* did not even deign to review the excellent *Kiss Me Deadly* and *The Brothers Rico*.

The hope that we may get back to the roots of our humanity may be a sentimental one, but it is far from the grandiose designs of tragedy, even the romantic-neurotic kind like *White Heat*. The fifties hero does not have tragic stature, and the content of the films is either plain sordid or cannot elevate itself from the muck of human contingencies. The heroes who are forced to act instinctively achieve only a limited understanding of what they have undergone and are too routinely reconciled to their world. There is no catharsis through recognition. Experience, at best, is humbling, and it is sometimes in doubt whether the hero learns even that much. All sense of triumph is modified. Moreover, we are always conscious of a scriptwriter's or director's viewpoint determining the hero's actions and behavior. Unlike the classic gangster, whose mere presence dominates our sense of any uses he is being put to, the fifties hero seems more in service to an a priori conception. Instead of gathering the image to himself and toward us, he seems rather to pull away from us and back into the image. We are always given a perspective on his movement and energy. It is not he but what's behind him that controls the film. What he achieves is thereby subtly compromised.

Most important, the now-archaic vision of hope that the conclusions of most of these films hold out is offered within the mature consideration that whatever of value has occurred the world goes on and we have to live in it. There are no expanded horizons. The world has simply quieted down and returned to normal. The hero of *The Big Heat*, purged of his hatred, goes back to his unglamorous job. Everything seems the same, except that he can instruct someone to "keep the coffee hot" without our shuddering (boiling coffee is no longer something that gets thrown in people's faces, a real enough change from when the film began). The question remains, though, whether Bannion is oblivious to the meaning of his experience (knowing Lang, the ambiguity is likely to be intentional). John Patterson, in *The Phenix City Story*, assures us all from the statehouse that the work has just begun. Ernie Driscoll, in *99 River Street*, achieves perhaps the clearest, most distinct triumph, and that amounts to realizing that he will never be a "champ." He accepts his limits and settles for the love of a woman and owning a gas station. No great vistas open up; the world just suddenly becomes habitable because he has come to his senses. In *Pickup on South Street* Skip is still a three-time loser, and the old, irrelevant battle between Tiger and himself continues. Fuller suggests, though, that nothing else matters but the look Skip and Candy exchange. That is triumph enough. The humanization of Eddie Rico in *The Brothers Rico* comes after irremediable disaster. He and his wife finally adopt the child, but only the dimmest viewer could imagine that to go on living as Eddie Rico, after all that he has been responsible for, will be an easy business. The doctor-hero of *Panic in the Streets* walks resignedly back toward his economic frustration, but less ego-ridden and with a new attitude of acceptance toward his human lot. The couple at the end of *The Big Combo* is a black silhouette walking slowly into a thick mist that promises a difficult and uncertain future. And there is of course *Kiss Me Deadly*, a film that ends on a vision of total destruction. But even that film has as its major focus, is *concerned* about, the distance we have put between ourselves and our human origins. Lily (Gabrielle) has lost the instinct that would make her close the box. In a film of ultimate gestures, Christina's ultimate gesture of spreading her arms out in front of Hammer's speeding car is memorable. We too, like Hammer, "remember" her. The film wants us to be appalled by what we see. In the fifties, it is the genre's pervasive humanism in a context of overwhelmingly contrary priorities that earns it the label "sentimental," a quality never more apparent than from our present perspective.

Pickup on South Street (1953)

Pickup on South Street is a signpost of the fifties crime film. With the collapse of the traditional gangster figure and the slow phaseout of the *noir* sensibility, the genre stands as an inviting blueprint of structure and imagery ready to be revamped. The fifties provides an opportunity for directors, within limited budgets, to specialize and make their mark in the crime film (Phil Karlson and Don Siegel, for example). The *noir* unity of style and sensibility (the film as its own reason for being, in the absence of any alternate certainty) is shattered to permit the binding of action and incident to moral and ideological statements. The stylish, decorative aspects of *noir* are replaced by a blunt, roughhewn, argumentative energy and urgency. Fuller's pickpocket is an unusual, but not an unthinkable, gangster hero, and he is not fated to die like the old-time gangster but is rather forced to deal with emotional conflicts that lead him to a moral (and, incidentally, political) choice. Where *noir* used brutality as an embellishment, it becomes the bread and butter of the fifties crime film. Fuller's climactic subway fight and Joey's roughing up of Candy have a crunching precision and explicitness noticeably different from the refined brutality of most *noir* films. To register the impact of violence, visual style becomes nervy and hyperbolic and, in combination with simple, elemental themes and emotions, often seems baroque. A film like *D.O.A.*, in comparison with *Pickup on South Street*, has a light touch; it blows its bile around with a loose, jumpy abandon. The fifties crime film has a more measured pace, and the weight and texture of cement. Fuller's agile camera creates a false illusion of speedy narrative. Behind his dexterity lie conceptions and sequences as immovable as boulders.

The hero of *Pickup on South Street* is a hard-working pickpocket named Skip McCoy who is an outcast by choice as much as circumstance. He lives in a (barely) converted tackle and bait shack overhanging the river. It is connected to the mainland by a long plank. His home is a symbol of his independence. Inside is a comfortable clutter minus all bourgeois comforts. He keeps his beer in a box and refrigerates it by dipping it into the water. He has no electricity, and the main piece of furniture is a hammock in which he sleeps. He is in good physical shape, and his senses are keen (he recognizes Tiger's footsteps sneaking up to the shack). He takes life as it comes and takes his chances every day on the subway. He's a three-time loser, but it doesn't faze him. He enjoys his life, even when the heat's on. He has style and humor and vitality. Technically, he is one of society's victims, but we do not regard him as a poor unfortunate. He lives the way he does because be likes it. It leaves him free and unsuffocated. He's a "skipper," with a light, easy way about him, and he's for real, the "real McCoy."

By living outside conventions, he has kept himself from becoming a machine. Being a small-time crook just interested in making a living has kept him human. Fuller seems to imply that although survival is mechanical, it is basic. Skip, Moe, and Candy are not criticized for trying to subsist, but they are shown, initially, as oblivious to any other reality but that. Under pressure, the film reveals that all three will move in a human direction—as opposed to everyone else, who all move in inhuman directions. Being marginal to the society, and any of its respectable forms of success, they can

Pickup on South Street. Skip enters the film, doing a day's work. The sassy back belongs to Candy, watched by camouflaged FBI men.

still care. Fuller's affection for his trio of underworld eccentrics is obvious. (His cops and Feds are either colorless, distasteful, or mocked, and his Communists are loathsome villains.)

Because they can respond to each other as human beings, Moe, Candy, and Skip are the only ones who can get anything done. Fuller focuses on them, presumably, because the straight society is not worth looking at. It is not human; it is not capable of taking meaningful action. The position on outsiders has shifted. They used to be, by definition, bad—murderers, pillagers, and so on—or bad/good—people with theoretically valid but unreasonable demands. In *Pickup on South Street*, and in many fifties films, the outsider is seen as the only hope for good and for change. We identify with those who are illegitimate because legitimacy has become a rationalization for one or another kind of dehumanization.

Fuller is not against communism as such, but against "isms" in general. Moe dies, and Candy almost dies, not because they hate communists but because they love, and are loyal to, Skip, an individual human being, one very pointedly disconnected from his own society (which is threatened by communism). Throughout the film Skip ridicules abstract concepts of politics and patriotism, and one expects that by the end he'll see the light. It seems that Skip and Candy, however, couldn't care less about having helped the fight against communism, and Fuller implies that's all right. In the political climate of 1953 it is surely no accident that a Communist plot is nipped in the bud. Americans feared communism. But it is not Tiger nor the FBI men who will protect us from Communists. It is the outsiders, whose resistance to communism is made possible by their belated emotional loyalty toward each other, who get the job done. It is only they who have any humanity left to assert and it is that hu-

Focus on

Feeling

187

manity that puts a stop to both communism and the destructive, selfish pattern of their own lives, a pattern created by their society. Fuller uses communism as the catalyst that will summon forth what remains of human feeling and the instinct for freedom, but he implies that it can no longer be located within the legitimate and that it is buried deep even within the illegitimate. When one stops being human it doesn't matter where it is or what it's called. That communism, and what in the paranoid imagination it stands for, presents a serious threat at all is a sign that America's defenses are none too secure. And it is not our lack of an opposing political philosophy but our lack of human values in the life we lead that leaves us poorly defended.

Fuller's position on communism is best illustrated through Moe (Thelma Ritter). Moe's anticommunism (like Skip's and Candy's) is underlined as ignorant. She doesn't know anything about Communists, only that she doesn't like them. Her instinct senses the kind of person Joey is, or has become. Undaunted by his threats, she tells him, "You pant like a dog." Her response might be read as symptomatic of the period's uneducated paranoia, but I think Fuller stresses, rather, the sureness of her instincts, her gut awareness. Moe is a figure much like Charleston in *The Killers*, a victim at the slow ravages of underworld hardship and scraping by. But where Charleston drifts away, useless (as befits the vision of *The Killers*) Moe is given a moral role to play, one that affects the outcome of the film. Fuller shocks you by having her murdered—funny, sweet old ladies usually don't get their heads blown off—but her loyalty to Skip is the turning point in Skip and Candy's relationship. She speaks her piece, implants her choric wisdom, and gets killed. Her death allows the emotional communion of Skip and Candy, now "motherless" orphans with no one to turn to but each other. (When Skip returns after burying Moe, Candy is lying in his hammock.)

Moe sells "ties," obvious symbols of human connectedness. The FBI man, Zara, buys one to humor her. When we see him later in the film, he is back to his own conservative preference. Skip knows Moe has sold him out when he searches Candy's purse and sees the tie, but he tries it on, even as he mutters "crummy tie." When he throws Candy out, he hurls the tie after her, but—and for thematic reasons only—Candy keeps it, shoving it into her purse. The symbol of Moe's business reminds us of what her business is—holding the world together.[2] What she knows about Communists is that they threaten the unity of man and man, and when she confronts Joey, she feels the reality of it. (Much is made of Joey's automatic recourse to his gun—he shoots both women. Skip, in contrast, says that he's never held a gun in his life.) On the other hand, if it is a waste of time even to try selling Joey a tie, she can still hardly give them away to her normal clientele and dies amid their dangling disorder.

When Joey threatens to blow her head off, Moe says, "You'd be doing me a big favor." She dies assuming she will be given a pauper's burial in potter's field — after a life that, as far as she knows, has added up to nothing. Skip is a three-time loser. Candy is a "half-assed hooker" (Fuller's phrase). Tiger and Skip are engaged in a stupid, meaningless rivalry, a mechanical opposition. All are driven by self-seeking obsessions within a knee-deep corruption. They are a conniving, mercenary lot, imprisoned by roles that mask their feelings. Fuller understands

Pickup on South Street. Consulting her price book, Moe explains the realities of inflation (fifty dollars for a "cannon"). Tiger feels the pinch.

that they are forced to be that way to survive, but he sees it as a dead-end situation. The human cost of living with nothing but survival in mind is too great. "Gotta eat" is not enough. The cat returning to the garbage has "gotta eat" too. It is a reductive image, and the "gotta eat" theme is surely parodied in the scene with Candy and Lightning Louie.[3] It is hard to reconcile *Pickup on South Street* with views of Fuller as an apologist for the American way of life. Fuller may believe in America's potential, but in giving us its facts, he has been one of its most consistently severe critics.[4]

Everybody sells each other out. Moe sells information to Tiger, and Tiger's professional ethics are bent to keep a kitty for her services. Lightning Louie sells Moe to Candy, Moe sells Skip to Candy, Candy is seduced by Joey's four hundred dollars into going back to get the microfilm from Skip (Fuller brings her from shadow to light, exposing her venality). Skip is playing everybody for his big score. Given what the world is, the behavior of Fuller's people is logical — the Communists are merely at a vile extreme. We see the characters initially in their worst light. They tend to accept the lowest versions of each other, a philosophically "safe" position. A bizarre coincidence, however, unpredictably criss-crosses individual fates, creating new possibilities the characters resist but finally give in to. Fuller achieves, by the end, a powerful sense of release, his characters at last liberated from their walled-in, self-serving states. If Skip and Candy remain socially rootless, they have come at least to trust their passions and feelings, and Moe has gotten the decent burial due her. That Skip finally trusts in Candy and can love, is, however, an individual and not a communal triumph. The world goes on as before. The Communist business and what happens to the microfilm are left loose-ended, as though they were inconsequential. Tiger tries for a fourth conviction, fails, and is again the butt of Skip's smirks and sneers (although Skip's attitude, now that his life does not solely take shape around his antagonism with Tiger, is less belligerent). There is no reconciliation, no handshake, no speech about the horrors of treason, no cushy future on the horizon. Skip is a brilliant pickpocket and presumably returns to his trade, only now, with Candy, he will be less bitter and lonely. If Skip's status remains the same, Candy's theoretically sinks. She moves from Joey, who on the surface is a respectable, decent-looking, reasonably successful young man, down to Skip. But Joey was a facade that kept *her* a facade. When she breaks through it, she becomes emotionally free.

By placing his story in the seedier locales of the urban jungle and by choosing a grubby set of characters from the rubbish heap of humanity, Fuller grinds our noses in some of our self-created dirt and tests our humanism. His antiestablishment, antibourgeois outcasts elicit his sympathy, and he seems to know them and their milieu from the inside. His old lady informer, his pickpocket, and his whore are fully developed characters (ordinarily, these types would be allowed minor roles). Fuller's detailing is not just psychological. Underworld paraphernalia, speech habits, and body language are carefully delineated. The characters' workaday lingo, gestures, and movements are observed (and performed) with notable relish and become, in an odd way, "educationally" absorbing. Fuller's unusual attention to these matters makes his characters extravivid among surrounding stereotypes—visually gangsterish Communists and dullish law enforcers doing their knee-jerk response to subversive microfilm. Both sides have a similar disregard for human values and for the human beings who have accidentally become entangled in their political skullduggeries. Skip mistakes Tiger's cops as holdup men, and Candy mistakes Zara for a Communist tail. Zara and Tiger willingly use Candy as a guinea pig. They stare her down like villains, the tightly framed point-of-view shot from below emphasizing the grossness of their heads. Candy has no choice but to agree to be their pawn, and she almost gets killed while they lose Joey. Fuller's cut from the police commissioner's "I want an arrest when he passes that film" to Candy, bruised and battered in the hospital, underlines the law's unconcern. Without Moe, Candy, and Skip, the cops would have gotten nowhere, but they don't count as human beings. Skip's cynicism may be personally damaging to his human potential, but he is right in assuming that there is nothing in it for him to abandon his ways. Appropriately, he is not rewarded and shows no sign of reforming.

America is turned over on its ear, and so is Skip. He is an exceptional man, a great pickpocket with hands like an artist's. (When Candy asks Skip how he became a pickpocket, Skip retorts angrily and defensively, "Things happen.") He is proud of his talent; it gives him self-respect. He is always trimly dressed, like a proper businessman, and he talks about his arrests as the "red side of the ledger." His assessment of his own skills borders on conceit, but he makes good his boasts by lifting a large handgun off the unsuspecting Joey with virtuoso technique.

Fuller likes Skip too much to leave him where he began. All his valuable qualities—his external crookedness—must stay intact, but his internal kinks have to be straightened out. Skip can stay a pickpocket as long as he changes as a man. To live as he has done is to accept the world's terms, to exist automatically. Without an allegiance to something other than himself he cannot be a hero worth taking seriously or worth making a film about. Skip must discover his own identity, work through his alienation, and make himself whole. The road to self-discovery is hard, but in the fifties it is a moral imperative. The old gangster had to die. If he learned anything, it was always too late, since his affliction either ran too deep or the damage he had wrought upon others was too extensive and/or permanent. The gangster can no longer be grandly conceived as an epitome, and the battle between himself and society has been leveled out along with everything else. His inflexibility is now of the same kind as the society's. Skip is typical of the scaled-down fifties hero who, being mostly at war with himself, does not have to be destroyed by what is outside himself. His violence is a process of transformation and leads to action symbolic of the potential for change.

The message of the genre in the fifties is that human priorities can be rearranged only through violence. Fuller doesn't just use violence; he believes in it. His partiality stems partly from his background (crime reporter, war experience), partly from his showmanship in a media ideally suited to depicting violence,[5] and partly from a conviction that violence is (a) a curative agent for internal conflict and frustration, (b) a primitive but effective and honest means of communication, and (c) a moral necessity under certain circumstances. Fuller's heroes are often brought to a point of murderous, righteous rage, and their adversaries are pummeled to a state as close to death as possible. We are not shown what is left of Joey after Skip gets through with him, but it is assumed that Skip stops short of murder. Skip, fighting in revenge of Moe, and

Pickup on South Street. Fuller's idea of a tender love scene: Skip and Candy in a look-each-other-over moment that promises, if the emphatic tilt is any indication, that violence will soon commence, until this brutal downtown docks version of "Gettin' t'know ya" runs its course. As they take turns coming out of the clinches, Fuller tacks on some incomparably sleazy dialogue. They whisper, so listen closely. (Museum of Modern Art)

for Candy, finds a useful outlet for his own frustrations. His human instinct, long repressed, explodes into unrefined, unreasonable violence. His anger, like his professional skills, must serve as a means to his personal liberation.

Fuller's love scenes are as brutal as most other directors' action scenes. He is a master of broad vulgar effects—Skip smiling upon discovering that he has just punched a woman in the jaw and pouring beer into Candy's eyes, Candy's bruised face in close-up as Skip mashes his mouth on hers while gently stroking her discolored face with his delicate fingers—but there is a "truth" to his male-female encounters. Skip and Candy's erotic feelings are resuscitated by violence—one can't remain too blasé about a woman one has just beat up. (Candy later knocks Skip out with a beer bottle—for his own good—but it's nice to see her get her licks in.) The now-a-punch, now-a-caress seesawing expresses the characters' emotional confusion about the risks of love. They exhibit the need to feel, and the fear of feeling. If loving is dangerous, Fuller makes it explicitly so. Both Skip and Candy are attracted by the wounded quality that they sense in each other and by their surface baseness. Skip is excited by the bruises he inflicts and by what he knows are her lies and corruption. Candy is taken by surprise by his violence and submits. The characters' vacillations keep the audience wondering whether the feeling they display is fake or genuine. The characters themselves don't seem to know, but pushed together and not having the time for a drawn-out, trial-and-error courtship, they can't decide whether to succumb to or resist their emotional and physical needs. They get to know each other fast and quickly exhaust the hypocrisy that lovers might otherwise slowly accumulate. Skip kicks her away, but his fury indicates a level of temptation that seriously interferes with his mercenary goals. At last, there's nothing left to hide and no cause to playact; Skip's courage and Candy's loyalty can unite. The violence of their relationship has burned away pretense and guile. Under hard confrontation, the true nature of each bursts free from its protective shell.

Fuller's belief in the efficacy of violence carries over to his style the most audaciously blatant of its period. The outrageous dialogue alone ("Look for oil and you hit a gusher") suggests that Fuller's treatment is not realistic. Fuller is not given to verbal subtleties; "literary" critics scorn him. But Fuller is not an intellectual, and there is no reason why his dialogue should sound like Oscar Wilde's or Edward Albee's, or even Joe Mankiewicz's. Fuller's dialogue must be judged as succeeding or failing within his very idiosyncratic movies, which do not resemble the slick, smooth, studio craftsmanship of "prestige" Hollywood or the art cinema. Fuller's movies are awkward, clumsy, vulgar, low-budget affairs, usually populated by wooden, second-string actors and actresses. Fuller's vision of the flawed hero/heroine in a flawed America, however, seems to have deter-

Pickup on South Street. Skip prepares to lift Joey's gun. What may pass as Fuller's wit is the sign on the subway doors that comments on the action.

mined his overall style, including his yeasty way with dialogue. (Fuller's films make you fight through their problems; what's "wrong" with them is part of their effect. *Pickup on South Street* is one of his more polished films, but with many of the others questions such as what if he had had more money or what if he had had a more gifted cast or a better script inevitably arise only to be answered by the films themselves. The film we may have wanted out of habit would have been a lesser, or certainly a less interesting, film.)

The comic-strip expressionism of the dialogue extends to the visual compositions. Skip and Candy's exchanges are bordered by a hook and chair on the left and a thick, rough rope on the right. As they kiss, the camera pans left so that the hook splits the frame down the middle, "separating" the characters at the moment they "join," creating an aura of violence and visualizing the tensions between them (*Park Row* uses a similar device). Fuller gets close to his characters but remains observant, free to comment. Fuller's movies have an expressive, nonnaturalistic edge; nothing is contingent, everything essential. He will go to any lengths to increase dramatic impact, to charge his mise-en-scéne with meaning. At the hospital, Candy is shown lying in a bed pushed against the wall. The next shot is from behind her head. This is literally impossible, but Fuller wants to shoot Skip's face divided by the bars of the headboard. He pans slowly, so the bars can cross his face as Candy explains how she got beat up. Skip is still out for the money and doesn't trust her. When he finally realizes that Candy suffered in protecting him, Fuller shoots from the same position, but Skip's face is now clear of the bars. It is an obvious metaphor, but it works. The whole sequence suggests a carefree attitude toward verisimilitude.

Fuller will mix long takes with rapid cutting, static with moving camera in

Focus on

Feeling

193

surprising ways. No one, except possibly Ingmar Bergman, has used the close-up so fearlessly. The wordless opening, with its series of quick, detached close-ups in the crowded space of a subway car, is cinematically free in a way few commercial features of the period are. Fuller is not noted for his restraint, but the pacing of this scene has to be just right to work, and it is.[6] The spacious, high-angle long shot of Candy that follows is an effective, disorientating contrast. Fuller then switches to a low-angle shot that shows Candy approaching the camera from a distance. When she searches her pocketbook, Fuller dollies in to an extreme close-up and then out to follow Candy's movement into a phone booth, without a cut. The high, almost perpendicular shot of Tiger watching Skip get out of the car from his office window expresses Tiger's power over Skip, who seems pinned to the ground. At the Communist hideout, after Candy's soliloquy, Fuller cuts from Candy to Joey, then to the other members, in rapid succession. The long take of Candy honors her as a complete character, one of integrity. The quick cuts, going from close-up to extreme close-up (Fuller could have just as easily panned around the room for a reaction shot), imply the disunity of the group. Each person is disconnected, and a threat to the other.

Fuller may be flamboyant, but his decisions within tight shooting schedules are invariably sound, and many of his scenes and shots are as carefully thought out as those of the most intellectual directors. The long take of Moe, Tiger, and Zara is a model of how to get by a talky scene. The camera, kept moving, eases the dialogue, takes some burden off the actors, and maintains the momentum of the opening scenes. During the murder of Moe, the camera's restlessness increases the tension; it stalks the characters, seems right on top of them, and, to some extent, distracts from the horror of the act. The camera sometimes anticipates the characters, moving before they do, its unexpected prerogative signaling implicit and often impending violence. Fuller's greatest moment, though, is with the fixed-camera long shot of Skip picking up Moe's coffin from the barge headed for potter's field. The stationary camera traps the viewer into accepting the macabre and solemn event. We have to wait out the transfer. Moe's coffin is at the bottom; others must be lifted off to get at hers. We watch it lifted from one boat to the other, accompanied by some of Fuller's best dialogue. "What are you going to do with him?" "I'm going to bury her." (The insistence on gender reminds us of Moe's death scene. Moe propped up in bed against her pillow, surrounded by a litter of male ties.) A close-up of Skip (to show his feeling) would have destroyed the eeriness of the scene. Fuller lets the camera roll and keeps us at a distance, watching the action unfold, the mood build, a black, sad mood, its grim humor overwhelmed by a kind of dignity. The dark waters slosh around, the men do what they have to, Skip what he has to, and the sight of Moe's coffin brings everything about her back into the film. (We recall Moe's "bye, Skip," and Skip's refusal to even turn around for what would be his last look at her.) Fuller gazes at it from afar, steadily and soberly, as though it were an important rite he has no business disturbing.

We never see Skip bury Moe. This is Moe's funeral, and there is no funeral scene in film more brilliant, more original, more intensely felt. Prior to the fifties, neither the genre's tough norms nor its separately boxed sentimentality permitted so rich a demonstration of feeling (and had it done so, it would not have mattered to anyone as much as Moe's death matters to Skip). The fifties crime film is marked by many scenes in which the loss of a human life is keenly felt in dealing with the problem of living life more humanly and basically; the genre could not continue an emphasis on the cheapness of human life characteristic of *noir* despair and cynicism or the rat-tat-tatting mayhem of the early period. And as Fuller does in *Pickup on South Street*, it restores to death a primal importance that the march of civilization has rendered commonplace and a passionate coloration it has anesthetized.

CREDITS *Pickup on South Street*

(Twentieth Century–Fox, 1953, 80 min.)

Producer	Jules Schermer	Cast	Richard Widmark (Skip McCoy)
Director	Samuel Fuller		Jean Peters (Candy)
Screenplay	Samuel Fuller (from a story		Thelma Ritter (Moe Williams)
	by Dwight Taylor)		Murvyn Vye (Tiger)
Photography	Joe MacDonald		Richard Kiley (Joey)
Editor	Nick De Maggio		Willis B. Bouchey (Zara)
Art Directors	Lyle Wheeler and		Victor Perry (Lightning Louie)
	George Patrick		Milburn Stone (Winoki)
Music	Leigh Harline		Henry Slate (MacGregor)

99 River Street (1953), The Phenix City Story (1955), The Brothers Rico (1957)

In a decade of hard, ugly crime films, no director made harder, uglier, less visually ingratiating ones than Phil Karlson. The fifties' sternest moralist, his films lack the fun and romantic rebelliousness of Fuller's and the brisk, chilly agitation of Don Siegel's. A plain, seemingly graceless stylist, his rather unpalatable movies, full of rabid, sloggingly orchestrated physical pain and psychic damage, picture crime as a monstrous, miasmal evil, divesting it of any glamour it ever had. He is the key figure of fifties violence, specializing in foreground placement of smashed, bloody faces. Karlson's movies are grueling, disenchanted journeys through suffering, and their violence is disturbingly infectious, since the necessity for counterviolence is always forthcoming. His heroes stagger dully about as life's punching bags, until they can't take it anymore and go haywire, strike out in a reasonless frenzy. Karlson and Fuller share a nightmare vision of the American status quo and a desperate hope that it can be purged of its evil. Fuller wants to rid America of its bourgeois hypocrisy and ideological divisiveness. Karlson wants it made safe for a normal, decent life. His stress is almost always (deceptively) local—the family, the community, the town, the individual. Fuller is much the more flexible of the two, can roll with the punches and crack a smile. For Karlson, criminals are the lowest scum on earth, and crime must be thoroughly destroyed. His hatred runs deep, and his cheap, sleazy, action movies are dead-serious assaults upon the audience's automatic receptivity to screen "entertainment."

In this section I will deal briefly with what I consider to be Karlson's three best works in the fifties. All three illustrate the repositioning of the genre's conflicts that is typical of the fifties and, in sequence, form a triptych of progressive horror and hopelessness.

In the first, 99 *River Street* (1953), the emphasis is on individual infection. The hero's melodramatic race against time is one we are pretty certain he will win. The film is dark—not a single scene in daylight—but the hero's journey is of the archetypal Aeneas-through-the-underworld-for-his-own-and-everybody's-good kind. There's light at the end of the tunnel. The action is emotionally charged, and the film has a hothouse eroticism. In *The Phenix City Story* (1955) a whole community is diseased, and the hero cannot prevent the loss of significant lives. His race against time is nearly lost, and the community nearly sinks away in a bog of corruption and apathy. Its visual look vacillates between capturing, openly and candidly, the depressingly banal ugliness of a real, medium-sized American city and a dramatic deployment of a thick, stark, *noir* night world. *The Brothers Rico* (1957) shows that all is lost. The hero acts, but clearly far too late. The infection has spread to national proportions. The film has a fresh, clean, spacious, well-scrubbed look; the camera is reserved and distant. We have emerged from the tunnel into a radiant facade of vast geographical extent. The film culminates in a dark, cramped candy store on New York's Mulberry Street, but its convictions about what the world is really like lie elsewhere.

99 River Street. Ernie Driscoll, a not-so-young man full of rage, checks the impulse to clobber Linda James, his momentary deceiver. Dynamic confrontations at close-up range establish a valid stylistics for low-budget filmmaking.

99 River Street takes place in New York. Its hero, Ernie Driscoll, is an ex-prizefighter with a damaged eye. Barred from the ring, he drives a cab for a living. A heavy pall of lost hopes hangs over his marriage. The discovery of his wife's unfaithfulness throws him into a bitter rage, from which he is distracted by a plea of help from Linda James, an actress-in-distress who claims she has just killed a man. It turns out to be a trick —she has used Ernie to help her perform in an audition. He socks a few theater people and they put out a call for his arrest as a publicity prank. The actress, contrite, seeks him out. Together, they find his wife's dead body stashed in his cab, placed there by her lover, Victor Rawlins, who has killed her and wishes to frame Driscoll. After working his way through some hostile entanglements with Rawlins's underworld acquaintances, Driscoll, with Linda's help, tracks Rawlins down before he is able to escape the country and beats him to a pulp. He and Linda marry and look forward to successfully managing a gas station.

The film is about so many things that it is difficult to decide which is uppermost. Its general theme is that one must accept one's limits. Its general method is a narrative that keeps clotting with betrayals and deceptions that the viewer, too, is victimized by. Its central metaphor is Driscoll's bad eye which looks and looks but does not see. Its bias is that sophistication is deadly, that one must descend to the primitive.

99 River Street opens with a hard-slugging boxing match. We watch the action aware of the obscene disproportion between the announcer's relish and the bloody images. Soon, a voice-over tells us that we are watching one of the "Great Fights of Yesterday." A slow-motion replay takes us by surprise. We are told that the challenger for the title, Ernie Driscoll (John Payne), has "never been knocked off his feet" and that his eye is so badly cut he can't see. He is "fighting on instinct alone." The camera pulls back to reveal we have been watching TV. It pulls back further to show us, from behind, the head of a man. He has a scar over an eye, which twitches involuntarily. He watches the screen

Focus on

Feeling

intently, almost not hearing a voice that reminds him of his dinner. It is Ernie Driscoll, watching his own self getting destroyed; he is fascinated, mesmerized. The camera reverses after a female hand clicks the TV off, and we are shown the full setting from behind the TV—Mr. and Mrs. Driscoll's apartment, dinner waiting on the table.

Ernie's obsession with his past seals him off from his reality. The visual confusion perpetrated on the viewer is the truth about Ernie's life. He could have been the champ; that he never made it haunts him. He thinks of himself as that person he can never again be. His wife Pauline (Peggie Castle) works in a florist shop and has a similar syndrome. In her mind, she married a "pug" instead of going on in show business. She says to Ernie, "I could have been a star." Ernie reminds her that she was "just a show girl." They are separated from each other by their fantasies. Ernie would like to patch up their marriage, but the opening sequence tells us he is too psychologically crippled to do so. It is too late anyway, since his wife, as we soon learn, has transferred her emotions to someone else—a slick, erotically persuasive thief. She has helped him steal some jewelry and plans to flee with him to France as soon as the stones are fenced. He kills her.

99 River Street is a film full of "I could have beens" and "ifs." Ernie and Pauline aren't young kids, yet they still believe that the big chance is there for them to grab. The present is a quagmire; all possibility lies in the past. Life is pervaded by myths. Ernie insists on believing in his marriage when it is evidently dead; Pauline, prodded by her past dreams, thinks she can run away. Victor Rawlins (Brad Dexter) thinks he can escape to France. Linda James (Evelyn Keyes) thinks she can be a great actress. The disease that goes by the name of the American dream infects all the characters. As Ernie tells Linda: "A chance at the top is the most impossible thing in the world." This is a fantasy the film destroys and then rebuilds in altered form. The film gives Linda and Ernie a new life only when they recognize that their fantasies are impossible. The future is closed only to big dreamers. Dreaming big dreams is what has closed it off so fast.

The gangster/crime genre documents America as a failure. The experience of failure, as reflected in the progression of his films, is cumulative. *99 River Street* gives us an America that has worsened in time. Its myths are used up. The frontier is closed; there is no space left. America is prematurely middle-aged and must face its middle-aged problems. The two people who try to escape it, Victor and Pauline, cannot. There is nowhere for them to go. They can't go West, so choose to head for France, the old world. This is, of course, a desperate backtracking, a return to the seat of the corruption. But it was only a delusion anyway that we were ever free of the corruption from which we sprang. Victor makes a great effort to board a ship that's in dry dock. There is no way of escaping the corner we have backed ourselves into. Ernie battles Victor on a plank that connects the ship to the land, high above the ground. The extreme long shot is a symbolic tableau. We're stuck in the middle of the bridges we have built. The fight is never finished; the police drag Ernie away and calm him down, and we are kept at a distance that implies the futility of it all. There future has no room for high expectations. Ernie and Linda's talents and ambitions are put under the pressure of real situations that they cannot adequately handle. An immense effort of will barely earns them enough time, and the intensity of the effort burns their unreasonable dreams away.

In *Pickup on South Street*, Richard Widmark's Skip McCoy has a lot of brash charm and exhibits more than a trace of the appealing hyperactivity of the thirties gangster. In *99 River Street*, John Payne plays his glum, drab dupe with a rigid sorrow and despair. He is a powder keg of tensions that he can't release. Ernie Driscoll's life is pure hell, and there is no legitimate way he can break out of it. His wife tells Victor that he "broods about things" and is dangerous because "suddenly he explodes." Ernie is vaguely aware of his dilemma. When his wife leaves him, he tries to be a fighter again. "I gotta hit," he says. He takes a long look into a mirror, trying to decide who he is and chooses to go back into the ring. He's got murder in him. He even roughs up his friend Stan (Frank Faylen), the film's voice of reason. Stan keeps advising him to take it easy, but that's easier said than done. When life punishes you, you want to punish it back. Ernie Driscoll has to learn to be reasonable the hard way, by a purgation of his anger and pride; he has to learn through his gut and not his head. The bland, settled Stan can't do him any good. He's got to beat his way to a peace of mind, and the violence he both inflicts and receives is a form of self-therapy, the stinging pain that it is necessary for him to feel at the death of his old self. As is common in the fifties, it is the woman Linda's loyalty that is instrumental in his change.

Linda's problems are analogous She thinks she is a great actress, but both of her "performances" in the film tell us she is not. The first, in which she fools Ernie, and the audience, into thinking she has killed a man, is by far the more complex. Karlson plays on all the shifting relations among theater, life, and film. We have a sense that Evelyn Keyes, the real actress of the film, does remarkably well, but we are not quite sure by the end what "remarkably well" even means. Linda is using Ernie as a prop in her audition, but we (and Ernie) don't know this. We know she is an actress, but we think she is being real. Yet Karlson stresses the *threatricality* of her response, which is fine in the theater but extremely mannered in the cinema. Karlson follows her movements in a very long take and in medium close-up. It is a grotesque tour de force, strained, exaggerated, brutally revealing. But whose tour de force is it—Evelyn Keyes's

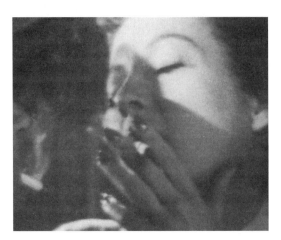

99 River Street. In an unsparingly sleazy sequence, Linda "acts" the sexpot for Vic, to no avail. *Noir* refinement has given way to aggressively direct, bare visuals that Karlson invests with rare intensity and thematic resonance.

or Linda James's? The transposition of theatrical skills onto the movie screen, where they seem glaringly inappropriate, makes us feel there is something wrong. Yet Linda James is an actress, and it is possible, maybe even likely, that she would maintain a role even under such circumstances, as a way of dealing with her fear. Ernie believes her and so do we, but not because we are really convinced. When Karlson reveals it as a hoax, we are startled, but also understand why we were "bothered" by the performance. It really wasn't very good—or, however acceptably it might have worked on a stage (like the one it is on), it was deafeningly unsubtle for the screen. When Linda drops back into being Linda, she naturally becomes "realer" than ever—at that point in the film, an obnoxious opportunist. The point isn't simply that she is not a great actress but that in trying to be one she treats people badly. Later in the film, she gives a performance in a real situation, when her life and Ernie's are on the line. In a waterfront bar, she tries to seduce the killer, Victor Rawlins, by coming on as the sexiest broad of all time. It is a lousy performance, and Victor doesn't bite. She finally drops the act and names Pauline, and that rattles him. All her acting gets her nowhere; it is the touch of reality that reaches him. When Ernie's vision blurs during the fight with Victor, it is clear that he can never be the champ he wants to be. Similarly, Linda's failure with Victor in a situation that is a matter of life and death, suggests that *her* talent is more limited than she has thought. The American myth of success dies hard but die it must if the society is to become less self-destructive and more mindful of the nature of reality.

The themes of *99 River Street* are distinctly interrelated with its visual strategies. The deceptions of Linda's first performance, and of the boxing match that seems real, are perceived as realities before they are exposed as shams. They are the realities of characters who cannot see reality as it is. That the audience is tricked as well suggests that these characters' flaws are not unusual; reality has become difficult to perceive. It is as though we are watching the world through Ernie Driscoll's shattered optic nerve. No character in the film has an adequate knowledge of reality, and they often share with the viewer the problem of seeing things clearly. It is impossible to distinguish reality from facade because their merging has become the basis upon which life is lived. Christopher (Jay Adler) wears glasses. When Victor comes to demand the money, Christopher behaves as though Victor's threats are not a reality that could affect him.[7] Victor raps his face, knocking his glasses off, after which Christopher sees he must comply. Mickey (Jack Lambert) has a nervous habit of putting his glasses on and taking them off, a means of changing his own reality as well as seeing things literally, but he mistakes who Driscoll is and is prevented from double-crossing Christopher. He beats Driscoll up for no reason. When Driscoll starts beating *him* up and asking questions, he

99 River Street. Visual deglamorization of violence. A battered head, thrust brutally at the viewer, occupies a large portion of the frame. From the angle of the shot, the audience anticipates more blows to come its way.

responds with a look of disbelief. The brutality of both question-and-answer sessions is of the classic "I'll make ya talk" kind, except that neither character knows what is going on or why he is being asked questions that are apparently absurd. The old situation is given a new twist by a reality that fails to correspond to one's assumptions about it.

Christopher runs a pet store as a front to his fencing racket, but it is not an old-style front—mask and reality, black and white. His legitimate and illegitimate work are visually integrated. Trophies and awards decorate the walls of his back room. When we first enter it, Mickey is there, in white uniform, grooming a dog. Christopher is busy out front nursing a pup. He is a character who seems remote from his own evil. Karlson must have liked the irony of Christopher nursing a puppy. He uses this unexpected image to convey his violence. As the nipple is forced into the squealing pup's mouth we feel the vast extensiveness of violence in the world of the film. Nothing is free from it. What should be handled tenderly is brutalized.

The novelties of 99 *River Street* cannot be understood except as part of a general context of the questioning of reality common to its period. The film can no longer assume that there is a static reality out there to be recorded. The difficulties the characters experience come from a loss of instinct that renders all perception of reality uncertain. Ernie's confused groping is paradigmatic. It is the older figures only who feel certain about anything—and their knowledge is either mistaken or useless. Stan shakes his head after Ernie departs. Pop, the fight manager (Eddy Waller), shakes his head after Ernie leaves the gym.

Focus on Feeling

Christopher shakes his head after Victor's departure, implying both that Victor's a hopelessly ignorant punk to think he can outsmart him and that he doesn't have the brains to stay away from women.[8] He knows certain things for sure.

Accompanying the insecurity is a view of the past as a golden age—an age of faith, hope, trust, decency, and a shared sense of reality. Ernie recollects Pauline's beauty and her happy laughter. He tells Linda, "When I was a kid, I thought I'd grow up and meet a girl who would stick in my corner no matter what. Then I grew up. Things aren't the way you think they're gonna be when you're a kid." Pop warns Ernie that what the new managers think of is 33 ⅓ percent of the cut, and that's all; they won't even bother to wash the resin out of his eyes. But there is no turning back the clock, and future hopes cannot merely be a reprise of past ones. The world has changed, and since the nature of reality can only be known by what men picture it as being, we can see how and in what ways it has changed by the evidence on the screen. Even as it points to a happy future, the film does not depart from its premise that the nature of things is difficult to perceive. It simply alters its tone toward the comic. The presentation of the images continues in the same vein. We see a boxer's gloved hands in practice and we think "Ernie," remembering that he had decided to start boxing again. We know it can't be, since that would go against the meaning of the film, but the image tells us nothing. The camera moves to show us Pop and Ernie watching the boxer. Now we know. Ernie mentions his new business and a partner. The camera moves to show us Stan, talking very businesslike. We think, "Him? But where's Linda?" The camera pans slightly to the right to show us Linda talking with Stan and make clear that she, after all, is the partner—as we had assumed until the image tricked us into momentarily thinking otherwise.

The genre has obviously shifted its assumptions and content over a period of twenty-five years, but its basic purpose and structure are still intact. Ernie Driscoll has to be separated from and put in opposition to his society, and the kind of individual assertion he makes carries those qualities that are in conflict with the status quo. The gangster is not now the center of interest. He is an aspect of society that people get mixed up with and require violence to get clear of. The hero's violence against the gangster resembles the old gangster's violence against the society, but there are new distinctions made about violence in the fifties and 99 *River Street* is not content to leave them implicit, as most films of the period do.

The problem of seeing clearly is connected to the problem of feeling clearly. The script makes explicit at the beginning and at the end that "there's something critical the matter with Driscoll's eye" and that he is "fighting on instinct alone—yes—on instinct alone." Violence based on instinct is good; it represents a basic will to live, to be human. Violence that is mechanical, impersonal, cerebral, staged—Christopher's, Mickey's, Victor's, the violence of the theater and of the boxing ring—is bad. It cannot be fought on its own terms, but with guts and feeling. The fifties hero, most often, uses his fists and hands. There is only one shot fired in the film that hits its mark—Victor shoots Driscoll, but it doesn't stop him. Victor kills Pauline with her scarf, in a pervertedly erotic manner. Ernie bangs out a future for himself with good old-fashioned knuckle power. Since the police are associated with the rest of the society, and are in fact chasing after an innocent man—the only one who can enact a true justice—they are pictured as irrelevant when they are not in fact unpleasantly obstructive. They have no knowledge of what has occurred, and proceed mechanically. At the end, they show up in a swarm when everything's over. In *The Phenix City Story* they are dangerous.

In June of 1954, Albert A. Patterson, the Democratic candidate for attorney general of Alabama, was shot dead outside his law office. It looked likely that he would be elected, and his ambition once in office was to prosecute the syndicate that controlled the vice industry in Phenix City and put an end to a notorious corruption that had lasted over a hundred years. *The Phenix City Story* (1955) is a generic dramatization of the actual events leading up to Patterson's murder and the subsequent calling out of the National Guard. Like many cold war films, it exacerbates some horrible actuality to a state of generalized paranoia. The point of the film is not to make us feel bad about vice in Phenix City but to warn us of our deadened sensibility.

The film's situation is a metaphor for the erosion of American values (read: human values) and our mechanical acquiescence to an enveloping and deep-rooted corruption. In an atmosphere of bland, accepting conformity, we cannot see the evil in our midst and how it is poisoning us. As Patterson (John McIntyre) himself says early in the film to vice lord Rhett Tanner (Edward Andrews), "I don't think at all. Don't want to. More relaxin'—and *safer*." He tells his son, just returned from Germany, not to get exercised over the state of things and that "we live a long way from Fourteenth Street." It is an attitude that leaves us unprepared to deal with criminal syndicates, delegations from outer space, and Communists. To ward off these dangers, an eternal vigilance is required. (The reporter, Ed Strickland, informs us that the syndicate still exists a year after the attempt to smash it and is trying to come back.) Unfortunately, however, we are a society of sleepwalkers. It takes the genre's mainstay, the outsider, to take things in hand. It is John Patterson (Richard Kiley), who comes back to America after living in Germany, who spearheads the movement against Tanner. Fighting Tanner, the police, the political machine, his apathetic community, and his own ideals and feelings, he is the center of the

Phenix City Story. Gothic version of election day in a southern town.

film's conflicts. Coming from the outside into an old struggle between established vice and powerless virtue, the currents of the situation jolt him with a fresh impact. The murder of his father makes him see what needs to be done. He finally unknots himself by acting out his emotions and tries to strangle Tanner.

The Phenix City Story is one of Karlson's most savage films. It has a raw, documentary atmosphere, all the more menacing for seeming authentic. Like all of his crime films, *The Phenix City Story* is a version of American Gothic, its use of sleazy natural locations and its string of petty, cowardly, ugly gangsters giving crime a narrowing and horrifying feel. Nothing is prettied up in this movie or caricatured. And there is no explicit commentary from Karlson. There is no need. The crime and corruption he shows are so repellent he is free to objectify himself, to blend his moral fervor completely with the material. As late as 1975, the film has university audiences cheering for the National Guard (unlikely, but true). It has no humor at all.

Karlson brings to his film an element of sordid horror. His environments are noisy, crowded, fetid. The sky over Phenix City is cold and dismal. The musical number at the Poppy Club is an antinumber, coarse, unprofessional, talentless. A dead child is thrown from a car onto a lawn. Voters, men and women, are beaten up at the polls and stagger into the street, dripping blood. The "heroine" gets killed, as does her pleasant young suitor. A crippled lawyer is shot in the mouth. One almost can't believe what is happening on the screen; the horror of it suffocates. We are not *shown* reality; we are assaulted by its dramatic re-creation. We are made to see by being made to feel. At last, when the tide begins to turn against the criminals, the viewer must face the horror of his own lust for retaliation. The film exposes us, our own capacities, much more than it does the "reality" of Phenix City. We are bombarded into an awareness of our own condition. The film doesn't just expose what people preferred to ignore; it exposes the fact that people were ignoring.

The Phenix City Story is a message to the American citizen. As one interviewee says, if you shine a light on a rat, "it will run for cover" (and it might run into city hall). This is not enough; one must beat the rats to death, and since they are always ready to come back, one must keep on beating them, ceaselessly. The movie makes you want to kill and robs you of the satisfaction. That it arouses the urge is a credit (discredit?) to its power. We, as viewers, have to be pulled back with the force that Zeke (James Edwards) uses to pull John back from strangling Tanner. Zeke's biblical remonstrances are well taken but frankly unwelcome. A true justice requires that Tanner die. The film allows us, like John Patterson, to live through a healthy anger as a form to vengeful release, despite our theoretical adherence to the laws of a democracy and our abhorrence to the shedding of blood. We must not kill, but to be made to want to kill should rouse a citizenry to take up a strong, if less dramatic, fight against crime or against its own numbness. The film is not cathartic. We leave concerned, angry, full of pent-up antagonism. Our frustrations are relieved only when John finally starts socking people around, unable to stick by his rational convictions. But he doesn't sock hard or long enough.

The Phenix City Story implies that without John Patterson's courage and eventual plunge into irrationality, conditions would have remained the same. The strong, extraordinary, honest men are few. The average American citizen is unkindly pictured. Good men turn away, morally lethargic; others are corrupt or indifferent. A parallel is made with Germany, from where John has just returned upon finishing his work prosecuting Nazi war criminals. Things were safer in Germany; the "war" here is more hellish. We are in the grip of a dictatorship of evil. John finds it hard to believe what he has come back to and finds the apathy even harder to understand. The police and the politicians are all bought off. The syndicate is, in effect, a mirror of the society. The *good* people say, "Let's get out of here, the cops are coming." John's father becomes the necessary sacrifice to the community. His martyrdom is garishly staged at night. Shot in the mouth, point-blank, he climbs out of his car and lugs himself down the street on his crutches. He staggers, but remains upright long enough to project a shocking image of destroyed integrity to the people slowly gathering. When he falls, it clinches our attitude for good, yanks us into the film with an appetite for action.

Karlson's confused heroes must batter their way out of their stagnant rationalism. John, like other Karlson heroes, is not only ordinary but rather hard to get behind because of his ambivalent position and the ease with which he takes certain notions for granted. He doesn't read the situation correctly, imagining that rational, democratic principles of law and justice can be applied. It is only when his father is killed and the rest of his family threatened that he realizes that conditions are too severe to be fought rationally and that he must let his true anger run its course. Karlson arranges his films to give his heroes a taste of humility, to make them confront their static assumptions and unrealistic shortsightedness (Eddie in *The Brothers Rico*, the Jeffrey Hunter character in *Key Witness*). They become as problematic as what they fight against. His characterizations are nonheroic and therefore nonassuring. The rage of his heroes is terrifying and forbidding but is preferable to self-delusion and ignorance. By giving way to it, they reach their humanity and cut a path for human goals. That their credibility and the credibility of what they accomplish, is discreetly suspect is the sign of an honest pessimism that refuses to be crowded out.

Much is made of the events being true. The film does exert a fascination from being based on fact. But the power of *The Phenix City Story* rests not on its "reality" but on its being a well-made fiction making imaginative use of the genre's structure and elements. The opening fifteen minutes of stilted "real life" interviews should make any viewer thankful for what follows (an hour and a half of *that* would be too depressing for words). The film moves into gear only when Karlson takes over, superimposing on the actual material a blatantly fictional style (its blatant movieness accentuated by the news interviews that precede it), coaxing convincing performances from his actors (however sincere, the real people of *Phenix City* are awfully dull), and beginning the rhythmic buildup with a climax in mind. Incidents are tied together like a closely wound spring and dramatic pressure is gradually increased. However timely and "true," *The Phenix City Story* is a triumph of craftsmanship, of artistry, of economy of means. Karlson gives us just what we need to know about what Phenix City looks and feels like, enough to understand how Fourteenth Street came to be and why it continues, and why it has to be destroyed —and he does it swiftly and vividly.

Despite the apparent victory of John Patterson, the film leaves us emotionally astir. There has been too much horror, too many innocents killed and wounded. Phenix City has a long way to go; the cleanup is a long-term proposition. The newsreel footage of the gambling machines being smashed and burned is gratifying to an extent but is visually a spectacle of destruction similar to what has preceded. The oppressive evil of Fourteenth Street lingers in the memory, and there are ominous hints that the corruption is controlled by people we never see on the screen and who remain unconvicted. Moreover, the film insists that we carry away with us a concern about our own personal and social realities, the facades of which need to be penetrated by the eye and annihilated by our feelings. The genre has assumed the task of awakening us to ourselves. *The Brothers Rico*, not surprisingly, is about a man who is completely out of touch with everything and the disasters that condition creates.

The dark, dank, claustrophobic world of *99 River Street* was humanized by pain, suffering, and feeling. Its black mazes were charged with heated action and ultraexpressive camera work. Its stylized, Gothic treatment of locales, its nocturnal frissons, made it heavy with atmosphere. Each scene boiled under exact, intense pressures. Where *99 River Street* sizzled on top, *The Brothers Rico* (1957) sizzles underneath, and the sound is almost inaudible. Its pressures are invisible, often unseen within the image. The score of 99 *River Street* was loud and obtrusive; the score of *The Brothers Rico* is minimal and unemphatic. The film presents its material with a mordant matter-of-factness. With calm and restraint, it lets the situation build to a *sickening* point, and we experience the horror of its clean, bright, ordered, undramatic world without being shown anything that is conventionally horrifying. The visual look of the film implies that the more evenly and fully you illuminate, without distorting, the world through light and shadow and unusual angles and compositions, the more horrible it becomes. It looks sane, pleasant, and healthy (unlike the world of 99 *River Street*), but its condition is now cancerous. *The Brothers Rico* is typical of the genre in the fifties in that while it works on an immediate level—the syndicate is evil and must be crushed—it embodies much larger concerns.

*T*he Brothers Rico is about Eddie Rico (Richard Conte), a former syndicate accountant who has been out of touch with the world of crime for three years and underestimates its heartlessness. The death of his two brothers, Johnny and Gino, finally provokes him to fight the organization led by Sid Kubik (Larry Gates), his uncle that he mistakenly trusts. He succeeds in killing Kubik, and the syndicate, with its head chopped off, will presumably breathe its last when the DA (never seen) starts prosecuting using Eddie's testimony. Karlson has in Richard Conte the perfect actor for the part—a family man who runs an honest, successful laundry business in Florida, a character with no obvious "hero" flair but who nonetheless looks like a gangster and promises, despite his well-mannered composure, to be successful when goaded into action. He and his wife Alice (Dianne Foster) in their ten-year marriage have been unable to have a child (two miscarriages), and his brothers' danger interferes with a long-awaited adoption procedure. The film implies that only when the syndicate has been smashed is there any hope for children and families, and the conclusion shows the adoption carried through. Eddie's lack of awareness contributes to both brothers' deaths—the price he pays for his obtuseness. Without their deaths, however, he would have not had the resolve to kill Kubik. Nonetheless, the terrible due exacted for his blindness, the character's helpless grief, and his belated vengeance, have a Euripidean pain and implacability.

Eddie Rico is a recognizable modern American man. He typifies the culture's middle-class norm. He represents a credible facsimile of our desires, wishes, attitudes, and capabilities. He is a respected man who has put a shady and economically insecure past behind him. His secretary "sirs" him, his wife obeys him (albeit with a sense of irony), he speaks and acts with authority. In the course of the film, this at first commanding figure loses all his conviction and is ruthlessly exposed.

The Brothers Rico. The childless Ricos, perhaps to compensate, are given an active sex interest in each other. The meticulous organization of this luxurious bathroom contrasts sharply with the living styles of all the other Ricos—less affluent but warm, soft, comfortably and comfortingly familiar, full of signs of the family's long history of special moments, icons of old-world piety (in the still above, it is all mob-money sheen, with high-end toiletries and plenty of space if you don't mind weaving about, despite the illusion of more space created by a giant mirror—all of which reflect Eddie's success, all bright and going somewhere in his intoxicating world of what "clean" laundry money can buy). (Museum of Modern Art)

The film opens with a shot of Eddie and his wife sleeping peacefully in bed. The light of dawn shines softly through an expensive picture window, illuminating their modern bedroom. The phone rings, waking Eddie, and he gets up to answer it. The syndicate wants him to hide a fugitive. His wife asks where his loyalty lies, precipitating a mild but, we are given to understand, long-established domestic conflict. The sequence continues through Eddie reassuring Alice that "nothing's going to happen," taking her amorously to bed —after which they both wake up chipper and less tense—the reading of a letter from Eddie's mother, and Eddie's morning preparations prior to leaving for work. Their relationship is warm, loving, sexual, but the atmosphere since the phone call is tense, and the commonplace conversation and activity (Eddie shaving, she playfully biting his back, he pulling her into the shower) have both a forced quality and an undercurrent of the ominous. Karlson establishes in this long (and odd) sequence an intimacy, what seriously threatens it, and Eddie's obliviousness to the danger. This quiet, slow opening, with its long, relaxed takes, is characteristic. *The Brothers Rico* bides its time. The pace of the movie is in keeping with the now-subdued nature of organized crime.

The film is divided into about ten long sequences, all of which involve Eddie (he is present in the frame at least 95 percent of the time). Brief linking shots and scenes provide transitions for Eddie to bring one established conflict to bear upon another. Toward the end, the sequences shorten, the editing accelerates the film's tempo (there is even a montage of Eddie eluding the organization's dragnet), and the film is suddenly over before we know it. This curious method is antithetical to the demands of action cinema, with its typically blunt exposition and careening, continuous activity. Karlson wants to put Eddie through a series of encounters so we may discern his character and see him gradually abandon his false assumptions. The true climax of *The Brothers Rico* occurs at the hotel in El Camino when Eddie realizes that he has been used and that he is powerless to prevent Johnny's execution. After this, Karlson seems to lose interest; the tragic potential of the film is exhausted, and all that remains is for Eddie to mop things up, rather miraculously. There is some effective action—the banging of Gonzales's head against the sink is a devastating piece of brutality, especially since the wait for violent action has been a long one, Phil shot in the eye—but both climax (the killing of Kubik) and anticlimax (Eddie and Alice at the orphanage) are unusually swift and abrupt, implying that Karlson has already said what he had to say and is just routinely bringing things to a close. In any case, the moral problems of Eddie Rico are at the center of the film.

As the oldest brother, with his own prosperous business, Eddie naturally assumes he knows what is right and that his younger brothers are overreacting and haven't sized up the situation properly. They try to warn Eddie that the syndicate wants their heads, but Eddie insists that Uncle Sid (indebted to their mother for his life and something of a substitute father) would never betray the Ricos, his adopted family. He uses the same line on both brothers: "Did I ever steer you wrong?" and causes, or at least accelerates, the death of both. He advises Gino to go back to St. Louis, as Sid wants. Gino knows it's a one-way ticket but is caught trying to flee the country. When Eddie defends Sid, Johnny (James Darren) sends him away with: "Maybe I'm gonna die. You've got even bigger problems—you're gonna live." Upon returning to the hotel, Eddie discovers that Johnny was right and that Sid's treachery, however unthinkable, is a fact.

Eddie is understandably self-assured. He is a self-made man, with a hundred thousand dollars—"clean" money—in the bank. He has age and experience on his behalf. He drives a fancy convertible. He is living the American dream, oblivious to the realities of the American nightmare and to the truth about himself. In the long conversation with Kubik it is easy to see how he gets duped. Kubik almost convinces the audience with his gentle manner and white hair. We are made suspicious, but discreetly. As Eddie enters Kubik's suite, the camera glides in long shot to pick up the space, the elegance, the slightly ostentatious decor. Most of the talk is in close-up and two-shots, creating an intimacy between the two men. (The decor, however, which the characters naturally ignore, continues to function for the audience as a distraction in counterpoint to the conversation, keeping it on edge and making it question the development of the scene.) Kubik is apologetic, sincere; he calls Eddie "son," says "I believe in families," and of Mama Rico: "I worship her." There is no apparent reason why Eddie should not trust him. Kubik's strategy is impeccable. He smoothes a path to his own ends, doing most of the talking, controlling the situation. He subtly flatters Eddie by treating him as his equal. As men of the world who understand things as they are, they can understand each other. Eddie is putty in his hands. He follows Kubik all around, and the camera tracks with Kubik's movement. The audience even wonders if Kubik isn't on the up-and-up until, after Eddie leaves, we see Gino being beaten up in a room down the hall. At this point we know for sure what Eddie doesn't and must wait in frustration until he discovers the truth in a painful way.

Eddie is a man suddenly confronted with a lot of decisions to make, a man who has retreated into a complacent frame of mind and must now face some unpleasant truths. One of the advantages of the B movie is that it is possible to construct situations of moral and psychological ambivalence for the hero that no star of A features would tolerate. One cannot imagine a Wayne, a Tracy, a Cooper, a Gable agreeing to enact a character so played upon, so confused about his loyalties, so helplessly agitated sitting out his brother's death in the hotel at El Camino, so victimized by external pressures and internal guilt, about which he has only the dimmest awareness. Also, an ignorant hero is a foolish one. Richard Conte as Eddie appears confident, manly, and competent, but these qualities in the service of folly and vanity are considerably less positive. What draws the viewer to Eddie is the insecurity behind the confident exterior. He is a hero who does not know what to do and from whom a great deal is demanded by in turn his wife, Gino, Kubik, Malix, his mother, Johnny, the sheriff, Gonzales. They freely offer either their advice as to what he should do or their opinion of his character. Eddie is too strong to pity, but his difficulties gain our compassion. He is finally forced to make a choice he himself confesses should have been made twenty years ago.

The Brothers Rico exposes why that decision was never made and why it has become too late to make it. To put it bluntly, it is because America is living a lie, as the life of Eddie Rico demonstrates. Eddie thinks he can start life anew by denying his past. He covers up his guilt by a naive and unenlightened belief in his innocence. He is a basically good man who foolishly thinks he is a pure man. Eddie may have quit the rackets, but he is smeared with its dirt. His cleanliness, precision, order, and efficiency are shown as compulsive. His business is a laundry. We see him shower and shave. His wife goes to hand him the soap on the sink, thinks better of it, and opens a fresh bar. His convertible gleams, vividly reflecting his and Gino's images while they talk. Gino wears a dark suit and looks a bit disheveled. Eddie sits trim, stiff, and tight-lipped in a light suit behind a white wheel. His office has a gleaming sterility; everything is spanking new and clean and perfectly, geometrically arranged. When he disturbs some of Malix's clothing in an argument, he smoothes and pats it back to neatness.

Eddie also thinks he is infallible and that he is better and wiser than other people. When he gives advice, he expects people to take it. He has figured the world out like a good rationalist. Everything he does in the name of reason is shown to be profoundly, humanly ignorant. He ignores his mother's fears as expressed in the letter—sees it as part of the potpourri of aches and grumbles that aging mothers give vent to in letters to their children. He responds to his wife's fear by likening her to a "superstitious peasant from the old country." Gino's fear earns him this rebuttal: "Feelings like that are for old women." It is not that Eddie doesn't have feelings, anxieties, or instincts, he has just cut himself off from them and from his emotional roots in family. He thinks Kubik is family because he can't *feel* Kubik. Kubik makes sense to him, as one successful man would to another. He tells his mother that Gino is a "crazy" kid, and, as for Johnny, that it is necessary to "put some sense into his head." When Johnny tells him that he's "got a *feeling*" about Kubik "this time," Eddie counters with: "What must I do to make you *understand*?" Eddie's unnatural control over his feelings, his body, his tone of voice, his marriage (his wife runs to fetch his slippers and kneels to put them on), his life is an unconscious effort to deny that he's part of the corruption. His mother's uncooperative irrationality and lapse into religion irritate him but Kubik's ritzy suite and rational assurances impress him. Eddie Rico is a modern man, a machine. He thinks he is in charge of himself and of his life, but he doesn't know what either is anymore. At one point, someone asks him how he likes Florida and he replies, automatically, but revealingly, "It's a great life."

When he learns the truth, he tells his wife, "I gotta get it out of my system." It is a confessional speech but he never seems to break out of his psychological pattern. It does not shatter him. His response is deliberate and rational, a ritual transformation from wrong to right reason that does not involve his emotional depths. Unlike other fifties heroes, he is incapable of getting in touch with himself. He is too stamped by the way things are to change. When he goes after the organization, it is a decision, not a burst of uncontrolled feeling. The movie lets us know from the beginning that Eddie will not be carried away and, as we would wish, carry us away.

The movie works on the strategy of our getting the message very early and Eddie getting it very late. By the time Eddie acts, our faith in him has been so undermined that we can't put much stock in what he does. An idle exchange between Eddie and one of his truck drivers early in the film says it all. The driver notices Eddie arriving to work in the morning and asks, "Little late, aren't you?" Eddie replies, "I guess I am."

The prosperous, inhuman syndicate is a symbol of aspects of American life that sever man from man, children from parents, brother from brother, man from woman. One assumes that Eddie has gotten Gino and Johnny into the organization (and then pulled out himself). Uncle Sid is a substitute for the father long dead and gone. Eddie has left the Italian ghetto of New York for

The Brothers Rico. Old and new. Grandma, deaf, laughs at a flying saucer movie, while dapper Eddie stands uncomfortable and incongruous amid an outmoded, warm decor.

sunny Miami. He is removed from his mother, who still gets by running a store on Mulberry Street with her crippled leg. He is a proper son, expiating the guilt of his emotional detachment and real unconcern in typical ways. He sends Mama a new refrigerator (which looks absurdly inappropriate in her old-fashioned decor) and a big TV to keep Grandma, deaf, feeble, and unable to understand a word of English, amused. He advises his mother to send Grandma to a rest home. His mother refuses, despite the difficulty of caring for her. His mother, too, is confused—a victim of the modern world. She admits that she doesn't know right from wrong anymore and doesn't know what to do. But she lives amid realities, unlike Eddie. Her home is a haven of religious, human values, two steps away from the dark violence of the city. Eddie's mental suburbia keeps him insulated from the realities of both good and evil.

The phone call that interrupts his sleep suggests that Eddie's past is very much alive and that his meticulous and meticulously run laundry business was begun with dirty money. Once he starts after Johnny he runs into several people who know him, remember him, and deal with him on the basis of past associations. One particularly revealing moment occurs in the hotel at El Camino. La Motta (Harry Bellaver), Kubik's man who runs the town, tells Eddie to cool it about Johnny's execution—it is a foregone conclusion. Eddie, who has just realized that he has been used by Kubik like a dog on a leash to discover Johnny's whereabouts, is still moaning and cursing Kubik. La Motta, impatient with Eddie's unreasonableness, says, "You listening to me, or am I just talking to myself?" At that point, Eddie, who has been on the bed the whole scene, gets up and sits in the chair La Motta has comfortably occupied all the while. The switch in position unites them. Eddie's earlier protest that his role in the rackets had never involved killing has been punctured by La Motta's "You knew what was going on, so don't start playing holy with me now." The fact that Johnny is Eddie's brother doesn't impress La Motta either: "So, he's your brother. We're all brothers, aren't we? Did that ever stop anything?" Eddie's situation tugs at our sympathy, but his naiveté is distressing. He later assumes responsibility for all the disaster, saying, "It was my fault," but he does it in a perfunctory way that is very much in character. The script's

clincher, though, is when Johnny, over-
joyed at just becoming a father, bubbles
over the phone to Eddie, "Congratula-
tions! You're an uncle." There is only
one other uncle in the film—Uncle Sid
Kubik—and the phone call is to set up
Johnny's execution, moments later.

It seems that Karlson can't end the
film with Eddie sitting on the bed, not
particularly crushed, but immobile,
after Johnny's execution—the point at
which the film perhaps should end.
This being so, he nonetheless appears to
have tried to modify the upbeat conventions he has to follow. La Motta tells
Eddie that he can scream his head off if
he wants but that "it changes nothing."
That is what we are made to feel.

For one thing, when Eddie boards

The Brothers Rico. Big-city big brother Eddie Rico, hosted by little-farm little brother Johnny Rico, Johnny's pregnant wife observing with a worried look. Eddie: "Did I ever steer you wrong?" Johnny: ". . . No, but Eddie . . ." His instinctual fear turns out to be more accurate than Eddie's faith in reason. As soon as Eddie leaves, Johnny's executioners arrive. The last Rico left to battle Kubik's organization is Eddie, at the moment still Kubik's dupe. (Museum of Modern Art)

the plane with Gonzales to be taken back to Kubik, we really don't know what
frame of mind he is in. It is possible that even after all that has happened he
has simply given up and will return to his business, still the "property" of the
syndicate but a little wiser and less smugly know-it-all. Even when Gonzales
mentions Gino's death Eddie seems to take it in, and settles back in his seat.
It is only later made clear that the death of brothers has finally made him want
to act on his emotions, however futile the results might be. But the context in
which his heroism is placed is overwhelmingly pessimistic. On their first and
only meeting, Gino snaps at Eddie, "It was too late what you told me." Eddie
says to his wife that he tried to prevent his brothers' deaths "but it was too late."
His wife replies, "It was always too late." Mama, looking straight at Eddie, says,
"My boys are dead. What's there to live for?" When Eddie replies, "There's a
new life ahead, for all of us," Mama doesn't look at all convinced. The deaths
of Johnny and Gino cannot be undone. Johnny's assessment is accurate;
Eddie's problem is that he is going to go on living.

The film's emphasis is that nothing can change. The conventional structure of such a film is made curiously lopsided. Almost all the film is devoted to
slowly waking Eddie up. Then there is a rapid ending in which we are told
things can change. It happens so quickly, though, that there isn't enough time
for the viewer to get adjusted to the switch in position or to savor it properly. It
seems a perverse application of formula. One wants a real encounter between

The Brothers Rico. Anguish turns to fury as Mama Rico catches sight of the treacherous Kubik. Her hysteria creates the distraction necessary for Eddie to make his move.

Eddie and Kubik, wants Kubik torn limb from limb. Eddie just shoots him. We don't even get a reaction shot, giving us Eddie's emotion, something implying a sense of release, of accomplishment. But given the film, it almost has to be this way. To make a big deal out of the ending, to let us feel Eddie's emotions, would be false to both theme and characterization. We understand why Eddie has been so cold and controlled a hero. In the world of *The Brothers Rico* to have made Eddie suffer would have been beside the point. What good would groveling and agonizing do? We are no longer in a world where those responses would make any difference. The film gets *us* mad. We want Kubik *more* killed. We fill in the emotions it is not possible, or not convincing, for the character to have.

We are given a character who basically doesn't change. The film plays on the viewer's frustration. Everything theoretically works out right, but we are left, as in *The Phenix City Story*, dissatisfied. The effect is to undercut the patterns of conventional illusionistic cinema. The usual prolonged action of car chases, gunplay, and suspense is kept to an absolute minimum. Malix, Johnny's wife's brother, who at last agrees to help Eddie bust the syndicate in court, is made priggish and unlikable. The new start provided for Eddie and Alice is a qualified one, and it is qualified by everything the film shows us is the truth about America. The coda, with Eddie and Alice adopting the child, is of course comforting but is awkwardly handled. The film seems aware that what we must be shown about Eddie is his newly gained humanity. He says he is "worried" about the adoption going through, and he has forgotten that his wife has the letter from the DA that he is fumbling for in his jacket. This is a different, humanized Eddie, a far cry from the blindly confident automaton who started the film. We have been shown, however, an entire country, from east to west, tied in corruption and evil, and the memory of that cannot be effaced by ten seconds of goodwill and lighthearted pleasantries.

America *is* one big happy family—the syndicate, which functions as a metaphor for our way of life. It is juxtaposed against the Rico family, which it destroys. Kubik calls Eddie "son" and Eddie accepts him as a father. Phil, Kubik's right-hand man, refers to Eddie as "Eddie boy." Even La Motta calls

Eddie "son." From his luxurious suite in Miami's Excelsior Hotel, Kubik runs the complex, inhuman (Eddie twice calls Kubik "animal"), impersonal network of crime, a large, perverse family that is bound together by fear. It is the family, and the business, of all the brothers Rico who have left Mulberry Street to get up in the world. It is the new structure that binds human beings together, replacing the family, the neighborhood, and ties based on feeling. The film implies that just about everybody belongs to it or might as well belong to it. Eddie travels from Miami to New York and across to California. Everywhere he goes, the syndicate is there—at airports, in cabs, hotels, banks, on the streets. Kubik has a pipeline to the DA's office. There is not a city or a town where he has not placed someone. One excellent shot in a hotel lobby showing two identically dressed men with curious looks on their faces synthesizes the film's paranoia—we are not told one way or the other, but the effect of the shot is to make us think that one of them is syndicate, the other not. There is no way, though, of telling which.

The syndicate follows Eddie's trail to Johnny. Karlson creates out of the geography of the whole country a closed universe. Eddie can go anywhere in the United States, but he's trapped. Once part of the syndicate, you are owned by it forever. The film does not explain how so many people became involved. One is left to infer that at some point or another, either with or without your knowledge, you become indebted, either directly or indirectly, to something the syndicate has a hand in. Then you are obliged for life. La Motta and Gonzales arrange for Johnny to get killed with utter nonchalance. If they disobey, they are dead, so it is nothing even worth thinking about. A moral sense is a luxury they can ill afford. La Motta is not hideously evil, he's just resigned, and it is his absolute acceptance of the situation that gives us the shivers. Gonzales is his echo, "You can't buck the system." La Motta orders dinner while Eddie holds his head. Organized crime may have had its origins in the urban ghettos, but it has come a long way since. It is not tied to any nationality. Gonzales is, presumably, a Mexican-American, and Kubik is made deliberately nonnational. He can't be typed, and he is given no history. All we have is his name, which suggests the hard, angular, rectilinear surfaces of the world the film shows us we live in. The only environment in the film that is distinguished from the rest is Mama Rico's—warm, comfortable, cluttered, a hodgepodge of rich wallpaper, old lamps, unpretentious chairs and couches, rounded tactile shapes. The store that is a home; the home that is a store.

What shot after shot suggests about the rest of the world is its severely ordered and clean appearance, its characterless neutrality and modernity, and its mechanical hardness. Kubik's suite is a precisely laid out and chicly incongruous blend of tile, glass, wood, expensive drapery, and Japanese silk screens. Eddie's home and office are equally immaculate and designed. The film is full

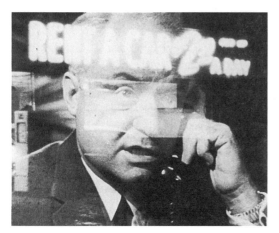

The Brothers Rico. Superimposition: the head of Sid Kubik and an emblem of the world he controls.

of long hallways and rectangular doors. Eddie and Gino drive up to a white glistening beach beneath geometrically swaying rows of palm trees. The interior of the Phoenix Airport—its floor being swabbed to a sparkle by a lone, unobtrusive black—appears as an uncannily logical arrangement. Its men's room features an array of sinks and urinals in rigid, glittering formation. Eddie stops his car beneath a mechanical stop/go sign that seems to have been included only to amplify a view of existence that isn't really lived but rather keeps clicking in and out of place. People walking in the film—at airports, on streets—have a stiff, somnambular quality. The facade, whether it is the interior of a bank or a hotel lobby, is always one of order, smoothness, imperturbability. *The Brothers Rico* contains very little violence because crime isn't like that anymore. It doesn't show its face. Crime is Sid Kubik pretending to be all heart but heartless underneath. He is the bureaucracy and the technology that have taken over. At El Camino, Eddie tries to reach Kubik by telephone and can't. Realizing he has been betrayed, he shouts, "My dear Uncle Sid!" and smashes his fist into the telephone. Sid Kubik is a telephone.[9]

Karlson records the American landscape with a diabolical equanimity. We see the environments as actual and authentic, but in the context of the film we see them with a fresh perspective. They are the rot-disguising fronts and facades we live among, and that makes them more sinister than any diagonalized dark alley. Karlson's sobriety constitutes his most lethal critique. A visual opportunist like Aldrich would have invested the Phoenix Airport with a special filmic excitement. Karlson refuses to make it any more or less interesting than it is. It is just there, like everything, like crime, and crime is everywhere.[10] Verisimilitude is being used for special ends. The film's method does not allow us to ask whether its view of America is true; it is so clear-sighted, level-headed, and undramatic that we accept it as true. We cannot undermine its effects by citing impatience, hysteria, an idiosyncratic shooting style. It makes us confront the accuracy of what it depicts. It is as clear and unmistakable as daylight, and it uses its audience's vision as an X-ray

The Brothers Rico is so unsentimental (compared to earlier fifties films) that it cannot end without making it explicit that the values of the old world are irrevocably destroyed. All it can do is to suggest (unconvincingly) that there must be a way of living in a syndicate-image society without succumbing to the grossly evil nature of a syndicate as such. That is all that seems possible toward the end of the fifties. Kubik is forced to come down to Mulberry Street in person to search for Eddie and is destroyed there, at the place of his origins. But Mama too is crushed, her values violated by Kubik's treachery, her sons murdered. It is through the old grandmother, however, that Karlson suggests the permanent passing of an old way of life.

She is in two scenes. The first (a comic scene) has her watching the TV Eddie has sent, a big, large-screen monster that sticks out like a sore thumb in the surroundings. Grandma loves it and watches it all day.[11] She mistakes Eddie for Gino and is vaguely aware that his presence is a special event. She babbles in Italian, and Eddie dredges some up for the occasion. Eddie and Mama, after the formalities, leave her glued to the TV. She is the old world on its way out, eased out by the great modern distraction, television. Near the conclusion there is a briefer, gloomier version of this scene. Eddie, escaping Kubik's men, runs into the store on Mulberry Street. He passes Grandma, still sitting in front of the TV, on his way toward his mother with the news that Gino and Johnny are dead. Eddie pauses for a moment to exchange a formal greeting with Grandma and hold her hand, which she extends. He moves toward the rear of the frame, back to camera, to face his mother, and when he lets go of Grandma's hand, her arm travels in a lazy arc across the bottom of the frame in the foreground. She mumbles something afterward, but that is the last we see of her. The movement of her arm is a gesture of farewell. It droops listlessly out of the frame and may be read as expressing the death of the old world.

The Ricos may go on living but not on Mulberry Street. The new Rico—Johnny's son, Antonio (named after the father)—is born on a California farm and will not have a Rico for a father. The legitimate line stops there, since Eddie must adopt. It is all over for the Ricos and for a particular chapter of American social life. The film takes perhaps an ambivalent position on its disappearance. In a sense it had to go, but its going involves a human loss. From the evidence the film gives, however, there is nothing to replace it, except the world we have been shown, ready to resume its course after the ripple has died down. The shop on Mulberry Street may close, but there will be a new tenant for the suite vacated by Kubik at the Excelsior Hotel.

Unlike the old days, the defeat of the villain (and the success of the hero) does not seem to resolve anything. Simple resolutions are out of the question in a world in which the conditions of humanity are so precarious and our perceptions of reality so confused. There are no clear labels on anything, and we leave the film disturbed. We haven't conquered *noir*'s jitters, merely pushed them below the surface. *The Brothers Rico* is as true to the life of its period as *D.O.A.* was to its. It gives us the surface, and looking at it gives us the jitters. There is no cure for these jitters and the unease we feel toward the film's matter-of-factness and its unsatisfying conclusion, we must carry with us back to life, creating an echo chamber between film and reality. The world outside the film is more entrenched than the world of the film, and it is too set in its ways for us to make it any different. After all, if the movies can't do it for us, it is a sign that it can't be done.

CREDITS **99 River Street**

(United Artists, 1953, 83 min.)

Producer	Edward Small	Cast	John Payne (Ernie Driscoll)
Director	Phil Karlson		Evelyn Keyes (Linda James)
Screenplay	Robert Smith (from a story by		Brad Dexter (Victor Rawlins)
	George Zuckerman)		Frank Faylen (Stan Hagan)
Photography	Franz Planer		Peggie Castle (Pauline Driscoll)
Editor	Buddy Small		Jay Adler (Christopher)
Art Director	Frank Sylos		Jack Lambert (Mickey)
Music	Emil Newman and Arthur Lange		Glen Langan (Lloyd Morgan)
			Eddie Waller (Pop Durkee)

CREDITS **The Phenix City Story**

(Allied Artists, 1955, 100 min.)

Producers	Sam Bischoff and	Cast	John McIntyre (Albert Patterson)
	David Diamond		Richard Kiley (John Patterson)
Director	Phil Karlson		Edward Andrews (Rhett Tanner)
Screenplay	Crane Wilbur and		Kathryn Grant (Ellie Rhodes)
	Daniel Mainwaring		James Edwards (Zeke Ward)
Photography	Harry Neumann		Lenka Peterson (Mary Jo Patterson)
Editor	George White		Biff McGuire (Fred Gage)
Music	Harry Sukman		Truman Smith (Ed Gage)
			Jean Carson (Cassie)
			Meg Myles (Judy)
			John Larch (Clem Wilson)
			Otto Hulett (Hugh Bentley)

(Columbia, 1957, 92 min.)

Producer	Lewis J. Rachmil	Cast	Richard Conte (Eddie Rico)
Director	Phil Karlson		Dianne Foster (Alice Rico)
Screenplay	Lewis Meltzer and Ben Perry		Kathryn Grant (Nora Malix)
Photography	Burnett Guffey		Larry Gates (Sid Kubik)
Editor	Charles Nelson		James Darren (Johnny Rico)
Art Director	Robert Boyle		Harry Bellaver (La Motta)
Music	George Duning and		Argentina Brunetti (Mama Rico)
	Maurice Stoloff		Paul Picerni (Gino)
			Paul Dubov (Phil)

Kiss Me Deadly (1955)

Mike Hammer (Ralph Meeker) picks up Christina Bailey (Cloris Leachman), who has escaped from a sanitarium. They are surprised by a group of faceless men who torture Christina to death and nearly kill Hammer. Hammer, intrigued by Christina's remark, "Remember me," decides to forgo his usual business of investigating divorces to pursue the case, figuring that it must be something big. He refuses to cooperate with the law, which is also unusually eager to follow up the murder. After a long, complicated search, he discovers Christina's secret, an atomic box hidden in a locker at an athletic club. Not knowing what it is, he leaves it there. The box is stolen, and Hammer's secretary/mistress, Velda (Maxine Cooper), is captured. Hammer goes after Velda and eventually discovers the criminals' hideout, a beach house on the ocean where Velda is being held. He is shot and is unable to prevent the opening of the box. The house gets blown apart in a series of explosions that continue as the film ends. Hammer and Velda try to escape, but it appears that they too are blown up.

Kiss Me Deadly invites us to ponder our worst fears, a vision of universal annihilation. Its style makes us live through what the world looked and felt like just before apocalypse. It is a cacophonous, cryptic world, upside down and in reverse. From the first shots, and then the credit sequence (the titles run backward) on, the movie takes us continuously by surprise. The credit gimmick works. It is the premise from which everything else follows. It sets us up into seeing things the way the film would have us see them, which is brazenly at odds with the way things are normally seen. We respond to the credits by trying to correct them; we are compelled to adjust them back to normal. But it is impossible. We are trapped. We must read them as they are given to us, even as we make the effort to "translate" them. While we are preoccupied at dealing with the credits in reverse as they slant away from us, a supplementary anarchy of sound and image is producing further, more disorienting, tensions. The panting of a terrified woman, naked under her raincoat, is mixed in with a song playing on the radio of the sports car that has picked her up and the loud, droning roar of the car itself driving rapidly through the most impenetrably black of *noir*'s black nights. The shot is taken from the rear of the car, and the portion of the frame brightly lit is the white line of the highway seen through the windshield, wriggling provocatively like an abstract animator's sensory fantasy.

Kiss Me Deadly's use of the atomic box puts the genre's iconography into a futile, sardonic perspective. If the world is going to blow up, what can guns, fast cars, being tough with women, or any of it mean? When the box is discovered, we understand why Hammer's macho image seemed to have a comic edge, why Nick was so funny-crazy, why we couldn't hold back a shout of laughter at Sammy's tearful "no more va-va-voom," why Christina started poking holes, without so much as a howdyado, in Hammer's ego, why Hammer's showy handling of his car seemed kind of silly, why the dialogue was so unpredictable and mannered, why the beach house—one of the key icons of forties melodrama—had an air so familiar and antiquated. The genre's standard equipment seems beside the point in an era of nuclear hazard. The explosions at the end of the film make all that has preceded—the "mystery," the tough action, the investigation, the gangster/crime and private eye film's entire sign system—meaningless. *Kiss Me Deadly* is a thesis film about the "great whatsit" and the human desperation it creates. So many are willing to die and for what? The film illustrates the mood announced by the lyrics of its theme song ("The night is mighty chilly And conversation feels so silly . . . The world is very frightening The rain begins and then comes lightning") and the sentiments voiced by Velda: "They. A wonderful word. And who are they? They are the nameless ones who kill people for the great whatsit. Does it exist? Who cares." In his greedy quest, Hammer stumbles on the truth. The film shows that his activity has as much meaning in the era of the bomb as all the accumulation of culture the film constantly refers to—none at all. In a movie that comes at you in a series of ferocious spasms, Aldrich has captured the terror and fear behind the fifties' spurious calm. It is the film the genre has been winding up to, and its tone and style anticipate the genre's most frantic and comedic cultural broadside, *Point Blank* (1967).

Kiss Me Deadly is a reprise of *noir* and its consummation. We are in LA once again, where *noir* stylistics and settings had their finest hour. *Noir's* stylized lighting and compositions, however, are taken to an extreme that exhausts their potential or, at least, seems to define their limits. Mike Hammer, like a good detective, tries valiantly to put things together, and when he does, they do not make any sense. It turns out that the world is speeding toward destruction, and all his efforts merely rock the boat a little without altering its course. Hammer is as impersonal as anyone else in the film and is always subject to a cosmic point of view. Nor is he like the worn-looking forties private eye who sets his small, grubby daily fee and peels his way cunningly through nasty situations. Hammer runs his business with efficient, amoral expertise. An affluent "bedroom dick" with an elaborate technology at his disposal, his vestigial humanity is central to the film's criticism of American society and culture.

Aldrich's use of natural locations is the opposite of the documentarist's and bears little relation to the goals of a fictional verisimilitude. The film's look is surreal, the world is carefully and fastidiously distorted. *Kiss Me Deadly* has the cold design of a modernist painting in black and white. No other film in the genre looks or feels quite like it. One senses its oddity immediately in the opening shots of a woman emerging out of total darkness, garishly spotlighted and running breathlessly toward the camera, and it is confirmed when Hammer and Christina pull into the gas station, which glares with a painted phosphorescence in the pitch-black night—a gas station of the imagination. Each shot is a challenge to the viewer's eye and understanding. The dramatic lighting, ultrasharp focus, jarring angles, the dazzling, perverse geometry of the compositions, the oily glitter of the night scenes, the elliptical narrative—all make it impossible for the viewer to relax. While our eyes are busy taking in the conflicts between angular, hard-edged shapes, our ears must strain to hear the characters, whose conversations are typically competing with background noises and voices. Most films, in one way or another, coddle the audience they are aimed at. *Kiss Me Deadly* is most unfriendly. From scene to scene, the audience is asked to screen out material that interferes, often obstreperously, with its penetration of the film's meaning, story, characterization, and continuity. Layers of extraneous sound and visual matter are placed between the viewer and the pertinent action. The characters behave as though everything is as it should be, but it's hell on an audience. We are shown a world in its final spasms whose condition is related to the characters' unawareness of it and adaptation to it.

Ominous, frighteningly vivid high contrast dominates; no chiaroscuro, but boldly outlined slabs of black and gray and white whose confronting and intersecting planes have the calculated weight and balance of something sculpted. The characters, too, are rigid with an emblematic torpor. They are not creatures of flesh and blood but hard rubber objects erratically animated by the will of the filmmaker. Even in pain and death their reactions are catatonic—the close-up of Nick beneath the falling car, the morgue doctor after Hammer jams his fingers, Carl Evello stabbed on the bed, Sugar twisted in the chair, the first shot of Diker's damaged face, Christina's dangling legs, Lily consumed by fire. Their screams, too, seem disconnected from their bodies. In the "love" scenes, Aldrich often shoots from over Hammer's right shoulder; we don't see his face or any sign of reaction. The women are made to seem slightly idiotic, their passions "prepared," their techniques the more ludicrously stilted for being wasted on a mannequin. The unknown actresses (this was Cloris Leachman's debut) have, as must have been intended, a similar hard, glazed appearance, and invest their lines with an inured senselessness, as though a congealed inner chaos had found its proper syntax and articulation. The iconic severity of such film-melodrama fixtures as Albert Dekker, Jack Lambert, and Jack Elam is exploited in frozen high relief, and Wesley Addy's long, ill-natured face is given a rancorous, waxen inflexibility. Hammer's face is frequently blacked out of the image; he never achieves genuine contact in his encounters. He is a presence and a shape, half listening to the soliloquys of others without learning anything.

Aldrich and photographer Ernest Laszlo appear determined to get the camera into places it has never been before. It is perturbing to get a corpse-eye view from a morgue locker. We become the car as it rushes down on Nick. One gasps at the overhead long shot of Hammer, a dot in the maze of staircases at the Jalisco Hotel, partly out of disbelief—where was Laszlo shooting from?—and is doubly startled when the camera reverses 180 degrees from an extreme high-angle shot of Lily going down the stairs to an extreme low-angle shot of her rushing down them toward the camera. In general, both the camera's rapid switches in viewpoint and the places and positions from which it shoots are highly disconcerting. Not only is the environment deranged into something horrible, unreal, and nightmarish, but the properties of vision are altered and convulsed. As in all the stages of the genre, the way the world looks is correlated with how it is felt.

The clean sterility of the images rules even the scenes of violence."[12] The excessive violence of *Kiss Me Deadly* is purely ideational. The screams, pain, flames, Hammer's hands are free of the lurid naturalism characteristic of most violent films. They coil into a continuous statement of lethal logic. Aldrich's use of violence is formal and intellectual. His aesthetic control over each instance of stylized brutality has a chilling, dehumanized quality absent from typically "involving" action. The effect is a kind of therapy through fear. In the film's catastrophic context, one feels the violence behind things—the potential of violence in Hammer's hands during an embrace or in the back of a broad-shouldered black man who parenthetically crosses the frame.

If Aldrich spares us the details of Christina's torture, it is only to make us supply our own fiendish possibilities. The film is an occasion for Aldrich both to work the audience over and to free the violence of his own sensibility. Certain scenes appear to exist for the sole purpose of giving Aldrich the leeway to express his feelings and attitudes through the staging of violence too deliberate and relished to function merely thematically. They strike one as personal excesses, of the kind that run through the films of, say, Josef von Sternberg. The excesses should of course cohere with the point and purpose of the film, as they do here. Hammer slams a man's head repeatedly against a building; the man slumps pulpily to the ground, his head sliding down the wall. A moment later he gets up and flings himself at Hammer. Hammer socks him down a shockingly long row of stone steps; the camera, positioned at the bottom, catches every bounce of his limbs on the way down. It is unlikely, to begin with, that the man could have mustered the strength to attack again and the violence that ensues has no purpose other than to assault the audience and, by assaulting them, twist their level of awareness from the what-happens-next conventions of the thriller to the what-is-this-I'm-seeing of an awed contemplation. In another scene, Hammer breaks away from Charlie and Sugar and runs toward the ocean, presumably to escape (impossible). Charlie and Sugar grab him in the surf and, trading blows, pound him like a beach ball, then drag him, in a spectacular long shot, up to the beach house. Hammer's escape attempt has nothing to do with story logic. Aldrich wants to have his hero beat up—to give him a taste of his own medicine—and to enact another brutal episode, this time in an ironic, elemental setting (also ideal for visual extravagance). (Hammer's beeline for the surf is also symbolic. His instinct makes him struggle to reach the ocean, the natural element of water, as it does at the end.)

Once again, we have the major polarity of the fifties: science, reason, mechanism, bureaucracy, detachment from self, civilization versus instinct and feeling. It is no longer a contest. The conflict in Mike Hammer between the flicker of humanity he has left and his need to repress it is an uneven one. He gives us his credo: "What's in it for me?" and sticks by it until it is too late. He is tough and fearless, but partly out of ignorance. Diker tells him: "If you knew, you'd be afraid." Hammer is an image of his world—cold, cynical, vicious, unprincipled, callous, emotionally repressed (but not vacant). *Kiss Me Deadly* is a film without any warmth or sentiment. Its characterizations are harsh and unpleasant. Hammer is the surliest, most sadistic private eye in film history. But he is in the hero slot and shows a hero's spunk, determination, and independence. We automatically side with him as he begins to unravel the mystery. Then the bottom drops out, for hero and viewer alike. When Hammer, in a daze, tells Pat, "I didn't know," Pat turns to him with, "You think you would have done any different if you had known?" The charge, we must grudgingly allow, is accurate.

Hammer may be repellent, but we are asked to understand him and be alert to his contradictions. His face is smooth, unlined, rather innocent; when he smiles (rare) he looks boyish. Hammer's face gives a false impression of being a blank, insensitive mask. It is actually a very sensitive register of feelings that must of necessity be held back. Aldrich has Ralph Meeker play the character for complexity. He follows Hammer's slow movements; his camera lingers on his face. We are forced to consider what is going through the character's mind and what his feelings are, since the camera would presumably not be staying there if there wasn't something to reveal. He is offered for interpretation.

Hammer is not a blind robot; his repression is a choice. Everything about him provokes the humanity that he has had to sacrifice in adapting to new modes and codes of survival. He lasts as long as he does because he has made himself tough. When he picks up the distraught Christina, he seems unnecessarily coarse and brutal toward her. It is not an "act" but a strategy of human relationships that has become second nature to him. He lays the belligerence on thick, but he has to if Christina is not to get the wrong idea. The film implies that if he weren't that way in the world as it is pictured he would be a goner, as Christina, whose defenses have collapsed, clearly is. That he picks her up suggests there is still something human

Kiss Me Deadly. Mike Hammer listens to Lily's nasal recitation of a Rossetti sonnet—maybe wishes now he'd kept those English 101 notes. A rare parenthetical home run blast for literacy, and a key moment for establishing near-universal critical agreement on Mike Hammer as *one stupid guy.* (Museum of Modern Art)

left in him. It would be dangerous, though, to give in to it fully. He appears to have made his choice long ago to be self-seeking and self-protective. Christina demonstrates what being real and human will get you. She represents *feeling*, what in the fifties (the genre tells us) is being killed off, and has been declared "crazy." Only someone as tough as the world can be its antagonist, and Mike Hammer's plenty tough.

He is so tough he survives being pushed off a cliff in an exploding car. His survival is symbolic, unbelievable—nobody could come through that alive. Hammer is like Walker, in the later *Point Blank*, a character who comes back from the dead because it is necessary for him to question and expose his world. At the hospital, he wakes to a new reality. We see no scratches, no scars, no bandages. From that point on he is treated as a mythical figure undertaking a mythical quest. It is death and resurrection. He lies in a coma for three days, then revives. Pat jokes about almost having had to "finance a new tux to bury the corpse." Nick says, "My friend just returned from the grave," like Lazarus. The theme is first announced when Soberin lectures Christina's torturer: "Who do you think you are that you can raise the dead?" Evello says that he should have been dead twice over. The allusive density of *Kiss Me Deadly* suggests that Hammer is the inheritor of a superfluous culture and a superfluous role, a modern, ironic Galahad whose quest leads him to a fire-breathing atomic box.[13]

Hammer's occasional kindnesses are in character, and his violence can be seen as a positive aggression against hypocrisy and cowering fear (his murderous hands as agents of a merited localized destruction). The inklings we have of his humanity are not to be underestimated in a world that demands the strongest of personal defenses. He comes to the scared Christina's aid, he helps the old man carry the trunk, he is bothered by Nick's death and Velda's danger, he gets along with the blacks in the nightclub. There is a decency the culture provides little outlet for. There are many references to friendship in the film—most of them ironic—but Mike does have friends. People seem to like him, often want to help him, and can talk to him. He is not the *cause* of people's terror and corruption, despite the violence he inflicts. He has to deal with them in the state he finds them in. He is out for himself, but the movie hints at the kind of man he might be if the world were different. Hammer's instinct leads him to be with people, depend on them. His manner of dealing with them—unresponsive, reticent, brutal, coldly direct—is determined by the nature of the society, which he has perceived and taken to a philosophical position. When Evello's half sister Friday throws herself upon him, he cautions her to learn how to say no, "because one of the best ways to be friendly is to know when to say no."

Hammer's negative qualities are inversions of positive ones. He is a mooch and a grub, lifting Pat's cigarettes, drinking Wallace's beer, Trivago's wine, receiving Velda's passion—a guy who takes but never gives, as Christina is quick to recognize. But the impulse toward human contact—however warped and perverted its signs—and human sharing is there. He is appreciative of Trivago's singing, and tastes his wine and spaghetti. He sits down at the dinner table with Wallace's family. He joins Eddie Yaeger in admiring his new boxing prospect. When he wakes Velda up to tell her about Nick's death, he finishes the milk she has left on the end table, and he is there because she is someone he can talk to. After Nick's death he drowns his sorrow (and his responsibility, too) in drink, in a bar where people know him. He lets Christina hold his hand and protects her at the roadblock. The way his hands are treated in the film is illustrative of how everything basic and human about Hammer has become infected. Once past the roadblock, Hammer snidely asks, "Can I have my hand back now?" Hands have rich positive associations—hands build, make, touch, create, caress. Hammer's hands kill and destroy. They are more lethal than guns. (Guns are old-fashioned in a world where everything has been transformed into a weapon of murder or assault—a pair of pliers, a car jack, dynamite, a truck, popcorn, sleeping pills, a desk drawer, Hammer's hands, and of course the atomic box, the murder weapon to end all murder weapons.) But hands nonetheless belong to the human body. Hammer's power is connected to his physical self.

If Hammer is a man of qualities, they are suspicious ones. The complexity of his characterization resides in his being made to convey human aspects on the verge of extinction while simultaneously remaining a charmless, vicious, greedy, ignorant, and uselessly reckless boor. Pat calls him a "slob." Christina puts him down as a male pig. He cares more about his expensive sports car than the person it almost runs down. The head of the Interstate Crime Commission orders a window opened after Hammer leaves the room. His flair with cars is admired by his Greek friend, Nick, who gets killed because he investigated for Hammer. His specialty is divorce cases; he and his secretary Velda use their own sexual persuasiveness to gain compromising evidence. His playboy apartment is a sanctuary of male materialist taste, containing the many technological tools of his unsavory profession. He cultivates a self-centered, stony male mystique. He is contemptuous of poetry, and his interest in classical music is strictly for clues. While he is getting drunk, Velda is captured. Nick is killed in the time span when Hammer takes Lily to his apartment, to protect what he thinks is his investment. She makes a sucker out of him. He always turns Velda's affections off by giving her some dirty work to do. However, as Pat says, "He's got a nose," and no one else has the sense of curiosity and adventure to open things up.

Mike Hammer is actually the clearest, simplest element in a most difficult film. Interpretations of him may differ, but the outlines of his role are fairly distinct and discernible. We see him holding back, and we know why he holds back. He mistrusts and refuses to commit himself, and the reasons are supplied. At the end, he lets himself go, becomes crazed, ferocious. Velda has committed herself to him, and it is his responsibility to act for Velda, rescue her. His passion for destruction acts as a personal release, a form of self-gratification (after being made a fool of). He must correct the consequences of his self-interest, and he realizes, finally, that Velda is what matters. The sterility of their relationship is transformed at the end by the primal cry of man for woman, woman for man: "Velda!" "Mike!" Hammer's derangement is made very clear at his second encounter with Diker, and in his treatment of Doc Kennedy at the morgue. He becomes a typical fifties hero; he goes crazy, violently crazy. He wants to tear the world apart. One finds one's humanity in an insensate rage. Where it used to make a difference, it doesn't anymore.

It is the rest of the film that is hard to assess—the weird, thick detailing, the meaning of numerous baffling shots, the tone of crucial episodes, odd characterizations and dialogue, the particularity and variety of its locations and techniques, the mirthless humor, the politeness and formality with which people in the film do the most awful things to each other, the fact that we get to know everybody's full name. It appears that the film wishes to leave nothing out, to crowd in as much as it can to create the effect of the senselessness of modern civilization, the chaos on the eve of its annihilation. The method of *Kiss Me Deadly* seems to follow the example of Pat's description of certain nuclear testing sites to a bewil-

Kiss Me Deadly. A surly and distrustful Hammer questions Carmen Trivago, an opera singer who has seen better days.

dered Hammer: ". . . just a bunch of letters scrambled together, but their meaning is very important. Try to understand what they mean."

Aldrich and writer A. I. Bezzerides imply that one of America's problems is that it has no cultural tradition. Our "respectable" culture is on loan—German music, African masks, Italian opera, Greek mythology, French painting—and our connection with it is superficial. America turns such culture into a product, a consumer good. Its true culture is the automobile, the tape recorder, and the rest of its impressive technology. The film's use of ethnics is sad and despairing. America has not been good to them or their culture. The new world gobbles up the old. Trivago lives in a dream of his rapturous operas, the beauty of the music in strident contrast to both his hovel and his manic accompaniment. Hammer smashes his records. Nick the Greek is out of his mind, deranged by the speed and noise of cars—there is nothing Greek left about him at all. Nick's mania separates him from his mild assistant, Sammy. When Sammy cautions him, Nick responds tartly, "You play your guitar, Sammy, boy." (Sammy later weeps over Nick's dead body, crushed by a car.) There is the garrulous old man lugging trunks his own size up flights of stairs for a living, whose repetitious lament of people who "never stand still" is thematically related to Velda's outburst on the "great whatsit." This old immigrant (he responds to Hammer first in Italian, checks himself, and goes on in English) may be insignificant and un-American in being resigned to his menial, physically strenuous job, but his steadfastness and survival are given a religious significance. He talks to Hammer under an arch behind which are stained glass windows and doors. His presence transforms the apartment house into a church or a cathedral. Home is something sacred; roots are important. He says that he has stayed for sixty-three years in one place, the house of his body, and cannot understand the people who are always moving, always coming and going. His life isn't much, but it is sustained by an old truth. The blacks in the film are no better off. They drink and assuage their lot by listening to the blues in "their" nightclub. (It is significant that when Hammer *feels*, he goes to the black nightclub where his sorrows fall on sympathetic ears. As is typical in the genre, the only humanity that exists exists outside the social mainstream. In *Kiss Me Deadly* being outside means being black, female [Christina especially], foreign.)

Eddie Yaeger is advised by Sugar and Charlie to shut up or die. Hammer suggests that he is in the habit of throwing his fights for the moneymen. Aldrich, unlike Fuller, has no faith in America as the nation that unites all other nations, the great family-of-man government. The fear, intimidation, and brutality that permeate his film are an altogether different reading of the McCarthy period of our history. For Aldrich, America is destroying itself. There is no unity, even in personal relationships. Velda and Hammer's exchange — "You're never around when I need you." "You never need me when I'm around." — may stand as a paradigm of the culture's discordance. Hammer's very livelihood depends on widening the rifts between men and women.

The brainy Soberin takes on the dumb Lily/Gabrielle as an accomplice and assumes she will be easy to ditch. Lily may not be too bright, but she is as determined as Hammer. Soberin babbles on about Pandora, the Medusa, Cerberus, and Lily looks at him like he's crazy. All she cares about is what is in the box; whatever it is, she wants half. She smells a double cross and kills Soberin. Now all of it is hers. She opens the box. It hisses and burns. Despite the pain and fear, she continues opening it. Aldrich underscores the perversity of the act. Lily's fascination leads to her death by fire. She could close it fast, but she lifts the lid higher and higher, looking down at what will burn her alive. The human race wants to destroy itself. The incompatibilities of the film — knowledge and ignorance both operating without a moral context and in detachment from human instincts, the literary dialogue sounding peculiar in a genre noted for its tough talk (even Jack Lambert's Sugar comes out with "Life on earth's such a brief span . . .") — are indications of an extreme situation that cannot be brought into line. Lily shoots the one man who can save her; his warning goes unheeded. The fear of world destruction has caused breakdown and madness.

The clue "remember me" — Christina's final plea — is from a love sonnet of Rossetti's that contains the portion quoted in the film, "tell me of a future that you plan." The film's last shot implies there will be no future — and it is not just the fault of foreign powers, eggheads like Soberin in their employ, or modern, unwitting Pandoras. It makes no difference who gets the "great whatsit," them or us. Its existence, period, is madness, the ruthless pursuit of it doubly so. It is Pat and his boys who are holding Christina in custody when she escapes. Aldrich tries to make Velda's key line a throwaway. Groggy from sleep, she disgustedly half mumbles it, back to camera in long shot: "Everyone everywhere is so involved in a fruitless search for *what*?" That's the mood of *Kiss Me Deadly* — frustration, desperation, uncertainty, spiritual emptiness. Velda knows it, but she is tied to Hammer. She too loves what destroys. If she can't get him to bed, she'll make do with mothering him and grumbling.

Kiss Me Deadly. Velda keeping fit for Mike in her nifty office/home arrangement, a nicely ordered world of fashionable linoleum, snazzy striped workout top, and the period's obligatory black leotards. Everything is clean, tasteful, and in place, including the well-behaved and no-doubt pampered pooch. The mammoth file cabinets do not loom or disturb, seem content with the space allotted to them. The fanatic Hammer, heedless of the surrounding order, pushes his butt carelessly onto Velda's desk, thrusting his male ego into her space to grill her at close range, his face almost at the contemptuous scorn it so often wears. Neither Velda's body nor her feelings can sidetrack him; he's only interested in information. (Museum of Modern Art)

The women of the film are at the end of their rope and, as Raymond Durgnat points out, are oddly aggressive, acting with a "forceful, exasperated, clitoral sexuality."[14] All of them want to soften Hammer, and they all fail. They have to be aggressive since the male is sexually undemonstrative. Velda's last name—Wakeman—suggests it is her function to rouse the morally and sexually inert Hammer. She criticizes his self-centeredness, but instinctively pursues her physical attraction and motherly concern, with no results. Where all else fails, her capture does it, but it is too late; unlike earlier fifties films, she cannot save the hero, the hero cannot save her. Lily is Christina's alter ego. They look alike and are naked under identical raincoats. When Christina (female/good) dies, Lily (male/evil) takes over. Christina is named after Christina Rossetti. Lily's real name is Gabrielle, a feminized version of Dante Rosetti's middle name. Hammer, intrigued by the genuineness of the former, gets taken by her double, who calls herself Carver (an ugly name, suggesting, in context, castration). The view of men is summed up in Christina's disappointed look at the garage attendant after his innuendo. If that is all that can be expected of men, then they are hopeless, and women must take the initiative, provoke men's loyalty and concern, as Christina does with Hammer (she gets through to him enough to make him follow up her clue). Sexual hostility and mistrust, though, are like everything else, too aggravated to be cured.

Hammer's quest takes us through a world of contradictions and discrepancies, grotesque pretensions and insidious facades. Everything is counterpointed: Charlie and Sugar and their dames bickering at gin rummy by Carl Evello's elegant swimming pool; Hammer's neat, organized apartment, which belies the sordidness of his line of work; Velda, with her poodle and ballet exercises, the abstract art hanging on her walls, her mobiles, silk bedsheets, intellectual airs, and precise articulation, is always on call to use her body for Hammer's corrupt business; Raymondo's riddle-without-an-answer, which Trivago recites; Christina, named after the poet Rossetti, a scientist mixed up with evil and tortured to death; Wallace, quaking at the dinner table in front of his family, a college pennant pasted on the background wall; the horse-race announcer on the radio letting loose with "joyous dances of victory" and other rhetorical embellishments; Trivago, singing his heart out, surrounded by his hanging underwear; Eddie, the fight manager, admiring the "beautiful" and "lovely" moves of the new young boxer he will sell out when the time is right. *Kiss Me Deadly* is a sinister evocation of a leisured, acquisitive society that is cankered beneath its show of cultured possessions, its hypocritical and skin-deep appreciation of art and beauty.

If *Kiss Me Deadly* is about the death of culture, its cheapening; it is also about the mask of culture, its lure. Christina's apartment is lined with books; the radio is tuned to classical music; paintings adorn her walls; African art is part of the décor. The cultured airs of the desk clerk at the Hollywood Athletic Club collapse immediately when Hammer smacks his face. Hammer walks through Harold Mist's Gallery of Modern Art, past Matisses and Picassos, while Mist, hearing the noise, hastily swallows a bottle of pills. His radio is also tuned to classical music, to which his dying snores enact a ludicrous counterpoint. Hammer, hoping for something to click, tunes in *his* radio to classical music. A tape-recorded message threatening his life cuts harshly through the lovely, archaic, incongruous strains of Brahms's C Minor String Quartet. *Kiss Me Deadly* reflects the period of American life characterized by a veneer of culture, a period when the consolidation of upper-middle-class and middle-class taste included an ersatz interest in art and pseudo-art — art as a reasonably inexpensive (given a high standard of living) luxury, something "fine" that could be turned into a display of its owner's discrimination. It was the era of mass-produced Van Gogh prints hanging in living rooms, of paint-by-number canvases of Picasso's *The Three Musicians*, of encyclopedia hustling, of mobiles, Mondrian linoleum, and the middle-class invasion of the concert halls after the hi-fi boom. Art made democratic by consumerism. The real art is part of the world's "fabulous treasures Soberin refers to, the "something very valuable" Hammer seeks. Man's destiny is to seek the "great whatsit"; he accumulates and digests cultures and civilizations, and their knowledge, to that end. To what avail that knowledge? What good does it do Velda to know Mike's name in Greek if Mike is always pushing forward and never looking back? Soberin laments, "How civilized this earth used to be" and proceeds to kill and torture to get what will blast it to pieces. That is the paradox. We have come to a point where going forward means going back. Which brings us to Dr. Soberin.

Dr. Soberin is the film's most eccentric, fascinating character. He is the only one within the movie who understands the movie. Understanding *Kiss Me Deadly* involves understanding him. He is the mystery. We do not see his face

Focus on

Feeling

until the end of the film, but we hear his voice—strong, superior, urbane, in-different—caustically philosophizing. All of his little speeches are interesting and pertinent to grasping the film, but one, especially, is a true crux. Soberin has captured Hammer and tied him facedown on a bed. Before administering a truth serum, he addresses Hammer (and the audience and himself) with amused contempt:

> Who do you seek? Someone you do not know, a stranger. What is it we are seeking? Diamonds, rubies, gold? Perhaps narcotics. How civilized this earth used to be. But as the world becomes more primitive, its trea-sures become more fabulous. Perhaps sentiment will succeed where greed failed.

The point behind these precise distinctions seems to be that a certain phase of civilization, the phase of "greed," is over. The earth used to be civilized when men sought diamonds, rubies, and so on—things of known and measured value, "treasures" that could be had, possessed, by exercising the rational emo-tion of greed. Soberin accurately assesses that it is this kind of treasure that has motivated Hammer, who has a very minor-league notion of the "great whatsit." Soberin knows what it is, but since he possesses everything else, there is noth-ing left for him to do but seek that which it is impossible to have. The world has become primitive by wanting the "fabulous"—the exotic, the supernatural, the thing that has no name and no known worth. Man is moving beyond civi-lization, through to its other side, back to primitivity and the seeking of un-knowns. Soberin has Velda captive, which he hopes might stir Hammer's "sen-timent," by which he means—in opposition to his former greed—his irrationality, every powerful gut urge a human being has. Man is a creature of powerful rational *and* irrational urges. Soberin's speech is a confession that he has become irrational, and since Hammer's greed has failed—if only for being inapplicable to the matter at hand—he may be prompted to become irra-tional.

Soberin is presented as the embodiment of human history. He is the man all human history has worked to create. He is its apex. He understands human history and his place in it. He is aware of his own sickness and evil. With a weary, cynical, but unperturbed amusement, he remarks to Lily/Gabrielle (the effect again is of someone talking to himself—and given Lily, that is what it amounts to anyway). "There is something sad and melancholy about trips. I al-ways hate to go away. But one has to find some new place, or it would be im-possible to be sad and melancholy again." He cannot bear feeling good; he has the "sickness unto death." And death is what he seeks.

Soberin's hard-core neuroticism seeks for those conditions that would make him miserable, and his philosophical epigram seems to fit human life as

Kiss Me Deadly has shown it. It is not a psychopathological instance, but a bizarrely rational precis of the inevitability of human misery.

Death is the "great whatsit," the great unknown. The only direction a man as civilized as Soberin can go is toward the treasure he knows is death. We know about everything else except death. Death is the greatest exoticism, and it requires the greatest exertion of all our faculties to know it. To have power over death is to have total power, the power of a god. Soberin doesn't want money, and his politics are really of no account—they are never mentioned. He seeks what he knows no human being can possess. He is in love with death. That is what *Kiss Me Deadly* is about—a world in love with death.

Although Soberin's urge has become primitive and irrational, his behavior remains civilized and rational. He is trapped in his neurosis and lacks real will. Knowing what he knows, he cannot succeed and he cannot live. He is in an if-you-win-you-lose-and-if-you-lose-you-lose situation. He seems aware of how absurd his own calm, methodical processes are, yet acts as though he is the master of the situation. I suppose we are meant to see the limits of his own understanding, have a perspective upon his own large perspective. He *thinks* he understands all human history, but the facts of his situation are more absurd than he imagines. He gives Hammer the truth serum, but the joke is on him, since Hammer knows nothing. He thinks he controls Lily because he thoroughly understands her, but she takes him by surprise and shoots him. Soberin does not acknowledge his own vulnerability. He knows the deadly nature of the treasure but thinks he can control it. The desire to be a god is a primitive urge, a myth that modern man believes can be made into a reality. For all his irony, Soberin must feel, deep down, that he can be the one exception—the man who can know and hold and possess the "fabulous." He *understands*, but as Lily's actions demonstrate, understanding is beside the point in the absence of instinct.

In *Kiss Me Deadly* all the issues of the genre in the fifties are brought to a crest and then drowned in a tidal wave of pessimism. The hero who questions the status quo becomes its victim. Women, who are explicitly defined as creatures of instinct, fail to assert it. Soberin is the ultimate version of the gangland boss who aspires to godly control. His death scene implies that there is no point any longer in suppressing his understanding of his own understanding—that the "great whatsit" is not a treasure but a nothing until it is opened (and it cannot be opened), that he has been courting death all along. He dies with no regret, no resistance, and no complaints about the manner, place, and circumstance of his death. His response to being shot is to make a speech. He warns Gabrielle not to open the box and falls to the floor.

If Soberin is at the highest end of the continuum of rationality (about to come full circle with primitivity), Lily/Gabrielle is at the lowest (the civilized

Focus on

Feeling

Kiss Me Deadly. Lily/Gabrielle, terrified but mesmerized, gazes into the atomic box whose fire will consume her.

greed for palpable treasures—diamonds, rubies, and so on). She is firm and laconic about her wants: "What's in the box? . . . I want half." Soberin points out for us her "feline perceptions," the "creature comforts" she has given him. He knows about women's sure instincts and about their impulses and curiosities (he cites Pandora and Lot's wife). Gabrielle, as a woman might, goes to open the box. There is nothing exceptional about that. But she continues opening it, and that tells us that even women have lost their instincts. They are no longer men's salvation; like men, they are in love with death (Gabrielle caresses the box). The box is *hot*; when Hammer opens it and gets burned, he clamps it shut immediately. Gabrielle keeps lifting the lid and staring straight down at the white fire that consumes her. She couldn't be expected to understand Soberin's intellectual patter, but this is something that requires no understanding. It is not even an instinct but a reflex. Anything human and animal knows to back away from heat and fire. The viewer, who presumably has more instinct left than Gabrielle, watches horrified.

It all sounds outlandish, and it is—outlandishly ambitious, outlandishly good. One could discuss forever the meanings and implications of *Kiss Me Deadly*'s visual, verbal/aural detailing, and, given the immensity of its theme, what piece of weirdness, or tonal incongruity, or unexpected emphasis couldn't in some way be accounted for? Chaos has no boundaries. In a world that is going off the deep end, everything can be made to fit and fall in as either cause, result, oblique argument, or appropriate mood. And it all does fit: Christina's address (325 Bunker Hill); the singing bird that Carver lets die; Velda's poodle and the cat at Soberin's answering service resting on pillows; Nick's "va-va-voom"; the Hollywood Athletic Club, whose initials are flashed on the screen—HAC (a reference perhaps to HUAC—Bezzerides was blacklisted); the sound of the surf so loudly mixed in in the beach house scenes; Soberin's first and middle initial, G. E. (an allusion to the firm whose familiar motto is "Progress is our most important product"?) and his hideous parody of the bedside manner when he pats Hammer's leg after administering the needle; the recurrent "x" patterns—outside Hammer's apartment, at Nick's garage, in the repeated shot of the beach from under the house, and in many other images; the unusual number of reverse angles, and even characters reversing their position in the frame, the way the framing often separates parts of the body and treats faces and limbs as compositional components; the prolif-eration of names in a world where people are strangers to each other, names that the characters themselves disregard or qualify as of no account (Hammer introduces himself to Lily with "My name is Mike Hammer, if it matters," and Soberin says to Hammer over the phone, "You probably will wonder who this is, but it does not matter"); the street lights flashing on and off outside Diker's house; Velda's obscene and sexually frustrated aposiopesis: " . . . and hang by the . . ." (while revolving her hand down a phallic exercise pole). There is much to tease us into thought for a long time to come.

CREDITS *Kiss Me Deadly*

United Artists, 1955, 105 min.

Producer	Robert Aldrich	Cast	Ralph Meeker (Mike Hammer)
Director	Robert Aldrich		Maxine Cooper (Velda Wakeman)
Screenplay	A. I. Bezzerides (from the novel		Albert Dekker (Dr. Soberin)
	by Mickey Spillane)		Wesley Addy (Pat Murphy)
Photography	Ernest Laszlo		Cloris Leachman (Christina Bailey)
Editor	Michael Luciano		Gaby Rodgers (Lily Carver, Gabrielle)
Art Director	William Glasgow		Nick Dennis (Nick)
Music	Frank DeVol		Jack Elam (Charlie Max)
			Jack Lambert (Sugar Smallhouse)
			Paul Stewart (Carl Evello)
			Juano Hernandez (Eddie Yaeger)
			Percy Helton (Dr. Kennedy)
			Marion Carr (Friday)
			Mort Marshall (Ray Diker)
			Fortunio Bonavona (Carmen Trivago)
			Jerry Zinneman (Sammy)

Contemporary Colorations
The Modernist Perspective

Kiss Me Deadly was noir's belated climax and, as well, a film in which the moral fervor of the early fifties gasped its last gasp and gave up. After Kiss Me Deadly, the genre enters its modernist phase. In the late fifties and early sixties the genre makes fresh starts and explorations and strikes new attitudes, however tentatively. Burdened by cheap production and by the obligation to break new ground, the films are often not as confident as one might wish, but they supply the artistic and tonal foundations for the more popular, surefooted, lavish, and ceremonious (though not necessarily superior) genre films of the late sixties and early seventies.

The label "modernist" is somewhat voguish and unsatisfactory, but may serve to cover the strategies of films as distinct as Bonnie and Clyde, Point Blank, The Godfather, and The Godfather II. The term signifies, in the main, an articulate and consciously conceived nonillusionistic cinema. The genre from the late sixties on is marked by films that prevent the audience from nursing the illusion that they are watching a real world. The nature of the relationship between art and the audience (and art and reality) undergoes a major shift. The quality of involvement/detachment integral to the *meaning* of a film like *Bonnie and Clyde* is a generic syndrome of the decade 1965–1975. Broadly speaking, even through the fifties, the world on the screen was something to *believe* in for an hour and a half. Creating an illusion of reality was a dominating principle. Elements of nonillusionism that threatened it remained incidental; they were properties more than principles. Certainly, watching *Bonnie and Clyde* (1967) is nothing like watching *99 River Street* (1953) or *Gun Crazy* (1949) and very different from watching *Little Caesar* (1930). The experience of *Bonnie and Clyde* is *weird*, and its weirdness can only be understood by postulating a working assumption about art and reality made possible by the development of the genre. To go from A to C you have to go through B.

The photograph is so much a replica that it becomes a subtle distinction to describe any kind of commercial feature film as nonillusionistic (paintings in comparison can be designated rather easily). Also, the nature of the medium as a public commodity determines, to a very real extent, the limit of radical gestures. No John Cage could exist in Hollywood. A modernist sensibility would proceed with discretion, even in 1975. The economics of moviemaking may have somewhat slowed down the feature film's emergence into modernism, but it could not prevent it. From 1945 on, the audience was carried gradually to the point where it was ready to "see" a film like *Bonnie and Clyde*. Hindsight shows us that *Bonnie and Clyde* had to come at a specific point; it could not have been made before.[1] It took the audience where it was ready to go.

By the late sixties the genre enters, along with the rest of cinema, an age of uncertainty. It is forced inward, toward its own procedures, which become increasingly sophisticated. It used to be that well-established procedures could be used to move outward toward an audience they could securely engage. Now the audience must be seduced into accepting new aesthetic resources and complex (and at times schizophrenic) attitudes. The outlook of films like *The St. Valentine's Day Massacre* and *Bonnie and Clyde* is not easy to fathom; their mixture of tones and cartoonish characterizations suggests that a contemporary sensibility working with gangster material cannot achieve a certainty of vision, statement, or judgment. In *The Grissom Gang* (1971) Robert Aldrich gives the audience a slobbering cretin to identify with. The first section of *Point Blank* is virtually incomprehensible.

But *Point Blank* didn't happen overnight. A few other short runs anticipated some of its qualities. Two major strains are evident: period biographies of historical gangsters (*Baby Face Nelson* [1957], *Machine-Gun Kelly* [1958], *Al Capone* [1959]) that stress their neurotic aggression, and a new type of cold, restrained, psychotic hero who must master a complex environment—recognizably our own—in a context that eliminates right and wrong (*The Line-Up* [1958], *Murder by Contract* [1958], *The Killers* [1964]). (*Bonnie and Clyde*, *The Grissom Gang*, *Bloody Mama* [1972], *The Godfather* [1972], and *Dillinger* [1973] derive from the former; *Point Blank*, *Dirty Harry* [1971], *The Mechanic* [1972], and most contemporary police films derive from the latter.) The main difference between them is that the early gangsters are shown as out of control, the contemporary heroes as very much in control. In both, the accent is on behavior; we are not concerned with what they believe but with how they perform. The dramatic qualities of black and white photography are not exploited; environments are generally kept neutral. The thirties figures are undone by their abnormality, the modern ones by some freak of circumstance that confounds all their surveying of the situation, their precise, calculated, poised, unflamboyant, and controlled application of resources, and their effective disguise of normality. In works with modern settings, the silencer comes into its own, its quiet, impersonal pffft in accord with the daylight merging of crime into the social mainstream (the white, clean look of *Machine-Gun Kelly*, the public locales of *The Line-Up*). (The old gangsters could be heard a mile away, nor did they hide behind roles.) Only the briefest explanations are ever given of why the characters are disturbed; primarily, we watch how (without being much concerned with why) their behavior reaches toward or departs from understood norms.

In *Bonnie and Clyde* displacement into the past functions to provide an "un-reality." The opposition between inside and outside the society, the individual versus the system, cannot be set up in present terms or in visuals on the screen that are meant to be understood as real (one has only to recall the credit sequence). To comment on the present, it is necessary to use the past. Reality can't be seen straight on, but indirectly, out of the corner of the eye. The state of our society and our place in it are incomprehensible via "showing" things as they are, the facts—because nothing is clear-cut. Meaning in *Bonnie and Clyde* emerges from the discrepancy between the story imaged and told and the feeling with which it is done (and our attitude toward it). Meaning, as perhaps inadvertently accomplished in *The Phenix City Story*, happens in us, off the screen. The reality is in our complex of reaction rather than in the events, action, or the characters as set up on the screen (the furor over *Bonnie and Clyde* suggests as much). Our removal from the story, our detachment and our impotence and our not caring, is a sustained happening in us during the film.

A whole other mode of consciousness is operating. We don't think about the meanings and implications of the story; we don't analyze rationally and categorize, because we sense that these are useless routes to understanding. The technique of the film works against the assumption that reason and logic, or the exposition of facts, will reveal what needs to be revealed. Realization comes from other sources, in our own dim awareness of how we are, something the film aggravates off the screen, via the work not in the work. In *The Brothers Rico* the problems remained firmly within the film. We may have been implicated in the character's inability to respond adequately, but it was *his* inability, *his* moral problem within the view of life the film showed us. In *Bonnie and Clyde* nothing coheres into a view of life; there is nothing to reflect on, only to react to. We sit, and watch, and interact. Here we are amazed, there we are shocked, but the film moves right on. The human reverberations of any event are withheld, moral reverberations eliminated. In *Little Caesar* Flaherty is part of a well-defined moral scheme. In *Bonnie and Clyde* Hamer has no morality, nor does anyone else in the film. The vicariousness of *Bonnie and Clyde* is a trickery. The film, in preventing us from caring about the characters, at the same time bending over backward to involve us, forces us to be involved in ourselves, our present individual existences. It draws out our own tensions.

Everything in the movie is a fait accompli, much as it is in classic tragedy or in *Little Caesar*, but our emotions are manipulated differently. There is no bad versus good. The shadings of those categories are absent. Neither morality nor justice is an issue. We are asked to perceive what used to be a tragic situation as drained of reality and emotional consequence within the film. Yet the results are vivid and powerful; the film gains strong reactions. We are made to watch an old story in a new way. It is narrative but not narrative; it is the star system but not the star system; there are characters but there are not characters; there are values but there are no values. We believe in a character played by John Wayne because we believe in John Wayne. We believe in Eddie Rico because Richard Conte is just a name, like in a telephone book. In *Bonnie and Clyde*, however, we swing back and forth between reacting to Warren Beatty and Faye Dunaway and the characters they play. *Bonnie and Clyde* is a striking departure for the genre because instead of shedding or clearly transforming all of the "givens," it uses them as stark conventions in a context of impotency. We can't do anything with *Bonnie and Clyde* except *watch* it.

In retrospect, it is possible to hypothesize that the brouhaha over *Bonnie and Clyde* was caused by audiences (and critics) being not entirely sure about what they felt, however strongly they felt it, and, as well, by an inability to reconcile what they did feel with what they were supposed to feel. The content of the film feeds nicely into all our "right" humanistic values, but somehow we can never quite fit them, and their related feelings, to the film. Blanche in prison interrogated by Hamer, Buck with his head blown apart, the massacre of Bonnie and Clyde—it is as though we are immune to the horror of these events. Violence became the central issue about the film because we were bothered by it but not really bothered by it. And we were bothered that we could be both. Moreover, it was impossible to locate our feelings in the characters or the issues in the film, because in one sense there weren't any. It all happened long ago, and to people it would make no sense to care about. (The meaning of the events resides in the conflict between the audience and the action and is not between conflicting forces within the film. We don't get "lost" in the film; we know it is a film all the time.)

In *Point Blank* everything assumes an unreality, and the inevitable mode of storytelling is the dream—the literal dream presented as the reality. Dream logic and time and space dislocations usurp a mechanical, ordered structure that presumes rational coherence. Truth and meaning are to be found only in a hallucinatory reality. We can't comprehend *Point Blank* as it unfolds in time; we must apprehend it at each instant. As the fate of its hero demonstrates, reality is unknowable and unmanageable.

By *The Godfather* (1972), the merging and blurring of the genre's conflicts evolve into a presentation of a single world. There is no set of major oppositions in conflict. Minor differences aside, the world on the screen is not split according to values or desires. We are given one world—the underworld (supposedly). We have gone from lawful society to those outside the law to the implication that the distinction doesn't hold or isn't meaningful to only one world on the screen, and the conflict or opposition that is crucial to the meaning of the film occurs between the audience and the world of the film, not within the

Contemporary
Colorations

239

film. The world of *The Godfather* is one unified minisociety in which the conflict of values within that world is less a source of enlightenment than the mixture of emotions evoked by the conflict between our values as against those in the world of the film. The recognition of similarity between the drives of the "family" on the screen, supposedly horrid, and ours, is the place of enlightenment. In *The Public Enemy* and other classic gangster films, there were two worlds on the screen, with parallels drawn between them. In *The Godfather* there are also two worlds; one is there in the film, but the other is not visible.

None of the three films can be called representational art. Separation between the work and its audience is bridged; factors outside the work are integrated into the work. The illusion that what you are seeing is real (suspension of disbelief) is carefully and deliberately destroyed. A mirror of life is impossible. Movies have existed long enough to have become an inescapable ordering or disordering of conventions. Most movies now, whatever else they go on to try to do, seem to rely on our perception of images and behavior as conventionalized. At the same time there is no shared system of picturing, narrating, or characterization. In an aesthetically self-conscious and sophisticated climate, a free network of aesthetic possibilities produces markedly different films, as the three that follow. The gangster (and the gangster film) is no longer to be confused with reality but is obviously an imaginative accretion of the culture's schizophrenia and five decades of finding out how celluloid can be used and joined. The genre no longer records, or elaborates on headlines; it fashions poems, dreams, epics, myths. Its characters do not have a strong individual identity; they are paragons, studies, imprints, not "real" men and women. They are not people whose emotions mean anything (the last weak sign of that seemed to die with Mike Hammer) but *signs* of emotions and qualities that we have learned to view detachedly, in part because we have become curious about them in ourselves.

The substitute for characters we can care for and a reality we can believe in (the lack of which in the films corresponds to our actual problems of knowing and feeling) is the creation/depiction, through one or another aesthetic strategy, of that condition on the screen/in the theater. If there are no more stories to tell, if there is nothing it makes sense to be involved in, what do you put on the screen? What becomes subject matter? The genre's response is to deal with what you can't do anything about at all—the past—which doesn't function as subject matter of intrinsic interest but as a means of creating an emotional point off the screen (*Bonnie and Clyde, The Godfather, Point Blank, Dillinger, The St. Valentine's Day Massacre, The Grissom Gang, Bloody Mama, The Valachi Papers*—almost every major gangster film of the period), or it creates characters and heroes who can scarcely be defined as human (in the old sense)—Harry Callahan (*Dirty Harry*), Michael Corleone (*The God-*

father and *Godfather II*), Charlie Strom (*The Killers*), Walker (*Point Blank*) — utilizing the stone-faced, laconic, murderous stillness of actors like Lee Marvin, Clint Eastwood, and Charles Bronson.

A way out of both torpor and bewilderment for both the characters on the screen and the audience that watches them is to increase the level of violence and also to create highly aggressive fictions that have little regard for facts. The credits of *Machine-Gun Kelly* state that "the title character upon which this story is based is true." That cannot be argued with, but the rest is a very free treatment of history. The film's low-budget carelessness in fact reveals its passions and attitudes. Frenetic thirties music alternates with modern jazz; distractingly contemporary location shooting mingles with period-flavored interiors; the characters go about their business with the unreflective dynamism of past heroes but pause to telegraph their neuroses. At times inadvertently, at times quite consciously, the film announces that, although it is set in the past, it is talking about the present. This is always implicit in period films, but in *Machine-Gun Kelly* (and in many other genre films from the late fifties on) it is on the surface. It is not necessary to cite the myriad excesses and inventions of violence in recent gangster crime films, and the different kind of audience connoisseurship they create and/or presuppose. Forties violence was quick, surprising, and often bloodless (a car cigarette lighter pressed into the driver's eye in *Thelma Jordan*, Burt Lancaster's arm released from traction in *Criss Cross*). In the sixties and seventies violence is protracted and graphic and the "wasting" of human life is cheered, applauded, and laughed at, as well as shuddered at. The distancing aesthetic exaggerations of films like *Bloody Mama*, *Bonnie and Clyde*, *The Godfather*, *Dillinger*, *Mean Streets*, and others (of which an assaulting violence is but one part) are signs of a modernist consciousness successfully grafted onto popular entertainment.

Two other aspects of the genre's modernist phase are important: the use of color and the emergence of a director's cinema. The gangster crime genre, perhaps more than any other, seemed suited for black and white. During the fifties, when many B productions in other genres (musicals, Westerns, sci-fi) were in color, the genre remained black and white, the accepted mode of cinema "reality" (for many years, color was associated with spectacle, triviality, and fantasy). Given traditional and automatic associations of black and white, each shot contained an aspect of morality as well as mood. It may be more than circumstance that the genre succumbed to color at the point where its content was being treated more and more amorally, since color abolishes an automatic moral-dramatic spectrum. The genre uses color to violate a sense of reality (the surreal intensity of *Mean Streets*, the distracting period "beauty" of *The Godfather* and *The Godfather II*), to convey psychological states (*Party*

Contemporary
Colorations

241

Girl, Point Blank, The Killers), for irony (the lulling Technicolor of *Bonnie and Clyde*, the pastels of *Dillinger*), for lurid emotiveness (*Bloody Mama, The Grissom Gang*). Whatever its uses, though, whether for tone, emotiveness, or psychology, color is morally disengaging.

The days when every genre B picture looked more or less the same as any other as they came off the assembly line are gone, and one reason the gangster/crime genre offers so distinct a variety of product since the mid-sixties is the felt presence of the director. In the past, one had to hunt for niceties of individual expression; a director nowadays has a bolder freedom of expression and a greater share of publicity, making his presence, and our awareness of it, more noticeable. Martin Scorsese's verité of the emotions in the enclosed, allusive "movie" world of *Mean Streets* is unmistakably individual. Roger Corman's movies are marked by a comic-conservative juxtaposition of sensationalized freaks and staunch norms and what can be argued as his misogyny. Peckinpah's romantic iconoclasm (in *The Getaway* they get away) is leagues removed from Aldrich's hostility and disgust (*The Grissom Gang*, ugly and pugnacious all the way, seems like the director's answer to *Bonnie and Clyde*). By now, Don Siegel's interest in the professionalism of borderline psychopaths is a trademark, and Francis Ford Coppola has become the De Mille of the genre (*The Godfather* tapping the audience that used to stand in line for De Mille's spectaculars), or at least the underworld's court painter, chronicle weaving and pictorializing on an epic, public scale. ("Michael is America," he has said.) All these directors make films that are tours de force, that depend not on the nuances of verisimilitude but on broad, and often eccentric, filmic styles. We never lose sight of the films as films, conscious manipulations of our attention. They cannot address us otherwise because, like modern art in general, they can only reflect the truth about a contemporary relationship with reality, that of paralysis—a condition from which there is no escape and that art, to sustain itself, must find new ways to articulate. *Walking Tall* (1973), made by an old-fashioned moralist like Phil Karlson, is an exception. A loose remake of his *The Phenix City Story*, it calls for action. The film is based on real incidents, but the hero, Buford Pusser, unlike John Patterson, becomes a pure animal, a pair of eyes through a mask of bandages, a mythic hero leading the community's retribution. He does all our fighting for us, becomes a grotesque spectacle we are awed by. Our response to his good deeds is not much different from our response to the death of Bonnie and Clyde, of Slim and Barbara in *The Grissom Gang*, of the death of the Barker gang in *Bloody Mama*. We gape at the tornado of violence in the film, much as the gaping and gawking crowds, echoes of ourselves as viewers, watch the perversion and carnage in *The Grissom Gang, Bloody Mama*, and *Bonnie and Clyde*. It has often been remarked that art awakens us to our true condition. The genre's main purpose now is to address our boredom, passivity, and ineffectuality. As the big events of the underworld pass before our eyes, it is with a discomfiting sense of their inconsequentiality to us and ours to them. It is always an open question, however, whether the films are simply reflecting that condition or bringing it to a point of awareness. The methods of analysis seem within reach, but they are always overwhelmed by emotion, the need to produce emotion in the audience. Perhaps the ancient distinction between art and propaganda, mimetic versus didactic, still holds firm within a barrage of sophistications, and no film can afford to become a treatise. The premise of this book has been that within our pleasures we may find instruction, however much the nature of both keeps changing in the genre.

Bonnie and Clyde (1967)

*B*onnie and Clyde is one of the most important and popular films of the six-ties.[2] Coming eighteen years after *Gun Crazy* (the similarities between the films in structure and incident are strong), it shows that the assumptions of Lewis's film can no longer be held. Bart and Laurie were restless, confused, and itching for excitement. *Bonnie and Clyde*, after what the fifties demon-strates, must regard a similar state of urgency as explicitly pathological, and where Lewis seemed to get behind the feelings of his young people, Penn seems remote. The film's mixture of tones reflects the frayed sensibility of the late sixties. Warren Beatty and Faye Dunaway are so obviously more intelligent than the scatterbrained characters they are asked to play that their perfor-mances become charades, impersonations. The characters of Bonnie and Clyde contain unresolvable contradictions. Bonnie is an introspective sensualist who sublimates her passions into stiff doggerel. Clyde's infantile vitality compen-sates for his impotence. Lewis's point of view was complex; Penn's seems in-decisive, as it perhaps must be. It is not that he wants to take a position and can't; it would be pointless to take a position. And so we veer from high-spirited comedy to ironic deflation to sentimental celebration, and so on, until the lyri-cal atrocity of the ending, which, like the rest of the film, leaves us more dazed than illuminated. Bonnie and Clyde see into each other, we see into them, and Penn sees into us, and shoots accordingly. One is not altogether sure what all the seeing adds up to, however. The film seems to operate on a level of rea-sonless necessity. The film must happen, but there is no telling why. The con-ventions of narrative and characterization, so inventively intensified by Lewis in *Gun Crazy*, are all awry in *Bonnie and Clyde*. Bonnie and Clyde are less au-tonomous characters than Bart and Laurie, and *Bonnie and Clyde* is not an ac-tion movie at all because the action is always embalmed within an idea or an attitude. Action, narrative, or emotion don't build because there are no values or meanings toward which the material can accumulate. It is all essentially static film kineticized by frantically edited set pieces

Penn knows that to make this old story work, a new approach, a new mode, is required. Simply plugging it into the cultural climate (which he does very deftly, and which most films manage to do anyway) is not enough. The film demonstrates that he has grasped that there are certain things that cannot be believed about movies anymore—that since reality is questionable, he can go to a period by now unreal (the thirties) and stress its unreality, that he can cre-ate characters who are not spontaneous, that he can work on the discrepancy between action and stasis, attitude and fact, that what there is to say about the present is the feeling we have about the past we watch in the film. Our impo-tence to alter the past is evident. The *present* of the movie (and this explains the film's enormous and controversial impact) *happens* in our feelings, not *on* the screen. The film is not about Bonnie and Clyde. The truth, for the genre in the sixties, resides in its finding a vehicle to create a psychic and emotional happening between the audience and the screen that makes sense (as a psychic and emotional happening, not a rational understanding, not something accessible, perhaps, to textual analysis). Penn elicits numbness, detachment, noninvolvement, pointlessness *through* the logic of depicting what is wholly over and having us watch it run its course as a stylistic tour de force.

Bonnie and Clyde. Bull's eye. Fun-loving neurotics Bonnie and Clyde share an early moment of high spirits.

In *The Killers* (1946) or in *Kiss Me Deadly* the indifference to human life, the cruelties of death, the cynicism are all within the film; they belong to the characters in the film. In *Bonnie and Clyde* these emotions and attitudes are ours. We don't resist them. The conception depends on them, reinforces them. The thrills of vicarious experience exist in paradoxical combination with the feeling that none of it makes any difference. In *Gun Crazy* it makes sense for Lewis to have us care. By the sixties it makes no sense to have us care. Art becomes not an escape, a dream, an entertainment in the old sense but a means to counteract boredom. Penn says, in effect, *look* at this, tune in. It is impossible for you to care about it, but it is something to do.[3] His distancing into the past is a choice motivated by entirely different conceptions than, say, *The Roaring Twenties* (1939). It is used basically to ensure nonillusionistic effects as opposed to vicarious involvement in and nostalgia for another era. We are kept from participating by being reminded that we are watching a movie.

In the credit sequence, the small print that provides brief histories of the actual Bonnie and Clyde is virtually irrelevant. What are of note are the undisguised operations of the medium—the click of the camera accompanying the photographs, the credits turning from white to red, the sudden substitution of the actor Warren Beatty in a photograph resembling the actual Clyde Barrow, and finally Bonnie's huge red lips, the intensity of the image abolishing our sense of what has preceded. (She is also using the camera lens as a mirror, and when she turns to a real mirror, the effect is quite disorienting.) This cannot be confused with reality or "realism." It insists that what we are watching is something on a movie screen—that we are here, and it is there.[4]

Bonnie and Clyde takes its immediate cues from the senselessness and chaos of the mid-sixties—the country's divisiveness over the Vietnam war, the inroads of the youth culture, and the generation gap. (Certainly, most young viewers in the audience knew, when C. W.'s father exploded over his son's tattoo—he couldn't care less about the blood-splattered Bonnie and Clyde—what that was all about in 1967. The film also catches some of the spirit of the period's unstable idealism—the tensions of the society vented in comic release [the Yippies as a corrective to anguish, solemnity, and the stultification of instinct, performing the ancient function of clowns and fools with ritual mockeries of politics and social mores; the development of communes; the invocation of Eros; the entire medley of liberating, antiestablishment gestures].) What the Barrow gang does is senseless. Their occasional generosity toward people and their hostility toward institutions is not what motivates them. All that is incidental to their genuine desperation, their utter hollowness. (The impromptu vigilante group that, yahooing, berserkly destroys their car, is made up of people Bonnie and Clyde would like to think are plain folk like themselves.) Their slaughter is equally senseless. Hamer and the ambushers slowly approach to examine what is left of Bonnie's body through the window of the demolished car. We peer at them through the same window from the other side of the car. Their blank faces suggest that they don't know quite what they've just done. There is no insight gained for victims, executioners, or viewers. Their death is really irrelevant—like Bonnie's poetry, Clyde's sexual triumph, Hamer's vengeance, Blanche's religion, "I love you," having dreams, desiring to act. Nothing resonates. Penn, wisely, knows what he must do—prolong the fact and the moment of their death.

Bonnie and Clyde's ideas about possibilities are pitted against what we in 1967 know. They have an illusion about themselves that we know is an illusion. They lack a sense of reality, ours as well as theirs. However admirable Clyde's will may be, we cannot help but see the folly of it. The impetus to roam free, to govern the land, to move westward has no object anymore, but the American psyche still wishes to see it enacted. Penn gives it to us in a context of ironic detachment. We may be pleasurably amazed to hear the banjo music start up again—albeit in more limping fashion—after the escape through the swamp, but it tells us Clyde is a hopeless case. His "rushing toward death" cannot be treated tragically like Roy Earle's; it is too absurd. One *feels* for Earle; one is incredulous at Clyde. Bonnie and Clyde, both youngest children of their families, are infantile, narcissistic lost souls. They can't go home again, and they can't really speak to a modern sense of aimlessness or revolt. Clyde's impotence, we are given to understand, is a self-inflicted one. The world hasn't made him impotent. The action of the lovers in *Gun Crazy* meant something; Lewis gave it a sense of necessity. Bonnie and Clyde are more obviously mixed up and naive, despite their appealing glamour and ebulliency. Clyde's vitality ("Ain't life grand?") is always closely connected to his naiveté and mental disturbance. Ivan Moss tells C. W. that "they ain't nuthin' but a couple of kids"—and he is right. To a modern sensibility innocence can't be heroic or tragic. *Point Blank* and *The St. Valentine's Day Massacre* were also released in 1967, and there is no reason to suppose that Penn or his audience would regard innocence unironically. Bonnie and Clyde remain oblivious of Ivan Moss's treachery. They go into town casually, like any normal couple. When C. W. disappears, Clyde revealingly refers to him as "that boy," the way a father might protest his offspring's incorrigibility (and we have just seen C. W. partaking of the ice cream his father has brought back after setting up the ambush with Hamer). The innocence of this couple is too radical for a knowing modern audience to support. It is part of a world that no longer exists, part of the *essence* of the past the film gives us—placid, empty, cityless, and where state lines mean something—a world so far away as to be unreal.

Bonnie and Clyde is not in the least nostalgic. The past seems dead and frozen; the thirties takes on a ghostly ambience. The environments are severely functional and have little force of their own. This is not typical period re-creation; it is not a "full" world we are asked to believe represents the actual atmosphere of the 1930s. The world is seen as a place of opportunity for Bonnie and Clyde; it is an abstraction based on their psychology. They go through it like a hot knife through butter. The period is distanced, impalpable; it is not present as a felt reality but resembles a stage backdrop. No environment can compete with the mental and emotional input the characters bring to it. The characters do not have to confront or deal with anything but each other in a succession of static settings. The visuals of the film are unrealistic, having neither the density nor tactility of real life nor illusionist methods of picturing reality. The general effect is like a Tom and Jerry cartoon, everything flattened into a pure surface.

Penn's strategies serve to keep us detached from actions we would, as a matter of course, become involved with. The banjo music often supports tone and attitude, but sometimes works against them, and it disrupts illusion by working as a device to separate episodes. The film could even be criticized as overcalculated were its calculations not entirely pertinent to its purpose. Penn's compositions are static. Things seem to come as in a pattern, carefully staged beforehand. It is too "tasteful" a film to be gripping in conventional ways, and its tastefulness is a result of a deliberate artificiality. Even in action sequences, Penn doesn't compromise his compositions. He is not giving us, primarily, a story and characters to believe in, but pictures to look at.

What seemed like awkwardness, and at times incompetence, in *Machine-Gun Kelly*, is here done with great skill and confidence. *Kiss Me Deadly*, for all its virtuosity, hid its seams within its density, clamor, and forward momentum. In *Bonnie and Clyde* the seams all show. Each transition, from the credits to Bonnie's mouth on, smacks of directorial decision. Penn's technique is exaggerated, overwrought. Each new element—C. W. Moss, Buck, Blanche, the succession of settings and locales—is not integrated. The egregiousness of the art direction and the attempts of the secondary cast members to burst into prominence give a disjointed effect. At no time does the purpose seem to be to reflect a coherent image of reality. Even Bonnie and Clyde are pitted *against* each other visually, as if to vie for the viewer's attention. Bonnie is loose, long-legged, soft, her clothes accentuating the flowing lines of her body always provocatively posed or in motion, her sensual neck and throat highlighted. Clyde's dress and movement, in contrast, suggest repression—shirt buttoned right to the top, tight suit; he is all angles as opposed to Bonnie's curves. Their wardrobe and movement are in character, but the effect is to split the focus of interest. One's attention is directed more to what they look like than to who they are. But there is little point in making the audience care who they are, as we do with Nick Bianco or Joe Morse, or want to care, as we do with Swede (and are prevented).

Bonnie and Clyde's long walk down to the center of town, C. W.'s gas station aria, Hamer's sadistic interrogation of Blanche—these scenes are like animated cartoons. Penn's lighting stresses the faces and bodies of his cast; they are always firmly outlined against a thirties background that is like an evocative shorthand and has none of the density of a full-bodied recreation of a time and place. Characters dominate settings by being photographically favored and conceptually quotation-marked. The gas station is too picturesque; the grocery is unreal; the kitchen of C. W.'s house doesn't feel like a kitchen; the main street in West Dallas is unnaturally lifeless; the hamburger joint has the airlessness of a TV studio set; the motels lack the ambience of motels; even the cars lack presence (all we feel is the people in them). In his long shots, especially, Penn conveys a kind of fantasy emptiness. In contrast to *Gun Crazy*, setting, action, character, and behavior do not seem solidly welded. For Lewis, the action is its own significance. He builds his characterizations *through* action. Penn's action confirms what we already know or suspect about the characters. Action represents not the means out of a trap but the chaos of living within one.

Penn lets his characters run away with the film as if the world they moved through was of no consequence, as if, in fact, the characters were not part of that world at all but actors who have been asked to impersonate certain temperaments that can be potent in combination with others—the world become a stage. Thus Gene Wilder's hilarious stint alters the tone of the film, but *what* he is as a person in that period is unessential but for his "undertaker" punchline. Penn uses him, then dumps him. Gene Hackman, Estelle Parsons, and Michael J. Pollard similarly respond to their roles as histrionic opportunities, going to excess where they might have modulated their style for a less off-balance effect in a more illusionistic film. Like Beatty and Dunaway, they pose, savor, mime, soliloquize—for the camera (again, *Gun Crazy* provides a useful contrast). In Penn's film everything is posed, everything is for the camera. Many shots are held for a distractingly long time with the result that our attention wanders from the content. Scenes are blocked in a very mannered fashion. The scene at the first hideout is particularly unsmooth. Everyone is slotted into some physical posture or activity that clangs a loud bell of "personality." The

Bonnie and Clyde. Memorable characterizations of Clyde (Warren Beatty) and Buck Barrow (Gene Hackman) as jolly lawbreakers helped secure the antiestablishment attitudes in favor at the time. Absent is Michael J. Pollard's C. J. Moss, the runt squirt who occupies the bottom rung of this bank-robbing trio. Penn's nervous, undermining demonstration of male egos makes it clear that this early ain't-crime-a-hoot meeting masks the sexual insecurity underneath all the activities of the Barrow gang. (Museum of Modern Art)

intention may be to show the untogetherness of this group arbitrarily thrown into mutual dependence. This suggests that Penn is trying to convey the awkwardness and tension of five psychologically isolated individuals sitting, talking, and moving about in a way that belies their obligation to honor their sudden and notorious unity.

One only has to think of performances at the peak of the star system to recognize how Penn's direction of his cast, with the likely cooperation of their own inclinations, produces vastly different results. Players like Cary Grant and Katharine Hepburn, Joan Crawford and Clark Gable developed a smooth acting style—the result of training, craftsmanship, and talent—that pulled us into the film to share their passions and emotions. They were not us, but we could imagine we were them, on, if not off, the screen. Beatty and Dunaway are neither naturally convincing nor professionally authentic. Nor can they be. By the late sixties and the high forties enactment of emotion and delivery of dialogue seemed impossibly stylized, even false. Its enchantments were the contents of dreams we could no longer have (and, as well, the thrill of thunderous kisses followed by fade-outs of great erotic fantasy could no longer satisfy a more knowing [and gnawing] sexual curiosity). The era of coherent acting personalities, and of the evasion of human awkwardness and incoherence, is, if not over, then certainly reconstituted. In *Bonnie and Clyde* the performances drift toward the comic, the inadequate, the designedly awkward. The actors project a strain, an inauthenticity, as though they had newly graduated from acting school. They seem alienated from their roles. This, perhaps, is part of Penn's desire to keep idealization to a minimum and to suggest the nervousness, insecurity, and nonintegrated personalities of his characters. He gives them a touch of caricature, a slight amateur air that corresponds to their amateur rank as bandits and prevents a significant degree of identification. (These new performance codes did not, of course, develop overnight. In the genre, one can see classical acting style modified and subverted in films as diverse as *Kiss Me Deadly*, *Machine-Gun Kelly*, and *The Brothers Rico*.)

The performances in *Bonnie and Clyde* do not carry us away; like the rest of the film they are there to be *watched*. The film as a whole is full of references and tools that stress aspects of seeing and watching that make us conscious voyeurs. People look at each other through windows; we look at them through windows. There are mirrors and eyeglasses. Bonnie and Clyde are always *on view* to others in their society. The Barrow gang may be fun, engaging, vital, and sensitive, but they are also grotesques, and we observe them as such—C. W. in long johns, Blanche munching a doughnut, Clyde flailing at Hamer in the river, Bonnie posing with cigar and machine gun. There are several scenes of people taking pictures. The extraordinary scene in the movie theater makes it impossible to view the action straightforwardly. The conflict among Bonnie, Clyde, and C. W. is almost drowned out by the sound track from the Berkeley clip, and Penn shoots to ensure that our interest is split between the film and the film within the film—at one point, the old movie takes over the whole screen. In one shot, the producer of the show watches the action on stage from a seat in the theater, and it appears that he is watching Bonnie, Clyde, and C. W.—and we are watching them watch him watch the show. One can infer that these are new ways to keep the audience interested in rather moth-eaten material that has lost all of its former attributes. Besides, *Bonnie and Clyde* is a long movie, and where Joseph H. Lewis could count on breezing through his eighty-seven-minute programmer in a representational style understood as pertinent between himself and his audience, Penn has to pump and pump, to assault and to abstract, to gauze his lens, to make the telephoto shot to end all telephoto shots, to knock 'em dead with slow motion, to get the audience going immediately by a fierce interest in Dunaway's nakedness. His attentiveness becomes our attentiveness, and our engagement with narrative and drama is displaced into an engagement with technique—whether we understand the nature of that displacement or not.

Burnett Guffey's images are more beautiful than dramatic, and their adroitness and elegance summon forth an independent appreciation. One of course *hears* the extended conversation between Bonnie and Clyde at the beginning, but one also admires and feels the effect of the slow and artfully interrupted track down the street—especially pleasant in conjunction with the cool blues and greens of the color scheme—in which Beatty and Dunaway are given a voluptuous observance that no doubt pleased them, and pleases us. Guffey's work under Penn has a slight excess of eloquence that calls attention to itself in, for example, the tableau composition of Bonnie leaning against the bedpost in the awful silence of failed sex, the light dull and soft through the pulled-down shade—the effect is like a painting. The canvas-still style is perfectly employed in the long shot of the car alone in the field at Dexter, Iowa. It is dawn; the birds are chirping, everything seems peaceful. Then we hear gunfire, and the violence erupts to shocking proportions. Penn has set us up cleverly with quiet and scenicness. The car, though, seems vulnerable and out of place in the shot. There is a stirring split second when it becomes evident that something is going to disturb this unnatural peacefulness, though we know not what. It is a beautifully designed shot.

Penn's favorite device to reduce and redirect our involvement is to undercut glory, happiness, and contentment with disaster, disappointment, and death. Bonnie thinks Clyde is hot stuff—she finds out that he can't perform sexually. C. W. thinks Bonnie and Clyde are too clever to get caught—their flesh and blood splatter across a country road. The Barrows pull a big robbery—and get away with peanuts. The potential for continued peace and calm is instantly undone by external threats and internal strife. As the "legend" increases, death casts its shadow over the latter half of the film—the blasted cornfield with the sun-blotting cloud, the picnic with the children playacting death, Eugene the undertaker, the farmer promising to bring flowers to their funeral, Bonnie's ballad, the shot of the car traveling at night (at slower speed), the increasing blood and agony and screaming, the group whittled down to the outcast pair and C. W. sidelined into an unwitting betrayal, the banjo music suddenly dragging to a dirge, Bonnie and Clyde's lovemaking juxtaposed with Ivan Moss's treachery, the laughter of the child at the Okie camp, which brings irony and indifference into a portentous, solemn context.

The freedom of Bonnie and Clyde is an illusion; it is an attempt to escape from reality, an escape that isn't possible. There is no way out for Bonnie and Clyde, and even the attempt to live, to be, is joyless, tense, and insecure. Bonnie knows it well. Right after their most successful (in terms of execution) bank robbery, she complains, "We rob the damn banks—what else can we do?" She knows she had better go see her mother before it is too late. Like women of the fifties she *knows*, but her knowledge does no one any good. Just before being shot, Clyde sends her a look that perhaps implies an understanding that this is how it had to be and that their mutual loyalty and love, however difficult to sustain, was the best that either could have hoped for out of life. Their relation-

Bonnie and Clyde. An evening at home with the Barrow gang. Bonnie sneaks toward Clyde in bed for some affection while C. J. Moss sneaks a peek. (Museum of Modern Art)

ship, however, has been characterized by major confusions and frustrations. The lovers in *Gun Crazy* took a positive charge from their sexual relationship. In the sixties, Bonnie and Clyde are conceived in the light of modern sexual attitudes and problems. The inadequacy of their sexual relationship may elicit sympathy (and perhaps empathy), but it reduces our confidence in the characters.

The sexual disharmony is neither subtle nor occasional, but in the forefront of our perception. The "new violence" of *Bonnie and Clyde* was an aesthetic strategy by which the genre could be transformed into a Pennian vision of the association of violence and sexual difficulties (Cawelti comments on the massacre of Bonnie as her long-awaited orgasm).[5] By the late sixties, the sexual "revolution" was in full swing, its options creating a dither among young and old alike as to how sexual relationships could and should be conducted. The sexual failure of Bonnie and Clyde can be received as a paradigm of the problems of living together, married or unmarried, when cut adrift from old conventions and faced with the obligations that a freer climate creates. They illustrate the consequences of classic sexist role adjustments that the late sixties was confronting. Clyde wants to deal with his impotence and his fear of Bonnie's sexuality, and Bonnie copes as well as she can with her frustrations. Their candor about such matters creates a welcome but disquieting intimacy of a generalized kind, more applicable to our condition than to theirs.

Much has been written on *Bonnie and Clyde*, and justly so. The film's great popularity and wide academic acceptance suggest a timely cultural intervention. A good deal of highly specialized criticism exists, and many of the film's details have been explicated and interpreted. *Bonnie and Clyde* set the example for contemporary period re-creations in the genre by adopting a paradoxical detached/involved attitude toward genre material and by shifting attention from the illusionist appeal to reality to a consciousness of the functioning of the medium, to that which produces a movie reality (editing, photography, performance, and so on).[6] It makes a clean aesthetic break from the past, unlike the fifties films, which struggled in transition. Penn was clear-sighted enough about the modern psyche to substitute one kind of involvement for another, to recognize that the material of the genre needed this to be able to function pertinently within the even low-intensity dispersal of modernist perceptions of art and reality in popular media. These newly evolved aspects gave the genre new life. In *Bonnie and Clyde* the genre can be seen confronting and incorporating the conditions that validate its continuation. The film opened doors that have yet to close.[7] Critics and intellectuals found an action movie that catered to their sophistication and allowed them to enter an American genre movie into the significance lottery without excessive apologies, and its overwhelming success with the public made it possible, after nearly two decades, for high-budget gangster films to be produced. It was not simply the violence that created impact but also the film's profound engagement with the culture's anomie. It got a response because it was true, and its truth had nothing to do with the thirties, or with gangsters, but with what it was proper for a movie to be for audiences eager for an art that would correspond to, probe, and give a just and unsentimental account of their psychic condition.

CREDITS	*Bonnie and Clyde*		
	(Warner Bros., 1967, 111 min.)		
Producer	Warren Beatty	Cast	Warren Beatty (Clyde Barrow)
Director	Arthur Penn		Faye Dunaway (Bonnie Parker)
Screenplay	David Newman and		Michael J. Pollard (C. W. Moss)
	Robert Benton		Gene Hackman (Buck Barrow)
Photography	Burnett Guffey		Estelle Parsons (Blanche Barrow)
Editor	Dede Allen		Denver Pyle (Frank Hamer)
Art Director	Dean Tavoularis		Dub Taylor (Ivan Moss)
Music	Charles Strouse		Gene Wilder (Eugene Grizzard)
			Evans Evans (Velma Davis)

Point Blank (1967)

When I saw *Point Blank* during its first run in 1967, my wife and I were the only people in a theater that seated close to a thousand. In the creepy solitude, we watched this unheralded, fly-by-night movie, cryptic, coldly luxurious, tonally baffling, maliciously witty, dart perplexingly before our eyes. It had its moments, but we dismissed it as too smart for its own good and a bit preposterous. *Point Blank* has since been "discovered" by viewers and critics alike. Like *Kiss Me Deadly* it was a film ahead of its time. Its peculiarities are still dismaying, but there is no doubt that *Point Blank* was a serious attempt to bring the genre conceptually and aesthetically up-to-date.

A logically sequacious criticism—the overprized mainstay of academic discourse, whether it is practiced by Christian Metz or Vincent Canby—is, alas, inadequate to deal with *Point Blank*.[8] The film as much as claims that to explicate according to conventional assumptions is useless. An outmoded critical discourse, however, is all we have at hand (and tenaciously protect), so what follows, the best effort and intention notwithstanding, is bound to do ill justice to a film that has outstripped present, available methods for dealing with it. The critic who has inherited an orthodox mode for making sense has no choice but to emulate the film's hero, who is irrelevant and out of his element altogether, like a summer bug going at an electric light bulb.

A man named Walker has been double-crossed by his friend Reese, who has shot him and run off with Walker's share of robbery money and his wife. The film is about Walker's attempt to regain his money and his wife and take revenge on Reese. It is an old-fashioned revenge plot, but director John Boorman and writer Alexander Jacobs have given it some spiffy new twists. Walker's personal vengeance is archaic in an impersonal world. He doesn't get the money, he doesn't get his wife, and he is outwitted by a reality he wishes to subjugate to his will. The narrative mode is imitative of dream because dream is the only mode in which the hero's situation can be put. The film *is* Walker's dream.

Point Blank pulverizes the classical genre style by underlining the anachronism of genre elements and by revealing their irrelevance to the nature of modern crime (modern life). The film confuses us because the world we expect to be present in the film isn't there, is negated by both form and content. As our expectations are denied, we must scramble to deal with what in fact we are given, which we feel makes deep sense but is not something we can arrive at by our ordinary distinctions. The film's emphasis on dehumanized characters and its deliberately disordered exposition align it with elliptical, antinarrative, antipsychological trends in other media. Boorman's cinematic excesses, inversions, and disjunctions construct a context in which his quixoti-

Dreams &

Dead Ends

254

cally determined hero approaches absurdity. The film plays havoc with what
is real and what is not, and its environments are visually distorted to reflect
Walker's subjective state. It is possible,
also, that *Point Blank*'s satiric extravagance extends to parodying the mannerisms of the art film by yoking them to
the vulgar ways of the gangster crime
genre.[9]

Walker is played by Lee Marvin,
that menacing actor synonymous with
nasty force. He is a highly authoritative
star, but not an assuring one. His backlog of sadistic, ferocious villains brings
an ambivalence to his "hero" role. His
viciousness in *Point Blank* may be justi-

Point Blank. Los Angeles again inspires a *noir* mood and setting as
Yost (Fairfax) offers to guide Walker, his obsessed dupe, to Brewster.
A subhuman murderousness seethes beneath a temporary acceptance
of mutual utility.

fied, but it is also off-putting. It will not do to identify too closely with so frightening a figure. His qualities, moreover, are undercut. He gets chided by the
fussy suburbanite Brewster. He is used and tricked by Yost Fairfax. His primitive directness, the cause of much excitement, is nonetheless futile against an
organization that is programmed to correct itself. It is implied that he is homosexual. (In one scene he is oddly feminized by being dressed in Chris's robe
and shown powdering his bruises with the puff from her compact.) He dresses
conservatively. He has few thoughts and few feelings and speaks few words; he
simply follows the scent toward an elemental justice that is finally not to be
had. As he dies, he imagines a potency that was never his in life—he imagines
the film we see, which is his dying hallucination. Marvin is well-suited to por-
traying an animated cadaver. The zombie stillness of his body and his rigid savagery are chilling and surreal.

Walker's symbolic range is widened considerably by his being dead—or as
good as dead—and the hero's magical qualities are thereby made more expli-
cable than is customary. Of course Walker escapes miraculously and effortlessly from several unfavorable situations—he is dead, so how can he be killed?
He is shot (in the opening moments) point-blank, and lives, a sign that the film
will not follow an ordinary logic. Boorman reminds us often that Walker is
dead, creating a very strange effect, for there, after all, is the character doing all
sorts of things as though he were alive.

We are told no one has escaped from Alcatraz as we watch Walker plunge
into the water (the recording on the sight-seeing boat tells of a past escape leading to a "watery grave"). Walker's wife, presumably projecting her own internal

Contemporary

Colorations

Point Blank. Walker, seat belt secured, test-drives dealer Big John Stegman's car against the supports of an expressway, "killing" it. Big John, who hasn't belted up, gives Walker the information he seeks.

state but addressing Walker nonetheless, intones, "How good it must be, being dead." The waitress at the nightclub asks, "You still alive?" Chris says, "You're supposed to be dead," and later, "You really did die at Alcatraz." Her sarcasm over the intercom at Brewster's can be seen as Walker's own thoughts reminding him of his real condition: "You're played out, it's over. Why don't you just lie down and die." The ghostly echo of Chris's voice coming out of the speakers in the empty house underscores its unreality—she is one of the many people he has made up? But Walker holds firm, his desire overwhelming his reason. He comes in from the pool, insults Chris (the agent of his own fears), and stands up to her pummeling like a stone. She slumps to the floor, exhausted, beaten, and Walker, having disposed of his bothersome thoughts, turns casually to watch TV like any normal, living man who has some time to kill. When Chris conks him on the head with a pool cue, he reverts to a semiconscious sensuality, delirious and painful, closer to his actual condition, at which point the sexual partner of his imagination—the wife who is not his wife, the faithful one, not the betrayer—Chris—in an exquisite conceit, rotates in necrophilic sequence with the dead Reese and Lynn, performing intercourse in paired combinations of the four characters.

At the end, when Fairfax invites Walker to take his money, he slips back into the shadows, his wish fulfillment no longer capable of being sustained. Throughout the film, one never sees Walker getting from place to place. He simply appears. Only in fantasy can the routes to one's desires be so quick-cut. There is one sequence in which Walker penetrates the "Fort Knox" of Reese's penthouse via elevator that points to the character's invisibility, although visual decorum demands a heavy emphasis on chance. However, the scene is shot to make us feel that Walker himself is not especially worried that he might be seen. His calmness smacks of the dreamer's prerogative, and also of primitivism, myth, magic, and the supernatural. *D.O.A.* questioned what was real or unreal and also had a hero who was dead but alive. Its method of storytelling, however, merely raised the question. In *Point Blank* the premise has fully affected the form, and the film's structure and technique convey how meaning can emerge only from madness, not order. The "truth" of Walker lies in his irrational, sensual, semiconscious being. Bigelow still reasoned things out; his best guess counted. Walker's best guess is irrelevant. Both content and form reject it.

Walker has no first name; his last resonates with meaning. He is The Walker. He pursues, with old-fashioned tenacity, on foot, a dinosaur in a technological world. Reese and Carter occupy strongholds accessible by elevator only. Brewster hops from airplane to car. Big John Stegman gloats over his fancy automobiles. Walker is defined by his first decisive action, the forceful, regular stride down the seemingly endless, art-lined corridor of the LA airport, the clang of his heels echoing long after the image has passed. Boorman's shot, though, makes it seem that Walker is not getting anywhere. In action movies, the character's energy is often the one clear, distinct value we can depend on, but in *Point Blank*, a negative irony accompanies Walker's will. Walker's embodied ghost causes some minor upheavals, but the system he hopes to disrupt goes on despite his efforts. At the end, he fades away, having accomplished nothing. The genre's classic ironies and metaphors about prison (in films like *I Am a Fugitive from a Chain Gang* [1932], *20,000 Years in Sing Sing* [1933], *Brute Force* [1947], and many others) depend on a firm distinction (reinforced visually) of being either on the inside or the outside. *Point Blank* both inverts and annihilates the distinction. Boorman makes every environment look like a prison—Lynn's and Chris's apartments, Reese's penthouse, the nightclub, the storm drain, Carter's office, Brewster's house, the mirrored bedroom, LA architecture in general.

The old concept of prison is extinct. Boorman presses the point home by using an actual prison structure as one of his settings—the abandoned Alcatraz. It is, fittingly, the place where Walker, one of an old, dead breed, dies. The obsolescence of Alcatraz is not a matter of mere physical decay. The recording on the tourist boat reminds us that Alcatraz was a prison impossible to escape from—the perfect prison, a supposedly surefire remedy for dangerous gangsters. Now it is part of recorded history, an object for sight-seeing. It is no longer in use, except as a drop point for the organization, a place where modern gangsters occasionally transact business. The irony is self-evident. Alcatraz is a symbol of the way things used to be, and Walker, "escaping" from it, can't begin to be aware of the nature of what he sets out to oppose.

The world of *Point Blank* is no longer a mechanical world but a technological, self-generating, closed-circuit world that runs by itself. The organization (the society) is impenetrable (except by magic/dream) and remains impenetrable. It is, in essence, computerized for profit. Its members, high and low, have no identity outside their function to the organization (or, more accurately, that is where their real identity lies). Walker demands money in a credit card society; there isn't any to be found. He roughs up several individuals, but they can't

257

comprehend what he is doing and why. The film implies that the whole point of living seems to have been lost. Nobody seems to know quite what he is after (not like the old gangsters, at any rate). There is the Multiplex Company (what the organization calls itself), which people serve and perpetuate—an impersonal, sourceless, boundaryless entity that determines the nature of life and controls human beings and their efforts. Walker assaults it with demands, but, as he is told, "There's no one man." He knows exactly what he wants, down to the last dollar, but nobody uses money anymore, and no one is empowered to make personal decisions. The runaround Walker gets is not out of malice or animosity. It is the nature of things. He is chasing shadows, and ends up exactly where he began. The film's title covers both Walker's quest and everyone else's existence; life is pointless, blank.

Walker, nonetheless, is one of the most powerful antiestablishment figures of the sixties. He demolishes facades we wish to see demolished. The film is too honest to let him win, but in exhibiting the character's nausea, hostility, and alienation (and his integrity and skill as well), it justifies his position against the business structure of crime and the technological deadening of life. Walker is not really a gangster; he is sucked into one heist by his friend Reese (John Vernon) and betrayed. The absence of information about Walker prohibits an account of him in conventional terms. He is a force, motored by a few basic emotions. The "gangsters" are a ruthless but comic assortment of conservative WASP businessmen whom Walker ruffles enough to force into situations where they can kill each other off. *Point Blank* is witty in its portrayal of the dullness of criminal life (as Brewster's bodyguard comments, "another day, another dollar"). Crime is a business, a bland, bureaucratic Monday morning affair. The organization, like any well-run corporation, offers money and security, rewards loyal initiative, is highly competitive, and seeks new talent. Brewster (Carroll O'Connor), its co-head, is a fat little guy worried about his shrubbery and the temperature of his pool. Carter (Lloyd Bochner), the other kingpin, lives an affluent, Republican-respectable life. In one scene, he is shown at a business convention in an auditorium mingling with whitehaired senatorial types, behind him an American flag. Fairfax alone retains an aura of the old-time gangster. Cruder and seedier than Carter or Brewster, he reminds us of the brute origins of crime, which in his case have not been permanent-pressed to invisibility. We know him as Yost and assume he is a cop. At the end, Fairfax presumably takes over the organization, but one suspects higher-ups never seen. The gangster's human functions have been taken over by technology. Walker's true enemy is not the men themselves but the technology they are expendable extensions of.

The response to Walker is amazement at his gall. They can't understand his insistence upon the measly sum due him and all the useless trouble he is creating. His cash hunger, his classical motive of revenge, his anger at betrayal, the directness of his violence are an embarrassment. They underestimate him as a mere fly; he underestimates their imperviousness to force. Crime is just a machine with replaceable parts; the criminal looks physically like a human being but has no internal or instinctive life. Crime used to be an arena of special excitements. In *Point Blank* it is no different than any other bureaucratized activity. Walker expends his violence to no

Point Blank. Attitudes toward technology: in an act of futile but gratifying violence, Walker drills Brewster's phone.

avail; these are not men worth shooting—there would be little satisfaction. Walker kills, but he does not kill men.[10] He kills cars, he shoots adulterous beds, he destroys a shelf-load of pills and lotions, he breaks the neck of a telescope, he rips tape from a tape recorder, savagely unplugs a variety of kitchen appliances, pumps lead into Brewster's phone instead of into Brewster (Brewster, alarmed by the noise of a real gun at close range, starts sweating and agrees to help Walker get his money. But Walker has already lost. The revelation awaits him that Yost is Fairfax.)

Walker, his wife Lynn (Sharon Acker), and Mal Reese are seen as rather ordinary people seduced by life's corruptions. They are lured from their natural paradise of friendship and love by the prospect of a slick, stylish life. All three are beset by guilt, and the disharmony of their sexual lives is their latent corruption brought to the surface. Lynn narrates that Walker "found Mal and brought him home," thus creating a divided loyalty. It is suggested, however, that she is the intruder in the relationship. When Mal goes to shoot Walker in the cell, he pushes Lynn aside. The killing is orgasmic for Mal; he derives a sensual pleasure from drilling Walker. The flashback (intercut) showing Mal convincing Walker to go in on the robbery is a sexual overture. Mal, at a crowded, noisy convention, throws Walker down on the floor amid a sea of feet and legs and, lying on top of him, implores hysterically for Walker's help—it is a kind of rape. (The flashback of the odd mating dance between Lynn and Walker on the pier is the only sexual attention we see Walker pay his wife, and they are surrounded by a sizable group of Walker's male coworkers.) Chris, Lynn's sister (Angie Dickinson), becomes for Walker another version of his wife—all women are associated with his betraying wife. Mal, it is implied, rap-

Contemporary Colorations

259

idly ditches Lynn soon after the robbery and lusts for Chris, who is so like her sister that her conquest would be a repetition of what he stole from Walker and thus indirectly an expression of his longing for the man. (The film appears to be making a statement about the homosexual overtones of male competition.) Chris says that Mal makes her "flesh crawl," a clear sign of sexual revulsion. Walker responds with "*I* want him." The killing of Reese is sexual, the passive Walker now becomes the erotic aggressor. There is a cut from Reese's hand moving down toward Chris's behind to Walker's fingers edging obscenely upward along the window drapes. When he surprises Reese, Reese demands, "Let me get dressed." Walker insists, "I want you this way," and straddles him. Reese, underneath Walker, begs, "Kill me. Kill me."

The film's sexual perversity is connected to its picture of a systems-dominated world where instincts are warped and sexual outlets and satisfactions are at a total remove from the sexual organs proper. Walker empties his gun into a bed. Reese empties his into Walker. The backhoe excavating his wife's grave site is a phallic ravaging of the earth. Stegman looks at the body of a curvaceous customer and fondles his car. The black singer handles a phallic microphone into which he shrieks one repetitive note. Chris spends herself punching Walker and dealing him with her purse. The woman in the TV ad tells us, "All I did was cream twice each night with Pond's cold cream." The film's most perverse moment is when Boorman gives us an enticing shot of Walker's wife lying face down, partly on her side, in bed; her dress is pulled up to her slightly raised buttocks, and she is presumably asleep. The eye darts to her revealed flesh and fixes there. It turns out she is dead. In a lighter mood is Walker's tying together of two homosexuals whose enjoyment of the bondage game is greater than their fear, and also a funny cut from Chris to a pair of Reese's guards that Walker has tied up, heads over the balcony ledge, posteriors sticking ludicrously out in tandem.

Like sex, crime is robbed of its traditional stimulations and liberating possibilities. Crime is omnipresent and fully merged into the business structure of the society. The criminal bigwigs and their employees exist at such a remove from the directness of crime that they actually feel respectable. There is no difference between the criminal and the businessman; facades can mask realities so thoroughly that they are lost sight of. This is an old theme of the genre, running strong from *D.O.A.* on through the fifties. *Point Blank* shows that the continuing development of that phenomenon, analyzed in films of the fifties, hasn't stopped. It has only become that much more unstoppable. If Walker can't interrupt it, it is a safe bet that no one can. In a film like *The Big Combo* (1955), it is the old instincts that can defeat the organization, and it is felt that lack of human input is why it crumbles. People need something more than what Brown imagines they do—including himself. However perverted their need has become, Brown's men, Fante and Mingo, need each other. In *Kiss Me Deadly* there is no human instinct left to use in combat. In *Point Blank* it wouldn't matter anyway, since the technology has outrun its users. It keeps going on its own, whether the men who serve it get killed off or not. Neither reason, feeling, nor force can break its electronic circuits.

Through Walker, *Point Blank* encourages violence as something preferable to the complacent, nonhuman status quo. The film reflects the political frustrations of the period—the protest against the war, the rise of the counterculture, black power, the attacks on computerized universities, the long-dormant resentment toward a whole way of life finally erupting—a period in which violence against the system was justified because the system would otherwise ignore its critics. Walker is a man who doesn't "go through channels." He invades the inner sanctums of power, ready to kill, with ultimatums on his lips. In a world in which nobody handles money, his demand for hard cash is a kind of integrity. His violence against the organization is a deep fantasy of the late sixties, and it is gratifying to see Walker make as much of a dent as he does. But he fails; the organization holds and presumably continues as before. What audiences seem to resent most about the film is its futile hero. Boorman puts a lot of anger into Walker but realizes how entrenched the system is. The character's heroism resides in his refusal to be assimilated into the organization and what it stands for, but the film insists that he is powerless to affect it. Walker senses this, and at the end slowly backs away. In doing so, he regains some of the dignity he lost in his confrontation with Brewster (who scolds him as a grown man might a child, reducing Walker to a feeble mutterer) and a touch of mystery, but whether Boorman means the conclusion to signify defeat or merely a stalemate is not clear. Perhaps it is neither, since even Walker's necessary violence cannot alter the situation. It can't get at men. Walker kicks down some doors, but he doesn't get at people. To speak of his "defeat" is perhaps to fall back on precisely those distinctions the film says are outmoded. Walker was never a "real" force anyway; he might as well have been invisible. Fairfax leaves him be without any concern. As far as he is concerned, Walker is less troubling than a flea.

Walker's origins are twofold. He comes from the "watery grave" of the sea and the dark womb of an abandoned Alcatraz. Alcatraz recalls the days of the old, passionate gangsters; it has color and tradition. Its present disuse is symptomatic of absent splendor. Dark, rusty, cavernous, its echoing decay has a harsh tactility. Its resonant past no doubt helps induce Walker's dying fantasy of rough revenge. Only at Alcatraz do Boorman's colors warm, the orange-brown hues in explicit contrast to the rest of the film. The credit sequence contains a series of still shots of Walker making his escape. He is caught in stark and mythic poses, at peculiar angles and focus, distorted by queer lighting and special lenses. We believe in Walker's escape in a way we might not have if it had been handled more conventionally. We see it happening, but we are distracted by the credits themselves, by the eerie music, and by the pervasive aura of fantasy. We are given an abstract of the escape, out of time. It keeps us guessing. The transition to the film proper, with Walker, neatly dressed, gazing down from the boat upon his own swimming body, is a sign of how free Boorman's cinematic narrative is going to be. Walker murmurs, "A dream, a dream," but it is not until the end that Boorman confirms it. The camera, in one continuous movement, rushes up from an overhead shot of Brewster's body at the site of the drop, up past the open roof of the building, and then pans right to San Francisco, then left to Alcatraz. As the island is brought closer, its telephoto shimmer matched to the quaver of one disturbingly held note in the score, the film ends. Walker dies at Alcatraz unnoticed. But what is real and what not? The last camera movement has taken us from night to day, from the palpably dead body of Brewster to a remote, insubstantial image of an island prison we know has not been in use for years. Is Walker really dead? Did he ever exist? Since the film makes it virtually impossible to answer such traditionally important questions, they are perhaps not relevant or meaningful. They arise from ways of understanding that are no longer functional and that the film's technique attempts to obliterate.

The four still shots of Walker in the credit sequence show him as more a creature than a man. In the first, his shoulder exaggeratedly hunched in the foreground, he bends his head toward the vast corridor of receding cells he must traverse; he resembles an emaciated Swamp Thing newly risen from the muck. In the second, his body is photographed from below the feet, through a grate. Hulking, unnaturally elongated, and hard to make out through the narrowly separated bars of the grate, his humanity is again lost in his physical grotesqueness. In the third and most remarkable shot, he looks like a painted savage, his face harshly lit, an intense, natural, fauve monstrosity caught by an anthropologist's lens. The fourth shows him in long shot hanging onto a barbed wire fence, arms and legs widely separated, a huge crab or spider. These are all stages in his escape. A nemesis figure, Walker returns to put a wrong to right. His inhumanity in the course of the film fits his symbolic function.

Most often, Walker waits and listens, spurred to action only when the particular justice he is there to enact is blocked or would be hastened by a show of force. At Lynn's, she asks all the questions Walker should be asking while he sits numbly on the couch without responding—as though what she had to say didn't matter at all and the saying of it was for her benefit alone. Walker is traumatized by betrayal, and bitter, but he is also one of them, implicated by his choice of going in with Reese (he wears their "uniform" too). His cause may be right, but it is modified by his brutality and guilt. He repeatedly relives the moment of his death in the attempt to assign it a meaning and to whip his resolve, but also to punish himself, to remind himself of the folly of his trust. The world may deserve Walker's aggression, but he is too violent, remorseless, and contemptuous for us to support wholly, which is maybe why he too is shown to "lose." "Losing," though, implies that somebody wins, or could win, but Walker, like all of the characters in the film, is unreal. Whoever, or whatever, wins isn't a person, isn't real.

Point Blank. The bedsheets indicate a busy night, but neither party much wants to face the other. Sex as revenge, as a desperate escape from self, as attempted within the chilly confines of Brewster's motel-like bedroom: a meaningless activity between two emotionally closed-off and momentarily impotent survivors of a painful past. (Museum of Modern Art)

The film is full of voices over loudspeakers, megaphones, intercoms, telephones, disembodied voices talking through electrical devices, technology as echo as well as extension. Sound, speech, and image echo frequently in Walker's mind. Stranger, though, is how the reality of human presence has been altered toward an unreality of person, object, and environment, in spectral interconnectedness. Walker backs into shadow until he is no longer visible. Chris abruptly drops out of the film at a point where her utility is being advanced. She has no utility, though, to anything other than herself. Stegman listens to his own commercial on the radio while Walker destroys his car. Walker's violence toward Carter is expressed toward the curtains in his office. His violence toward Reese makes specific use of the penthouse setting. People are attacked via the systems that represent them, have become them. It is as though the world of any individual man is his own projection; reality = himself. Everything outside oneself is oneself. One cannot imagine reality as separable from a sense of oneself. Nothing, no one, can be touched or held. Everything is an echo of ourselves. Everyone exists in isolation; identity is a kind of mocking feedback.

It is no wonder, then, that human feeling expresses itself as mechanized violence that, as it expends feeling, simultaneously deadens it (action does not invigorate, as in most gangster/crime films). One is either inert or one attacks. Sex is associated with death and violence—Lynn's attractive corpse, Walker's erotic dream of Lynn falling to the ground in seductive slow motion, as though in death (a repetition of Walker's entry into the apartment and knocking down

Contemporary Colorations

of Lynn, but using shots we haven't seen before, and decidedly more sexual), Reese dragged naked from his bed and whirled off a penthouse balcony, Walker in bed with Chris fantasizing sex with the dead Lynn and Reese, Chris and Walker able to have sex only when all feeling has been drained away by violence, the hit man's appreciation of Walker: "Walker's beautiful, he's just tearing you apart," Chris and Walker's casual, postcoital acceptance of each other as bodies, not selves—"What's my last name?" "What's my first name?" (an epigram, perhaps, on the sexual morality of the late sixties).

What keeps Walker from being a monster is his vulnerability.[11] He is haunted by his mistake, he cannot totally suppress his desire for his wife, he returns to Chris's apartment for no apparent reason other than concern and perhaps companionship, he reaches some level of awareness at the very end. He is not a pure automaton like the members of the organization. His compulsiveness is rooted in emotion, however destructive. He has a sense of humor. Although he doesn't behave like one, in the long run he is a victim. The look on his face as he retreats into shadow is not easily deciphered. Disgust, incomprehension, caution, understanding—whatever the combination, he is forced to fall back. By this point it makes little difference whether his greed was a pretext for justice or vice versa. His alienation is complete, his efficacy halted for good. It may be tempting to regard his refusal of Fairfax's offer as a sort of triumph, but it is made clear that whatever Walker does makes no difference to Fairfax. Walker's withdrawal is not based on fear or insight or any of the common forms of human emotion or knowledge. He experiences a mild metaphysical shock. He hangs back, unconsciously realizing without fully understanding that he is "played out," that the money (presumably real this time) left there for him to take is not the issue at all, as he had thought, and that it cannot be central to the experience he has had or fantasized. His withering of purpose is accompanied by a dim recognition of the world's impenetrability.

The film closes, then, on an imponderable. Walker cannot combat Fairfax, nor can he die, because neither has any meaning. In the face of reality, one simply retreats. Walker is too useless to be crushed. As a figure of romance—misplaced, tarnished—however, he gives mythic expression to contemporary metaphysical uncertainties. Walker's qualities, his positive and negative aspects, lose their definition in mystery, in an enigmatic synthesis of the sad, chivalric, animal, elegant, brutal, and cynical. There is nothing to gain and nothing to surrender, only a condition that needs articulation.

The complexities of *Point Blank* are forthright and highly informed by method. Boorman's slick, darting intelligence encapsulates a history of genre conventions and, inspired by the art cinema of modern Europe, constructs with sophisticated dexterity an alternative to the often square-jawed hypotheses of the genre. He succeeds admirably. What could have been a pearly nuisance, a murky, exasperating novelty, is, in fact, one of the least affected existential statements of modern film. Rarely has the genre been served so handsomely, thoughtfully, and with such visual originality.

A moralist and a humanist may lurk somewhere in Boorman, but *Point Blank* is in the main very analytic and formalist. Its curiosity about color,[12] structure, sleek modern surfaces is evident, and the abstract sensuality of the image and the witty working out of tone and dialogue keep the emotional climate rather frigid. Its experiments follow naturally from its assumptions, among the most important being that of aesthetic primacy, that the medium can be only capable of aesthetic solutions. The medium must be reinvented and our awareness of it reinforced. Its only realities are its operations, and it can make statements and attempt expositions only by an appeal to its *processing* of material. *Point Blank* is modernist in its assumption that "plots" are no longer necessary or stimulating. The viewer's struggle to make sense is part of the adventure of the film. There is no ready-made "sense" that the film can provide. The film is free to be unique. Walker and his violence are treated as a theme-and-variations in an essentially open context. (The history of the genre is present, but it is blurred and blunted as a tool for comprehension.) First he smashes into his wife's apartment, then he smashes up Stegman's car, then he lays out some thugs in a nightclub, and so on and so forth, until in desperation, he shoots Brewster's phone. These episodes do not advance a "story" but rather intensify an attitude by repetition. The pattern stops when Walker is blocked, when what seems to have been purposeful action is shown as purposeless (by the usual standards of goal-minded narrative and character achievement). The cold-shower coda puts the preceding action into perspective; in effect, it negates what little logic it might have had. One does not feel that a story is coming to an end; one senses and observes a formal farewell of a sensibility that has revealed itself.

The nightclub scene will serve to show how Boorman stays within and goes outside the genre simultaneously. It is patterned on conventional lines. Walker enters in the midst of a musical number, sits at a table, and converses with an attractive waitress. There are volume switches from laconic dialogue to musical background, the act on stage intercut with Walker's activity. A sense of something about to happen is implicit. When Walker goes to leave, the impending violence breaks out and is culminated. Cut to next scene. Into this common framework, Boorman injects large creative energy and satiric bite. The perennial cocktail lounge (or bar), piano-accompanied vocalist (or bouncing chorus line), urbane and snappy dialogue are replaced by a mixed-media onslaught, a choking crowdedness, earsplitting volume, and a kind of cultural death throes. The nightclub is a whirling hell of tensions. If the world above and outside is colorless, reserved, and "cool," the modern nightclub is the place where debased energies and drives are sadomasochistically unleashed. Boorman creates a sardonic vision of late sixties art—a basic rhythmic riff pounded to death, the minimal song lyrics ("yeah"), the black vocalist putting on the caricatured white middle-class audience (his contempt disguised as sing-along-with-me entertainment), a go-go dancer's attitudes utterly divorced from the movements of her body. Walker and the waitress must scream at each other to be heard. The sequence is a metaphor of cultural chaos and disintegration, of amplified technological frenzy, a hideous interpretation of modern man at play. The noise of the fight merges with the noise of the band. The violence becomes (for the viewer) part of the act. The dancer's discovery of the body elicits a scream that goes unheeded, and Boorman cuts there, having said what he had to say. The culture's oblivious self-castigation parallels Walker's own. Even its pastimes are senseless, the reflex response to a general chaos. The false "liberation" of the late sixties and its true psychic distress are superbly evoked. The elements of the scene are quite familiar and shared in common with many other films, but Boorman's daring, fiendish variations are unique.

Boorman uses the iconic authority of Lee Marvin's persona to glue the film together (and make it marketable) and to free him to experiment with full force. Marvin provides such a strong visual center that Boorman's oblique, splintery presentation of the world accumulates around him into an effective complementary imagery. The landscape and the mise-en-scène of objects and environments are filled in not as backdrops to dominant action but to form a small, broken-rhythmed dream poem of their own, a personal, surreal vision of the inhuman America Walker confronts. Reese's penthouse, Chris's apartment, the storm drain, the sight-seeing boat, Brewster's suburban retreat, the McDonald's-type takeout joint, the high-rise hotels and office buildings, the beauty parlor with its rows of contraptioned heads, Lynn's color-coordinated apartment—an interior decorator's finest hour—whose gray walls perfectly match Walker's drip-dry shirt, the abstract patterns of LA's neon glare (one of the few night shots in the film), the Dixie cups, the bored, strobe-inflected body of the gyrating go-go girl—all have an antiseptic sensuality, a sinister clarity neither beautiful nor ugly, an amoral, exact poetry.

With *Point Blank*, the gangster/crime genre shows that its basic themes and patterns can withstand a battery of innovations. Boorman's ways with the genre have been subtly influential. *Point Blank* is too eccentric a film to be directly imitated, but some of its qualities have seeped into the work of other directors, especially British ones. Mike Hodges's *Get Carter* (1971) is certainly indebted, as is the Donald Cammel–Nicholas Roeg *Performance* (1968, released 1971). American films in the genre have been less severe and brittle in both content and style, less lean, less prickly in tone. Boorman's fastidious attention to color, to the score,[13] to making widescreen composition of existing urban environments and architecture apropos to the genre is a lesson in directorial risk and integrity that should not go unlearned. The genre, by its very nature, can least afford to turn staid or grow fat or abandon tough-mindedness. The slightly corpulent pictorialism of recent American gangster/crime films may be a profitable but aesthetically unwieldy direction for the genre to travel.

CREDITS **Point Blank**

(MGM, 1967, 92 min.)

Producers	Judd Bernard and Robert Chartoff	Cast	Lee Marvin (Walker)
			Angie Dickinson (Chris)
Director	John Boorman		Keenan Wynn (Yost Fairfax)
Screenplay	Alexander Jacobs and David and Rafe Newhouse (based on Richard Stark's novel *The Hunter*)		Carroll O'Connor (Brewster)
			John Vernon (Mal Reese)
			Lloyd Bochner (Carter)
			Michael Strong (Big John Stegman)
Photography	Philip H. Lathrop		Sharon Acker (Lynn)
Editor	Henry Berman		Sandra Warner (Sandy)
Art Directors	George W. Davis and Albert Brenner		
Music	Johnny Mandel		

The Godfather (1972), The Godfather II (1975), and After

The success of *The Godfather* and *The Godfather II* indicates that the genre is picking up a powerful vigor. The rash of gangster/crime/*policier* entertainments in the early seventies (prestige ones among them) makes the period analogous, in output and visibility, to the early thirties and the years immediately following World War II. A decade ago, in the early sixties, the genre was lethargic and directionless. If in the past its staying power seemed on occasion suspect, there is now no doubting it.

The Godfather and *The Godfather II* are certainly among the genre's major achievements. Their impact has been considerable. They have been very successful commercially, and critics have been lavish in their attention. A full-scale analysis would be of monograph length, but ignoring them altogether won't do either, hence the following expeditious list to indicate those aspects that matter most. It would seem that both films are imbued by a modernist emphasis that produces effects that are in line with a five-decade evolutionary process.

1. Both films lack the genre's typical brisk efficiency. Together, they are a rhythmically ponderous domestic epic about the consequences of American capitalism on family life. The effect, however, is not analogous to a soap opera intimacy. We watch a pageant and are kept detached. Or, if we are involved, we are involved with our own detachment. What with the slow pace and the absence of episodes that sustain a forward movement (the wedding in *The Godfather*, for example, doesn't move forward but circles in on itself) or any prolonged action, we lie back and watch pictures cranked slowly before our eyes.

2. Both films have a generally petrified air, a lifelessness that keeps us at a distance. Even private emotions are treated ceremoniously by style. They are weighted, lengthened, rendered as abstractions; they become components of a continuous, solemn exposition. The past is projected not as a reality teaming with verisimilitude but as a tableau, artificial "conception" (*The Godfather*), or with a muted, textured, archaeological fondness (the young Vito sequences in *The Godfather II*) and a vivid postcard glaze (the Lake Tahoe section of *The Godfather II*). The presentness of even past action that we feel in most films is absent. We feel the content as that which has happened, not as something that is happening. What used to be accomplished by voice-over narration is now embedded within directorial attitude and photographic style. *The Godfather II* insists on its past tense by written information that is casually dropped once the viewer has been sufficiently oriented. (The contrast with a film like *The Roaring Twenties* [1939] is sharp. There, after the intrusions of voice-over narration cannot dispel the vital presentness of the action. We know the twenties is some-

thing that has happened, but we feel it as happening. Better production has nothing to do with it [*The Godfather II* is better produced]; it is a matter of attitude and sensibility. John Milius's *The Wind and the Lion* [1975] tells us again and again that it is taking place in 1904, but its action has extraordinary presentness.)

3. We do not enter into the characters and their world but sense that they are apposite to our own existence. The conflict of opposed worlds that occurs between the audience and what is on the screen is now fully developed. On- and offscreen factors are merged. In a very different way than past movie "cy-

The Godfather (Part I). The elegantly accoutered Don Corleone (Marlon Brando) dispenses the foundations of Italian justice to a petitioner during his daughter's wedding. Robert Duvall is the grim-visaged overseer. (Museum of Modern Art)

cles" or follow-ups, *The Godfather II* depends on the audience's knowledge of *The Godfather*. Its effects are contingent upon our making the proper associations. The movie literally refers to something offscreen as well as on. However, what it seems to refer to is not so much its predecessor as such but the audience's recollection of what it felt when seeing it. When, after it has subtly evoked the sense of *The Godfather* present in us, it brings the world of that film back onto the screen in a brief sequence that feels like one of its outtakes; one can almost feel, in the theater, an immense interchange between the audience and the film. The effect does not revolve around the drama of the moment or our feelings for any of the characters; it arises from an accumulated sense of uselessness suddenly made aesthetically resonant. There are all these dead or might-as-well-be-dead people on the screen, whose relationship with their world and each other resembles nothing so much as our relationship with both films.

4. The success of both films lies in their intuitive grasp that there is a profound mood of uselessness in the audience that is ready to be exploited and sharpened to a point of pleasure. The audience never quite feels that it is either being instructed about the workings of the Mafia or that it is emotionally embroiled in the high drama of its participants. The material seems to be treated indirectly; it does not have an organic self-sufficiency. Our concern is with how the material is presented, and we take gratification that it seems, more obviously so than in traditional cinema, to be presented *to* us and *for* us. It is *we* who matter, not the survival of the Mafia. For its audience, the burning of Rome and what happened to Robert Taylor and Deborah Kerr in *Quo Vadis* (1951) mattered, as the film was being watched, however much the film could be passed off as an absurdity later on. In *The Godfather* and *The Godfather II*

Contemporary
Colorations

The Godfather, Part II. Group portrait, Sicily. Don Corleone (Robert DeNiro) presides over ritual honoring of family. He stares boldly at the camera, a man who will protect his family. (Museum of Modern Art)

the merging of the Mafia into the American economy and, through the marriage of Kay and Michael, into the American bloodstream, is a matter of indifference. We must shrug it off as something we have to live with. It is *there*, permanent, colorful, "wrong," destructive, apt—and all we are asked to do is watch it unwind, knowing what it is but knowing also that it is useless to get angry about it. The movie projects its listlessness and indifference upon the audience and catches the enriched rebound it has anticipated. The process intensifies, the ante being progressively raised as to what extremes it would still be possible to remain indifferent to, and those extremes are located in the culmination of both films.

The moral anger of fifties Mafia films and syndicate films is no longer appropriate. There is no way of working out of the condition of them being us and us being them. Gangster and non-gangster alike are immobilized in the vacuum left by the untenability of the American dream for a post-Vietnam, post-Watergate society. Nor are we left aghast by the situation. If Michael is a monster, we realize and accept why he has to be one. The man must do what he does; his choices are made *for* him and not by him. They have been made for him long ago by the competitive business society in which he lives. The audience understands, and regrets the *inevitability* of his situation, because the lines of its own lives have similarly rigidified after the evaporation of the dreams of the late sixties. Michael does not fall to pieces at the end; he is not shattered. He is burdened, lonely, and withdrawn, very much like ourselves, who act out the reality of our lives without a full awareness of what it signifies. The films are neither revolutionary nor masochistic. They elicit our curiosity in a context of stalled contemplation.

5. The elaborate production and sheer length of both films give them a dully stupefying grandeur and a glutted glamorousness that act as ironic, distancing filters, diffusing the potential corrosiveness of the implicit parallels, juxtapositions, and contradictions that are envisioned as being held in common by the ways of the Mafia and American bourgeois ideology. We are kept from being exercised by an inert mise-en-scène, long takes, *profondo* dissolves,

a highly embellished tapestry of life that oozes heavily and portentously across the screen. Prolonged silences create a restlessness dissimilar to conventional anticipation that is momentarily manipulated into a kind of circus hysteria by the methodical application of violence. The films lack the relish for violence present in any Fuller film or the horror of violence that a director like Nicholas Ray achieves with brief, baroque intensity in films like *Party Girl* (1958) and *On Dangerous Ground* (1958). In the absence of consequentiality, the pattern

The Godfather, Part II. Brains plus guts. A young Don Corleone (Robert DeNiro) taking care of business. (Museum of Modern Art)

is to seize the audience and let it go, again and again. This, presumably, is why the audience is there, knowing that the films can only ritualize into spectacle a shared sense of confusion, incoherence, and ideological collapse. This may be why their points are made so grossly and obviously, and why the relationship between meaning and technique is so explained, paused over, and underlined. We are not allowed to go into a trance or pursue nuances of meaning. The drama of the films lies in our awareness that they are there to come to us (and not us to them) and precisely how they will manage it. To claim an aloofness from content (beyond proof) leaves one open to the charge of inexactitude. Did we stand in line to learn how the Mafia works, or were we looking for a strangely interactive film experience that blurs outside and inside, one that forces an awareness of film as the medium that corresponds best to the puzzling feel of our existence? The latter, surely. This is a result of the cinema's growing knowledge about itself and about what is necessary to provide for its audience. *The Godfather* and *The Godfather II* are two films so fastidiously executed as to seem almost pleased with themselves, but that is both *where* their energy lies and where their aspiration leans.

Critical reaction to *The Godfather* was mixed; the more downbeat *The Godfather II* drew more uniform praise. Audiences, on the other hand, were stunned by *The Godfather* and more dubious about *The Godfather II*. The immense popularity of *The Godfather* (aided by the interest generated by Puzo's book, and by a beautifully designed trailer) suggests that it got a good many people into the theater who hadn't been there for a while. One can see why. It retained, as it modified, a strongly traditional appeal. It was controlled by a large, heroic, dignified character, whose efforts were on behalf of family unity and survival, and that struck a sympathetic chord in a fragmented culture. Don

Contemporary Colorations

Vito's obsolescence was a kind of purity. The film progressed linearly toward an undeniable achievement—a political marriage, the baptism, the destruction of family enemies, Prince Hal understanding the responsibility of kingship by both learning and choosing not to learn from his father. The family was a bunch of potential freaks who ultimately coalesced with our sense of normalcy (despite disturbing evidence to the contrary). In *The Godfather II* the family, settled into normalcy, appears more freakish and neurotic. The world of *The Godfather* moved toward something, however slowly and grotesquely. The sense in *The Godfather II* is that once there, there is no turning back, and nothing else to move toward. The film, accordingly, juxtaposes two pasts. There is no point in *hoping* for Michael; for him to succeed means that he must destroy the family, which he does. The continual references and parallels to *The Godfather* provide an ironic perspective on both films.

The Lake Tahoe gathering is contrasted to *The Godfather* wedding, Michael now assuming Don Vito's role in a similarly subdued interior that is played off against the gaiety outside—with major differences, of course. The family is now a sad, worn-out group that has lost its ethnic definition (neither the music nor the musicians are Italian, and the old-timer Pantangeli, who would have simply been part of the scenery at the wedding, is buffoonishly obstreperous in the midst of the pseudogentility. Brando, personal and virtuosic, gave a goitrous performance that threw *The Godfather* appropriately off-balance. Don Vito was a big man, and Brando's overplaying registered how the world of the film could be defined by him. Al Pacino's mannered soft-spokenness, small build, tight uncomfortableness, and minor-key presence suit the more reductive and darker vision of the sequel. In *The Godfather* the door is shut on Kay out of necessity and a macho propriety of means and ends audiences found agreeable. In *The Godfather II* Michael slams the door in Kay's face in a neurotic rage that underscores his compulsion, insecurity, and loneliness. It is a destructive not a constructive gesture. The stark, plangent theme for solo trumpet that helped solemnize and authenticate *The Godfather* is used basically as recall, being inappropriate to the mood and content of *The Godfather II*.

The Godfather II uses *The Godfather* analytically, linking the violence of Sicily, Vito's progress in America, and Michael's brutal reign as Don in a cumulative vision of the order of things. The world of *The Godfather*, it turns out, was not any better than the world of *The Godfather II*, past or present. It was a world in transition, however, a transition associated with values that created false options and induced an illusion of choice. All the time, however, we were observing inevitables.

The restrained pace and overrefined visuals of both films keep us unagitated and untroubled by existential givens. One may well ask what good it would do to arouse concern, since everything seems out of our hands. Cop-

pola's cutting, and graphic bloodlet-
ting—as subtle as a brass band—is a way
of supplying, by aesthetic peroration,
what will keep the audience absorbed in
a period of moral and political inertia. It
is not quite virtuosity in a vacuum; the
vacuum demands the virtuosity. The
lack of moral urgency, or a commitment
to statement, is reflected in the films'
temporal and narrative structures as well
as in their unrelieved stylization. Within
their noncommittal attitude, they can
go back and forth, stretch scenes inter-
minably, pan expansively, dolly at snail
speed, intersperse flurries of action with

The Godfather, Part II. An image borrowed from the documentary tradition. The romance of the immigrant who works hard and succeeds is a thing of the past. Now it's cautious, shielded lawyer-orchestrated hush-hush countering of criminal charges. (Museum of Modern Art)

long, static passages of characters staring at each other and whispering. They
can (and do) take their time because there is no point in hurrying to where
they have to go or in obeying the momentum of a strict causality. They cannot resolve anything for the audience, and so they take the "and then . . . and
then . . . and then" route and work hard to keep the journey to nowhere interesting. Aesthetic considerations and an acute attention to the medium are
forced into being by the absence of any other confident purpose. We are not
"moved" by Michael sitting alone as night descends over his expensive property and his burdened conscience, but we appreciate the beauty of the image
and the aesthetic finesse of the conception.

The international hour-and-a-half to two-hour feature film, despite its obvious use of art-cinema techniques (Griffith's *Intolerance*, Gance's *Napoleon*,
and Murnau's *Sunrise*, are three mature early examples of enterprising cre-
ativity geared to a general public eager for spectacle, drama, and romance),
still adheres to narrative conventions and expectations. *The Godfather* and *The
Godfather II* are painterly nostalgic tableaux of an irretrievable past. Their self-
conscious technique and revisionist impulses are signs of the cinema's late arrival at a full-blown modernism. Its early fling was short lived and, confined
mainly to experimental shorts, of no commercial impact. The feature film,
commercially dominant and perhaps wary of unprofitable innovations infil-
trating its well-developed formulas of success, skips past the inherent dangers
with a steady diet of dream-factory product, spiked occasionally by a borrowed
flourish of avant-garde style and/or attitude (a quickie montage or gratuitous
wipe or time-and-space-scrambling superimposition). Modernist viewpoints,
though sometimes implicitly hanging in the air throughout certain sophisticated films (*Singin' in the Rain, Scaramouche*, Ulmer's *The Black Cat*), had to

Contemporary

Colorations

The Godfather, Part II. Michael Corleone (Al Pacino) enjoying the fruits of his labor. The body language says it all. (Museum of Modern Art)

wait until the dismantling of the studios and the arrival of fresh, better-educated, and independent-minded cineastes who felt unconstrained about displaying the changes in visual and narrative understanding necessary to bring the medium up-to-date (Arthur Penn, Ingmar Bergmann, Wim Wenders). Only then do films, by and large, accede that significant shifts have occurred in assumptions about the making and viewing of feature films. So "modernism," quick to take over the galleries around the turn of the previous century, had a much harder time speaking its piece on neighborhood screens, content to make sparing, nonfundamental appearances as illusion-threatening transitional devices (montages, etc.), but destined, nonetheless, to become an intrinsic part of a seamless mastery of visual articulation when it peaks in what is sometimes referred to as the "high forties." By the time of films like *Point Blank*, *Bonnie and Clyde*, and *The Godfather*, the takeover is complete, and they can, without much risk, ask the audience to pay heed to and enjoy some new kinds of moviegoing experience.

CREDITS *The Godfather*

(Paramount, 1972, 175 min.)

Producer	Albert S. Ruddy	Cast	Vito Don Corleone (Marlon Brando)
Director	Francis Ford Coppola		Michael Corleone (Al Pacino)
Screenplay	Francis Ford Coppola and		Tom Hagen (Robert Duvall)
	Mario Puzo		Kay Adams (Diane Keaton)
Photography	Gordon Willis		Sonny Corleone (James Caan)
Editor	Peter Zinner,		Fredo Corleone (John Cazale)
	William H. Reynolds		Clemenza (Richard Castellano)
Production			Sal Tessio (Abe Vigoda)
Design	Dean Tavoularis		Connie Corleone (Talia Shire)
Music	Nina Rota		

(Paramount, 1974, 200 min.)

Producer	Francis Ford Coppola	Cast	Michael Corleone (Al Pacino)
Director	Francis Ford Coppola		Vito Corleone (Robert De Niro)
Screenplay	Francis Ford Coppola and		Tom Hagen (Robert Duvall)
	Mario Puzo		Fredo Corleone (John Cazale)
Photography	Gordon Willis		Hyman Roth (Lee Strasberg)
Editor	Peter Zinner, Richard Marks,		Kay Corleone (Diane Keaton)
	Barry Malkin		Connie Corleone (Talia Shire)
Production			
Design	Dean Tavoularis		
Music	Carmine Coppola and Nina Rota		

Toward the 21st Century
Frenzies and Despairs

7

This would be the right place and moment to say there isn't much difference between our latest underworld films and those powerful early talkies that elicited such censorious tremors of apprehension throughout a concerned, law-abiding citizenry, at the same time thrilling them with bold gestures of social defiance and raking in big dough during hard times. The conditions now are different, and we've seen many a criminal type come, momentarily hold sway, and then be given the choice of a ticket out of town or a bullet in the head. Films have fictionally documented, investigated, and taken positions on these real-life turnovers and their surrounding political contexts. Yet the kinds of stories they typically tell tend to simplify often messy issues by a fierce attention to emotions and by adhering to the clean, noble, time-tested patterns and structures of literary forms—tragedy, comedy, satire, romance—but adding their own appropriate variations and, it must be said, exercising all manner of expressive license. What works (i.e., makes money) gets repeated. The gangster, a fascinating public figure, was the subject of more than fifty films from 1930 to 1932, which suggested that he was plenty fascinating on the screen too, hence this period of his greatest popularity. He never had it so good again, but he has continued to sell tickets to this day—has, in fact, never been off the screen since his spectacular debut—and I'd guess that he makes some kind of appearance in probably 80 percent of American films. When he's not up front, he's lurking somewhere, and films will acknowledge his criminal and sinister presence within both law-breaking and law-abiding communities.

Basic, straightforward stuff. Those early films are much like our present ones in that they're easy to figure. There isn't that much to think about. The kind of complex considerations that *film noir* and then the morally resurgent 1950s demand from viewers has, in effect, been declared a sentimental dead end. Visceral excitement, the seductions of texture, sex, and violence no longer subject to restraints, a catalogue of charged sensations—these unite the two periods, along with a thinning out of implications. The gangster as spectacle. What's to understand? We gawk, maybe gulp, and find it sufficient.

The conventions and motifs still stand in place, one and all available, but take on different qualities in combination, and to select without self-consciousness is nearly impossible. All that's missing is the exhilaration, the intensity that a goal felt as possible brings out in the performer, the director, and the cooperative will of the audience. Our films now cannot provide that kind of satisfaction, which would, in any case, feel false. *Noir*'s bleakest moves we understand, but not the richness of its civilized pathos and corruption.

And the gangster's litany of high purposes and allegiances, of honor and family and public service, and clan loyalty doesn't hold water any more as a cover for the frequent exigency of butchering to conduct business for maximum profit. Greed (which often obliges a show of competition) is the bottom line, and all the vaguely infantile boys' club secret codes and mumbo-jumbo and in-house justice and community service can't hide the fundamental rapacity. There's no one to like or to pull for anymore. Crime is a business, a low-profile hierarchy of team players. The big bosses at the very top are rarely seen. The gangster's glamour and mystique have played themselves out.

Films either visit a retrospectively "poetic" past or fantasize a heroic present, locating within it a live, connecting current with the past, as what's actually at hand doesn't add up to much: pimps and drug lords at the excitable, kinetically flamboyant street level (both too seedy to serve as either profound or ecstatic cynosures), or high-level politics and intrigues where "respectable" lawyers, politicians, bankers, corporate bigwigs, philanthropists, and academics routinely go about their business—increasing profit (like more developed and attention-worthy clones of the Carroll O'Connor character in *Point Blank* [1967]).

Organized crime is a bunch of sober, solemn business executives, jockeying for power in conference, and, when they wish to make a particular kind of point, on the streets, backed up by the muscle and firepower of hired goons. The old films had a reckless enjoyment, and the gangster's crazy daring imparted a purposive forward movement. Rico, Tom Powers, and Tony Camonte—one has only to think of them and what stands out is how they savor their own energy and advance. And it's infectious; they pass it on to the audience. They were the antidote to our depressed stasis—every confident gesture expressed the gangster's difference from us in our lives. Contemporary versions are less fun because the gangster is stuck by all the once resourceful emulations of capitalism-in-action he had the hot hand to wield at historically opportune moments (Prohibition, The Red Scare, Hollywood, the Depression, political corruption in big cities). He can only succeed if he becomes like his enemy. He is no longer a free man, and he needs to use a tricky palette of protective coloration. Consequently, he becomes like the people he hopes to prey on, and they like him. Madness is his only route to distinction, but mad people are too dangerous and confused to be heroes, and so the gangster becomes that which must be destroyed. The kind of negotiations possible through to the 1960s—whereby we could identify with and even find liberating his unhypocritical lust for power and both concur with and enjoy his social antagonism— have gone the way of the singing cowboy. His readiness for violence, joined with his technological prowess, is merely frightening, and we are less likely to be indulgent toward his forgetting several key commandments.

The mythical status the gangster once attained is now in shreds, or fossilized as ancient history, or dispersed onto behavioral and sartorial sign systems that blend with irreproachable citizenship. Criminals and their frequently "legitimate allies" (corrupt or complicitous government agencies, cops, businessmen, media, the legal machinery) are more often "all-in-a-day's-work" types, their infringements necessary detours in the pursuit of steady, family-upkeep, dishonest work. One's moral sense, one's humanity, is scarcely an issue when work is undertaken out of a dourly dutiful obligation. The new tends to simplify the old (for occasionally powerful effect but overrelying on the often crazed and ruthless brutality of contemporary criminal aggregations or individuals); space for any kind of tragic-heroic incarnation, or for the sympathetic depiction of the many *noir* protagonists who must turn criminal, or for the ebullient action hero whose superiority to stay-put deadbeats is evident in a risky rambunctiousness marked by humor (John Milius's Dillinger in the 1973 *Dillinger* may be the last convincing one), is thin indeed.

Yet feelings are difficult to suppress altogether—one can be brutal/indifferent or indifferent/brutal only so long, and other, less rigid emotions leak out. In the gangster/crime/cop film there is a faintly melancholy sentimentality, as if a kind of remorse has set in for all the license we have given not only for gruesome excesses of violence but also for our acquiescence toward an unfixable world of universal criminality, a kind of petty swindling underneath the big-time scams involving murder and such that we allow if not also practice. Hardly any grandeur in that. One might say that we are making more sentimental films than ever before but ones with hardly any sign or moment of real sentiment. Movie commentator Bob Mondello of NPR, looking ahead recently at a batch of new films coming our way, rolled off titles something like this: *Smash, Blast, Slasher, Murderous, Switchblade, Throttle,* and the like. These will doubtless have sentimental conceptions standing in for outmoded, and no longer credible, sentiment (*Criss Cross, The Last Gangster, The Big House, Angels with Dirty Faces, The Big Combo,* and a video store full of others).

Since the decline of the studio system and the crumbling or reinventing of genre, there has not been a unifying style or production method for genre films. With no stable methods of lighting, shooting, editing, scripting, and so on, there are no established attitudes or techniques consistently at hand that might help a young director get his feet wet at little risk (the 1930s, 1940s, and 1950s had helpful conventions and practices, and there was the steady flow of genre films themselves). Television work, one could argue, is the present equivalent but is inhibiting, nerve-wracking, and goes at a lickety-split clip. Interesting hybrids result when each film makes its own idiosyncratic journey through the generic terrain, the director understanding that he must make it new. Genre, these days, has cachet if it can demonstrate its relevance by way of novelty. Hence commonplace frenzies. Thus *Reservoir Dogs* (1992) is like a cross between *The Texas Chainsaw Massacre* (1974) and *Kansas City Confidential* (1952) and amuses itself by being poised to go either way. Typical of contemporary habits in registering affection for old genres while conceding their inadequacy are combinations of derivatives, a little bit of this, a little bit of that, into, *voilà*, a "something else," which then becomes a new variant like *Pulp Fiction* or like Quentin Tarantino *per se*, a genre unto himself.

It is, therefore, a very free and open field, which makes it all the more surprising that so many ancient conventions and emphases remain so blatantly in evidence. A revisionist sternness replaces the creative elan so matter-of-factly maintained in the 1930s and 1940s. Production is sporadic, execution sloppy, performances arch and hammy when not amateurish, characters fashionably sour and hostile. There are few attempts to "move" us, which may be why one can hardly remember the film one has seen only a few days ago. Competent enactments of sex and violence seem to have usurped all other considerations. If the genre, even inadvertently, is mirroring our condition, what it's showing is a contemporary lack of faith in anything. Its task is to make this compatible with entertainment. The solution seems to be endless action sequences interrupted occasionally by hysterical crying and screaming and sweaty sex. Thinking doesn't have quite the same punch and doesn't film well. Hence commonplace despairs.

We still have, in the classic and enduring sequences of events, situations and voices common to the genre within which their larger patterning can take shape, a structure that effectively transmits the clang of seemingly inescapable contradictions. The somewhat guilty buzz caused by the gangster's unpunished behavioral license produces a quick (and steady) moral combativeness. The screen excitements of his meteoric career coexist with a kind of moral undertow; we seem strapped, as for our own good, to be the edified witnesses of the preordained comeuppances meted out by law and justice. This apparatus can be employed cynically (*The Killers*), angrily (*Brute Force*), sentimentally (*High Sierra*), high energy (*Gun Crazy*), low energy (*The Brothers Rico*), comedically (*Brother Orchid*), whatever. The gangster/crime film continues to cohabit with any and all political beliefs and states of feeling. It has welcomed both high jinks and high tensions. Its "radical" period (the early 1930s) wasn't very radical, and maverick reactionaries like Sam Fuller have done superb work under its influence. Its resilient there-ness throughout our history has helped produce more than its share of film classics and masterpieces, and at this late date it looks like it will go on being of use to some of our best movie minds. It has a deep, firm bottom and a volatile, hungry top, acting like a sturdy Bach continuo over which one can bring any number of instruments, solo or in concert, to add commentary, from the businesslike to the passionate.

The point being that working within a genre is a partnership — the age-old product of many people joined to your fresh contribution. No one can trail-blaze and invent for two hours nonstop, nor is it possible to start from scratch. A director needs to best-guess what he can count on the viewer to supply, and the viewer surely does not expect to be pelted by novelty. While it is liberating to get out from under a Do's & Don'ts list, one still should be intelligible. Genre helps us be intelligible and to use this freedom to heighten the work's essential impulses.

Everything is *neo*-something. This smorgasbord is the order of the day — in clothes, restaurants, education, museums, dance instruction, and cinema. Click and pick. There's no telling who will want to try their hand at a particu-lar option the history of the genre provides; the more independent-minded can aim for a new synthesis or blaze new trails. If there is a uniform purpose or message, it cannot pretend to ring with the clarity so common to the films of the 1930s, 1940s and 1950s. The "buried" or "I don't have to think twice" mes-sages — rebellion against poverty, ambition, acquisitiveness, testing one's met-tle, fame, riches, power-elevated self-esteem — are brought into play almost un-thinkingly as accepted plot and character conventions and are easily grasped as givens. What's happening is what's happening, and it's clear enough. Only *noir* and its spontaneous cultural need to protest its pessimism (1942–1949) in-structs us to speculate on what's being constructed on the screen. The films of the 1970s through the 1990s tend to give in to the *noir* premise, and we expe-rience them by means of this continuously confirming and uncontested out-look. The films of this period have little juice left with which to debate or un-dermine their downbeat attitudes. They are illustrations of an unavoidably despairing status quo.

A film like *I Walk Alone* (1947), on the other hand, with its severely out-of-sync hero (Burt Lancaster again!) and an at-base linear narrative arranged to withstand a number of nonlinear episodes, cannot be understood without some effort to grasp its conflicted statements, its nighttime confrontations being perfect demonstrations of the difficulties of knowing. What *is* happen-ing? What's the right or wrong or just or unjust about it? Can anything prevent a "worse" or "worst" from happening?

Such questions have been settled (despairingly) by the early 1960s, and are dropped in favor of a reflex, thought-throttling certainty of Cold War villainies and the cynical triumphs of international espionage. Bond territory. A debili-tating paranoia coexists with the certainty that the accidental push of a button could blow the whole show to smithereens. *I Walk Alone*, in contrast, is pri-marily metaphoric; we are involved in an intricate, hard-to-read sequence of events, certainties put into doubt as fast as we can entertain them. It's a famil-iar tale: Frankie Madison (Burt Lancaster) has just finished a long stretch in stir, having taken the rap for his bootlegging business partner Noll "Dink" Turner (Kirk Douglas). Turner has built up a hot nightclub with their bootlegging profits, one with a clientele too high class for him to want a sartorial embarrassment like Frankie hanging about the premises. Frankie insists it's only reasonable for him to get his fair share; Dink's response is to have him savagely beaten by the likes of Mike Mazurki and selected goons. Frankie gains the aid of Kay Lawrence, Dink's "girl," who also sings at the club (a made-to-order icon of the transitional stage of womanhood—she ends up cooking breakfast for Frankie!—as the club itself is of postwar leisure habits and social mores). She supports his going after Dink and exposing his evil, and she walks off with him into a less glamorous but more virtuous future. Unlike present-day action-oriented, disillusion-diagrammed crime films, *I Walk Alone* insists that our minds toss around questions like Where do women fit into the scheme of things? What values determine their actions? What can we depend on them to want to do? And, likewise, What should a young man be these days, and how should he behave? What does he need to understand? Hollywood was often forced to proceed by indirection, but it wasn't all evasion; it could also come up with thought-inducing solutions. Characters are poised on a slippery Where am I?/What am I? slope. Lancaster's Frankie Madison punches his way to a 1950s moral victory, but not before his 1940s identity gets hung out to dry. Beaten to a pulp, he takes it as a wake-up call. Old-fashioned armed-and-dangerous, he breaks into Dink's entrepreneurial dirty-money gold mine, his combination nightclub/fortress seat of criminally acquired power, gets him to go for his gun (a legal no-no the police have arrived in time to see), and rescues just-looking-for-a-clean-start Kay for a final walk together into thick fog. Neither the fog nor Kay (Lizabeth Scott, cf. *Too Late for Tears*, 1948; *Dead Reckoning*, 1947; etc.) offers much of a guarantee, but we must, having lived through it with him, credit Frankie for his victorious struggle over confusion (he has come a long way in recognizing how little the fantasy life he lived in prison has to do with reality), and we must admire Kay for switching allegiance from the soft (but imprisoned) life with Dink to face a scuffling but free and clean existence with Frankie.

Contemporary *noirs* like *Kill Me Again* (1989), *The Paint Job* (1993), and *Blood Simple* (1984) set in motion three or more disagreeable characters in an assumed no-way-out situation that predictably (if sometimes ingeniously) winds down to a nobody-gets-anything finale. Vintage *noir* heroes make us understand things, entertain doubt, but eventually come to know what course of action makes more sense (even if it just means rolling over and giving up the ghost). What is happening (or has happened), can be brain-spun to good purpose and contribute to an aura of possibility (suicide in *They Wouldn't Believe Me* [1947], moral regeneration in *Force of Evil* [1948], surrender to fate in *De-*

tour [1945]). If the shifting implications of 1940s *noir* don't manage to register, their density having passed you by, you can feel pretty lost. Contemporary versions tend to put a premium on violence and sex, which obliterates nuance in favor of riveting nakedness and action-powered destruction. After the crafty, "X"-avoiding montage of slipping and sliding bodies, and the hysterical acceleration of the pace of screen mayhem, one is sometimes left with a minus yield of meaning.

Perhaps putting brain work on hold is what people want. There has been a slight dumbing-down as the genre (in no danger of disappearing) gives first-time directors a shot at doing something interesting, and a market research audience which, if the films are any indication, will really watch *anything* that resembles the kind of movies they go for. There are exceptions, of course (two coming up shortly), but sensation has generally replaced reflection. Thus Oliver Stone's sensation-happy *Natural Born Killers* (1994) sends forth loud hints that we can leave our brains at home, and not to worry—it'll do our thinking for us or bypass that impediment altogether (as a good many wall-to-wall action movies considerably aim for and achieve).

Just as surely, all kinds of *noir* films of the 1940s and 1950s (the various minicycles are nicely judged by Frank Krutnik in his *In a Lonely Street: Film Noir, Genre, Masculinity*) ask for the kind of response described above for *I Walk Alone*. A thinking process is forced to take place, unlike the more informative (also informational), tragic-structured (and thereby somewhat borrowed-awkward), monolithic, 1930s gangster films, and the more visceral, amphetamine-driven, aggression-favoring, deep-end violent, neo-whatever genre products of the last three decades); if it fails to, the movie may simply prove unclear and uninteresting and irritatingly short on action. This is not to say the crime/cop melodramas of the 1940s and 1950s shortchange an appropriate violence. Indeed, they are celebrated for their virtuosic filming of new means of inducing pain. The difference is subtlety and nuance (the thug's bandaged nose in *D.O.A.*, thrown in for laughs? And "borrowed" perhaps by Polanski in *Chinatown* [1974], and *T-Men*'s Dennis O'Keefe getting his ears boxed after his heave-ho into the gutter from the gambling joint—personal affronts and humiliations not always easy to make up socially), and Bigelow's one-man terror squad after small-timers who have accidentally poisoned him in *D.O.A.* suggests the hot encroaching boredom that can craze a good citizen of the aptly named town of Banning.

All a-tingle, he plunges out of his backwater haven, whose very name suggests an obstreperous antagonism toward such things as weakness and desire. He escapes Banning's moral guardianship by "partying" with licentious conventioneers and boozing it up in sinister jazz joints. Exciting big-city trouble follows. Eventually, he goes to his doom firing away, with murder in his heart and poison in his guts, pausing only to deliver the possibly expiatory, but finally bewildered, yarn of his demise. Paula finds him genuinely regretful, but what other picture could he possibly paint? The cops think he's half-cocked. Only we know his secret!

This kind of madcap tale of an unfortunate citizen, with its inventive embroideries of violence administered and/or received, is character-specific, and feels suitably apt. It tells us something about the person. In the 1980s and 1990s especially, bullets whiz by, splatter, and punctuate what seem like entire environments and any luckless bodies in their path, but what any of it reveals about those shooting or those getting shot at is nil. Violence, so tautly held at bay in real life, is free to express its fundamental and frustrated transgressiveness on-screen, and films imply that violence, when it comes right down to it, is the only recourse, the only solution; those bullets rain logic upon us. Classic *noir* despair was never that nihilistic or inundating; it seeped its way through heart and mind and a highly personalized, however functionally representative, figure (compare the credibly creeping anguish of the Dick Powell character in *Pitfall* [1948] with the stiffly symbolic Michael Douglas character in *Falling Down* [1993] to feel the difference). The former film treats home and hearth and their disruption in a casually unostentatious way; but the latter feels like a treatise.[1]

The modified tones of these angst-revisited and combative remakes raises the issue of how ersatz the activity is. From the privileged plenitude of the Reagan years, one can risk making a loud noise, and, from the security of a plumply placid era of "unprecedented growth," can fiddle with despair, make its special wail, overload it with the combined science and aesthetics of special-effects bragging, and, with an almost careless largesse, reroute the whole show toward something more upbeat. This is only just; the new versions are part of *our* history. But there is a kind of sanity and clarity in the older films that visions of contemporary life cannot, in good conscience, manage. If we deal with the present, we can't trick ourselves with squirmy waffling about how bad things really are. Films of the 1980s about the 1980s give us the fat sow's diseased underbelly, festering and inedible. They aim to jolt and frighten, pelt and curse. Their impotence is underscored by sadomasochistic excesses. The romantic glory invoked is stillborn. Crime and *noir* are recovered as idiomatic of unrealizable romantic projections. Consider this short list of 1980s nonremakes: *Black Rain* (1989), *Body Heat* (1981), *Sharky's Machine* (1981), *Once upon a Time in America* (1984), *And Then You Die* (1988), *Bad Boys* (1983), *The Exterminator* (1980). The genre responds to Reaganomics with a succession of anticapitalist diatribes that makes one think that living in America is like circling the darkest regions of a Dantean hell. Everywhere corruption, everywhere the same moral blight. Was it that bad? Maybe so, as many more could go on that list. The 1990s offer more of the same: *King of New York* (1990), *Ricochet* (1991), *Deep Cover* (1992), *Romeo Is Bleeding* (1993), *The Usual Suspects* (1995). Time now, though, to take the measure of a couple of more recent canon-worthy films: Sergio Leone's *Once upon a Time in America* (1984) and Gary Fleder's *Things to Do in Denver When You're Dead* (1995), each carrying rich cultural and generic markings *en route* to constructing their own idiosyncratic visions.

Once upon a Time in America (1984)

A towering Everest of a film, Sergio Leone's years-in-the-making masterpiece is now available to all on videotape in its 227-minute cut. Slow, stately, meditative, it is the very opposite of the typical car-chasing, bullets-flying, tough-talking crime films that whip up a froth of gangster energies, and it brings to American aspects of business, crime, society, love, and right and wrong the perspective of an outside observer we may be impatient with and also mistrust (like we do French adulation of Jerry Lewis). His track record makes him the right candidate to tell and show about the matters at hand, having recapped our Western era as a period of soiled and brutal territorial acquisition and maintenance, yet heroic in its tenacity, one that led the way to our eventually being under the gangster's thumb. In *America*, Leone connects the rise and fall of the "gang" with America's own failure to be an example of anything. Gangsterism is typically right wing, partial to blow-'em-away fascist attitudes. But here it's an uneasy, awkward power ball they play. Leone stresses the eating away at itself by means of its own vicious aims and goals. He clearly deplores the way society and politics say one thing but swim happily in greed and corruption, and how the capitalism that gangster activity imitates breeds ruthless competition, power, rape, and murder, and buries tenderness, quietude, and beauty.

Once upon a Time in America goes beyond condemnation or celebration, replacing the "heroics" of the film's characters with the heroics of the film's director in the less frequently attempted but more profound realm of contemplation. Gone is the pleasure taken in the gangster's charisma, the whole gallery of entertaining, screw-loose, trigger-happy, pathologically driven, society-marauding, self-made men of action. Instead, Leone gives us an unexceptional, flawed, uninteresting group of thugs who take their ghetto life of hard survival as a springboard of how to get ahead: exercising power, generating fear, racking up profits, never thinking twice of the justifiability of violence, and casually willing to commit rape and murder as all in a day's work. This, I assume, is the capitalist paradigm that in the course of the film invisibly, off-screen, intangibly, and without challenge establishes its collusion with politics and cops and eventually finds room for its energies and values in high political office (it is the very air we breathe). At that point, "internal" problems demand the death of the character who has risen the highest, after which the character who has been forced to spend thirty-five years in exile because his act of friendship was about to imperil a million-dollar caper, decides to seek solace in an opium den.

Despite its gallery of far-gone infected characters, molded socially in a way that prohibits their human range and development, it is a moving film. The

Once upon a Time in America. Very little machine gun mayhem in this long, somber saga. Leone's interests clearly lie elsewhere. A shot like this is in the nature of a homage—a kind of respect rendered for the genre as a whole (the American western, of course, remains Leone's favorite poaching ground). (Museum of Modern Art)

plot, rather confusing from so many editing jobs designed to make the film presentable, doesn't matter much; it's the choices people make that create the real drama. Three young Jewish lads grow up in a Brooklyn ghetto and are joined by a fourth who is being threatened by the same gang. The solidarity pays off in a life of petty crime. Noodles and Max (the outsider) are both gang leaders but have different personalities. Max (James Woods) takes special pleasure in the excitements of a life of crime and is always looking to expand operations. Noodles (Robert De Niro) is sensitive, dreamy, wavering toward conventional respectability, and is coping with a crush he has on Deborah, a neighborhood girl, who enjoys his moonstruck attentions but has no desire to yoke herself to a destiny that seems either dead-end or calamitous. A rival gang leader is killed in a brawl; Noodles is charged with murder and spends years in prison. When he gets out, he's Robert De Niro, not the boy actor who played him as a youth. The gang is rolling in dough and welcomes him back. Drunk with wealth and power, we see the gang behave outlandishly, carelessly, indulgently, and maybe a bit idiotically—Max eating it all up but Noodles looking for something more than party life. Prohibition is over, the coffers are full, the life ahead high style and in the fast lane. But Noodles, even after twelve years in prison, remains shy, love-struck, and not as criminally eager. Though he will assume his rightful high station in the gang, he doesn't much feel like celebrating; and all the while the going is good, he seems aloof, somewhat morose, and not a little skeptical of where Max's reckless illegalities will end them.

It's all downhill from here. Noodles' destiny is to lose his closest friend (Max, who doublecrosses him), his great love (Deborah, whom he is driven to brutally rape), and his freedom (a lower east side heroic gangster is forced into a low-criminal, hedgehog exile in the anonymous backwaters of Buffalo). The film's concluding cadences are slow and solemn, and bleakly ironic. Noodles refuses to shoot Max, who has lived a life of imposture as a Mr. Bailey, moneyed and influential, and about to be exposed by an impending hearing, and walks out into the dark, empty streets.

A garbage truck rolls slowly by, busily grinding its most recent deposits, of which Max just might be one, some on-the-hook party making sure Max will not be showing up at any likely-to-be-incriminating hearing. Noodles, in an act of free will, heads for an opium parlor he has frequented in the past, where an attendant gently guides him into bliss. The film closes with a freeze frame of Noodles' opiate-widened smile.

This is a huge beached whale of a movie using numerous and well-worn genre elements in both a pragmatic/functional and commentative/rhetorical way. For a massive undertaking, it concerns surprisingly few people—people, moreover, who are essentially nobodies, nothing exceptional. It's sufficient that they have the usual human mix of strengths and weaknesses, pride and shame, appetite and restraint. Leone charts their cruelties and their kindnesses with equal poise and emphasis. His characters do not grow so much as

Once upon a Time in America. This is Max, Noodles's best friend, played to the hilt by James Woods. A study in contrasts: DeNiro's reasonable, well-mannered mobster against Woods's repeat-please, scary psycho. The scars are age-old underworld credentials—signs that you've already gone too far and are likely to do so again. (Museum of Modern Art)

exhibit their defining traits within various contexts. This is not a film of epic "sweep" or color. It is dark, drab, slow, interior, and close-up. Its music is plaintive and melancholy and anguished—Zamfir's Pan Flute, "Yesterday" (Lennon-McCartney, not Kern) stealing in now and again—and the long silence during the credits sets the precise funereal tone for this movie of dark frames and large empty spaces. Leone is sounding the genre's death knell. He has not adhered to the subject. This is his final say on America, an elegy that seems to take place in a land of dreams accompanied by eerie sounds and a stray song or two.

Leone allows Italian operatic emotion to color his presentation of a doomed love and a doomed brotherhood. Morricone's score is masterful and solemn, in keeping with Leone's dead serious account of the often rambunctious gangster here treated as a man of feeling and various sorrows, insecurities, and inhibitions (Noodles). His alternative, the extrovert, anything-goes Max, is more confident but also crazy. In the grip of New World opportunity, he becomes a personification of greed whose forward momentum cannot be

Once upon a Time in America. Noodles (Robert DeNiro), aged and weary, on the trail of a long-standing mystery. (Museum of Modern Art)

blocked, except by betrayal. Leone succeeds in giving all his disagreeable punks some charisma and is interested in the loyalty that can bind drastically opposing natures—Max: thin, wired, hysterical; Noodles: solid, easy-going, soft-spoken. But that's as much "community" as he'll concede. At the center of the film is the unhappy, guilt-ridden, lonely figure of Noodles. We wander around the Cinecitta set designs with him for long stretches of time. And he's withdrawn, reclusive, not inclined to open up. The first sequence, which visits different times and places in Noodles's past, is practically like watching a silent film (a ringing telephone links all the settings); we know very little, but shot duration gives us time to reflect, and contributes to a down mood as we accompany Noodles, revealed by his gait as a beaten man, toward some discovery—a dirge-like theme to go with his sad eyes.

Leone's structuring of the material, with its period overlaps, sharp soundtrack switches, as yet undefined characters doing unexplained things, all linked by a ringing telephone, is, right from the start, a sign that he wants to show the care he's put into it and expects the audience to hang on every nuance and soak up the mood. The plot itself is pretty standard stuff: characters with criminal histories perform criminal actions; disagreement over gang policy compromises friendship, gives rise to betrayal, which results in lives of misery; an accompanying love story illustrates, by its disintegration, that it must be a casualty of lives so erringly conducted. All these commonplace elements, however, have been ingeniously woven and present the material in large, unexpectedly sequenced emotions. De Niro's "old man," noiseless glide, painfully long pauses in speech, the developed numbness of emotion to keep pain under control, and soft, throaty voice governs from the beginning (after a couple of horrifying hooks of killing and torture—of characters we see later in the film) the gloomy tone Leone wants, as something we may wish to go back to as perspective. Leone wants to brood. He is not being nostalgic or offering yet another stimulating trip with characters we have long enjoyed cavorting murderously with. It's a settled-in, almost out-of-a-time-zone film, slow in movement and full of dark, heavy, brooding images. The film can take its time, for it has nowhere to get to except gloomier, heavier brooding. It is mesmerizing in the tireless investigation of such a state, its control of it. Only a confident director could have managed to go so against the grain at such expense (over $40 million). (The Ladd Company, understandably displeased to have already spent so much, decided that brooding was probably not going to be big that year and cut the film down to 137 minutes, thus increasing its difficulties by making it incomprehensible. But there's no getting around it. Leone's long version says you have to sit down for a long brood, and it's worth it, as no other film puts you in quite that kind of state.)

Boring it's not; it just places you in a different kind and at another level of attentiveness and awareness, as in a dream, dark and sinister, but gripping nonetheless, and on the edge of discovery. It is a film of enclosures and ghosts and indistinguishable noises. A dead world, old, crumbling, being torn down; De Niro's Noodles, a man looking to lie down somewhere and die (at the gang's ornate tomb, he closes himself in, wishing perhaps to rejoin spiritually the only worthwhile accomplishment of his life—a heartfelt friendship). The film is framed by two trips to an opium den, where Noodles assumes the identical lying down position to take the pipe, which he sucks at intensely (there is a maternal quality to the attendant's soothing ministrations dispelling pain). Noodles cannot figure out how pain can be otherwise endured, nor, perhaps can the director. Noodles's sensitivity distinguishes him from the other gangsters—or actually anybody—in the film, making him grieve acutely for lost love and lost friendship. No one else could or would react that way. Focusing on Noodles directs Leone to see how he is at the true sad center of things and determines the run-down nocturnal environments we walk through and sit in with him (in the Miami Beach sequence, he is the only one wearing a black shirt and bathing suit). Max is all job, and a go-getter. Noodles is reasonably content and worries about other things, mainly the absent Deborah. The coming betrayal (which again seems inevitable the way America works) destroys love and friendship both, causing lifelong grief and guilt. Max, the less sensitive, gets himself a life, and eventually a one-way ticket on a garbage truck. Noodles bears the pain.

Is it an advantage being Noodles and not Max? Hardly. Even his big love, Deborah, wanders over to Max and becomes his mistress. Leone is more interested in Noodles, the real sad case, the loser of losers, whose feelings do nothing but get him into trouble. He is the only seriously hurt character, emotionally. Like some stagnant remnant of a bygone gentlemanly era, he is stern and puritanical, preferring to idolize and idealize his *inamorata*. He is a "moral" man, one with standards individually developed that he expects others to recognize. Yet this makes him out of place; being a member of the organization, he kills if he has to, but it's just business, and he doesn't partake with any relish in his society's other tastes and entertainments. He prefers to nurture a vision of love and friendship that life can't possibly match. He turns

Once upon a Time in America. Noodles doesn't like to be called Noodles. This shot shows he thinks himself the "class" of the outfit. Max has a costly cocaine habit. Noodles spends a fortune wooing Deborah. (Museum of Modern Art)

stoolie to save Max's life, and it all back-fires. His current real-life woman is killed, a good friend tortured, and Max, in a deal with the cops, survives, while the other two gang members die. One could say that Noodles's human qualities manage to be very destructive; in such a pessimistic film, it is no wonder.

Noodles is a fool, but a sympathetic one. We see and hear and experience the film mainly through his consciousness (the whole thing may be an opium dream), and having unattainable visions isn't so terrible. He is a creature of his environment, of American society, and of a masculinist ethic. His "soft" side lets him choose to be bonkers over Deborah, but it also helps keep a real relationship from ever happening. To a gangster society, this is clearly weakness, and Max needles Noodles about his "head-in-the-clouds" behavior. It is woman's influence that makes him fink, and De Niro's soft-spoken gentleness imparts a romantic aura to his scenes with Deborah (Elizabeth McGovern). He also rates a lyrical Morricone theme that marks him as susceptible to tender feelings. Yet Deborah, eager herself to get out of Brooklyn and get a life, doesn't buy the heavy wooing, doesn't trust him, and figures he's going nowhere. She runs off, but not before a goodbye rape that hardly does him credit. He rapes her because he can, and feels it is his right after such longtime ardor and the spectacular romantic evening his wealth has just made possible. Thus he is a character cursed, and can only deal with the person he was destined to be, a product of the Jewish ghetto, a tough male criminal who understood that power made things happen, who treated women badly until chastened by sexual idealism misplaced on Deborah, and, obeying the contradictions of his character, chose a course of honorable action that proved devastating.

These flaws, though, can be shown to generate anger, pathos, laughter, contempt—whatever. Leone's choice is tragic-pathetic. Noodles's longing for Deborah has both the stateliness and frenzy of grand opera. In a world where the only true love can exist between men, as when friendship and trust build up over years of shared experience, Noodles makes a tragic choice in pointing his soul's compass toward a woman. In such a world, it cannot work, and Leone's treatment of Noodles's grand passion has both sympathy and irony. The film clings to his spare conversation and lumbering steps, and of course his laborious sleuthing, as though they were, above all, what mattered. The long last section of the film seems to last forever; it's a dying pace, as though the world was running down and darkening, the will utterly eroded, the completed puzzle bitter and ironic. If his opening sequences showed the director willing to try his audience's patience by presenting an oblique and scattered narrative, flickering motifs, and an unusually expressive technique of artful transitions, his despair-wrapped conclusion is even more taxing, if powerfully different, in its slow journey to absolute stasis. It is a romantic conception, honoring at the end by its sweeping strings and soaring voices, Noodles's choice not to abandon those personal convictions of right behavior and his failure to accept the easy pickings of corruption. He talks to Max, after refusing to kill him, of how it would be a shame, a "waste" of a lifetime's work, if he is imprisoned or killed, and he's serious. Max nonetheless chooses suicide, it is implied, by depositing himself in the grinding mechanism of a garbage truck. Or he is perhaps thrown in by the executioners he expects. His life, in any case, literally comes to waste, while Noodles goes on to seek a kind of peace in the hallucinatory medicine of perhaps a wiser culture.

Leone's romanticism, then, rests on the suffering he burdens his hero with, for which he is rewarded by a simultaneously beatific and twisted grin when the opium takes effect. These last minutes of anguish and release are among cinema's most moving, despite being lavished on a muddled thug who mistakes stubbornness with morality, ego with charm ("I have a way with women"), and emotional reticence with dignity. No matter. Morricone's solemn whole note strings have a kind of placid beauty as well as a funereal despair. Leone wanted that disparity to coexist, sorrow and beauty both. The closest other experience worthy of being its predecessor is Tchaikovsky's tradition-breaking Sixth Symphony, with its beautifully painful and slow last movement marked Finale: Adagio Lamentoso (and he means it). No symphony had ever ended on such a note of pathos, of willingness to die, winding down to a barely audible rumble in the brass. It is the saddest of symphonies, as Leone's *Once upon a Time in America* is the saddest of gangster films. Tchaikovsky, though, was expressing his private miseries, Leone the lamentable state of an entire country. But both found remarkably similar structural means to get at the heart of what they felt and needed to say. And just as Tchaikovsky injects a last spurt of vitality before the coming doom and gloom, so does Leone, in a brilliant conceit: the lights of the receding garbage truck grinding up Max's body dim, only to be precisely replaced by the headlights of a roadster carrying drunken revelers—an eerie apparition of the good old days that swiftly passes the hallucinating Noodles, Kate Smith's "God Bless America" ringing on the soundtrack.

It remains only to note, after suggesting kindred emotional states in figures as far removed as Leone and Tchaikovsky, that if the relief opium provides to the desperate ones acts as a framing device, appearing early and late, so too does Kate Smith's famous blessing come early and late, thus sharing framing honors. Quite the mix.

CREDITS *Once upon a Time in America*

(Warner/Embassy/Ladd/PSO, 1984, 228 min.)

Producer	Arnon Milchan	Cast	Noodles (Robert De Niro)
Director	Sergio Leone		Max (James Woods)
Screenplay	Leonardo Benvenuti and		Deborah (Elizabeth McGovern)
	Sergio Leone		Jimmy O'Donnell (Treat Williams)
Photography	Tonino Delli Colli		Carol (Tuesday Weld)
Editor	Nino Baragli		Joe (Burt Young)
Music	Ennio Morricone		Police Chief Aiello (Danny Aiello)

Things to Do in Denver When You're Dead (1995)

Gary Fleder's movie opened to mixed reviews and didn't get much of a run, but what a movie it is! A serious look at contemporary life, it is also a graceful carnival of hat-tipping homage to the situations, settings, characters, and motifs of the genre. Fleder and company have come to both play and ruffle some feathers. "Crazy" is the operative term here, inspiring a licensed mayhem. The world doesn't make sense, it's crazy. The criminal is in, as it were, his natural habitat, smack in the core of craziness. He can call the shots because he understands and accepts the terms life sets down. The title itself is beyond "sense," each half negating the other. It's a story that has often been told straightforwardly and with a straight face, but never with such intent cross-examination and ambivalent serrations.

"Crazy" is versatile, could be anything from serious mental illness to comic license. In *Once upon a Time in America*, Max practically froths with rage when Noodles dismisses him as crazy; a lot rides upon being mentally sound. In *Denver*, there is, arguably, but one person who is mentally sound—the hero, Jimmy the Saint (Andy Garcia)—and it's not a commodity of any market value. By the film's end, after many physical and emotional battles with all manner of craziness, he too flips, having reached his wit's end, and commits to a line of action in keeping with how the mob wishes matters to be settled, given its codes and the extent to which one could be punished for violating them. He of course goes under, though his qualities and the energy he expends to ensure their survival will, the film implies, be passed on via his seed, which he has made sure to plant before his execution, in the womb of a prostitute, Lucinda (Fairuza Balk). Lucinda loves Jimmy and, having just been perversely violated and severely beaten, is looking for ways to get out of hooking. She wants to get a legit job and be a mother and requests that Jimmy help by impregnating her. At first skeptical—he has looked after her for years as a friend, and there is no passion involved—when it's clear his own time is running out, he seeks her out at work in the streets and they copulate in his car, just minutes before he is discovered and dispatched by hired killers. Providentially, it's the right time of the month for Lucinda, and the film's coda shows her very pregnant and boarding a bus out of Denver and toward a new life.

All of this is right at the movie's end. Jimmy's saintliness, a quality frequently exercised despite a life of crime, is underscored by his final act of generosity (he also gives her ten grand, his share of the aborted job his failing business and the wishes of his creditor, the Man with the Plan [Christopher Walken], has forced him to take on); he more than earns his nickname. We are told he studied for the seminary but dropped out to be a criminal and ladies man. His associates look up to him as a learned and honorable man, a doer of good deeds, and a shrewd manipulator who talks a good line (he's also called "slick"). And they all want to talk to him, a square guy they can trust who will assure them their problems can be solved. Talking to Jimmy is like going to confession, and he is often put in a "Father" Jimmy position—which calls for sympathy, understanding, and wisdom. In comparison, the rest of the characters are unhinged and unable to suppress urges that are self-destructive. Somehow, Jimmy has kept cool and collected, runs a legitimate (but nonetheless slimy, exploitative, and cynical) business (preparing videotapes of the dying that will become gifts from the afterlife), and has severed his criminal ties, but the Man with the Plan has something urgent on his agenda, and thinks someone like Jimmy, someone temperate and classy, would be perfect. Jimmy can't refuse, as the Man holds a note on Jimmy's business.

Things to Do in Denver When You're Dead. The fetching good looks, sensitive facial features, and a carefully placed errant lock or two, mingle with a tumbled look in this publicity still from *Things to Do.* From the beginning, Hollywood saw the glamour of the gangster, and even the plug-ugly ones were knowledgeably tailored to receive flattering attention from any woman, even the most gorgeous. Check out photos of real gangster mugs: gargoyles and gorillas, mainly. Even the homeliest studio "bad guy" or villain of star value whose heroic campaigns were no more bloody than squabbles over who got which dressing room. There's usually one excessively mainstream-handsome and one excessively strange-ugly guy, and one can confidently assess the moral makeup of each along a spectrum of physical favor. The "ugly" one tends to steer clear of dames; the handsome one is always chasing or being chased by one or more human females.
(Museum of Modern Art)

But what are we doing in Denver? Why does the film want to be there? Well, it's a different town overrun by crime for a change (and by now "crime" is assumed to be a vast and multifaceted enterprise, including politics, law enforcement, business, town government, any network designed to maximize profits illegally by any means); this is not the Denver in the Chamber of Commerce booklet. The environments, by and large, are the dismal sites of urban decay where the outcasts and misfits live their dismal lives. Dark, wet alleys and crowded, smoke-filled interiors pop up regularly, and it is almost always night. The Denver we see here is not one we would want to visit; at base, it's like any other big city, full of sex, violence, racial tension, corruption, and the ongoing daily operations of crime. It is America failing once again under spectacular mountains and clean air. It is a

Dreams &
Dead Ends

294

sick city, its heart deeply infected, and the Man with the Plan is its symbolically crippled overlord, alternately mourning and avenging a long-dead wife and an adult, brain-damaged son who molests little girls in school yards who remind him of his deeply loved college sweetheart (about to be married to another man). Anger and anguish direct the behavior of both, but the Man with the Plan has the power; he calls the shots. Paralyzed from the waist down, he uses his breath to propel his wheelchair, and his continuing to breathe has but one aim—to get more power and control, the only compensation that assuages grief, which, by this time, is barely distinguishable under a terrifying and gra-

Things to Do in Denver When You're Dead. What's this? The *Things* cast sporting parodic tough-guy expressions and mannerisms? The promise, here, is one of spoofy frolic. There was obviously a question of how the film should be marketed. I suspect the goofball antics kicked it off but that unexpected pockets of seriousness had to be contended with, or wrongly denied. They're not denied. (Museum of Modern Art)

tuitous sadism. He owns Denver, and his evil and violence echo all around the Denver we are restricted to in this film.

One assumes there is a "normal" Denver functioning somewhere, but the script pays attention only to the dynamic pertaining to those who "work" and apply what they know toward criminal activity. The rules of the game, the behavioral codes, the rewards and punishments and risks involved are commonly understood and, make no mistake about it, you will get what's coming to you, and you must be prepared to accept it. It's often difficult to keep this in mind as we watch, but it does seem to hang over everything that happens. The story is a simple one. A criminal gang from Brooklyn has migrated (for some unknown reason) to Denver, where they have over a period of time found legitimate channels for getting by in life, or, having served prison terms, are still on the fringes of the law or subject to the constraints of parole. They consist of Jimmy the Saint (the acknowledged brain and leader), Pieces (Christopher Lloyd, a leper who projects films in a triple X movie house), Easy Wind, a black wheelman who has done some recent time (Bill Nunn), Critical Bill (Treat Williams), who has also done time with Easy Wind, and Franchise (William Forsythe), who manages a trailer park and has a wife and kids. It is not clear when the group arrived in Denver or whether the Man with the Plan came with them from Brooklyn, though it is suggested that Jimmy knew the Man's dead wife, Cynthia, and later that he and Franchise's wife had something going a while back. It appears that they all came together (the result of a purge or a recommendation from some big boss) and that the Man, stinging from the loss of his wife, flung himself into a life of crime with the intent of amassing the kind of power that would bring the city to its knees (he makes a big point of making people beg, then cursing them for begging), while the others floated in different directions, meeting only accidentally. But the many years spent together in high style and criminal accomplishment have formed a deep bond, a concern for each other's welfare, and a fantasy of them all retiring on a luxurious fishing boat, enjoying the good life (Jimmy is even said to be building up a boat fund). The Man with the Plan has succeeded in becoming the kingpin of Denver crime; he lives in a huge, cold, dimly lit mansion, attended by a nurse and two bodyguards—but he is stuck in a wheelchair and fluctuates between scorn, malice, self-pity, and murderous rage in his dealings with human beings. Unlike the frequent nostalgic camaraderie among Jimmy and his crew, he lives alone and apart, his hatred subsiding only when his "ten" nurse delicately strokes where his body still retains sensation.

As in many gangster films, the straight world is a dull, dumb morass, numbing to any that belong to it, a world that by its very boring, yes-sir-ing nature eliminates any live wire from staying within its boundaries. A counterworld of crime, deviance, and defiance arises as an alternative, attracting anyone with moxie, antagonism, and nonconforming, individualistic impulses. Crime is a world unto itself, with harsh standards and inexorable self-policing, and competitively cutthroat but in a more open way. This "other" world most of us are too timid to take our chances in, has always been exciting, even fun, to participate in from a movie seat, and *Denver* is very aware of this tradition of appeal. With help from a superb sound track, our journey with Jimmy as he scurries around trying to solve a sudden torrent of problems, has plenty of zip and bounce and entertaining episodes, but also hideous violence, disgusting revelations and unstoppable evil. How it walks that tightrope makes it differ from the traditional Runyonesque aggregations whose peculiarities and illegalities we easily indulge. These ex-Brooklynites are too dangerous, psychotic, and uncontrolled to take lightly. The result may be called oxymoronic: a bright black comedy.

This band of irreversible misfits is put into service when the Man with the Plan orders Jimmy to throw a scare into Bruce, the "orthodontist" that Meg, the longtime girlfriend of his mentally ill and acutely suffering son, is going to marry. As Bruce makes his scheduled drive to Denver, Jimmy is to somehow stop his truck, take him somewhere off the highway, and scare him so thoroughly that he'll never even think of coming to Denver again. Up until this point, Denver crime has respected Jimmy's attempt to go clean and live legitimately, including the Man's bodyguards who talk of good times past they've shared (but who will later, following the Man's orders, beat him up unmercifully—nothing personal); but the Man with the Plan, bitter to the core, and perhaps resenting Jimmy's quitting the racket (too much like a betrayal and/or a rebuke to his power), asks him to "do it for the old days. Do it for Cynthia" (his dead wife), and finally resorts to the threat of destroying his business. Jimmy has no answer for that (viewers by now understand how serious criminals are about collecting money exactly when it's due) and complies. It is hard to understand why he requests this crew, which he knows are a volatile bunch, often at odds with each other and out of practice, unless it's out of friendship and maybe the sense that they aren't exactly flush and could use the ten grand each. Or maybe he sees it as a chance to relive the old days with guys he can trust,

Things to Do in Denver When You're Dead. Meet "the gang." A grungier quartet of losers would be hard to find, but their present gigs are so lame and dead that they go for this last caper, which is "a sure thing." Until they get involved. Don't underestimate the genius of these marginal malcontents. (Museum of Modern Art)

friends (we see him early on frustrated at having to perform a business pitch to some skeptical customers). Feeling, certainly, takes precedence over reason. We see, though, the ruinous outcome in a beautifully directed, edited, and photographed sequence, in which the "asshole" Bruce refuses to comply with Pieces and Critical Bill who, dressed as cops, have pulled him and his truck over and have asked him to get out. Instead he insults them until Critical Bill loses his cool and drags him out and kills him. Meg, who was asleep in the back of the truck, suddenly emerges, and Pieces, in a panic, shoots her in the head. Hysteria reigns. The bodies are disposed of by a cooperative undertaker obviously an old hand at such things, but they are now all marked men, "buckwheats" (gangsters designated for slow, excruciating deaths).

Jimmy is an old character inventively refurbished for this film. His situation, and his being summoned by the Man with the Plan, is close to a direct steal of the opening of *The Brothers Rico*, and his frantic trying to make ends meet, the hard work his hustling demands, and the vision of the good life he sees as the payoff, are very close to the sweaty pressures making life difficult for Richard Widmark's Harry Fabian in Jules Dassin's *Night and the City* (as is his fate: "You're a dead man, Harry Fabian."). The others, too, come out of the tradition of eccentric cronies, and they too meet, each in their own way, horrendous "buckwheat" deaths. The title, however, has already announced this, and it comes as no surprise. The Man's son Bernard (Michael Nicolosi) also dies, stabbed to death by Jimmy under the guise of friendship, an act that is both a mercy killing and a way at getting back at the Man with the Plan, who, when told of Bernard's death, turns stone cold himself and, we are later told, "never spilled another drop of blood again."

Scott Rosenberg's glittering screenplay, bristling with witty details, makes this pantheon of loony misfits something repellently special. All the old heist outfits seem positively benign in comparison (excepting, perhaps, the bunch in *Reservoir Dogs* [1992]). They are, though, provided with great talk and an inventive string of catchphrases that express, in a kind of shorthand, their dreams, loyalties, and solidarity. And there is another prominent individual named Joe Heff (Jack Warden), an old, sporty type who, now and again, narrates explanatory matter in voice-over from a table he presides over at Moe's Malt Shop, where Jimmy visits regularly to settle his stomach with a malted. Joe is an ironic storyteller whose favorite subject is the past and Jimmy's heroic exploits in and around Brooklyn. He too has apparently stuck with "the good ol' gang" and come West to be their raconteur and choric interpreter (he often explains their obscure lingo). He has retired from the field but is ready, as the band's historian, to regale any interested party who wanders in with what they've done or are doing. Robinson's density of language (each character speaks differently) adds to the film's already complex visual style a further contrapuntal consideration—are we to see things as Joe does? How do we size him up? Is there another perspective we place over his? (Joe is like Finchley in *Criss Cross*, a man of criminal attitudes and insights but savvy enough not to get directly involved.)

Things to Do in Denver When You're Dead. It sure *sounds* like a comedy, but its farcical moments at last recede so that scenes of emotional force can take place. It is not unlike what Arthur Penn puts us through in *Bonnie and Clyde*, that unpredictable see-sawing between detachment and involvement, of our surrendering to illusions of verisimilitude (yes, such characters exist and that's how they talk), or, given a razzle-dazzle display of the medium's bag of tricks (this is artifice and creative hijinks, which we recognize have a postmodern freedom to create ever-changing surfaces, from the still to the busy, the dull to the coruscating, the past to the present, without any warning). Like *Once upon a Time in America*, the first half hour is difficult just to keep up with—forget about tying it all together. But Leone's behemoth can't maintain such a pace and slows itself down permanently, with no thought in mind to ever crank itself up to forego a satisfying oblivion. *Denver* constantly discovers means to kick itself along, and manages an exit mood both lithe and blithe. If it may be said that *America* evokes Proust (massive, memory laden, emotionally exhausting), then perhaps we might say that Faulkner (narrative freedom, groping turbulence, emotional responsiveness) is at hand here. A director needs to be alert and supple to follow and then realize scenes that as scripted have their own intrinsic functions but are also echoing past works and creating a referential texture.

Denver doesn't merely accumulate, unconsciously, aspects of settings, characters, and events that simply go with the territory and are bound to make their presence felt even without anyone's consent. It goes out of its way to saturate sound and image with film and literary history; it is like entering a giant museum of a particular genre that houses a great many things that look familiar, and helping us locate and anchor much of the film's "meaning" that keeps reconstituting itself in the swirl of the narrative. Yet the *way* of telling the story can afford to be experimental, using as ballast the continuity provided by expectation, allusion, and imitation. Fleder's direction accomplishes this in *Denver* as well as we could hope for. He lets everything in but never loses control. Camera position, angle, and depth are always what they should be. Each scene is as tight, fat-free, pointed, and economical as anything in *The Public Enemy*. The history of the genre he so generously acknowledges helps him create a disciplined work. It's not mere Tarantino smarts that push this film along—he has that in his hip pocket—but it's all that other stuff he's willing to learn from and astutely borrows that makes for such an impressive debut.[2]

Leone's is a hard act to follow, as it presents itself as the genre's funeral rites. A bad business. Case closed. The genre needed to recharge the territory, recover its narrative energies, and respond by a new sense of play, even horseplay. Leone's dark journey of the soul gives futility its most resonant container. *Denver* counters with black humor, restless narrative strategies, and a worrisomely entertaining cast of characters. The surface crackles with new life, fresh absurdities, novel turns of phrase. And why is Denver chosen as the site of a murderous underworld—for the unexpected incongruity? It's a local stop whose criminal business is run by exiled Brooklynites who bring that borough's virus into the foreign environs of healthy mountain air. It's a goofy show, something like "The Bowery Boys Go Skiing." In any case, whatever the exact parameters of its tonal range might be, it is a reprieve from *Once upon a Time*'s gloom.

Rosenberg's script is a marvel. It delivers a Shakespearian street poetry that is almost an independent pleasure but is completely geared to situation and speaker; each character is given its own particular eloquence, and each seems to be made whole (and not mere types or sketches) by having been heard. Everybody *talks* in this film because everybody has something to say; they are required to justify their separate existences, announce their fantasies, get out their difficulties, and, in general, communicate. They all seem to be thinking, and verbally *being* what they are, for it seems advisable to be capable of defining oneself. They all make their positions clear, explaining why they must do this or decide that and, in return, must listen to the others. It becomes a kind of debate that we hear, and we think things out along with them. These folkloric characters speak like Damon Runyon creations on crack, and they are probably the most warped quintet of lawbreakers yet put on the screen, top-of-the-line, marginalized sleazeballs of the American underclass; Rosenberg takes them seriously by giving them a vivid language, obliging us to follow suit and let pathos creep in.

These guys, a Flatbush fraternity of criminal exiles, are all leading desperate, uncongenial lives that require them to keep their nasty compulsions under control. They are a rough and disgusting bunch (one rapes young boys in prison, another eats shit for money) that make the old caper/heist congregations (as in *The Asphalt Jungle*, *Plunder Road*, and *Criss Cross*) look positively benign. Given the opportunity, they choose to go outside the law and against the social grain (important especially in the romantic subplot involving Jimmy and Dagney, a poised and educated "ski-instructor" he meets in a bar and falls in love with but has to tearfully abandon). Having once tasted the heavy liquor of comradeship combined with outlawry denied to a "straight" lifestyle, they cannot resist Jimmy's offer—the money, the urge for action, the joy of reunion. Their headquarters is in an out-of-the-way malt shop (!) where Joe Hess, now retired from a life of crime, regales customers with accounts of old jobs and skirmishes starring the near-mythic Jimmy the Saint. But *Denver* insists, as do most crime films, that the world of dreams crumbles upon contact with reality, whether you remain loyal to underworld codes or, as here, have tried to go straight while struggling against the restraints you have agreed to audition as a means of possible happiness.

The film's opening is boldly to the point. Children's voices at a school recess are heard during credits. An overhead establishing shot gives way to one of a large man looking in through the fence. This is Bernard, who we later learn is the mentally damaged son of Denver's crime kingpin, the Man with the Plan. His eyes fix on a particularly pretty blonde girl skipping rope that he longs to caress (we later see she looks very much like his longtime girlfriend Meg, who has left him for another man). It is clear he cannot help himself; it is broad daylight and he is certain to be apprehended, but he scales the school yard fence anyway. He is cursed to achieve happiness in this perverted, socially dangerous way. He approaches the girl and talks to her. Unimpressed by his adoration and unfearful of any harm he might do, the young girl turns on him with disgust and shoos him off with a nasty "What do *you* want, doofus!" Bernard is restrained, and this event "causes" the film's narrative. Bernard is an image of the state of things; the world is wrong, producing men like this.

Bernard's erotic intensity goes unchecked in the scene just discussed because his mental equipment doesn't convey to him it is inadvisable at that moment. So he climbs the fence. Our likely disgust for a child molester melts to a reluctant sympathy as the girl's fearless put-down sends him, hurt and reeling, exposed and humiliated, into the hands of the law.

It may be a tough call where sympathy lies. If he is not restrained, he might well rape her, yet Bernard is weak, disturbed, and no match for anyone who is strongly anchored in their sense of self or who thinks their society adequately channels their needs and energies. The wills of criminals, outsiders, disbelievers will shatter against the firm foundations of an untoppleable wall of reality. The reality principle triumphs over those naive enough to think they can outthink or outpummel it. Consider the backfiring of the plan itself. Dressed as policemen, they fail utterly in convincing Meg's orthodontist husband-to-be that they are policemen, or that he should be afraid of them. Indeed he is so persistently and obdurately obnoxious that when Critical Bill finally shuts him up by stabbing him repeatedly in the throat, we are not entirely displeased. He is the "asshole." But he represents the reality that will not budge, move over, or get lost when a criminal demands. In fact, those representatives of the straight world we get are all unsympathetic: the little girl, the orthodontist, the cop who works for the Man, and especially the "uptown motherfucker" who beats up Lucinda and who Jimmy, bursting into an executive board meeting, garrotes with his own tie (all in a day's work of lost causes—but we're really glad to see that human scum get it). It's an old move: make the people gangsters prey on viler than the gangsters themselves so that the straight route is blocked off without any necessary explanation (gangsters are shown mainly preying on each other, anyway). Even the malignant Man with the Plan displays flickers of feeling, perhaps believes himself generous, and has developed a kind of fierce pride in the face of his disability (his reverent recollections of his wife also suggest he really loved her).

Nothing, presumably, happens to the "uptown" swine who rapes Lucinda with beer bottles (that'll stay the same), but the Man with the Plan will suffer by the derailment of his criminal power, which he has built up from a hate-fed initiative. He is, after all, having no body left to speak of and confined indoors, now all brain, a manipulator, an outsmarter. His paralysis requires Bernard's virility; it is his link to a virile life and a psychological necessity to maintain. He enlists Jimmy to help preserve Bernard by restoring Meg. But it all goes to hell, and he ends up with no son and nothing to live for.

As if the film didn't have enough nuts running rampant through it, a few more arrive late, the most important of which is Mr. Shhh, a contract killer from El Paso the Man has lined up to "buckwheat" Jimmy's bungling crew. Played with sinister, grim panache by Steve Buscemi (for effects anywhere from menace to out-and-out laughs), his dark-suited, steady gait and mechanical gestures make it seem entirely possible that he has dispatched some 200 victims, as Joe Heff claims. We watch his progress with interest, anticipating professional-quality executions of the gang members. He eventually meets his match in Critical Bill who wastes him with a shotgun only to be fatally shot himself with Mr. Shhh's hidden handgun. But Mr. Shhh has already made short work of Pieces and Franchise, not to mention more than a few others not on his dance card. Ruthless and proficient as he is, he gets involved in two peculiar situations that suggest he is not merely job-oriented. On his way to find the whereabouts of Easy Wind, he comes across a gang of toughs beating up a guy on the street. He strolls over, kills one, wounds the other, and watches the rest flee. A few moments later, he is in the bar over which Baby Sinclair (Glenn Plummer) presides, and where Easy Wind, a fellow black man targeted to be "buckwheated," has, by an arrangement with Jimmy, been allowed to hide out. This remarkable sequence opens with Baby Sinclair holding court and explaining how technology will enable blacks to gain and exercise power over all "cities," a dream of finally being able to call the shots and seeing Whitey jump. Black takeover is imminent.

He lords it over his lieutenants, who seem impressed by his impassioned predictions. This contrasts with the weakening efficacy of old-style gang leader Jimmy the Saint, who cannot save his crew from extinction and whose vision of human freedom is having "boat drinks" on a fishing boat with his buddies. There's something maniacal about Baby Sinclair's apocalyptic harangue that sees white society as so weakened and dissipated that it is ripe for a black takeover, confirming the white world's worst fears. He has, though, to a degree, read the situation right. Jimmy and the Man, once unified, *are* now at each other's throat; division has replaced alliance everywhere. The wedding of "Slick" and his angelic ideal is not to be. Even she, after he fails at her request to satisfactorily execute the old Cagney signature expression "You dirty rat . . . ," says "No Sale." Baby Sinclair is certain that blacks will soon be running the show. As he is elaborating on that, Mr. Shhh enters the bar and asks for Easy Wind's whereabouts. He is polite but insistent, patiently enduring a number of insults. Finally, black arrogance turns him into a tornado of destruction, as he destroys a baker's dozen of Baby Sinclair's bodyguards and henchmen. After the carnage, he asks a second time, and it is implied that Easy Wind will be handed over. So much for the fantasy of black power, an entire roomful of revolution-minded soldiers swiftly dispatched, not by a white contingent but by an unassuming albino welterweight. When all the dust has settled it's the seriously crippled and seriously misanthropic Man with the Plan who is in charge. But in charge of what? Nothing. Nothing is left. Joe Heff tells us later that the Man with the Plan, having lost his appetite, did not care to continue his old ways.

At this point the film appears to be saying that there is no way to live, that nothing works, that life has its personalized raw deal waiting for you whatever you choose to do. But there is a hierarchy; the now-extinct Jimmy (he and Dagney meet under a dinosaur construction in the Museum of Natural History), most committed to extending the values of the old days into the inimical present, is clearly at the top, a man of honor (as opposed to the Man, who tells Jimmy "I'm a criminal. My word ain't *dick*!"), who nonetheless fails in his business, both legitimate and illegitimate. But he remains a human being who cares for others and helps when he can. The Man is the other kind of criminal—heartless, vicious, self-involved. Both use the term "citizen" with contempt, attracted by what promises to extract more of life's juices for one's efforts (or, as Pieces reiterates, "We did the things"). Being an "uptown motherfucker" is pure hypocrisy, and the worst of options.

The envisioned life of ease and brotherhood is a pipe dream, it can never pan out, and the romance of gangsterdom is part of history, not present actuality. The subject comes up between Dagney and Jimmy at their meeting in the museum. She asks what he does, and if maybe he's a gangster, given the way he looks (nice suit, slicked back hair) and the various moves he has made on her. Jimmy answers that he

Things to Do in Denver When You're Dead. Contemporary gangster films, whether set in the past (*Once upon a Time in America*) or in the present (*Things to Do in Denver When You're Dead*), represent romance as a pipe dream, letting it faintly flicker before relegating it to the large dustbin of aborted amours. Love backfires, turns sour, evaporates, betrays, has a thousand ways of causing grief and disappointment (especially to the young and unwary). Love leads not to salvation but doom. This lost-in-love moment, shared by Garcia and Anwar (like the idealized fantasy Noodles makes of his lust for Deborah in *Once upon a Time*—which culminates in rape and decades of regret), all the romantic trappings in place, has little chance of surviving either the incompatibility of their social allegiances or the sordid dangers of disentangled criminal indebtedness. (Museum of Modern Art)

didn't think they were around anymore, as though he understood what an anachronism he was with his commitment to romance, love, justice, honor, loyalty, and friendship, in a world spinning destructively with greed, brutality, race hatred (even within the gang, Critical Bill keeps hurling racial slurs at Easy Wind, a close friend in the past), madness, and cruelty.

It boils down to a struggle between good and evil, Jimmy vs. the Man with the Plan.

The "citizens" occupy an uninteresting, jumbled limbo that pretty much stays out of the fray (unless they're "asshole" enough, like Bruce, to try and push his position past what it can handle—he throws his knowledge of the law and *his* rights rather too aggressively at Pieces and Critical Bill and gets himself killed). Criminals are a self-perceived aristocracy, even in these polluted times, and their antipathies are settled internally, with the strictest justice. All the noncitizens have some sort of color, flair, and drive in the pursuit of specific satisfactions. Even the Man is intelligent and resourceful, although something of a psychotic nihilist. Pieces meets his end with a certain gallantry, and

Critical Bill and Easy Wind go out making apt summary statements or with flamboyant defiance. And Lucinda? Only the deep end hooker has a shot at becoming the Virgin Mary.

After it has succeeded in convincing us (in however lively a manner) that only bleak failure awaits those who want to live life outside the label "citizen" and all that implies of quiescent obedience, it shifts into a mellow gear, as though to say that even if the past can't be recaptured, the present is unendurable, and the future appears closed off, let's imagine it were otherwise. Immediately after the blaze of guns from the Montirez brothers (hired killers recruited from Albuquerque to replace the dead Mr. Shhh) signifying Jimmy's execution, a coda commences, the narrative voice of Joe Hess presiding. We are shown the pregnant Lucinda boarding a bus out of town, then Dagney with Jimmy's ring on her finger driving alone and presumably away from the "citizen" she was engaged to. Lucinda is carrying Jimmy's child and Dagney is taking sustenance from Jimmy's love. We then see the Man with the Plan, alone in his gloomy tomb of a palace, watching the videotape Jimmy has left for those he had cared for and the son he would never see, and he understands that he has been defeated. Finally, the camera enters an azure paradise of sky and sea and glides down to a fishing boat. This is what Jimmy and his pals were going for. With lyric grace the camera travels close in to the people on board, who we recognize but who look different, too—at ease, clean, unbruised, healthy: Jimmy, Critical Bill (scaling fish), Easy Wind (sprawled out), Pieces (pleasurably fishing), Franchise (mixing drinks). The sun sparkles on the water as Franchise announces "Boat drinks!" That word, so often heard, has worked its magic. Denver is no more. The dead have arisen. The time frame momentarily vanishes, and we are suspended out of time until a shot of Joe Hess, in the malt shop, returns us to reality, as we see him close the remarkable history of Jimmy the Saint, a man worthy of canonization. The last shot is a freeze frame of Jimmy doing his typical energetic entrance into the malt shop, accompanied by a reference to his halcyon days in Flatbush. Thus we leave him in his glory, not as a bloody corpse in a wet gutter. In the execution, all Fleder shows are the blazing guns, so we never see Jimmy dead. Like Keats's lovers in "The Eve of St. Agnes," Jimmy's benevolent and incorruptible high spirits remain free from the intrusions of time.

Fleder's direction makes sure we give Jimmy his due, and celebrates him as an honest, reformed crook. But this does not imply unthinking adulation, nor does sympathy lead to a whitewash. Like Leone's criminals, Jimmy's crew have done terrible things, and they all pay the price of leading risky, violent lives. They are all marked with flaws that cannot help but be transmitted by a flawed world. The film, to its credit, invites us to be wary of uncritical admiration of these characters. Joe Hess avoids being too sentimental a figure by the relish he takes in his anecdotes of sadistic gangland retributions; he offers the implicit wisdom that things will never change, but he's as much an old fart as he is a profound philosopher. "Malt," who runs Moe's Malt Shop, has the black man's skepticism about all these white guys' tall tales of heroic exploits. He tends to respond curtly to any question or request, and doesn't seem exactly thrilled to have this kind of crowd hanging around in a family establishment.

In order to juggle the variety of tone when Scott Rosenberg's lines are spoken, each shot has to be carefully composed, with the same imaginative freedom and craftsmanly concentration characteristic of movie making in its heydey, when everything was new and fresh. Interesting that after all these years it is criminal life that inspires the urge to make adventurous films, films that have something on their mind and need to be shaped just so. Scene after scene shows a talented director in charge, one with a strong, never loafing visual sense. It has plenty of pace when pace is called for but is at its best when slow and textured and beautiful, exploiting its numerous environments for their potential. The Malt Shop is, for one, a canny choice, since its functions are consistently put in peril while volatile gangsters perch on the stools. All aspects of it become motivically useful. One scene in particular extends the range of the set with intuitive pointedness, to show what an anachronism this Denver gang is and what a destructive course of action they will be taking. The attempt to settle their differences causes old hatreds to erupt in vicious fighting, this while a children's birthday party is taking place a couple of tables away. The fight is stopped but starts again a few moments later with greater vituperative volume and destructive force. The kids turn to look, but just go back to partying when Jimmy assures them all is OK.

Many important scenes take place there (Lucinda's affecting love and admiration for Jimmy, the sorrowful Bernard's gratitude for accepting his apology, Malt's realistic assessment of Jimmy and Lucinda's chances, Jimmy's battered face swigging down his last malted, as though that satisfaction would do for a note to go out on), and the ordinary aura that former mobsters are now used to hangs ironically over the film as something unattainable for men with their violent history. Any hope of living that life is illusory. (Its source may be Gordon Wiles's 1949 film *The Gangster*. Wiles, a former set designer, designed a beautiful neighborhood ice cream parlor that the local crime big shot Shubunka frequents both to collect payments and to feel like he belongs and is human. But he must finally leave to meet his death, and the death of his sentimental notion of the store as part of a community to which he belonged.) The police have nothing to do with this, no relevance at all in the struggle a true criminal has over what to do with his freedom. Their efficacy is nil. It is practically axiomatic that crime films show cops as "there" but dense; whether dealing with garden-variety lawbreakers, private detectives, or major criminals, they mainly interfere or mop up.

Fleder's film, then, updates in a spirit of homage. As an illustrious amalgam of the something old and new, it exhibits both a nostalgia for those freewheeling days of yore and a sharp contemporary sensibility at home with demented associates and the unexpected (?) satisfactions of disillusion. Fleder doesn't miss a trick, but you don't hear the genre's tried-and-true conventions clanking about or being trapped into place, because this kind of film's whole has been thoroughly reimagined and infallibly executed. Its in-your-face, up-your-nose, and through-your-ears perversities, and the violent set pieces probably prevented any word-of-mouth audience recommendations; but why critics were so lukewarm remains a mystery. The referential games it plays with the genre's past alone should have struck a responsive chord. Better late than never.

CREDITS **Things to Do in Denver When You're Dead**

(Woods Entertainment/CFI, 1995, 114 min.)

Producer	Cary Woods	Cast	Jimmy the Saint (Andy Garcia)
Director	Gary Fleder		Pieces (Christopher Lloyd)
Screenplay	Scott Rosenberg		Franchise (William Forsythe)
Photography	Elliot Davis		Critical Bill Dooley (Treat Williams)
Editor	Richard Marks		Man with the Plan (Christopher Walken)
Music	Michael Convertino		Easy Wind (Bill Nunn)
Art Director	Burton Rencher		Joe Heff (Jack Warden)
			Lucinda (Fairuza Balk)
			Dagney (Gabrielle Anwar)
			Malt (Bill Cobbs)
			Bernard (Michael Nicolosi)
			Mr. Shhh (Steve Buscemi)

Criss Cross: One to "Watch Over and Over."

We know at once in what category *Criss Cross* belongs: crime melodrama (*film noir* after French critical intervention). It is blithely reliant on genre conventions, using the recent successful star/director collaboration (*The Killers*, 1946) as active echo. Shot in 1948, released in 1949, it appears at the peak of the *noir* cycle, its stylistic sophistication and conceptual refinement giving this conspicuously evolved example an eerie luminescence beside its more ill-favored brethren. Self-aware, metaphoric, ironic, closed-off, inbred (people and events with more screen history than "real" history—Hollywood product being as much about its internal dynamics as any slice of actuality outside its gates it purports to render faithfully), it plays out a losing game with earnest, deadpan innocence. Having found the right roles for a talent pool as deep as in any 1949 Hollywood film, it was likely that time might eventually declare *Criss Cross*, in tinseltown parlance, a "major motion picture" (despite its thirty years of obscurity). And so it came to pass, as Jay Cocks startled the mainstream audience of *TV Guide* by including *Criss Cross* among his "Ten Great Movies to Watch Over and Over" (August 5, 1989). If one had to give it a rating, it would be something like 4**** (and improving).

Here are its bare bones:

Steve Thompson (Burt Lancaster) returns home to Los Angeles, having (he thinks) recovered from the breakup of his marriage to Anna (Yvonne De Carlo). He is living with his mother (Edna M. Holland), his brother, Slade (Richard Long), and Corky the dog at the family house, where Pop (Griff Barnett), who works with him at an armored car company, is often a dinner guest. He passes on going bowling, ice-skating, or seeing a movie with Slade and his wife-to-be, and revisits the club where he and Anna used to have good times. It's changed but still exciting, and when he drops in later that night and finds Anna herself, as provocative as ever, dancing to a wailing rumba band, he's hooked again. They meet, and Steve learns she is now gang leader Slim Dundee's (Dan Duryea) woman. Passion is rekindled nonetheless, and a chance encounter later on weakens Steve's resolve not to give in (despite strong objections from his mother and good friend Pete Ramirez (Stephen McNally), a cop, long eager to arrest Slim, who also thinks Anna is big trouble. After discovering marks left on her by Slim's beatings, Steve decides to protect her. Slim catches them together, and Steve improvises, with the excuse that he is seeing Anna (now Mrs. Dundee) to get to Slim, whom he thought might be interested in helping him rob an armored car company. Slim can't refuse a shot at such a major heist and, for the moment,

parks his jealousy. The robbery takes place, masterminded by the alco-
holic intellectual Finchley (Alan Napier), who agrees to come out of retirement in exchange for a standing order at the liquor store. His plan is
good, but the robbery is undertaken by fallible human beings. Slim betrays Steve by killing Pop. Steve betrays Slim by shooting down gang
members and wounding Slim, who escapes, hobbling on one good leg,
with half the money. Steve too is shot, comes to in a hospital bed, and
ironically is perceived as a hero, the company employee who successfully
fought off the robbery attempt and hung onto half the loot. Slim sends
someone to abduct Steve from the hospital, but Steve bribes the guy to
take him to Anna (who has agreed to hold the money). Anna is ready to
take off on her own, without Steve or Slim. When Steve arrives, his arm
in a cast, and is told as much (she can't drag a cripple around with her),
he sits stunned as she explains what life is all about. Before she can
escape, Slim, supported by a cane, emerges from the darkness of an
open doorway, pointing a gun. Anna screams and falls into Steve's one
good arm. Slim shoots them both. Sirens are heard as Slim turns to
leave.

Its most salient, other-than-narrative quality is an overarching *noir* vision
(tempered by irony and compassion). Good or bad, everybody loses, is a loser.
Reality is equally unknowable to everyone. *Criss Cross* is one of the purest examples of this thesis. Unlike many other *noirs*, however, it is not an angry, agitated film; it accepts that reality is unknowable, that all human aspiration,
wanting and planning, operates on a plane of random absurdity, and that despair is its apt, unshakable, companion. Hence its gallery of surprisingly goofy
lowlifes and decent but uniformly oblivious law-abiding citizens — all cut-rate,
scaled-down, finally impotent. The pathos of human life is that people must
nonetheless act as though they had figured something out, or will be able to.
That sounds pretty grim, but *noir* merely hastens the inevitable leveling
propensities of death, to which we are all, each in our own way, resigned. It
only asks, at checkout time, that we toss what tatters of illusion remain in the
trash.

The straightforward synopsis given above cannot track all of the plot's
twists and turns, double-crosses and criss-crosses, and fatalistic intertwinings.
There is a kind of tacitly agreed-upon interrogation of the crime-does-not-pay
story line, but its antiquated moral semiquavers occasionally leak through, perhaps to satisfy the censor. One could infer, but without much confidence, that
Criss Cross prefigures, in the fate of its characters, the conformist prosperity of
the 1950s, but only as the palest of afterthoughts. Consider the criminal life depicted in films like *Criss Cross, Gun Crazy, He Walked by Night,* and *D.O.A.,*

very different works but all united by a contempt for legitimate gigs that are there to be had and would guarantee a comfortable, economically worry-free life. All the traffickers in lawlessness in these films are shown with good jobs and solid opportunities for advancement in postwar America but flee or shed them for more thrilling underworld activity. Their jobs don't *satisfy*. This is not the depression malaise so eloquently brought to life in the cinema of the 1930s but rather a more inner, sinister, and undefinable one.

People either die or are stripped of their illusions. We feel this right away in Rozsa's gloom-sharp score over the credits, the aerial camera floating over the city until it drops down, in a movement simultaneously random and purposive, to isolate Steve and Anna illuminated by the glare of headlights in the parking lot of The Rondo. Rozsa's theme, with its repetitive figure that keeps trying but cannot really soar forward (tight and locked-up, as it were), and its mix of trilling violins and brooding cellos, encapsulates the film's "corrective" romanticism, its view of passion as dangerous but necessary folly. This is a dream-world melodrama, one of film's most magical moments (everyone has their own), the dream factory doing what it does best—transporting us to a super-reality of significant connection to our real lives and conflicts, but with a thinly glamorous glaze that invites rapturous contemplation and creates the risk-free confrontations we so willingly pay hard-earned money to undergo.

How to describe the mood of *Criss Cross*? Reserved, laid-back, calm, poised, lyrically despairing, analytically melancholic, bemused, austere, sympathetic? Contrast it with another *noir* of the same year, *D.O.A.*: urgent, cackling, bilious, raging, morbid, raw, violent, belligerent, frenzied, assaultive. Compare its nothing-to-lose hero with Steve, who imagines life will be meaningful again quite soon with Anna. In *D.O.A.* anguish topples over into comedy; life is ridiculous, and we can know and label it as such. *Criss Cross* is more given to metaphysical irony. Life is unknowable; philosophy comes away empty-handed, closed off. No bleaker, but in its own way more liberating, premise can be imagined. After *Criss Cross* and *D.O.A.*, *noir*'s visual style hangs on, but its conception/perception of the world withers and/or transmutes to a more conciliatory one. *Criss Cross* articulates a ground plan of inevitable doom, which cannot be avoided but is somehow just. One plays out the string of one's choices?

Style and outlook go hand in glove, criss-cross as theme, event, and sign coalescing with astonishing singularity of purpose. Chance and inevitability are synchronized with human will (and/or self-delusion) with a potency that feels like vicious intent. Steve and Anna cross paths at the train station despite very good odds of their not meeting. The counterman bends down for a pack of smokes (ah, the good old days when smoke swirling in the balconies of local movie houses was part of an era's mysterioso/seductive iconography); we're dealing with a preordained criss-cross (Steve applies a string of "ifs," but "ifs" are beside the point in a pattern that began long ago and is destined to work itself out). With rare exceptions, characters are trapped within the visual style (strong formal compositions, "fixed" shots, tight positioning, a diagonalist-inflected mise-en-scène) that controls their actions. "Inevitability" puts a burden on style; the what is given, so attention is on the how (Renoir's loose framing is often cited to note its aptness to the director's contrary predispositions—openness, growth, freedom). Yet edges can be blurred. Steve is trying to avoid Anna, but he really wants to meet her. So Fate gives him what he wants as he aimlessly wanders the city. This section doubles back on the account of his initial return (stopping in at The Rondo, but professing disinterest in Anna). Here his real desire gets ironically gratified. Siodmak's narration sandwiches and overrides Steve's anyway, the forty-minute flashback compromised by Steve's gullible point of view and making us recall and question the events that preceded it. So while Steve's narration invites us to concur in a sense of cosmic raw deal, the remainder of the film places Steve in a more objective framework, one minus his special pleading. We are asked to balance the one off against the other and perhaps recalibrate our sympathies.

While we do that, we might consider where we are with this film: near its heart or still noodling hopefully at its edges? The stirringly romantic visual/aural sweep of the credits leads directly into the passionate declaration that initiates the film proper and holds its major themes: that the world cannot be understood, that appearance and reality are easily confused, that subjective readings are often misreadings and unreliable, and that the world cannot accommodate intensity of that order. Impotency is a keynote, blocking the actualization of any kind of wanting, desire merely blind or willful impertinence. It frustrates the oblivious (Mom and Slade) and the aware (Pete), the cautiously wise (Finchley), and the recklessly naive (Steve) equally. Slim Dundee may be of a "rotten class of people," but his cynical "read" of things gives him a momentary survival edge. Steve, most naive, and thereby truly unfit, is first to go. Anna's charge at the end is correct: he "can't take care of himself." Yet Slim's shrewdness and cynicism also lead nowhere, and his initial "flare-up" (jealousy over Anna and the indignity of having to share power and control with Steve?) should not be discounted. There is something of the lover's frenzy, however dark and sadistic, at his core. He is interesting, like so many movie characters, because he operates outside the law and exhibits the kind of excessive behavior our timidity feeds curiously and often excitedly on. If Slim falls outside the good/evil, black/white certainties of moral judgment, if he too is some shade of gray, then gray must be the representative color of *Criss Cross*'s entire population—including the oddly sinister-looking but apparently benign doctor who we first see attending Steve in the hospital. If gray is our

Appendix 1

310

common color, does the film advise on how one should live? Is Slim wrong? Is Anna? Should Pete have minded his own business? *Criss Cross* implies that human crookedness is nothing compared to cosmic crookedness—a kind of Big Warp out there and up there. People are innocent, the world is evil. Our true condition?—we are pawns of an indifferent fate. Nobody knows or lives as though this were the case, but there are those who by their very nature, must test it, and they always pay the price of their effrontery. Steve, Anna, and Slim, who choose to play for big stakes, go down 1-2-3 at the end, in sequence, like fragile bowling pins, awaiting the speedy annihilation such uncalled for assumptions of privilege provoke. What could they have been thinking? All three think they have come to the right conclusions, have "figured things out," only to have their faces stamped with a similar uncomprehending look. All that falls under "life" or "existence" seems to effortlessly nullify human aspiration.

A "full" view of *Criss Cross* would involve pursuit of vague and vast categories like art, commerce, society, history, and the like, as well as more precise ones like the careers of its key personnel: Siodmak's other films, screenwriter Daniel Fuchs's shamefully overlooked novels of the 1930s, the "star" presence of Burt Lancaster, the opportunistic use of Yvonne De Carlo's inadequacies, the expatriate expressionism of Frank (nee Franz) Planer, the marvelously anguished/edgy romantic score by Miklos Rozsa (who studied with Bartok), the early stage of Anthony Curtis's (Bernie Schwartz's) groom job for stardom, and so forth. That's work, eventually, for many hands, especially since people seem to like and admire this film for a number of different reasons, indicating not thematic fuzziness or lack of structural clarity but a kind of existential maneuverability, the artist's response to the world opening a similar receptivity in the viewer.

Divergent cases can be made for the film being about this, that, or the other, both from within the field and without. More useful here to work from within the film, since the surrounding cultural contexts will still be there to investigate when we return from its singular inner landscape.

Let's start by dragging the highly peripheral Finchley to the forefront. His presence is so thematic and idea-generative that it alters the mood of *Criss Cross* considerably, rerouting it from its action formulae to a realm of philosophical contemplation. As the film's only thoughtful man, he is in sharp contrast with all the others, who live simply by following their urges and feelings and routine obligations. Although he serves a clear purpose in the plot's getting from one incident to another (he masterminds the heist), Finchley is not really a necessary character, something that alerts us to his significance. If the story can be told without him, he is probably there for some other purpose. Imagine his absence, and assess what, if anything, is lost. The film's main concern is with Steve/Anna/Slim, but maybe Finchley can help clear up what all the rest

Criss Cross. Dan Duryea's tie shouts a loud "NO" to its wearer's "Am I cool?" Contrast the working-class dignity of Burt Lancaster's outfit. Alan Napier, the retired intellectual dandy called Finchley, gives special "nerd" instructions to an unlikely gang member, while Yvonne De Carlo misleads everyone by showing only a mild, background interest in the proceedings: she wants it *all*. (Museum of Modern Art)

is driving at. His age makes him a candidate for a mentor figure, a source of wisdom (perhaps outmoded), a voice (cautionary, and as a rule, ignored) of experience. The film's criss-crossing is complemented by frequent up-and-downing, and Finchley occupies the film's highest point (the gang members seem to climb forever before they reach his room, high above the rest of the world). In a kind of retreat, Finchley has made himself inaccessible and camouflaged but also above it all, his life the result of dignified personal preference, not externally dictated degradation (or if it is the latter, he behaves as though it were the former). One guy thinks he's dead. By choice, it seems, he has stopped participating in life, thereby avoiding its dangers and challenges. But he does not forego its pleasures, though he has whittled them down to two: liquor and chess. And one might have to include the mental stimulation of planning the robbery without being fool enough to be in on its execution (two stages of brain activity). Alan Napier plays Finchley as a man of bearing and high intelligence, an aristocratic sensibility that looks on those he sends to their death with a gentle contempt, his philosophical superiority tainted by the acknowledgment of his own weaknesses. (Does he take on this caper because he finds it especially challenging, or is he just hard up? A bit of both, perhaps?) The excitement of criminality without any of the consequences may figure into it also. *Criss Cross*, with possibly a deliberate forgetfulness, takes no pains to bring him to justice. He blurs out in medium long shot, content in his sudden isolation (the others having hurried off to die), savoring the raised bottle's promise of an 80-proof oblivion, soon to arrive.

The gang interrupts Finchley's chess game (it is with himself—a game he cannot lose or win?), but he continues right on playing as he concocts a sure-fire robbery. It is with reluctance that he allows himself to be coaxed into contact with "real" action or people, and he treats the gang as pawns, as abstractions, as fodder for his analytical urges—and accepts a modest legal reward for his troubles, a supply of booze from his local liquor store. He has long sensed the risk of physical visibility, especially in a life of crime, and has in effect been playing dead to survive (the problem is that to "play" dead, you sort of have to *be* dead. The film isn't exactly advocating Finchley's behavior or outlook—to have to cut yourself off from life is only another instance of failure—but it allows him to survive and score minor meaningless triumphs. *Noir* winners are losers anyway—for what's to win? Finchley's way of being "stuck" is offered as an option and contrasted most particularly to those who think they can, by doing this or that, get unstuck. He plays chess with himself presumably because there is no other competition, but also to illustrate life as a never-finished puzzle; you don't fight life, you keep playing it. Most people are like Steve, Slim, and Anna: they want, fight, struggle, move forward (or wish to—the narrative structure of *Criss Cross* makes that impossible). Finchley, being his own opponent, plays a game that never ends (but that's the level at which you can safely engage)—if you get too smart, you beat yourself. The last move cannot be made. Stuck. Deadlock.

Perhaps Siodmak identifies with Finchley? Finchley's shabby room is lined with books—suggesting a cultivated intellect, a man of sensibility who can do something with his awareness of human futility. Finchley enjoys his chess, his liquor, his "direction" of the robbery. Siodmak enjoys the game of making movies, even disreputable genre movies at the least reputable of the major studios, Universal. It is hard to tell, without absolutely knowing, if *Criss Cross* was a plum assignment. It is, after all, a retread of *The Killers*—heists, gangs, nightclubs, obsessional love, and Burt Lancaster in another undershirt. But *The Killers* was a great film, and a hit, nothing to be ashamed of. The "a la Siodmak" tag was already in place, an honor of sorts for the inimitable execution of his *noir*-ish inclinations. If this assignment was an insult, it was clearly one Siodmak could live with, and even turn to his advantage (his star was about to start fading—only *File on Thelma Jordan* of the remaining American films is close to it in quality).

The gang humors Finchley, think they've got the upper hand, have sucked him in by the promise of booze, but it's he who orders them around and has the last laugh. His aesthetic connoisseurship matches Siodmak's rendering of all the generic paraphernalia in *Criss Cross*, a film that bespeaks great involvement, energy, and purpose but which also exposes film's fundamental unreality. The audience is entertained as expected but also undeceived. You can have your Hollywood cake and eat it too. *Criss Cross* is not as "serious" or as poignant as *The Killers*, but it is more sophisticated and intellectually resonant, a follow-up with cooler textures and less agony.

Finchley's presence in *Criss Cross*, then, allows us to entertain wisdom of an unconventional sort. His female counterpart is The Lush, a boozing sideliner with more of a front-row seat at the fray—a barstool with her name on it. The Rondo epitomizes the restless, energetic, suddenly cash-flow postwar nightclub, a kind of entertainment center not terribly mindful of class distinctions (though Slim lords it nicely in his private wing). But The Lush is both of it (a social manifestation?) and apart from it (off to the side and glued). Finchley's choric counterpart, she is also something of a tainted Sibyl, her knowledge both ridiculed and found erotically fascinating by the floundering Steve. She has made a choice not to participate; life swirls around her and she watches it all, detached. The problem of knowing, of assessing things properly, is that you end up like The Lush and Finchley—drinking life away, a decision not to be sneered at. Lush wisdom: "You shouldn't bet if you can't afford to lose" (she misreads Steve's troubles, but the metaphoric sweep of the caveat covers Steve's blundering aptly).

Anna, as played by Yvonne De Carlo, an experienced but inconsistent actress, cannot bring that elusive extra dimension the role calls for, but her blankness expresses the reality-as-indecipherable idea surprisingly well. *The Killers* made Lancaster an instant star. De Carlo had made twice as many films in twice as many years as Lancaster, but mainly Bs, and, alongside Lancaster, she couldn't help but appear shallow. Lancaster had depth and charisma, making the waste that becomes Steve's life in *Criss Cross* that much more lamentable and undeserving than Anna's. De Carlo seems limited to expressing what the scripted role instructs. What she brings to the role is neither terribly personal nor professionally inventive, but as a wobbly icon of the femme fatale she is perfect for this film. Lancaster's less greedy character and still-rising star gets the lion's share of admiration, passion, and sympathy. We feel for this guy with the nice smile who must take the fall. (Steve's mother offers this backhanded tribute: "In some ways she knows more than Einstein"; her son Steve she ranks considerably lower in the brain department.) Anna keeps us guessing all the way, entering "masked" by the glare of a car's headlights in The Rondo's parking lot (alluring enough to mesmerize Steve), but the viewer has the option— a wise one—of keeping clear of Steve's infatuation by recognizing her character's antecedents, ancient (the Biblical Eve) and recent (last week's leading lady), all ready to assume the role of full-time seductress, or (in close-up) a starkly iconic question mark, real only in a hallucinatory way. We are pulled in, but not far enough to become a sap like Steve. We question her sincerity, which makes her more interesting than dangerous. We watch Steve helplessly succumb and understand how creatures like Anna can spell doom for enchanted males. Is she sincere? Who knows? It's in the film's best interest that Anna remain as much of an enigma to us as she is to Steve. (Why are sincere people uninteresting? Not to say "unreal." Would we watch a film about Steve's brother Slade and his girl? I don't think so.) It's not that she surprises us with her self-serving instincts at the end—we expect as much—but that her position is as understandable as it is reprehensible. Hounded by Steve's mother,

blackmailed by Pete the cop, beaten by Slim, loved unwisely by Steve, what's a poor girl to do? Anna, of course, is a sign of internal alterations in postwar American society. Men have gone off to fight (Steve returning from his wanderings collides with a changed world similar to the one awaiting returning vets), and women have usurped their place in the labor force and have become less wifely overall. Anna works (salesgirl), is independent and self-sufficient, and is used to material benefits and the pleasures of greater affluence. She likes clothes, jewelry, perfume, nightlife. Is it wrong for her to be out for herself? Men are, always have been. Should she retreat historically, be submissive, let Steve dictate her fate? Human beings perhaps can be divided into two groups—those who like to live it up and take risks and those attracted to domesticity, placidity, security. The postwar world as defined in *Criss Cross* has plenty of both types. Anna likes excitement—dangerous situations, dangerous men. Not for her the life of good wives shopping at the new supermarkets or using extended leisure time to lounge at the beach. This kind of new identity Anna isn't interested in. Steve has a foot in each world; the two impulses are at war in him. He plays the male protector well enough: "You're not eating well, Anna," "You're getting fat . . ."—but he craves excitement too, the excitement Anna stands for. And he knows it; he's already been married to her, and he comes back for more! He knows well enough that Anna was never into managing a household, and that she'll eat too many sweets and put on weight. He complains about how they were always running around (unlike his mother—as though Anna should be like his mother). And this beats lying around the house aimlessly flipping through the newspaper—bored, if a bit wistful on observing Slade and his bride-to-be enacting a parodistic version of a typical male/female romantic ritual of male dominance and female submission. But this is self-delusion; Slade's scene can never be his.

Moreover, Anna genuinely wants him, desires him, would remarry him. This confuses Steve. She writes, calls, initiates, encroaching on his male prerogative. He changes his attitude when he invites her swimming. Eventually, too many things (marks from Slim's beating her, threats to "remove" her by his mother and Pete—both of which activate his protective urge and misapplied, outdated chivalric attitudes) conspire to prevent his staying away from Anna, including a kind of perverse resentment toward those who would want to control his life. Steve, after all, is expected to be, upon his return, the man of the house, freeing Slade to marry. He revolts against that. With Anna out there representing something else, the kind of home life that awaits him as a tethered mama's boy clearly won't do. The altercation with Mom catapults him toward a certain doom. These are the film's conditions—either/or. Live or vegetate. When push comes to shove in Anna's world, however, you may not survive. Childhood buddy and mom, on the other hand, would stick by you (though he is exasperatedly dismissed by both).

A few remarks about Burt Lancaster are in order. He was one of several (Douglas, Mitchum) physically powerful actors tailor-made for the kind of punishment, of the body and of the psyche, that *noir* loved to dish out. Seeing men that strong be duped and bite the big one was surely humbling. Occasionally, Lancaster's strength would be harnessed toward violent and/or futile heroics, as in Jules Dassin's romantic *Brute Force*. Under the unromantic Siodmak, he was considerably more subdued and pathetic. We may note his physique here as accentuated by a kind of trademark undershirt. Period male cheesecake.

Burt as pinup is of unquestionable sociological interest, but that would mean abandoning the film of which more needs to be said, if briefly. Perhaps a shorthand list of some matters criticism might wish to pursue will be sufficient. How the film handles location versus studio shooting—how, once in the "real" world, not the world of the gang's mental designs, space opens up dramatically, and with this invasion of actuality a sense of danger magnifies. This is followed by the bizarre chaos of the robbery itself, directorial lucidity at the service of depicting major confusion. The caper is actually a partial success, but its failure to go according to plan is symptomatic of the misreading, despair, and paranoia that follow profusely in its wake. The final "false" romantic imagery of lovers enlaced in death points, indeed, to the viewer's susceptibility to idealizations.

The Rondo: Its sections—bar, dance floor, banquet room, washroom—exist in perplexing relation to each other. As the shot moves away from the door to the street, with obscuring light streaking in, the club becomes more unreal, more a place of fantasy, a maze, an enigma, one's bearings uncertain. The name itself designates a musical form that's linear but also circular (ABACA), always returning to A, repetitive and locked in, resembling the image patterns of the film, its narrative method (a kind of willful plot retardation), and the helplessly compulsive habits of the leading players. Its deceptions and disrelations are emblematic.

Pop/Mom: older generation with no useful wisdom to pass on. Steve is responsible for Pop's death—and as the representative figure of the mature male in his world, Steve's behavior and fate suggest we're all in deep trouble. (This will change in the 1950s.)

Pete (and Re-Pete—he pops up several times to warble the same dirge) says, "I don't care anymore," yet he shows up at the hospital, and his explanation is all cockeyed—he's got it wrong. Not much to hope for there. Can any individual or institution dispense or represent justice? All the characters seem to have limited knowledge. Do the various images at the end simply overwhelm any idea we have about Pete's usefulness (Nelson's meanly glinting eyes in the rear-view mirror, the dark sky hanging over the beach house, a climax with a hysterical Anna, a limping Slim, and Steve with an arm in a cast, from which scene Pete has been removed as of no account)? Probably, but it takes almost the whole film to discredit Pete. His simple sense of right and wrong produces both misreadings and questionably legal harassment tactics. He and Anna both are left with the same words for Steve: "I'm sorry." Do we therefore reject his do-goodism? Not totally. He has, unlike Anna, a fixed hand to play, and it is just not adequate. He abruptly materializes out of the mist and fades away, seeming to walk out on Steve, as though he were scarcely real, but something Steve himself conjures up, as he does Anna dancing at The Rondo (the impression created by lighting and editing). Pete may be able to see much of the picture, but he's ineffectual; the total design of things eludes him. Nor can he, in or by his detachment, avert anything. He sees, he cares, he is the counter to the withdrawn Finchley, but it's futile because what will happen will happen anyway. At base, he is what *film noir* needs (but can only fail) to do with the Pat O'Brien priest figure holding the pious fort amidst Warner Bros.'s busily rehabilitating 1930s underworld as the Depression lifts. Unlike Pete, who is ambivalently portrayed, perhaps even discredited, Pat always gets the job done. *Noir* and blarney, however, don't mix.

Realism. Despite its eloquent intensifications, *Criss Cross* also aims for a kind of authenticity and gravitates toward a visual "norm" in its handling of space and composition when "drama" isn't an insistent factor. It gives us the life of a certain kind of people, how crime and legitimacy could mesh and overlap and criss-cross in the "neighborhoods" it records. Thus we have a mother who's a "real" mother and not a sentimental fiction or grotesque harridan, a *femme fatale* who's getting a bit blowzy and overweight, a big shot whom waiters are allowed to undercut, and so forth. We should not underestimate its value as a record of its time.

But that is an incidental attribute. We cannot long escape the Steve-Anna-Slim triangle and the implications of its history and outcome. Anna when we first see her in the parking lot, Anna dancing, Anna behind the screen at the cottage—all these Annas seem to be projections of Steve's romantic imagination. He ought to know better—he's been married to her! He may know the score intellectually, but he can't help himself emotionally. His need is so great it penetrates the very evidence he gathers around him like a shield. Slim is not much different in assigning a symbolic value to Anna and killing her for betraying him. (Anna, though, has not only dumped Slim but Steve too. Having lined up alone, as a separate self, her final shriek at Steve to protect her reverberates ironically around them all.) Anna doesn't ruin Steve or Slim—they ruin themselves. Anna is the mystery that fires male purpose and desire, something ordinary (which we see) made extraordinary (which we also see), a something idealism produces out of the nothing it refuses to accept. Anna, like the

Criss Cross. It may be sunny California outside, but inside there's *noir's* signature darkness, rooms, objects, people in shadow where evil, jealousy, violence, and caprice overwhelm past scruples and deal you a bad hand in a high-stakes showdown, and you have to muster all the guts you have and call the bluff so you can have the pleasure of just seeing and knowing that it had all been set up long ago, whatever happened "in the cards." Anna's injured glowering and Steve's helpless solicitousness are played out in a patchwork of light and shadow that scrambles will and motive, right and wrong, sufficiency and nothingness. Vertical masking increases the pressure, but there is, simultaneously, an environment that invites our extension of it, that has space to expand into a counterforce to emotions that would be gripping via close-up, bringing into prominence, instead, the flimsy curtain, cheap radio, and soiled wallpaper. The problems being worked out between Anna and Steve get somehow less urgent, their fates of less importance, the mutual despair captured in a frozen long shot, a tableau that says "We're losers in the game of life."
(Museum of Modern Art)

robbery, is a gamble, a temptation. Steve knows Anna, yet he goes ahead anyway after a weak show of resistance. There is little hard evidence of her hold over him—she is the routine object Steve transforms to give his life a purpose. Steve's nature is criminal, criminality in *Criss Cross* being the region you pass over into when you individually care enough about something and act on its behalf. Crime is not given any special or pejorative moral coloring; it is, as a character in Huston's *The Asphalt Jungle* remarks, merely "a left-handed form of human endeavor."

California. Palos Verdes. Steve sits with his back to the ocean, up against it. The sky glowers over the calmly rippling water. Nowhere to go, no more going ahead. The black, open doorway is a metaphor. The setting and atmosphere are existential. One cannot be enclosed, protected. You need to let what's out there come in, and deal with it. But you can't. Here, it's Slim with a gun and an only partially correct view of Anna and Steve as romantically involved double-crossers. He misreads her flinging herself on Steve as making a choice driven by love, and that sparks enough of a desire for vengeance for him to pull the trigger. Steve and Anna lie in each other's arms—a lie to any ignorant viewer of the scene (they are no Romeo and Juliet or Tristan and Isolde). Steve holds death in his arms, a nothing. Slim leaves the frame, leaves them behind. We are not to linger on them, despite Rozsa's big theme starting to resound again. They are blocked from view by Slim's large head in the foreground (same shot, no cut) until he realizes he too is subject to forces he can't outwit, and slowly leaves the frame, giving us another glimpse of the doomed lovers—all three playthings of a capriciously malevolent universe.

Who can say exactly what that ending signifies? There are no visible cops—just the siren's whine, the sound the world makes when it's about to tell you you're small change, a thought that has yet to cross Slim's vain mind. Siodmak's ending mixes comedy, despair, and sadness in equal measures. The cops can't mop this one up—best to leave them offscreen.

"I can handle Anna," Slim assures Steve before the robbery (and us), but the film shows how her symbolic range outstrips any means he has of controlling/dominating her, including beating her. Anna's agenda focuses on material security, pleasure, and high living, and if that means giving up love, she will; if it means accepting Slim's courtship (and hand), she will; and if it means having to dump them both, she will. The film locates an insecurity about women that has yet to seriously dissipate. Anna is so confident of her improvisatory skills that she wanders around bored, filing her nails, and eventually falls asleep while the gang makes big plans. She lets the men work things out, has an unclouded faith that her erotic allure will serve her well when the time comes. Slim mistakes her as a mere woman, no match for his authority. His fate is to look out, at the end, into a black, blank void; nothing is to be seen, there is no knowledge except that of failure, of having failed. There are no heroes or antiheroes (the terms are meaningless). The conclusion of *Criss Cross* violates our expectations of closure and foregoes the usual elements of melodramatic climaxes. All the turning of tables endured by the characters lends a certain absurd quality to their behavior. Slim's dazed and worried final look caps off the film's unsentimental view of human longing and ambition. Indeed, from a certain philosophical perspective (Finchley's? Siodmak's?), the application of intensity to life, the know-nothing folly of persistent hope, is comic.

Paranoia is woven deep into the fabric of *Criss Cross* (climaxing in our step-by-step infection by it in the hospital scene), but the film's pessimism lies far beyond it; paranoia is a mere stage—disagreeable but not by nature insurmountable or fatal. There's nothing bad to be seen, nothing particular or definable, just a void. You can't control what you can't grasp. Paranoia is often unavoidable but useless. Slim is finally addressed in a manner eschewing words or pictures, by a noise that says to him "you're nothing, despite what you thought." Life isn't complicated, or absurd, or unjust—it's nothing, and you can't make sense out of nothing. Even the momentousness of death is denied. Slim's is a look combining bewilderment and disenchantment. This is not how he pictured any final moment of reckoning, or how any of us might, either in real life or in the movies (the conventions of masculinity, of showdowns, of triumphant justice, and established order). Steve just sits there and painfully absorbs what Anna and Slim have to dish out, killed by her words long before Slim's bullets arrive; Anna is dead as soon as Slim appears, but she has to do *something*, so she flings herself on Steve, adding a special deceitful twist to the traditional romantic tableau (this is a death of lovers who are not lovers—Slim

Criss Cross. Classic *Noir* Situations, #9A: Out of the hospital's darkness comes your worst nightmare. The man you thought was harmless, passing every credibility test you threw at him, was a great actor, and is now gazing down on your sap-of-the-year gullibility with cynical sympathy. The nurse has gone to that party in Monrovia. "You and I have a date with Dundee." (Museum of Modern Art)

is taken in by it, and so might we be, if we didn't know better); Slim discovers the futility of erasing Anna and Steve by a stern reminder of how he may be the biggest sucker of them all.

In guiding our sympathies, *Criss Cross* leans toward ceding that it's preferable to be like Steve and Anna and Slim, to give it a shot, go for it, rather than be like the penny-pinching pods who chit-chat about where it's cheapest to buy tomatoes in town while thousands and thousands of dollars pass through their incurious hands. People so mummified and comatose deserve, among other things, never to have movies made about them. But be prepared to have your illusions rapidly evaporate as they come into contact with chaos—the state of things about which no adequate sense can be made. Steve says: "I'm no bowler." Got it. Good luck.

The first scene of *Criss Cross* (Steve and Anna's breathless, adulterous rendezvous in The Rondo's parking lot) is the scene a straightforward movie would build up to. How the world is represented and narrated, with its system of qualifications, the finely honed, unostentatious but resourcefully varied style, suggests a deep-grained treatment of genre, a using of genre as a means of contemplating the human condition. *Criss Cross* tactfully lets us see, feel, and help construct a worst-case scenario about life having any purpose, meaning, or justice. We are shown figures, weak and strong, knowledgeable and dumb, but all equally helpless and unable to avert disaster. Plans go haywire, Pete gives up, Pop is sacrificed, love gets wrecked, crooks grim ("I don't think it's so beautiful") and tender ("beat it, dear") die with impartial dispatch, nice guys like Steve, who plays with his dog, and sadistic slime like Slim, who'd as soon plug a dog as pet one, receive the same harsh comeuppance, Mom and Slade live on out-of-it, shielded by the lie of Steve's "heroism," all of it prefigured early on by the Chinaman placing his bet "too late." Something this downbeat perhaps needs to be beautifully made to give great satisfaction, and *Criss Cross* is. Its difficult blending of tones is perhaps the most masterfully managed among all *films noir.* Its conclusion brings off something close to impossible: high passion and a parody of it. It reverberates poetically yet is chillingly logical; it has unmistakable eloquence and pathos at the same time that it questions the very idea of eloquence and undermines its pathos—by absurdity. It mimes emotion in a triumph of style that comments, by its own analytical lucidity, on the emotion it strives to create. Its visual vocabulary belongs to *noir*, but its tempered anguish and serene pessimism is like something out of Sophocles, one of those jolly choruses that reinforce for the simpleton or incurable optimist what the play's action is unmistakably illustrating. Resignation is a keynote, and the gist amounts to "Count no man happy until dead. Best is never to have been born. Second best is to return to an unborn state as soon as possible." *Criss Cross* drags Pete in once again to ice it: "I should have been a better friend," he says, distraught, and exits the film in a defeated state. But it would not have made a difference. His name comes up again, at the cottage, as though he still might be a factor in how things turn out (the siren heard at the end probably has something to do with his ongoing duties as a cop, but its sourceless, unvisualized, abstract nature signifies an agency that's weak, ignorant, unfathoming, insufficient, and always "too late"). Destiny does not play fair, is partial only to caprice. Against goodness, compassion, reason, and law, it opposes indifference, amorality, chaos, and the arbitrary. Being invulnerable, it cannot lose.

I've been tinkering with *Criss Cross* since 1975 or so, delighting in its visual sheen but wary of trying to critically define its uncanny emotional equilibrium, the ease of its sleights-of-hand, its expert selection and tailoring of genre elements, its witty/melancholy shift of emphasis from the sad poetry of human failure to the bracing triumph of film poetics. In the first edition of *Dreams and Dead Ends*, it got tucked away in a guilty footnote. With the advent of the VCR and rental tapes, David Thomson, in the May/June 1990 issue of *Film Comment*, wrote a beautiful essay, one sharply tuned in to the film's special ambiance, tonal balance, and team effort. His insightful reading of the film seems to fuel his enthusiasm to surprising heights. But on the verge of declaring it a "great" film, and rescuing Siodmak from the auteur doghouse of Sarris's Expressive Esoterica, he backs off. His essay helped gain *Criss Cross* new respect; no critic can now ignore it in any overview of *noir*. Yet it remains to be said that the film transcends its genre, probably by a total studio effort in which all personnel involved seem to be having what in sports are called "career years." Thomson earlier ventured where I feared to tread; time now to return the favor.

Criss Cross adds to *noir*'s compendium of downbeat particulars some philosophical finesse, achieving clarity of utterance with material often fogged by sentiment, distorted by brutality, moralized by good intentions, tenderized by personal warmth, or detoured toward upbeat finishing points. *Criss Cross* spreads its culminating despair around quite indiscriminately and gains, thereby, a comprehensiveness of vision more cosmic than geographic, economic, or social. Perhaps it is a case of the critic needing to justify his labors, but *Criss Cross* is looking more and more like one of the best American films.

(Universal, 1949, 87 min.)

Producer	Michael Kraike	Cast	Steve Thompson (Burt Lancaster)
Director	Robert Siodmak		Anna (Yvonne De Carlo)
Screenplay	Daniel Fuchs		Pete Ramirez (Stephen McNally)
Photography	Franz Planer		Slim Dundee (Dan Duryea)
Editor	Ted J. Kent		Finchley (Alan Napier)
Music	Miklos Rozsa		Bartender (Percy Helton)
Art Director	Boris Levin, Bernard Herzman		Vincent (Tom Pedi)
			Walt (John Doucette)

Appendix 1

322

Gangster/Crime/*Noir*/Post-*Noir*: The Top 14

Everybody loves lists. The internet is swarming with them, naked messages of what pleases or displeases or stupefies, rooftop shouts of guilty pleasures, calls of the vile, road maps to movie heaven. Time to unveil, then, my previously secret but now "officially" registered Top 14 in the Gangster/Crime/*Noir* category. Low-budget films dominate because that's what gets me most excited, provides special, incalculable thrills, leaves me lost in admiration. Anybody with millions to play with could put something relatively watchable on the screen. It's those cheapo wonders I turn to again and again, where directorial genius makes something out of nothing, where style is at a premium as financial tightness leads to artistic economy, and a powerful starkness may result. Why 14? Because one always feels the need to go beyond 10, an arbitrary limit that spawns unnecessary difficulties. There's always a small bunch seriously competing for that last spot; I am allowing leeway for that final spill and tumble into four extra spots that will make you sleep better, unhaunted by one or another unjust exclusion that will cause your public mortification. So 14 is ample, allowing for a last-minute throw-in without any intimations of the weak will that simply had to go to the next level, 15, at which point uneasiness over a flabby grip may be starting to settle in; 14 is the perfect solution: gentlemanly generosity within sensible limits.

1. *Detour* (1945—Edgar G. Ulmer). In a class by itself. A few tweaks of visual panache, and then Ulmer seems to just let it happen. Ann Savage's leechlike performance continues to astonish.

2. *Gun Crazy* (1949—Joseph H. Lewis). File montages. Bit players doubling in minor roles. No name stars, but who cares? John Dall and Peggy Cummins, cameraman Russell Harlan, and Lewis throw themselves into this one as though there were no tomorrow. One-time magic. Nothing quite like it ever again.

3. *Criss Cross* (1949—Robert D. Siodmak). A film of such relaxed intelligence that it feels more amiable and serene than it really is; the definitive *film noir*, so fully loaded it can range both sadly and wittily over its grim premises and for good measure add a philosophical finesse to its mastery of style and despair-modifying ironies.

4. *99 River Street* (1953—Phil Karlson). Karlson's best film, and a veritable clinic on direction, on how the special qualities of film can be brought into play and make exciting what could prove tedious under a less imaginative filmmaker.

5. *Blondie Johnson* (1932—William Wellman). Typical Warner grit and darkness and social criticism, but fascinatingly transposed. What must change, what can stay the same, given the sex switch? Who can resist

Joan Blondell, Warners' bounciest, most life-of-the-party working girl, as a mob leader? Not I.

6. *The Grissom Gang* (1971—Robert Aldrich). An act of courage all the way. Aldrich's most undervalued film is also his riskiest, throwing at us a truckful of nasty characters who, through absolute mastery of technique, keep us enthralled in their unpalatable midst for two grueling (and at times hilarious) hours. A couple of gutsy, career-stifling performances from Kim Darby and Scott Wilson. (Who knows what they might have done if it weren't for this?) Aldrich thought he would be cashing in on *Bonnie and Clyde*, but it flopped. I think it's better.

7. *Raw Deal* (1948—Anthony Mann). *The* great female narrator *noir* film. Moody, beautiful, moving, painful. A compendium of *noir* devices expertly employed. Perhaps the most Bergmanish of American *noirs*, it is, in any case, a masterpiece. Mann and cinematographer John Alton's finest hour together . . . or was it *T-Men* . . . or *Reign of Terror* . . . or *Border Incident* or?

8. *Kiss Me Deadly* (1955—Robert Aldrich). Enough said.

9. *Angels with Dirty Faces* (1938—Michael Curtiz). The greatest American actor gives his greatest performance, transcending even the perfection of Curtiz's direction. With a radiant Ann Sheridan and an encore triumph for the Dead End Kids, he sails above it all, untouchable in his tribute to the gangster figure in this high-flying melodrama. Rocky Sullivan's extraordinary human qualities distinguish him not only from Humphrey Bogart's saturnine Bugs Moran (all swindle, sneer, and greed) but also show him much the superior of even Pat O'Brien's streetwise reformed priest, a surprisingly "heroic" reading of this heretofore socially dangerous figure. Perhaps the best argument to be found for the studio system in any genre, and the pivotal film of the gangster's dignified atonement, the menace-to-martyr transformation all the more credible for being achieved through the same actor (cf. *The Public Enemy*, 1931).

10. *Dillinger* (1973—John Milius). AIP gave Milius his head, and, instead of coming back with the studio's typically scruffy stuff, he delivered a rollicking re-creation of the thrills of bank robbing in the 1930s. The violent lifestyle of select celebrated outlaws (*Pretty Boy Floyd, Baby Face Nelson*, others) seems to stimulate contradictory impulses in Milius, so we get bizarre, infectious energy, mordant wit and comic extravagance continuously overlapping. It's a heady mixture that happens very fast and has visual style to burn. The critics were not especially kind—dismayed perhaps that the state this whirlwind of a film

left them in was so tough to judge and not at all prone to stay put and be helpfully apparent. Yet nobody found it boring.

11. *D.O.A.* (1949—Rudolph Mate). Perhaps *noir*'s zaniest crime site in both story and execution. Rumor has it that actress Beverly Campbell, asked by a journalist what she thought of *D.O.A.* (her film debut), answered that she didn't think it would get any Academy Awards, a harmless enough statement that couldn't possibly cause a stir. The film's producers, Harry and Leo Popkin, took umbrage nonetheless and made sure industry doors were closed to Miss Campbell. Such minor events, nay, nonevents, like the above absence of team spirit, may serve as an index of Hollywood's paranoia over its behavior during the years of the Red Scare and political witch hunts. The Popkins' paranoia showed how subversives would be handled. If true, the self-protective climate it illustrates would clam up any semifractious statement that might be construed as unpatriotic. Campbell didn't say anything particularly keen or disloyal; any sentient human creature could have uttered something as harmless (and, one might add, safely irrefutable), yet a quiet blacklisting occurred (she went on to television fame as Beverly Garland).The film *D.O.A.* is charged with an atmosphere of Cold War paranoia—the hero's "Why me?" "What did I do?" and "What *did* I do? symptomatic of just how careful one should be, given how unanticipated the arrival of disaster could be. By the time of *Kiss Me Deadly* (1955), this implicit subtext can be more overtly and angrily clanged. Interesting that a close-up shot of a hotel register includes, among its guests, the signatures of the film's crew just horsing around—or, a political act? But signifying what?

12. *Night and the City* (1950—Jules Dassin). Incredible. Richard Widmark's Harry Fabian is the small-time urban hustler at fever pitch. Dassin brings both flamboyance and hysteria to material most filmmakers would leave seedy and distanced. Widmark's energy is exhausting; one feels quite drained afterward. If not the best *noir*, it is the most febrile and garish. (The 1992 remake eliminates the harshness of the original. Harry's girlfriend's role is much expanded, and with that there's hope for the future! Whatever happened to Hollywood's spine?)

13. *Tight Spot* (1955—Phil Karlson). Not exactly a comedy, but it may be the funniest of crime/mob films anyway. Edward G. Robinson, with a blacklist cloud hanging over his head, and a long-in-the-tooth Ginger Rogers are as good as good can be and, helped by Brian Keith, make William Bowers's script scintillate like it was Oscar Wilde's. Phil

Karlson supplies a desperately needed equanimity for a film full of surprises and nonstop tonal swerving. Shot by shot, a B film gem that bears repeated viewing.

14. A tie! (which means we'll get to 15 anyway, but via a legitimate struggle). First *Murder by Contract* (1958—Irving Lerner). Vince (Ben Casey) Edwards's hit man antihero, morose and mentally sharp, undone by Johann Sebastian Bach, a tough female pianist (his victim), and the precariousness of his own sangfroid. It was one of Scorcese's "guilty pleasures." Made for about a buck and a half, it stands at the forefront of the "killer-by-choice," murder-as-business cycle and has never been bettered. Second, we have *Henry: Portrait of a Serial Killer,* a film recently vilified by Nanno Maretti in his *Caro Diario* (1994) as a worst offender contender for gratuitous and sensibility-damaging violence. Well, violent as it is it still doesn't come close to the actual horrors people commit on other people all over the world, but it does give you worry and some chances to write to your congressman or mouth off in an editorial. Henry is what's emerging from an unmonitored and ignored underclass. Played by Michael Rooker, Henry kills to fill voids caused by boredom, disconnection, emptiness. He's not dumb and has picked up a minimum of social mechanics. But his sickness is uneradicable and incurable. The film, exercising a near-reflex misogyny, somewhat blames it all on a loveless whore of a mom, but with a parenthetical half-heartedness that suggests it too thinks it's a pretty cheesy explanation. (As we experience the film, it becomes clear that following that line would do about as much good as thinking a few afternoons at the Police Athletic League every week could have straightened *this* Henry out as a kid). His rage is deep and scary and not likely ever to be plumbed. These killings are for stimulation and not vindictive. They are as nonchalantly undertaken as buying a ticket for a movie. The absence of context, of information, comes from our failure to take note of the Henries proliferating around us, a disaffected underclass whose random killings are like ugly retaliations for being overlooked as also existing. Henry doesn't care if his murders are stomach-turning and senseless, or whether we find them tantalizing or revolting. I'd caution against watching it alone, as we are not put in a comfortable position and at points may even flop over from horrified citizens to reluctant allies. Henry murders capriciously; he lets the need build, then goes out to find a victim—it's sort of like some horny guy looking to get laid. Such a killer can only be caught by accident, and the film leaves him at large and us with a double trouble response, left as though we had

been slapped in the face again and again for our voyeurism. We've come a long way from the *noir* hero's implicit recognition of moral transgression. Maretti is right to be appalled, but the daily papers tell us there are more Henries out there than we think, and our ability to understand them is advancing very little, if at all.

50 Post-*Godfather* Gangster/Crime/*Noir* Films Worth a Look

After Dark, My Sweet. 1990. James Foley

After Hours. 1985. Martin Scorcese

And Then You Die. 1988. Francis Mankiewicz

Bad Boys. 1983. Rick Rosenthal

Bad Lieutenant. 1992. Abel Ferrara

The Big Easy. 1988. Jim McBride

Black Rain. 1989. Ridley Scott

Blood Simple. 1984. Joel Coen

Body Heat. 1981. Lawrence Kasdan

A Bronx Tale. 1993. Robert De Niro

Bugsy. 1991. Barry Levinson

Capone. 1975. Steve Carver

Casino. 1995. Martin Scorsese

Cop. 1987. James B. Harris

Dead Again. 1991. Kenneth Branagh

Devil in a Blue Dress. 1995. Carl Franklin

Donnie Brasco. 1997. Mike Newell

Falling Down. 1993. Joel Schumacher

Fargo. 1996. Joel Coen

Get Shorty. 1995. Barry Sonnenfeld

Gloria. 1980. John Cassavetes

Goodfellas. 1990. Martin Scorsese

Hoodlum. 1997. Bill Duke

Hustle. 1975. Robert Aldrich

Kill Me Again. 1989. John Dahl

King of New York. 1990. Abel Ferrara

Kiss the Girls. 1997. Gary Fleder

The Krays. 1990. Peter Medak

L.A. Confidential. 1997. Curtis Hanson

The Lady in Red. 1979. Lewis Teague

Lepke. 1975. Menahem Golan

Manhunter. 1986. Michael Mann

Married to the Mob. 1988. Jonathan Demme

Men of Respect. 1991. William Reilly

Miller's Crossing. 1991. Joel Coen

Mulholland Falls. 1995. Lee Tamahori

Natural Born Killers. 1994. Oliver Stone

New Jack City. 1991. Mario van Peebles

One False Move. 1992. Carl Franklin

Pulp Fiction. 1994. Quentin Tarentino

Red Rock West. 1992. John Dahl

Reservoir Dogs. 1992. Quentin Tarentino

Romeo Is Bleeding. 1994. Peter Medak

Scarface. 1983. Brian De Palma

Seven. 1995. David Fincher

Sharky's Machine. 1981. Burt Reynolds

True Romance. 1993. Tony Scott

Underneath. 1995. Steve Soderbergh

The Untouchables. 1987. Brian De Palma

The Usual Suspects. 1995. Bryan Singer

Aging Well: 50 Vintage Gangster/Crime/*Noir* Films

Al Capone. 1959. Richard Wilson

Juicy Rod Steiger interpretation of Capone as inhuman monster. Heavy grinding of late 1950s moral axes complement Rod's departures from subtlety.

Beast of the City. 1932. Charles Brabin

Frustrated cop Walter Huston takes it upon himself to massacre a bunch of unruly thugs the courts keep letting walk. The "answer" to the rampart sinfulness of gangster life. Sounds like a for-extremists-only film, but dancing, dope, sex, and Jean Harlow give good accounts of themselves before being snuffed.

Beyond a Reasonable Doubt. 1956. Fritz Lang

The actors seem to have been either left alone or coached to a state of petrification in this Fritz Lang farewell to America. It lacks the energy of his early films, but its heavy Teutonic plod allows the ironies of the plot to accumulate slowly, and this is what interests him most, what really matters. It's the kind of film whose very imperfections somehow seem to serve a grander purpose. A testimony, I guess, to Lang's track record of seriousness is that this no-budget offering can be so gripping.

The Big Combo. 1955. Joseph H. Lewis

An arrant stylishness only helps cement the reputation of this fascinating study of good and evil.

Big House, USA. 1955. Howard D. Koch

Broderick Crawford 5-star nasty in a pre–Highway Patrol starring opportunity.

Blue Gardenia. 1953. Fritz Lang

Nat Cole sings the moody title song in his usual cool, mellow manner, somewhat at odds with a film full of twisted emotions. Raymond Burr is in it. Rule of thumb: any film with Raymond Burr in it (up until about 1960) is excellent.

The Boss. 1956. Byron Haskin

Who is Byron Haskin? Where's the cult? *I Walk Alone, The Boss, Too Late for Tears, War of the Worlds.* Many a cult has been built on less. Volunteers?

The Bribe. 1949. Robert Z. Leonard

Pleasingly absurd shenanigans of an unsavory sort with an A-team of *noir* veterans avidly chewing the scenery.

Brute Force. 1947. Jules Dassin

Prison horrors. It caused a ruckus for its excessive brutality, but Dassin's emotionalism dictates that the prisoners' revolt against the sadistic Captain Munsey must happen, despite the catastrophic results. The action carries metaphoric weight: "Nobody escapes, nobody ever escapes." But before that discouraging conclusion, there is a fine frenzy of romantic rebelliousness creating several boiling points.

Christmas Holiday. 1944. Robert Siodmak

This keeps getting endless play during the Christmas season, as it sounds like appropriate holiday fare. Many a viewer therefore must have been unpleasantly surprised by this dark, perverse, psychologically sinister thriller and wondered how Deanna Durbin and Gene Kelly (of cheerful musicals fame) found themselves inside *noir*'s tenebrous labyrinths. It shows the full head of steam a *noir* outlook must have had by 1944 for Durbin or Kelly to have chosen (or been studio-coerced) into starring in such downbeat fare.

Cry Danger. 1954. Robert Parrish

The big crime here is Richard Erdman not winning a Best Supporting Actor Oscar for his booze-dependent ex-marine.

The Dark Corner. 1946. Henry Hathaway

One of the classic utterances: "I feel all dead inside. I'm backed up in a dark corner and I don't know who's hitting me." Life is being able to take a lot of punishment without knowing why.

Dark Passage. 1947. Delmer Daves

Highly watchable gimmick flick with Bogart's vocal and visual mannerisms in full flower. He has broken out of jail and we don't get to see his face, because he's going to get a new one, which is Bogart's! "An almost total drag," said the *New Yorker*. I think you'll like it.

Dillinger. 1945. Max Nosseck

Expatriate Max Nosseck, with no reason to wax sentimental over Dillinger, gives us a narcissistic, psychopathic brute. Monogram's greatest film.

Double Indemnity. 1946. Billy Wilder

Much admired, much quoted film, deserves all its plaudits.

Each Dawn I Die. 1939. William Dieterle

Neat pairing of Cagney and Raft. Together, they narrow the gap between cop and gangster (trying out each other's obligations) and greet the new dawn of social unity and national preparedness.

The File on Thelma Jordan. 1949. Robert Siodmak

Barbara Stanwyck invites pine-board-faced Wendell Corey into big trouble and pushes a red-hot sedan cigarette lighter into bad guy Richard Rober's eye. Go Barbara!

Five against the House. 1955. Phil Karlson

A thrown-together band of college misfits plan a heist of a Reno casino out of boredom. Kim Novak adds her gifted presence to the proceedings. And for that, thank you Harry Cohn.

Framed. 1947. Richard Wallace

(Statue-esque) Janis Carter gets a shot at playing a sexy femme fatale. Certainly worth a $2 rental.

The Gangster. 1949. Gordon Wiles

An art house film before art houses, and the most pessimistic portrait of the gangster and society to date. It trashes everything, even goodness. Nothing is left uncompromised. Barry Sullivan, asked to do more than usual, is up to it, giving a wonderfully intense performance.

Impact. 1949. Arthur Lubin

Engaging reactionary melodrama that seems more horrified at the sight of Ella Raines in a grease monkey's job and outfit than anything else. Definitely *not* what the lost and wandering Brian Donleavy wants in a woman. Not to worry—at film's end Ella's in a dress, much to the relief of all the males. No, it's not a comedy.

Kansas City Confidential. 1952. Phil Karlson

John Payne gets beat up. And beat up. And beat up. And beat up. Some heavy hitters in this one: Neville Brand, Lee Van Cleefe, and Jack Elam in one movie! Villain overkill. John certainly has his work cut out for him getting past those three. Hard to believe, but he does, only very painfully. Guess they needed Jack Lambert in there too (probably beating somebody up on another set).

The Killing. 1956. Stanley Kubrick

Highly self-conscious use of the genre's mannerisms and stylistic proclivities. May delight or irritate, depending on your mood.

A Kiss before Dying. 1956. Gerd Oswald

Rare color *noir* that presents the psychopath as that much more credibly invisible to other folk. Robert Wagner's sinister purpose is hidden by his bland blending into the environment. It gets pretty queasy. Remade in 1991 for no apparent reason.

The Last Gangster. 1937. Edward Ludwig

Sticky toward the end, as sentimentality yanks the movie away from its tough beginnings into a quicksand of treacle. You're sucked in, though, thanks to Edward G. Robinson who, unused to happiness, wails and moans over how short-lived it must be for those who live afoul of the law.

The Line-Up. 1958. Don Siegel

An electric film, set up by a long first half of "realistic" police muttering and routine (an *almost* miscalculation) that unveils Dancer, the professional killer, who steps up the pace to meet his deadline. Eli Wallach gives an inspired, core-of-the-character performance, which may have influenced the study of Mr. Shhh in *Things to Do in Denver When You're Dead*. There is a spectacular car chase (rear-projection and all), and an unsettlingly cool, amoral tone to the proceedings.

Little Giant. 1933. Roy del Ruth

Edward G. Robinson parodying himself as "Little Caesar." Gangster fun and games, which suggests that the gangster film did indeed peak and expire in 1932.

Machine-Gun Kelly. 1958. Roger Corman

What did Corman ever have in mind here? The portrait we get is not one we expect of Charles Bronson, even back then: to wit, an insecure, quaking, pussywhipped, chicken-shit, dim-witted, infantile, trigger-happy, loser—weakness unparalleled in the characterization of a notorious gangster. But the guy is such a cringing weasel, we feel sorry for him and dislike the trio of strong women who tease, insult, and stand up to him.

Marked Woman. 1937. Lloyd Bacon

Lloyd Bacon made a jillion films of every possible kind during his long stay at Warner Bros., but perhaps none as powerful as this story of brutal gangster exploitation of prostitutes. It's the late 1930s, so we find gangsters and the law given equal screen time, with the law eventually triumphant, but rarely with so bitter an aftertaste. Bette Davis and the women are the real heroes here and are allowed to verbally stick it to Bogart's comfortable liberal attorney who has, in his own way, patronized and exploited them. Nothing has been "fixed," and the women disappear into the mist like the walking wounded. Re: Lloyd Bacon: he never even got a listing in Andrew Sarris's *The American Cinema*. Consider the following sound films to his credit: *BrotherOrchid, A Slight Case of Murder, Action in the North Atlantic, 42nd Street, Footlight Parade, Picture Snatcher, The Oklahoma Kid, The Sullivans, Knute Rockne—All American, Larceny, Inc.* There's plenty of weaker stuff too, but what's a guy gotta do to get noticed!

Murder, Inc. 1960. Stuart Rosenberg, Burt Balaban

Grisly wide-screen treatment of the killing business, when business was booming, with authentic atmosphere. Peter Falk scary as Abe Reles.

Murder Man. 1935. Tim Whelan

Peppy period example of two milieus often with their noses in each other's business, with Spencer Tracy's "natural" acting skills evident playing a boozing star reporter mixed up with gangsters.

The Narrow Margin. 1952. Richard Fleischer

Charles McGraw, a premiere heavy, plays the lead: a cop with key witness moll Marie Windsor in his custody. It's as though a subplot suddenly took over the main plot. A perfect film, every shot carefully judged for maximum utility and resonance within a B budget. (Rule of thumb #2: any film starring a well-established "heavy" is worth catching. Examples: *Big House, USA, Crashout, Hangover Square, Johnny Cool, Black Angel*.)

Nightmare. 1956. Maxwell Shane

Smart-looking picture with hip visuals, no doubt keyed by its jazz musician protagonist. Jazz and the underworld often relate, usually at the site of the music, whether seedy dive or more upscale nightclub (*D.O.A.*, *Phantom Lady, Sweet Smell of Success, Out of the Past*).

On Dangerous Ground. 1952. Nicholas Ray

A class act. Rarely has spiritual burnout or self-disgust been caught so eloquently as in detective Robert Ryan's eyes and voice and body, and in the cynical brutality of his daily encounters with lowlife. He meets blind Ida Lupino, whose example of human endurance and love teaches and shames him to regain a faith in life. The snow-laden second half makes for an unusual setting but one credibly conducive to Ryan's spiritual rehabilitation.

Party Girl. 1958. Nicholas Ray

Ray's bizarre approach to the genre hasn't pleased many. *Party Girl* is a wide-screen Technicolor extravaganza kicked off, literally, by a florid Cyd Charisse dance number in the credits. It's a fantasia of time-worn motifs. A phlegmatic Robert Taylor is given a cane, a limp, and a law school education to play with and looks lost, as though he'd wandered in from another set. But Lee J. Cobb in an over-the-top ham (prosciutto, but still ham) version of an Al Capone crime boss stands out. Too startling to pass up.

Plunder Road. 1957. Hubert Cornfield

Late–in-the-game heist opus, standard "four losers lose again" formula, but nicely shot, and if you like rain (and there's no rain like movie rain), this has a lot of it, in Regalscope.

Quick Millions. 1931. Rowland Brown

The gangster deglamorized and cut down to size. The ways of a capitalist society make crooks of us all. Brown's sardonic script touches on the similar aims and aspirations of crime, politics, and business. The way the game is played, criminal deceit and strong-arming are just risky ventures embarked on through initiative. Bugs Moran is killed unceremoniously, almost parenthetically, as though he were a gnat. He just made a few wrong moves.

The Rise and Fall of Legs Diamond. 1960. Budd Boetticher

> Smooth, suave, handsome, graceful, Legs here seems more an emanation of Boetticher's matador mania than anything else. Ole!

The Roaring Twenties. 1939. Raoul Walsh

> You've probably seen it a few times already, if you've been living right. Walsh and Cagney connect with warmth and ease in this intimate epic. Walsh is the American Renoir.

Rope of Sand. 1948. William Dieterlie

> Underrated desert-*noir* featuring torture punishment of Burt Lancaster by sadistic Nazi Paul Henreid, punctuated by Claude Rains's droll villanies. Corinne Calvet's body heat does not go unappreciated.

Scarface. 1932. Howard Hawks

> Gangster as ape with feelings; preverbal, childlike, impulsive, vital, immediate, unaware, moronic, and a scourge it would be best to eliminate ASAP.

Scarlet Street. 1945. Fritz Lang

> Incorrigibly gloomy account of bank employee Edward G. Robinson being milked for all he's worth by crooks Dan Duryea and Joan Bennett. Ironic twists aplenty. Bennett is killed, Duryea executed, and Robinson is ruined. You know Fritz; he can't help himself.

Smart Money. 1931. Alfred E. Green

> Eddie G's a barber who fancies himself a great poker player. His customers stake him to take his chances in the big city. He trains in with a big roll and complications ensue. Irresistible. Green also is a director who needs investigation. *Smart Money*, *Baby Face*, and *The Dark Horse*, for starters, are wonderful entertainments.

Somewhere in the Night. 1946. Joseph M. Mankiewicz

> Everybody's favorite amnesia movie.

Tension. 1949. John Berry

> A surprise from M-G-M: something unwholesome and tawdry. Audrey Totter is the campy but perhaps definitive version of the snarling sleazo slut, here the sneering wife of four-eyed runt Richard Basehart, who is nuts about her. She's sick of his penny-ante drugstore gig and hooks up with rich big spenders, one of whom is found dead. Detective Barry Sullivan, of the perfect sneer and side-of-the-mouth wisecrack, steps in and solves the case. Tension is finally dissipated by a happy outcome, but not until much that is sordid has transpired.

They Made Me a Criminal. 1939. Busby Berkeley

> Garfield was the late 1930s James Dean, looking to "belong" but isolated by violence and sensitivity. Here a boxer on the lam thinking he has killed a reporter in a brawl, he runs into the Dead End Kids somewhere

out West (don't ask how *they* got there), and, with the help of Ann Sheridan, tames their unruly ways. A boxing match helps decide the ending in which everything — by a hair's-breadth — turns out O.K. It happens. (Garfield also boxed his way across the more famous and stronger *Body and Soul* [1947], which however does not have Ann Sheridan — always, for me, a consideration.)

T-Men. 1947. Anthony Mann

Starring John Alton.

Underworld, USA. 1961. Samuel Fuller

Fuller, the angry moralist, at his peak.

The Undercover Man. 1949. Joseph H. Lewis

Mild-mannered Glenn Ford gets the Big Fella on a tax rap. Not the most exciting fare, but those interested in the flexibility of *noir* stylistics will find much to chew on in this film's modifications.

The Web. 1947. Michael Gordon

Edmond O'Brien out of his league and in trouble again. Ah, temptation! This time it's Ella Raines. The film's sheen is connected to its theme. Plus, there's Vincent Price practicing his modest horror chops for the demanding decades to come.

Notes

Preface to the First Edition

1. The inaccuracies of Stuart Kaminsky's chart on page 32 of his *American Film Genres* (Dayton, 1974) I must assume result from just such a hasty classification.

2. P. W. Bridgman asserts that "it is impossible to transcend the human reference point" ("Philosophical Implications of Physics," American Academy of Arts and Sciences *Bulletin* 3:5 [February 1950]. Reprinted in *The Limits of Language*, ed. Walker Gibson [New York, 1962] p. 21). Werner Heisenberg's claim that "we always meet only ourselves" ("The Representation of Nature in Contemporary Physics," *Daedalus*, Journal of the American Academy of Arts and Sciences, 87:3 [Summer 1958]. Reprinted in *The Discontinuous Universe: Selected Writings in Contemporary Consciousness*, ed. Sallie Sears and Georgiana W. Lord [New York, 1972], p. 131) is also relevant. Stanley Cavell, in his *The World Viewed: Reflections on the Ontology of Film* (New York, 1971), does not presume to talk about the ontology of film from outside the context of his subjectivity.

Preface to the Second Edition

1. "Reconsiderations." That's a bit of a howl. When I first taught courses in film and pop culture, that was considered a renegade move by the administration (and some faculty), and their warmest wishes were not forthcoming. The provost, come tenure time, found it necessary to call *me* a "gangster," though I had taught many a standard lit and writing course. I wasn't in any position to rebut and engineer the kind of public shaming such a remark deserved, and so it went unchallenged. Some small satisfaction remains in seeing PBS embrace once-ridiculed classics like *Detour* and *Gun Crazy*, and to see the general rush to "reconsider" what was once judged unworthy of consideration by institutions of higher learning. But when I came up for a promotion recently (my "career" already having been thrice-stalled by ivory-tower-ish disdain for the kinds of work I study), all that nonsense finally hit the ironic jackpot, as I was taken to task for not continuing to write about films of the kind I had chosen for *Dreams and Dead Ends* but writing useless *poems* instead! Funny world out there. Chinatown. Politics.

Introduction

1. I would have sacrificed the poetic resonance of my title—*Dreams and Dead Ends*—had it not also been aptly descriptive. Dreams leading to dead ends is what much of the genre is about. The title also applies to all the aesthetic detours the genre has had to construct when its filmic assumptions have dead-ended. Finally, the title was chosen with respect to how the medium engages our consciousness, as a synthesis of dream and reality. (The arguments for this position are briefly rehearsed in Basil Wright's *The Long View*, 1974, pp. 4–22.)

The following remarks by Stanley Cavell epitomize how tangled dream/film equations can become: "To speak of film adventures or glamours or comedies as dreams is a dream of dreams: it doesn't capture the wish behind the dream, but merely the wish to have interesting dreams. But horror films specifically do infuse boring narratives with the skin-shrinking haunts of dreams" (*The World Viewed*, Re-

flections on the Ontology of Film, 1971, p. 67). One is hard put to decide, using Cavell's distinctions, on what side the genre falls or whether it occupies a perplexing middle. If the choice is between the kind of film that resembles our "wish to have interesting dreams" (films that *represent* the American dream and work like myths that substitute, project, explain, give an account of, and reveal our *fantasies*) and the kind of film that is infused with "the wish behind the dream" (films that take the dream to be the film and make it *real*), I'd opt for the latter. The gangster does not settle for the dream but must make it happen. In a sense, that is why he is a gangster. The gangster film takes the living out of the dream for its substance. There is a match between the dream within the gangster film and the dream that it *is* for the viewer, and our involvement is taken to the second power. I'm not sure, however, whether the distinction between myth and reality, between fantasy and the "haunts of dreams," can be precisely argued or critically applied. (More material on film and dreams can be found in George W. Linden, "The Personal World," in *Reflections on the Screen*, 1970, pp. 160–197.)

2. As a rule, American movies externalize inner conflict into action, cultural tensions into melodrama. Like other genres, the gangster/crime film, underneath its action-laden surface, works by implication and must be read between the images in a way that is consistent with its surface. The mechanism and material of genres let filmmakers establish an easy, unesoteric connection with the audience and from that assuring base work whatever variations their ideas and feelings provoke. Scratch any but the most obviously trivial American film and you'll find something "troubled," anxious, and sometimes subversive, tones and attitudes jostling uneasily with formulaic entertainment conventions. The "double" nature of many American films may even be seen as a virtue, prohibiting excesses of propagandistic ideology, didacticism, and elite obfuscation, with a corresponding increase in visual subtlety, conceptual refinement, and directorial inventiveness. (The propaganda is there, but so smoothly embedded that it operates subliminally.) One has only to recall how Douglas Sirk slid about ingeniously in the muck of soap opera, poker-faced, letting the sentimental plots and opulent bourgeois visuals of his films turn in upon themselves and provide their own bitter commentary. On the other hand, this view of Sirk's films would be hard to prove conclusively; it is a possibility for the predisposed. Sirk "straight" is effective, too.

3. Charles W. Eckert's analysis of *Marked Woman* is the best discussion of these ideas to date. "The Anatomy of the Proletarian Film: Warner's *Marked Woman*," *Film Quarterly* 27 (Winter 1973–1974): 10–24.

4. When the studio system was thriving and distribution under studio control, genre films came out with regularity; most had recurring studio personnel and crews, and, within limited budgets, there was unofficial competition as to who could turn out better pictures. With several films of the same kind most always around, genre, not surprisingly, was not a matter one could easily avoid, and it was handy for everyone in the industry to consider films as belonging to one or another commonminded group—discussion of themes and techniques and conventions and performers to come tumbling after a focus was established. One could do that then because clarity of outlook and execution were high priorities, both in filming per se (repetition making for increased technical polish in working crews, in the much-maligned

typecasting that resulted in the applause-worthy perfection of so many minor roles) and in those who wrote about them (deconstruction, postmodernism, performativeness, and the like not yet being factors). There was often a match between the apparent desires and values of the filmmakers and the unsophisticated, often poorly educated audience of all ages for which these films were made. The 1920s, 1930s and 1940s, and even some of the 1950s are decades with easily read genre product; unifying threads abound. Any "shift" would be felt by the whole unit. To belong to a genre was hard work, with little opportunity for individualized carrying on. It feels, in the films' relaxation, like it was a fairly satisfied society, all the reputed moaning and howling over compromised artistry notwithstanding (many good films managed to get made). The 1950s don't really turn to the 1930s for inspiration; their eyes are fixed on what's ahead, and the challenge of television. All the previous decades have a similar self-sufficiency (say up to the 1960s). The difference between then and now is that our genre films can be genre films by dipping into any part of their history at any time. No combination is impossible—hence the screwy, fatalistic, maudlin, and scatterbrained examples that constitute our present fare. You know what kind of film it is but don't really know what it's up to—and you wonder if *it* knows. Ideas arrive from everywhere and nowhere, and who comes up with what is anybody's guess. We seem to be facing a future nobody wants to face, one so dispiriting that even the thrilling exploits of a life of crime cannot justify a participating appetite, as the past has become a vast storehouse to pillage, and, increasingly, a guide to what it is we think we might be doing.

5. A weird segue, I realize. I seem to have unconsciously drifted over to the horror film in order to express how *noir* characters and events often feel. Sometimes, as in this case, it can be a shortcut to an interesting aspect of thefilm best left to specialists (if perhaps better secured by your average Joe or Jane). Here the genre teases our investigative know-how and the scholars' store of knowledge about erotic facets of the narrative. The horror elements express now *noir* characters and events often feel less palpable than those full-shot, space-gobbling, effortlessly physical bodies of the gangster film's early heyday. In the 1940s, the criminal is downsized, subject to the same vicissitudes as a grocery clerk, floundering in dark confusion. In the late 1950s revival of the gangster film, the history of celebrated tough guys is retold with outlooks and anxieties supplied by sexual gurus like Freud, Kinsey, and other angstmeisters qualifying as experts on sexual insecurity and abnormality. These are films in which each gender is suddenly fuzzy about what makes the other tick, and upset about how nothing adds up. (Compare this to how almost-not-there this business is in 1930s films or, to put it more accurately, how peremptorily each sex fulfills their, one might say, socially *inscribed* and sanctioned roles as gangsters, molls, cops, waiters, bartenders, mothers, etc.)

Chapter One

1. See Robert Warshow's writing on the gangster in *The Immediate Experience* (New York, 1964), pp. xxiii–xxviii, 83–106.

2. I use "ephemera" loosely, as things determined by the manner and attitude governing their production, marketing, distribution, rate of consumption, and by their degree of perishability. The American feature film was never offered under the

auspices of art, as something to be preserved and valued. Moreover, when viewing old films, we are distracted by what the world (and its people) used to look like, by the technical limitations of the medium, and by a recognizably period style. These factors combined do not promote an automatic "respect" but rather unconstrained opportunity for negotiable judgment and pleasure, free of the insecurity that often accompanies the effort to appreciate texts designed, or nurtured by others, for posterity.

3. For a concise discussion, see Stuart M. Kaminsky, "*Little Caesar* and Its Role in the Gangster Film Genre," *Journal of Popular Film* 1 (Summer 1972): 209–227.

4. There is *Scarface*, too, of course—a superb piece of craftsmanship and arguably the best of the early gangster films—but it has been so rarely seen that its reputation rests mainly on the testimony of its contemporary enthusiasts. Since relatively few of my contemporaries have seen it, I thought it best to concentrate on its two prestigious predecessors, which have been more widely circulated and are at present available in 16mm.

5. Kaminsky, "*Little Caesar*," p. 215.

6. Gerald Mast, *A Short History of the Movies* (New York, 1971), p. 276.

7. Curtis Lee Hanson, "William Wellman: A Memorable Visit with an Elder Statesman," *Cinema* 3 (July 1966): 22.

8. John Gabree, *Gangsters: from Little Caesar to The Godfather* (New York, 1973), p. 55.

9. *The Public Enemy*'s depiction of the gang differs considerably from *Little Caesar*'s. In the latter, the emphasis falls on ruthless jockeying for top position; very little comradeship is present. In *The Public Enemy* nobody seems discontented with his position. The hierarchy is one of proven merit and initiative. Neither Tom nor Matt covets Paddy Ryan's position, and Paddy gives due deference to Nails Nathan. Mobs savage rival mobs but remain content with the organizational structures of their own. Paddy Ryan is, as he himself claims, a "right" guy and does his best to help Tom at the end. He is willing to give up his stake in the racket if Schemer Burns promises to return Tom safely home. Friendship can go no further, and Paddy Ryan makes good his early promise to be Tom and Matt's friend, as well as business manager. Paddy becomes for Tom a substitute father. His greedy empire building is seen to grow out of the nature of the times. His kindness and loyalty imply that his crookedness is simply sound business practice, not a moral flaw. The friendliness of the gang of course permits a favorable viewer response. Neither comic butts nor malevolent overreachers (as in *Little Caesar*), the mob comes across as a bunch of likable, if legally delinquent, guys.

Chapter Two

1. The postwar crime film also featured a run of mentally disturbed criminals who shared emphasis with ordered documentary-style accounts of police investigations (*T-Men, He Walked by Night*). Law enforcement is a huge bureaucratic network that grimly and rationally tracks down what appears to be an enormous incidence of crime. The men who work this giant machine are galvanized into concerted action by the appearance of a particularly dangerous and elusive killer or racketeering activity. The criminal now is crazy and unpredictable. He has no clear goal, just a sick, consuming drive to injure people and society. The action of such heroes is a desperate attempt to forge a personal identity. Their emotions are brought to a boiling

point; they crack at the seams and commit acts of violence. The speed and bigness of the society has crowded them out, suppressed the life of instinct and individuality, and they retaliate with hostility, acting not so much *for* (as the early gangsters did) but *against* something. The police are organization men who must suppress their personal emotions and abide by their methods of investigation in order to triumph. They are allowed (usually at the climax) a momentary frenzy, but neither their triumphs nor their enemies' defeats are heroic. The police must "do their job," the criminal his, and both with a deglamorized compulsive exactitude. The harsh realism and precise observation of this strain of the genre give way to romantic culmination in the extravagant symbolism of *White Heat* (1949), the film that breaks the mundane deadlock between law and crime and releases the accumulated meaning of this group of films.

2. As in most caper films, both capers are successful, but neither film gives much attention to the caper proper, and the positive dimension of men outwitting institutions characteristic of post-1950 caper films is missing. The capers become merely one aspect of an unaccommodating reality, a reality that later caper films either mask out or exhibit marginally. *Noir* recognizes the urge to react against large, impersonal systems and institutions, but its pessimistic perspective de-emphasizes suspense and audience involvement. By the 1950s the shock of the war years had been somewhat absorbed and dispersed, and the caper film flourished by taking the urge and giving it detailed exposition, and decontextualizing it toward purer fantasy. *Noir* laid the groundwork—a motley crew united by a specific task, the concern with expertise and precise execution, the lone woman, aloof, still, but observant amid the atmosphere charged with male ego—but it was only in the psychological inertia of the fifties that the slow-fuse caper film took clear shape. The possibility of meaningful activity and freedom inherent to the caper was choked off in the fatalistic contexts of forties melodramas. One minor convention may illustrate the difference. In the fifties the audience is aroused and intrigued by the magnitude of the operation. It is daring, impossible, never done before. The participants' inevitable apprehension does not negate the audience's anticipation of excitement ahead and rooting interest. In the forties a different climate of awareness is created about the big job by having a participant relate a story of a failed caper in the past on the eve of the one coming up, a device that enforces a level of viewer detachment (*High Sierra, The Killers, Criss Cross*).

3. The Goodhues' odyssey seems on the one hand to smack of populist sentiment—a "we the people" flavor. On the other hand, what was stirring in *The Grapes of Wrath* (1940) is very distinctly compromised in *High Sierra*. The Goodhues degenerate toward middle classness, become trivial and corrupt. It is what the society demands they aspire to. *High Sierra* is typical of the schizophrenic muddle most American films manage to make of class issues. The Goodhues find a place in the social order, but Pa's values (seen as good) are not passed on. Pa understands Earle and Earle understands Pa: their values are equated. (Marie understands them both and everyone else she comes in contact with, in ways *they* don't understand). Earle, by his name, is tagged as an aristocrat, but it is a superiority he is trying to shed. We learn, obviously by design, the names of all the local cops who are involved in Earle's downfall—Charlie, Slim, Hank, Sam—all common names. They unite together in a cooperative effort to get Earle. They are the people who make up a democracy and they play an active role in safeguarding it. At the film's conclusion, Earle is kept in

middle and long distance—we are removed from his feelings. We are given close-ups of Marie, the radio announcer, the newspaperman, the cops. One expects to be brought close to Earle in his final moments, especially since the film has made us care about him. Instead, while Earle undergoes whatever he is undergoing, we get a close-up of Slim the sharpshooter, held long enough to acquaint us intimately with every one of his bad front teeth. In effect, we are not allowed to *be* Earle. We become not him but *them* or perhaps *us*. The camera angle enforces this view. We pull the trigger with Slim; we ambush Earle. It's a curious sensation. We admire Earle, but we cannot let him live in the world we live in. The shock of his death is double; we feel the loss of someone valuable in whose death we are implicated by the staging of the action. Marie smooths us over the jolt by leading us back to life, to prison. For her, it's a literal one; for us, a metaphorical one. The film appears to assert that living is worse than dying because the only structure left that can sustain life is a middle-class one whose values are corrupt. The hard grip of the cop's hand on Marie's shoulder signifies the burdens and oppression we will all, in one way or another, have to bear. Only Earle has managed to "crash out."

4. The scene where Roy and Velma gaze at the stars is artistically unhappy if taken as an attempt at deep emotion. Surely the studio could have done much better than the twinkling decorations we get. It is not that Roy's "poetry" is false and unreal, but that in the context of Velma it must be modified, even undercut. The whole sequence must be based on Roy's erroneous judgment about what it is possible for his life to become. As it stands, the scene tells us of admirable qualities in Roy at the same time that it supplies a context of absurdity and pathos. Perhaps the audience bought the sky mock-up completely and got all wet in the heart from the characters' warmth. If so, the rest of the film tells us they were set up.

5. One can imagine the mess that might have been made of Burnett and Huston's script, the mess Huston himself might have made in dealing with so goofy a subplot and so romantically dignified a hero. (*The Asphalt Jungle*, with its cold, timid humanism and its maudlin conclusion, comes to mind.) Walsh is tougher, more clear-visioned and acerbic, and also warmer and more emotional than Huston. The stylistic and temperamental repose of a film like *High Sierra* suggests that, notwithstanding his reputation as an action director, Walsh is the American Renoir, minus the Frenchman's sophistication. (I thought the Renoir comparison—even tucked away in a footnote—might be taken as too fanciful, or might cause some highbrow displeasure, or just be deemed unwise until I discovered that Manny Farber had anticipated it four years ago in a piece on Walsh [the best yet written] published in *Artforum*, a piece I hadn't known about until it was reprinted in the Winter 1974–1975 issue of *Sight and Sound*.)

6. I speak of complexities over and above the ambitiousness or lack of ambitiousness of a given script, of course. One can make the same claim of complexity, I suppose, for a director as different as Ingmar Bergman. A director like Bergman, however, carries the method to theoretical extremes and keeps his characters' emotional states more recherché and his own attitudes more consciously ambiguous. The feelings of Bergman's people are also less jiggly and less prone to "noise" and other interference, since they cannot travel very far in the closed chambers Bergman provides for them. Nothing can impinge on their clarity. In a Walsh film, film, they can be blown away by the wind, simply fall short of going the required distance, or get snagged

in the frill of a lampshade. Bergman seems to work out of a priori conceptions of spiritual alienation. His films are exactly structured models of uncertainty. The "confusion" of his characters is predetermined—although his actors and actresses are given enormous leeway to exercise their vibrancy. Someone like Walsh seems to have no ideas at all. His movies habitually suggest an unpredictably alert subversion of overtidy scripts by an impromptu on-the-set response to the talent of his players and the kind of space they inhabit. Bergman's showy skill, as in, say, the elaborate refinements of a film like *Persona*, makes certain that his ideas will not be compromised. Walsh's floating concentration on whatever interesting tangle of emotions has been induced within a scene often makes us forget what his movie as a whole is about.

Bergman worries his material like an artist. His films are close, intense transcriptions of his inner life. Walsh is less egocentric and less hard on himself. His muse is good-natured. He has a curiosity and respect for things going on outside himself and worth capturing on film—things that have nothing to do with the medium as such or with a "vision" of human life but with men and women, actors and actresses, trying to live under often difficult, demanding, and unideal circumstances, including Hollywood and studio realities. Bergman's contempt for the world is apparent in his harsh attitude toward his characters and in his frequent use of remote, isolated settings. His personal psychological burdens are transmitted by the cumbrous pacing of his shots. The springy movement of a Walsh film suggests a preparedness to consider anything of note that comes into the frame or that the camera can shift to pick up. He is not a modern director. *High Sierra* neither crawls, nor rushes, nor broods; it unfolds. The process of unfolding is a positive dimension that alters the pessimistic premise of the film. In the presence of any sign of a still vital humanity, Walsh will find ways of celebrating it. One wonders how he might have exercised his sensibility on a project like *The Killers*. Actually, for Walsh, it is an almost unthinkable project.

7. Paul Schrader, "Notes on *Film Noir.*" *Film Comment* 8 (Spring 1972): 13.

8. Edmond O'Brien is well suited to the role, one that became a specialty as he went on to portray similar figures in *White Heat* and *D.O.A.* His puffy but smooth face, his ordinary physique, and his voice with its restless cynicism, complements Reardon's opportunistic, self-serving character perfectly. Hard-nosed, fast-talking, and unfeeling, Reardon has a pushy self-satisfied quality that seems to express O'Brien's own attitude as a Hollywood actor. His would-be heroes have a sour charge perhaps symptomatic of his own frustration in these kinds of roles. His Reardon is an almost overattentive performance, as though the role could be transcended by talent and energy. But the film has him locked up tight. Every clarifying and intensifying touch O'Brien provides backfires (?) into exposing the character further for what he is, a man of rather credibly objectionable qualities, but ones that ensure him success in the present ways of the world.

9. The boxing scenes are especially ironic in the light of Swede's dedication. Grisly and savage—Swede gets viciously beaten—they herald the dawn of such angry boxing films as *Body and Soul* (1947), *Champion* (1949), and *The Set-Up* (1949). The fight game is pictured as a mercenary racket, belying Swede's naive faith in its validity. When they find he's through, his trainer and manager talk cynically of finding themselves a new prospect, cheap.

10. J. A. Place and L. S. Peterson, "Some Visual Motifs of *Film Noir.*" *Film Comment* 10 (January–February 1974): 35.

11. Perhaps the film omits the scene where Reardon and Lubinsky rehearse the roles they will play at The Green Cat precisely to permit an ambiguity about Reardon, to tantalize us about his motives. It turns out that he's playing it straight all the way, but all the film has to do is to make us feel that it might be otherwise to undermine our automatic notions of what is legitimate and what not and make it possible to infer a similarity between Reardon's activity and the gang's. There is also an intriguing dissolve from Kitty's flashback to Kitty and Reardon at a table in The Green Cat. An image of Swede and Kitty kissing passionately fades into a shot of Kitty and Reardon (their position in the frame reversed from the preceding image). The shots are linked by the candle on the table that burns at the center of Swede and Kitty's fading embrace (echoing the lamp between them at their first meeting) and is centrally positioned between Kitty and Reardon. Although the candle—Kitty's flame—has burnt low and is fluttering, it still works. Reardon is fascinated by her narrative, a narrative of evil and treachery, suggesting that if he were slightly less strong (or brainwashed) he could well fall under Kitty's control. He is, in any case, explicitly connected with Swede.

12. In the illogical schemes of *film noir*, the elderly man who wins the youthful, beautiful woman from the understandably uncomprehending younger man, is a common motif.

13. It is ironic that Colfax, the brains of the outfit, is revealed, and finally killed, by a man named Dum-Dum. Their special antagonism, though, is established early, as well as the fact that they both have "reputations" to maintain. The result of maintaining them is their elimination of each other.

14. *Criss Cross*, three years later, finds the director refining his theme by the very nature of illusionistic cinema and playing the game of making Hollywood formula movies. *Criss Cross* clarifies *The Killers* by giving the principle of detachment a philosophical application, by matching the *nothing* of a movie reality to the *nothing* of reality. Life cannot be defined by a presence of qualities but by an absence. Whether you sit in your room or come out of it, life will run its course independent of you. Only Finchley and The Lush, who watch other people act, have figured out how to play the game, and like Charleston in *The Killers*, they are drunkards (controlled drunkards). There are some people who will always be tempted. It is their nature to seek out an object on which to focus a drive that's there. They do not know that they can never control anything. Others have lost the will, have bought into a system that gives it no room. They live out their lives in unawareness. It is only the sideliners, removed enough from life to understand how it works and therefore free to play out a losing game with graceful interest, absorbed by and mindful of the rules, who survive and achieve what it is only possible to achieve, the pleasure of perceiving its codes. *Criss Cross* suggests that one could do worse than drink one's life away.

15. If the film has any defect at all (other than Rozsa's occasionally too emphatic score) it is that it can't breathe. Siodmak's control is perhaps too severe and confining. It would be unfair, though, to ask that an artist stop short of fully realizing his vision. *The Killers* may not be a particularly likable film, but it ranks high as being the most thoroughgoing example of *noir* style and outlook.

16. *Noir* accommodates, within its vast index of social pathology, a wide curiosity and appetite for violence created by the war. A shocking relish accompanies Richard Basehart's point-blank shooting of a cop in *He Walked by Night* and Raymond Burr's

ingenuities with fire in *Raw Deal*—to name only two of many money's-worth sadists of the period.

Chapter Three

1. James Agee, *Agee on Film: Reviews and Comments* (Boston, 1964), p. 376.
2. The Cagney-Robinson-Raft image of the short, glib human dynamo may be what pops into the mind when one thinks "gangster," but in truth the gangster comes in all shapes and sizes, races and nationalities. Also, the xenophobic strain that wishes to imply that crime is the property of the immigrant population and their spawn is not minimal but is less insistent than it seems, and WASPs appear to dominate the higher levels of corruption. Finally, the gangster does not have to die, and when he does, it is not always in a city street or gutter, or the chair or gas chamber. He dies all over the place, in varying tempos and volumes, in close-up and in long shot, alone and with others. It is a tribute to the early gangster films that their conventions were so gripping that they made an irrevocable stamp on the popular imagination and became the repertoire of mimics, caricaturists and farceurs, but a study of the genre in its totality reveals these emphases as period ones. By the mid-forties, extensive modifications have set in.
3. The sight of Victor Mature's hulking muscularity crushing Coleen Gray's teenage nubility limp must, I assume, also have been intended to be sexually provocative.
4. Lawrence Alloway, *Violent America: The Movies, 1946–1964* (New York, 1971), pp. 37–39, 63–71, especially.
5. Eric Sherman and Martin Rubin, eds., *The Director's Event: Interviews with Five American Filmmakers* (New York, 1972), p. 30.
6. I am not saying that poetry cannot be public or moviemaking private—they can be and they have been. I am referring only to their status in recent and present Western culture.
7. It is not too farfetched to suggest that it was Garfield's own guilt that was being conveyed in roles like this. Garfield retained his leftist ties and sympathies throughout his career. Being a leftist in theory and a wealthy film star in actuality must have been a hard line to walk. His old friends disowned him as a sellout, and he was too much of a maverick, an individualist, to survive in the movie industry. At last hounded and persecuted by HUAC, he died of a heart attack in 1952, at the age of thirty-nine. His lower-class, antiestablishment manner was something audiences were receptive to for well over a decade.
8. Andrew Sarris, *Interviews with Film Directors* (New York, 1969), p. 387.
9. Sarris, *Interviews*, p. 392.
10. There is an article to be written on telephones in a genre that seems suspended between Vince Barnett's wanting to shoot one in *Scarface* and Lee Marvin finally doing it in *Point Blank*. The suggestion is not an idle one (compare the uses of the telephone in *Little Caesar*, *T-Men*, *The Public Enemy*, *Gun Crazy*, *The Big Heat*, *99 River Street*, *Kiss Me Deadly*, *The Brothers Rico*, and countless other films).
11. Sherman and Rubin, *Director's Event*, p. 21.
12. Compare Fritz Lang's *You Only Live Once* (1937), an early outlaw couple movie in which sympathy is established for Henry Fonda and Sylvia Sidney by the absolute vileness of the people who reject, hound, hunt, and finally kill them.

13. The film is superbly photographed by Russell Harlan, whose talent more than meets the film's extraordinary challenges, his supreme moment coming in the eerie mist of the concluding shots.

14. Material on Lewis's technical experiments may be found in *Cinema* 7 (Fall 1971), which contains a long interview with Lewis by Peter Bogdanovich, provocative critical statements on the director by Paul Schrader, Robert Mundy, and Richard Thompson, and a complete filmography by Robert Mundy.

Chapter Four

1. Films are often cavalierly dated. *Gun Crazy* and *D.O.A.* are most often dated 1949, but, on occasion, also 1950. *The New York Times Directory of the Film* states that *White Heat* was released September 3, 1949, *D.O.A.* on May 1, 1950, and *Gun Crazy* on August 27, 1950. Assuming the *Times* as an authoritative source it would appear that I am treating the films chronologically backward. I don't think, however, that it makes much, if any, difference. Since all three films were made so close together in time and may have been in production simultaneously, it is unlikely that one would have influenced the other. (We do not know, moreover, just when each was *conceived*.) It was a period in which the genre was being both eroded and revitalized. It was wide open; one could make of it what one wished. The gangster crime film was being put to use in a variety of ways. It had no stable identity, as in the thirties. It is possible to see, though, that near-simultaneous films as different as *Gun Crazy*, *White Heat*, and *D.O.A.* were making intelligent explorations of the genre, keeping it useful, and taking it somewhere in a period of transition.

2. Eric F. Goldman, *The Crucial Decade: America, 1945–1955* (New York, 1956), p. 112.

3. Later, when Joe (the man whose nose Chester has smashed) chases Bigelow outside Mrs. Phillips's hotel, in long shot, we can see if we look closely enough a new white bandage on his nose catching some light in the general darkness. It is a gratuitous touch, since we don't exactly see Chester's blow land, but the tone of the film permits this nose joke twenty-five years before *Chinatown*. Unlike in *Chinatown*, next to nothing is made of it; it is almost unnoticeable. It's the kind of detail that goes with *noir*. *Chinatown*, in milking it dry, is merely doing what it has to—making it clear that it is, inescapably, self-conscious *noir*.

4. For more on this see Paul Jensen, "The Return of Dr. Caligari: Paranoia in Hollywood," *Film Comment* 7 (Winter 1971–1972): 36–45.

5. Bigelow never even considers going to the police for help; the film takes for granted the impotence of cops. On one occasion only do they come to his aid—when he gets off the bus and a cop shoos Majak and his men away for obstructing traffic—but unknowingly. This incident shows Bigelow's skill in using what means he finds at his disposal. The presence of the cop is fortuitous, not philosophically salutary.

6. Paul Schrader, "Notes on *Film Noir*," *Film Comment* 8 (Spring, 1972): 12.

7. There are good reasons behind the neglect of Walsh and why there is no satisfactory account (perhaps excepting Manny Farber's) of Walsh as a man who sees the world in a certain way and makes movies accordingly. A director asked to handle and to salvage so much junk throughout a long career is almost asking for anonymity. Besides, he efficiently disappears behind his characters and their world. Walsh at least

has been noticed, and his good films demand that we treat him as the equal of more recognized but less talented filmmakers. But one is never quite certain what to praise him for. An idiosyncratic director like Fuller or a pretentious perfectionist like Stevens never leave their admirers in doubt; one knows what is there to praise and/or love. But Walsh's straightforwardness, while it provokes critical regard, stymies critical analysis. Still, he has made too many wonderful films for the critics to abandon him.

Just recently, there has been a flurry of interest in Walsh, Richard Schickel's TV show on Walsh—the best of his "Men Who Made the Movies" series—in November 1973 was probably influential in stimulating a reconsideration. William Paul has done a three-part study of Walsh in *The Village Voice* (May 23, June 6, and June 27, 1974), and Julian Fox has a three-part career survey in *Films and Filming* (June, July, and August 1973). In 1974, over sixty of Walsh's films were screened at the Museum of Modern Art.

8. *White Heat* has absolutely no interest in revealing prison conditions, although a good deal of the film takes place in prison. Like all the film's environments, the prison environment is there to illuminate the character's psychology. The interest is not in "story" or in objective action. The film may be a narrative, but even techniques that advance the action, like the dissolve from Jarrett's head to his mother's, place emphasis on his mind in a way that overrides an automatic interest in the narrative.

9. The movie gangster is often reluctant to accept the breakdown of the family. Either he retains strong emotional ties or his struggle has repercussions within the family. In the pessimism of *D.O.A.* the family is not an issue—Bigelow has no family. There is no one to turn to. In *Force of Evil* (and Siodmak's *Cry of the City* [1948], notably) the family is divided destructively. In *Bonnie and Clyde*, which reconstructs an earlier period, family ties are stressed and are important to the development and outcome of the film. Buck separates Clyde from Bonnie, Bonnie separates Clyde (emotionally) from her family (C. W.'s removal at the reunion is a sign that he too is not "kin"). C. W. betrays Bonnie and Clyde at his father's insistence. Ultimately, family loyalty is firmer than gang (business) loyalty, not necessarily by choice but by a deep instinct. Ma and Cody are at the end of the line, both insane, but both stick it out to the bitter end in serving and sustaining each other.

Chapter Five

1. An important offshoot of the gangster is the juvenile delinquent, who came into his own in the fifties as a charismatic figure whose lifestyle and mannerisms were aped by admiring patrons of his own age bracket. Juvenile delinquent films (when they are not flatly exploitative) carry on the tradition of the socially conscious gangster film (the hero warped by social conditions, and so on, and deserving some measure of sympathy—a phenomenon to be *understood*, at any rate). The genre's structure is ideal for an account of the tough teenager who, perceiving the world he has been born into and its inadequate values, chooses, or is driven, to stand outside it and carve his own reality. A large number of juve quickies were released, and, in the era of burgeoning drive-ins, consumed. The thirty or so I've seen from this period are all worth watching (Mamie Van Doren's verbal digladiation with a bunch of nuns in Charles Haas's *Girl's Town* [1959] is especially not to be missed), though none (ex-

cepting Nicholas Ray's *Rebel without a Cause* [1955] and Laszlo Benedek's *The Wild One* [1954]) would meet anyone's criteria of a major film. The JD movie was revamped in the sixties into the bike flick, a spirited subgenre that is still occasionally grinding its gears.

2. When Tiger first mentions Moe to Zara we expect a man to appear, but there are no men that can function like Moe. She is interested in absolute basics—buying food, being properly buried, and even in her obnoxious line of work (informing), being human. This tired old woman's sense of fun and the good-natured warmth she maintains in the nasty sideline she must use to get by, is apparent in her first scene with Tiger and Zara, two glum sourpusses made to look forlornly inept by her knowledge, zest, and timing. Tiger knows he has to turn to her, that he's cut off from everything that matters. Moe tweaks him, "I thought you knew everything about everybody." This is the woman's function—awareness, a knowledge of things men do not have. (This is made even more explicit in *The Big Heat* and *The Big Combo* and is one of the genre's axioms in this period.) Joey sends Candy out to do his dirty work with the excuse, "If I had your contacts . . ." Where women, both by their nature and their social roles connect, men remain isolated. If it weren't for Moe and Candy, Skip's will to act for something other than himself could never develop. The sexist reflex is apparent. The only good comes from women, but it is the *man's* problem that has to be overcome. Moe dies, and Candy lies in a hospital bed, while Skip takes crucial action. Women may instruct, but only men have the ability (and opportunity) to bring about actual change. That men without women are lost, however, is so insistent a theme of the genre in the fifties that it amounts to an exposé, at least for the modern viewer, of sexist assumptions.

3. Fuller: "Lightnin' Louie was played by a card expert and magician from Chicago named Victor Perry. It was his first and last picture. I just happened to meet him. I asked him, "Are you good with your hands?" He said, "Am I good? Just watch my act!" I said, "What I want in my film is a man who is so indifferent to people that he has contempt for the people he's selling information to—especially if they interfere with him while he's eating. That's why I want a man like you, with a big belly. Now let me see you pick up some money with the chopsticks and just keep eating with them." (Eric Sherman and Martin Rudin, eds. *The Director's Event: Interviews with Five American Filmmakers* [New York, 1972], pp. 151–152).

4. *Pickup on South Street* is typical of Fuller in that the struggle for meaningful life is implicitly tied into the values of a place where one can live it—that is, a free America. His later films, however—*Shock Corridor* and *The Naked Kiss* in particular—find the director unable to sustain the political mythology his earlier heroes fight so painfully on behalf of (for example, O'Meara leaving the Sioux to give America another try in *Run of the Arrow*) and even implying that the hypocrisy and insanity of America crushes individual hope.

5. Only Fuller, as its spirited choreographer, could describe a scene where Skip pulls Joey down a flight of subway steps by his legs as: "The heavy's chin hits every step. Dat-dat-dat-dat-dat: its musical" (Sherman and Rubin, *Director's Event*, p. 149).

6. Fuller's notoriously restless camera—in and out, up and down, high and low—always works within a tight general design. Fuller never lies back, but he never loses control either. His fondness for symmetrical design works especially well in *Pickup on South Street*. The opening subway sequence is memorable visually but

also memorable for its denuded context. Nobody is identified; we have no idea what is going on. The sequence is repeated prior to the climax, except that now we know who the people are and the great amount at stake. A similar action takes place in a similar setting but we are now active emotional participants. Fuller doesn't disguise his manipulation. He even repeats the shot of the whole train roaring underground as if to remind us that what we are now about to see we have seen before. The effect is like an announcement: this is what you have been waiting for and I am going to give it to you. We see the movie taking shape before our eyes, a significant departure from traditional illusionism.

7. One interesting motif in the fifties is the gangster's fearlessness, which is seen as a specifically nonhuman quality. This is why, so often, the gangster is brought to a point of fear, of begging not to be killed or harmed. It is a trait, usually, of the *top* gangsters. Not to feel fear is a source of power; it keeps one invulnerable. It also keeps one separate from humanity and at a remove from one's own reality. When Driscoll holds his fist in front of Mickey's face, he produces, in Mickey, a healthy natural fear. Christopher's lack of fear, in contrast, is unnatural, creepy, inhuman. Rhett Tanner, the syndicate kingpin in *The Phenix City Story*, makes a point of repeating that he's not afraid of anything. He begs and grovels at the end. Human beings are not above good and evil; they are good and evil, and mortal. Brown, in *The Big Combo*, has made himself something other than a human being. He is a pretender to godliness. In the same film a character named Dreyer receives a phone call that should make him afraid. He decides he can be greater than that and conquers his fear. But that is to exceed one's human limits. He walks out the door and gets shot.

8. Christopher deals with women by not dealing with them. He is not, I suspect, a misogynist—he lights Pauline's cigarette with a grim, mechanical civility—he just knows that the threat women pose is the irrational. He works on a principle "I never do business with women." He is right. Women are creatures of instinct who will gum up male rationalism and mechanism. Ernie tries to get rid of Linda since she is living proof that his position on women—that they are all untrustworthy and ambitious—is mistaken and would have to be reconsidered. The film says, though, that without women, there is no hope of men ever coming to their senses, nor is any change possible. It is Pauline's interference with Christopher's business that leads to his eventual death. As the "boss" figure, he is the center of the film's corruption, and, like Brown in *The Big Combo*, he must be forced to play his hand. Victor's murder of Pauline enables him to demand money from Christopher and that forces Christopher to drop his sinister, passive control and go after Victor personally.

9. One cannot help noticing, as well, the proliferation of signs, and especially numbers—indexes of an ordered world. They would be tedious to catalog and have no specific meaning, but they reinforce the certainty and precision of many of the images.

10. There is no law in *The Brothers Rico*. The El Camino police are on the take, and the town's citizens take orders from La Motta. Since cops can't be trusted, Eddie can't seek help from them. If he tried, the syndicate would get to him first, anyway. Eddie, as the insider turned outsider, is the only one who can break the organization. They are otherwise untouchable. The law is either helpless (crime has gone legit) or corrupt. (After Eddie escapes from Gonzales at the Phoenix Airport, there is a sudden

shot of a police car that fills the frame. The film has so successfully inverted our habits of seeing and associating that the image produces anxiety and terror.) Like big business, the syndicate is concerned only with profit; the claims of friendship and family are of no account (Johnny is executed on the eve of his son's birth). Metaphorically, it represents the way of life the police are there to protect, so it is fitting that they play no role in getting Kubik. It is Mama Rico whose way of life has been superseded in modern America, who hangs on to Kubik's leg and holds him in place long enough for Eddie to take aim and kill him.

11. Grandma is watching, and laughing at a flying saucer movie—a dig at the period's paranoia over UFOs. It is an ironic allusion to a ridiculous preoccupation and anxiety. As the film indicates, we have plenty of real worries, but they have nothing to do with invasions from outer space. The enemy is right here, among us, and in us.

12. The remark is Raymond Durgnat's, from his chapter on *Kiss Me Deadly* in *Eros in the Cinema* (London, 1966, pp. 84–94), a chapter that illustrates how problematical film criticism can be. His remarks, as usual, are fascinating, but that is not the issue here. It is obvious that he has seen a print different from the one United Artists currently distributes in 16mm. The differences happen to be very important. Durgnat writes that when Hammer visits the opera singer he "starts smashing his collection of rare Caruso records, one by one." In the print I have been working from, he cracks one record and leaves. Now it happens that I have seen a print (some eight years ago) that contained the scene Durgnat describes and was surprised by its absence in the 16mm UA print. I recall the scene vividly because it was the high point of Hammer's brutality (he as much as kills the aging singer—who doesn't know anything to tell him anyway—by demolishing his records). However, Durgnat places this scene near the beginning of the film, and I recall that it occurred during his second visit to the singer, *after* he has been tongue-lashed by Pat. (Hammer, frustrated and furious, starts a second and less polite round of interrogation on the same people.) The existence of the scene is important in that it prevents any possibility of our romanticizing Hammer—he is merciless and vicious, like those he hunts. The placing of the scene is also important in the rhythms of the film and in revealing Hammer's no-holds-barred desperation.

Durgnat also claims that at the end "Velda and Mike stagger into the dark, rolling surf, and watch, and wait." No figures are visible in UA's 16mm print. A movement is initiated that could imply that Mike and Velda escape (they reach the door), but the editing suggests they blow up along with the house. At best, they could have just put foot onto the sand, which would make them dead anyway. Obviously, whether the hero and heroine are allowed to survive affects any interpretation of a movie. (Durgnat's mistakes: Nick does *not* drive the booby-trapped car, Mike does; Mike does *not* disconnect the dynamite, Nick does; the opera singer is Italian, not Greek. Mike does not "kill his doctor.")

13. Alain Silver in his article "*Kiss Me Deadly*: Evidence of a Style," (*Film Comment* 11 [March–April 1975]: 24–30), says on p. 25 that "Hammer is not another Galahad about to begin a quest for the grail." It might be more useful to grant that he is, or more precisely, he is what's left of one. This would correspond to our sense that a dynamic action hero is being ironically undercut. If Hammer didn't have heroic qualities, the scene with Pat would not have the effect it clearly has on audiences.

14. Durgnat, *Eros*, p. 90.

Chapter Six

1. As I imply, I believe that the process of development is to a large extent internal to the medium. Movies come from other movies; genres ultimately become self-conscious. However, a vast range of cultural factors—too many for one commentator to handle—also comes into play. My contention, however, is that one usually starts with the notion of what might make a successful movie by appealing to internal history and authority, and then applies the proper shadings and accents based on a reading of (or a feeling about) the culture, and not vice versa. It is not just TV and high prices that have reduced attendance. The movies have changed; they are not what they used to be. There is a whole class of people who simply don't go to the movies anymore, and it is not because they can't afford it, prefer TV, or are too busy. The aesthetics of movies are different and troublesome to the habitual moviegoer of, say, the fifties. In an attempt to recapture a large audience, the seventies has seen the return of a strong, genre-based cinema, but the genres are now recognized as genres, as distinctly stylized unrealities. It is the rare film, these days, that does not, in some way, question our relationship to it.

2. There is already a book of critical readings on *Bonnie and Clyde* edited by John G. Cawelti (*Focus on Bonnie and Clyde* [Englewood Cliffs, 1973]). It is a useful collection, containing a fine and thorough essay by the editor. It is remarkable that a film released in 1967 should by 1973 be given the kind of homage typically reserved for the hoariest classics.

3. Penn has said that he made "a distinct and conscious effort not to be boring, by alternation of effect." (In Joseph Gelmis, *The Film Director as Superstar* [Garden City, 1970], p. 222.)

4. Cawelti's essay, "The Artistic Power of *Bonnie and Clyde*" (in his *Focus on Bonnie and Clyde*), despite its many valuable insights, takes a position I disagree with. I don't believe it is possible to talk persuasively about "tragic power" in a film of such desperate comedy and ironic futility. Neither Bonnie and Clyde nor those who destroy them know what they are doing. If the film were a tragedy, it would not have been so controversial or bothersome, and its entire technique would have been different. Tragedy is noble, "safe," and passé. Penn makes it far less easy lot us and far truer to an exacerbated modern consciousness. To have gone the tragic-pathetic route would have been anachronistic.

5. Cawelti, *Focus*, p. 83. Also, Penn's remark that "everything in life comes out in the bedroom," is relevant (Gelmis, *Superstar*, p. 226).

6. Penn is not necessarily counting on a sophisticated audience—the ballad narrative structure he adopts is quite simple—but he is assuming there is a consciousness upon which his kind of film will register, an audience for whom the film will feel right without their necessarily knowing why. In some ways, his film is less complex than old-style genre films, the way in which, say, Ornette Coleman is less complex, but more modern, than Charlie Parker.

7. Even a very late film like Menahem Golan's *Lepke* (1975) is firmly in the mold. We watch Lepke's detailed electrocution in much the same way as the slaughter of Bonnie and Clyde. It is not "man's inhumanity to man," it doesn't produce moral outrage against capital punishment, nor are we "moved." We are forced to look at it because it is assumed that we are numb to its content and that by looking at it we do not look at a reality or at a character whose life and death makes any difference. It is not cynicism that operates but rather an inertia of the emotions produced by in-

significance that film, along with other modern arts, can combat by creating an anxious fascination with its processes and emphases. *Lepke* is a success.

8. The enthusiasm with which academics, especially, cluster around and defend the proliferation of new critical systems for their claimed discipline and objectivity is finally disheartening, since all these systems do is perpetuate critical and scholarly habits that are insufficient to deal with film. For the lack of anything else, they are of course useful, but one ought to use them with a full awareness of their limitations and not with an impassioned partisanship that may petrify them into competing orthodoxies in the search for critical "truth." What seems necessary is not more critical systems but a new critical language and sensibility that can accommodate our thoughts about our feelings and perceptions of film. Occasionally, I feel something like it happening in the work of people like Manny Farber and Raymond Durgnat, but my sense is that their orneriness is not in clear favor.

9. The lyrical interlude of Lynn's flashback, for instance, seems a parody of *Jules and Jim*, with its fluttery romanticism and voice-over narration.

10. Reese's death is an accident. The wind finds his bed sheet and whips Reese over the ledge. We do not see Walker push him. Chris later asks, "You let him fall?"—implying that he *should* have killed him. Walker may be indirectly responsible for Reese's death, but Reese has begged to be killed anyway.

11. Chris is the only other character who seems caught in the transition from human to machine. She is inured to her reality, her existence is comatose, but Walker's return and the possibilities opened up by naked, indiscreet violence urge her toward Walker and a shared sense of mission. She is heroine to Walker's "hero." These roles are, however, no longer possible in parody. Chris and Walker are shown sipping sodas. They are both really too numb to help each other. The organization has killed the man Chris was in love with (a jazz trumpeter); Walker's wife has committed suicide. They are drawn to each other for the same reasons men and women normally are, but they end up merely using each other as an antidote to that human inertia they sense in themselves as wrong but have no choice except to perpetuate. Walker treats her like dirt and can be reached only by being knocked unconscious by a pool cue. Chris apparently accepts a night in bed with Walker as the limit of their relationship and disappears from the film without any good-byes. She still assumes the woman's old function of humanizing when she attempts, in an extended pounding of Walker, to break through his hard contempt, but she is not, finally, successful. Walker regards her as an interlude and goes on with his urgent, futile business.

12. The March 1975 issue of *American Cinematographer* (56:3) contains an interview with Boorman by the editor Herb A. Lightman, in which the director comments specifically on his schematic use of color in *Point Blank*. "I decided to shoot each sequence in a different color—with the costumes, the sets, and everything in the same color. It was a kind of spectrum thing. The story was about a man who comes back from the dead and he sort of warms up at the end. I started in the cold colors, gray and silver, then went up into blue and green, and on up until, eventually, the last sequence of the film was a kind of rusty red" (p. 334).

13. Boorman comments, "The studio always wants to make an album because they always hear you can make a lot of money with a film score. So they set up to make this album, and it turned out 14 minutes of this atonal drone . . . (in an interview with Stephen Farber, "The Writer in American Films," *Film Quarterly* 21 [Summer, 1968]: 9).

Chapter Seven

1. It isn't quite fair to juxtapose films this way for the purposes of evaluation. We all "taste" differently; what makes me laugh might make you cry. Taste is protean, wavering, unreliable—subject to weather, diet, time of day. Thelonious Monk has a composition called "Ugly Beauty," and we all know individuals we find beautifully ugly. And tastes change, sometimes mystifyingly. Listen!—those are, indeed, the opening bars of *Eroica*, but where are the goose bumps? They may never return. Remakes should be enlightening, as they are attempts to transmit the magic of the original work, or at least have it float about the frames in a helpful way. Yet people are wary of them and expect disappointment. Contrast obviously is a useful tool in spotting cultural markings, clarifying aims, and arguing preferences. With remakes it's very hard not to start waving the evaluative yardstick. The gangster/crime film has had its fair share of remakes lately, a sign that present cultural concerns, the social mood, issues of ethics and aesthetics, and, even more broadly speaking, behavior and style, have an affinity with the feeling tone of a past culture as it has been preserved in its artistic documents. Remakes are useful strategies in coping with problems we can see previous generations trying to work out. Their art is instructive. The interactive impulse of the remake makes for a sympathetic transport of what continues to trouble and call for investigation. The various kinds of dysfunction currently in place look, perhaps, for some relief in past styles and comfort in familiarity. Just about all of the recent remakes that come to mind are far less axiomatic in despair than the hard-nosed originals. There is a general reluctance to accept harsh and final outcomes. Consider the softened judgments, romantic coloration, visual opulence, and hope of survival characteristic of these remakes: *Kiss of Death*, 1995; *The Narrow Margin*, 1990; *D.O.A.*, 1988; *Night and the City*, 1992; *Out of the Past* (*Against All Odds*), 1984; *Criss Cross* (*The Underneath*), 1994. These are not tight, ascetic, darkness-embracing, last-exit films. On the contrary, they have sexual allure, kinetic excitement, and a somewhat flagrant hope. (Most fascinating, perhaps, is Brian Helgeland's *Payback* [1999], a remake of *Point Blank* [1967]. It has the equivalent ill will and stylistic insolence but expires in a lunatic pileup of violent set pieces, a very Everest of wretched excess, and a gutless concession to Mel Gibson addicts, whose sensitivities are spared by having him survive, succeed, and get the girl, sending all *Point Blank* fans into a collective cringe.) They don't really want to face the music— not Miklos Rozsa's, anyway. But Phil Collins?—oh yeah, sure. All in all, the originals are a far tougher lot.

2. What famous novel opens similarly? It's time for a digression citing some of this film's extensive allusiveness and up-front homages. The answer is *The Sound and the Fury*, of course. William Faulkner's still-amazing tour de force begins with the idiot Benjy's account of a walk along a fence, a long section told from his limited grasp of things but alive with sensations and emotions, including a physical dependence on his sister Caddy. Like Bernard, he has strong sexual urges, but a weak, damaged brain. Eventually, he is gelded. Bernard too is a problem, his agony leading to acts of violence. His own father admits he's "crazy as a shithouse rat." His death, a mercy killing by Jimmy just prior to his own gangland execution, momentarily creates a moratorium, as the walking symbol of a world out of kilter is no more, and even the Man with the Plan is stunned into inactivity. Other allusions: (1) *D.O.A.* Nothing of significance. It's playing on a television screen, and we see, of all things, the shot of Raymond Rakubian's coffin. Just an affectionate nod, I suppose, and the

satisfaction of bringing to view one of its more obscure moments. (2) *Point Blank.* The flashback sequence of the happy outdoor party with Bernard and Meg, and the Man with the Plan, conveys the same point with the same techniques as the romantic flashback with a younger, happier Walker, Reese, and Lynne. It functions the same way, the memory of happy circumstances turning to bitterness from betrayal, both shot with filters and in slow motion. (3) *Night and the City.* Jimmy the Saint and Harry Fabian undergo essentially the same process. (4) Malt shops, Ferris wheels, natural history museums, steam baths, comic funerals, thugs with a knack for language, each and every characterization part of a gallery of known figures with defined histories. These others can work on. (Hint: the Ferris wheel is from a film later "novelized" by a writer whose initials are G. G.)

Selected Bibliography

Books

Agee, James. *Agee on Film: Reviews and Comments*. Boston: Beacon Press, 1964.

Alloway, Lawrence. *Violent America: The Movies, 1946–1964*. New York: Museum of Modern Art, 1971.

Barbour, Alan. *Humphrey Bogart*. New York: Pyramid Publications, 1973.

Baxter, John. *The Gangster Film*. New York: Barnes, 1970.

———. *Hollywood in the Sixties*. New York: Barnes, 1972.

———. *Hollywood in the Thirties*. New York: Barnes, 1968.

Bergman, Andrew. *James Cagney*. New York: Pyramid Publications, 1973.

———. *We're in the Money*. New York: Harper & Row, 1972.

Bonn, Thomas L. *Undercover: An Illustrated History of American Mass Market Paperback*. New York: Penguin Books, 1982.

Bookbinder, Tobert. *Classics of the Gangster Film*. Secaucus NJ: Citadel Press, 1985.

Bordwell, David, Janet Staiger, and Kristin Thompson. *The Classical Hollywood Cinema: Film Style & Mode of Production to 1960*. New York: Columbia University Press, 1985.

Brode, Douglas. *Lost Films of the Fifties*. New York: Citadel Press, 1988.

Cameron, Ian and Elizabeth. *The Heavies*. New York: Praeger, 1967.

Cameron, Ian, ed. *The Book of Film Noir*. New York: Continuum, 1993.

Cavell, Stanley. *The World Viewed: Reflections on the Ontology of Film*. New York: Viking, 1971.

Cawelti, John G., ed. *Focus on Bonnie and Clyde*. Englewood Cliffs, NJ: Prentice-Hall, 1973.

Christopher, Nicholas. *Somewhere in the Night: Film Noir and the American City*. New York: Free Press, 1997.

Clarens, Carlos. *Crime Movies: An Illustrated History*. New York: W. W. Norton & Co., 1980.

Cook, Pam, ed. *The Cinema Book*. New York: Pantheon Books, 1985.

Cross, Robin. *The Big Book of B Movies*. New York: St. Martin's Press, 1981.

Doane, Mary Ann. *The Desire to Desire: The Woman's Film of the 1940s*. Indiana University Press, 1987.

Dowdy, Andrew. *"Movies Are Better than Ever."* New York: Morrow, 1973.

Durgnat, Raymond. *Eros in the Cinema*. London: Calder & Boyars, 1966.

———. *Films and Feelings*. Cambridge, MA: MIT Press, 1967.

Farber, Manny. *Negative Space*. New York: Praeger, 1971.

Gabree, John. *Gangsters: From Little Caesar to The Godfather*. New York: Pyramid Publications, 1973.

Garnham, Nicholas. *Samuel Fuller*. New York: Viking, 1972.

Gelmis, Joseph, ed. *The Film Director as Superstar*. Garden City, NY: Doubleday, 1970.

Gow, Gordon. *Hollywood in the Fifties*. New York: A. S. Barnes, 1971.

Hardy, Phil. *Samuel Fuller*. New York: Praeger, 1970.

Higham, Charles, and Joel Greenberg, eds. *The Celluloid Muse: Hollywood Directors Speak*. New York: New American Library, 1972.

————. *Hollywood in the Forties*. New York: Barnes, 1968.

Hirsch, Foster. *The Dark Side of the Screen: Film Noir*. New York: Da Capo Press, 1983.

————. *Edward G. Robinson*. New York: Pyramid Publications, 1975.

Hossent, Harry. *Gangster Movies*. London: Octopus Books Ltd., 1974.

Jarvie, I. C. *Movies and Society*. New York: Basic Books, 1970.

Kael, Pauline. *Kiss Kiss Bang Bang*. New York: Atlantic-Little, Brown, 1968.

Kaminsky, Stuart. *American Film Genres*. Dayton: Pflaum, 1974.

Kaplan, E. Ann, ed. *Women in Film Noir*. London: BFI Publishing, 1998.

Katz, Ephraim. *The Film Encyclopedia*. New York: Crowell, 1979.

Kauffman, Stanley, and Bruce Henstell. *American Film Criticism: From the Beginnings to Citizen Kane*. New York: Liveright, 1972.

Krutnik, Frank. *In a Lonely Street: Film Noir, Genre, Masculinity*. New York: Routledge, 1991.

Lee, Raymond, and B. C. Van Hecke. *Gangsters and Hoodlums: The Underworld in the Cinema*. With a foreword by Edward G. Robinson. South Brunswick, NJ: A. S. Barnes, 1971.

Mast, Gerald, Marshall Cohen, and Leo Braudy, eds. *Film Theory and Criticism: Introductory Readings*, 4th ed. New York: Oxford University Press, 1992.

McArthur, Colin. *Underworld, U.S.A.* New York: Viking, 1972.

McCarthy, John. *Hollywood Gangland: The Movies' Love Affair with the Mob*. New York: St. Martin's Press, 1993.

McCarthy, Todd, and Charles Flynn, eds. *Kings of the B's*. New York: Dutton, 1975.

Martin, Mick, and Marsha Porter. *Video Movie Guide 2000*. New York: Ballantine, 1999.

Muller, Eddie. *Dark City: The Lost World of Film Noir*. New York: St. Martins Press, 1988.

Munby, Jonathan. *Public Enemies, Public Heroes: Screening the Gangster from Little Caesar to The Godfather*. Chicago: University of Chicago Press, 1999.

Palmer, R. Barton. *Hollywood's Dark Cinema: The American Film Noir*. New York: Twayne Publishers, 1994.

Peary, Dannis. *Cult Movies*. New York: Dell Publishing Co., 1981.

Pym, John, ed. *Time Out Film Guide*, 8th ed. New York: Penguin, 1999.

Rosow, Eugene. *Born to Lose: The Gangster Film in America*. New York: Oxford University Press, 1978.

Russo, Vito. The Celluloid Closet: Homosexuality in the Movies, rev. ed. New York: Harper & Row, 1987.

Sarris, Andrew. *The American Cinema: Directors and Directions, 1929–1968*. New York: Dutton, 1968.

Schatz, Thomas. *Hollywood Genres: Formulas, Filmmaking, and the Studio System*. New York: Random House, 1981.

Server, Lee, Ed Gorman, Martin H. Greenberg, eds. *The Big Book of Noir*. New York: Carroll & Graf Publishers, Inc., 1998.

Sherman, Eric, and Martin Rubin, eds. *The Director's Event: Interviews with Five American Film-makers*. New York: New American Library, 1972.

Shipman, David. *The Great Movie Stars: The Golden Years*. New York: Crown, 1970.

Silver, Alain, and James Ursini, eds. *Film Noir Reader*. New York: Limelight Editions, 1996.

Silver, Alain, et al., eds. *Film Noir: An Encyclopedic Reference to the American Style*, 3rd ed., revised and expanded. Woodstock, NY: Overlook Press, 1992.

Staiger, Janet. *Interpreting Films: Studies in the Historical Reception of American Cinema*. Princeton, NJ: Princeton University Press, 1992.

Telotte, J. P. *Voices in the Dark: The Narrative Patterns of Film Noir*. Urbana: University of Illinois Press, 1989.

Thompson, Peggy. *Hard-boiled: Great Lines from Classic Noir Films*. San Francisco: Chronicle Books, 1995.

Thomson, David. *A Biographical Dictionary of Film*, 3rd ed. New York: Knopf, 1994.

Tudor, Andrew. *Theories of Film*. London: Secker and Warburg, 1974.

Tuska, Jon. *Dark Cinema: American Film Noir in Cultural Perspective*. Westport, CT: Greenwood Press, 1984.

Tyler, Parker. *The Hollywood Hallucination*. New York: Creative Age, 1944.

Warshow, Robert. *The Immediate Experience*. Garden City, NY: Doubleday, 1964.

Wilson, Robert, ed. *The Film Criticism of Otis Ferguson*. Philadelphia: Temple University Press, 1971.

Wright, Basil. *The Long View*. London: Secker & Warburg, 1974.

Yaquinto, Marilyn. *Pump 'Em Full of Lead*. New York: Twayne Publishers, 1998.

Articles

Allan, Alfred K. "Crime in the Movies." *Adam Film Quarterly* 8 (February 1969): 21–25, 90–96.

Allen, Richard. "Brushing Classical Hollywood Narrative against the Grain of History." *Camera Obscura* 18 (September 1988): 137–145.

Armstrong, Michael. "On Violence." *Films and Filming* 15 (March 1969): 20–31.

Austen, David. "Out for the Kill." *Films and Filming* 14 (April 1968): 5–11

Bergman, Mark. "'This Will Happen to Your Kids Too.'" *The Velvet Light Trap* 8 (1973): 20–22.

Blum, William. "Towards a Cinema of Cruelty." *Cinema Journal* 10 (Spring 1971): 19–33.

Bobrow, Andrew C. "The Making of *Dillinger*." *Filmmakers Newsletter* (November 1973): 20–25.

Bogdanovich, Peter. "Karlson." *Movies International* (July/August/September 1966): 48.

Bourget, Jean-Loup. "Social Implication in the Hollywood Genres." *Journal of Modern Literature* 3 (April 1973): 191–200.

Brown, John Lindsay. "Islands of the Mind." *Sight and Sound* (Winter 1969–1970): 20–23.

Chappetta, Robert. "*The Godfather*." *Film Quarterly* 25 (Summer 1972): 60–61.

Childs, James. "Can You Ride a Horse?: An Interview with Raoul Walsh." *Sight and Sound* (Winter 1972–1973): 9–13.

Cook, Jim. "*Bonnie and Clyde*." *Screen* 10 (July/October 1969): 101–114.

Dempsey, Michael. "*Deliverance*/Boorman." *Cinema* (Spring 1973): 10–17.

———. "The Family Tree of *Film Noir*." *Film Comment* 10:6 (1974): 6–7.

Durgnat, Raymond. "Genre: Populism and Social Realism." *Film Comment* 11 (July–August 1975): 20–29, 63.

———. "Paint It Black: The Family Tree of *Film Noir*." *Cinema* 6/7 (1970): 49–56.

Eckert, Charles W. "The Anatomy of a Proletarian Film: Warner's *Marked Woman*." *Film Quarterly* 27 (Winter 1973–1974): 10–24.

Farber, Manny. "Raoul Walsh: 'He used to be a big shot.'" *Sight and Sound* (Winter 1974–1975): 42–44. First published in *Artforum*, November 1971.

———. "Coppola and *The Godfather*." *Sight and Sound* (Autumn 1972) 217–223.

Farber, Stephen. "The Writer in American Films." *Film Quarterly* 21 (Summer 1968): 2–13.

———. "The Writer in American Films, II." *Film Quarterly* 22 (Winter 1968–1969): 2–14.

Flinn, Tom. "*The Big Heat* and *The Big Combo*: Rogue Cops and Mink-Coated Girls." *The Velvet Light Trap* 11 (Winter 1974): 23–28.

French, Philip. "Cops." *Sight and Sound* (Spring 1974): 113–115.

Gale, Steven H. "*The Maltese Falcon*: Melodrama or *Film Noir*?" *Literature-Film Quarterly* 24/2 (April 1996): 145 (3 pages).

Hanson, Curtis Lee. "An Interview with William Wellman: A Memorable Visit with an Elder Statesman." *Cinema* (July 1966): 20–32.

Hess, John. "*Godfather II*: A Deal Coppola Couldn't Refuse." *Jump Cut* 7 (May–July 1975): 1, 10, 11.

Hess, Judith. "Genre Films and the Status Quo." *Jump Cut* 1 (May–June 1974): 1, 16, 18.

Hill, R. F. "Remembrance, Communication and *Kiss Me Deadly*." *Literature-Film Quarterly* 23/2 (1995): 146–150.

Hutton, Virgil. "*Easy Rider*: America's Bad Trip." *Western Humanities Review* 25 (Spring 1971): 171–178.

Jensen, Paul. "The Return of Dr. Caligari: Paranoia in Hollywood." *Film Comment* 7 (Winter 1971–1972): 36–45.

Kaminsky, Stuart. "*Little Caesar* and Its Role in the Gangster Film Genre." *Journal of Popular Film* 1 (Summer 1972): 209–227.

Kinder, Marsha. "The Return of the Outlaw Couple." *Film Quarterly* 27 (Summer 1974): 2–10.

Kleinhans, Chuck. "Types of Audience Response: From Tear-Jerkers to Thought-Provokers." *Jump Cut* 4 (November–December 1974): 21–23.

Lindsay, Michael. "An Interview with Arthur Penn." *Cinema* (Summer 1967): 32–36.

McConnell, Frank. "*Pickup on South Street* and the Metamorphosis of the Thriller." *Film Heritage* 8 (Spring 1973): 9–18.

McGilligan, Patrick. "James Cagney: The Actor as Auteur." *The Velvet Light Trap* 7 (Winter 1972–1973): 3–15.

Nichols, Bill. "Horatio Alger Goes to Hollywood." *Take One* 3/11 (1973): 11–14.

Orr, Christopher. "Genre Theory in the Context of the Noir and Post-Noir Film." *Film Criticism* 22/1 (Fall 1997): 21 (17 pages).

Paul, William. "Raoul Walsh (1): Speed and Grace." *The Village Voice* (May 23, 1974): 97.

———. "Raoul Walsh (2): The Poetry of Space." *The Village Voice* (June 6, 1974): 93.

———. "Raoul Walsh (3): The Limitations of Freedom." *The Village Voice* (June 27, 1974): 85.

Peary, Gerard. "Notes on Early Gangster Comedy." *The Velvet Light Trap* 3 (Winter 1971–1972): 16–18.

Place, J. A., and L. S. Peterson. "Some Visual Motifs of *Film Noir*." *Film Comment* 10 (January–February 1974): 30–35.

Polan, Dana. "*Film Noir*." *Journal of Film and Video* (Spring 1985): 75–83.

Porfirio, Robert. "No Way Out: Existential Motifs of *Film Noir*." *Sight and Sound* 45/4 (1976): 212–217.

Powell, David, and John W. Kline. "Criticism in the Present Tense." *Film Society Review* (January 1968): 42–46.

Robinson, George. "Three by Aldrich." *The Velvet Light Trap* 11 (Winter 1974): 46–49.

Rogin, Michael. "*Kiss Me Deadly*: Communism, Motherhood, and Cold War Movies." *Representations* 6 (Spring 1984): 1–36.

Ross, T. J. "*Point Blank*: A Stalker in the City." *Film Heritage* 5 (Fall 1969): 21–27.

Schrader, Paul. "Notes on *Film Noir*." *Film Comment* 8 (Spring 1972): 9–13.

Shadoian, Jack. "*Dirty Harry: A Defense*." *Western Humanities Review* 28 (Spring 1974): 165–179.

———. "*Michael Curtiz' 20,000 Years in Sing Sing*." *Journal of Popular Film* 2 (Spring 1973): 165–179.

———. "*Kiss Me Deadly*: Evidence of a Style." *Film Comment* 11 (March–April 1975): 24–30.

Silver, Alain. "Mr. *Film Noir* Stays at the Table." *Film Comment* 8 (Spring 1972): 14–23.

Telotte, J. P. "The Call of Desire and the *Film Noir*." *Literature-Film Quarterly* 17/1 (January 1989): 50 (9 pages).

———. "*Film Noir* and the Dangers of Discourse." *Quarterly Review of Film Studies* 9/2 (Spring 1984) 101 ff.

———. "Tangled Networks and Wrong Numbers." *Film Criticism* 10/3 (Spring 1986): 36–48.

Thomson, D. "A Cottage at Palos Verdes." *Film Comment* 26/3 (May–June 1990): 16 ff.

Van Wert, William. "Philip Marlowe: Hardboiled to Softboiled to Poached." *Jump Cut* 3 (1974): 10–13.

Vernet, Marc. "The Filmic Transaction: On the Openings of *Film Noirs*." *The Velvet Light Trap* 20 (Summer 1983): 2–9.

Warner, Alan. "Gangster Heroes." *Films and Filming* (November 1971): 17–26.

Whitehall, Richard. "Some Thoughts on Fifties Gangster Films." *The Velvet Light Trap* 11 (Winter 1974): 17–19.

Whitney, John S. "Filmography of *Film Noir*." *Journal of Popular Film* 5/3-4 (1976): 321–371.

Williams, F. D. "The Morality of *Bonnie and Clyde*." *Journal of Popular Culture* 4 (Summer 1970): 299–307.

Vogelsang, Judith. "Motifs of Image and Sound in *The Godfather*." *Journal of Popular Film* 2 (Spring 1973): 115–135.

Supplementary Material

Cawkwell, Tim, and John M. Smith. *The World Encyclopedia of the Film*. New York: World Publishing, 1972.

Halliwell, Leslie. *The Filmgoer's Companion*. New York: Hill & Wang, 1967.

Maltin, Leonard, ed. *TV Movies: 1975 Edition*. New York: New American Library, 1974.

The New York Times. The New York Times Film Reviews, 1913–1968, 6 vols. New York: *New York Times*, Arno, 1970.

Special issues: *Film Comment* 6 (Winter 1970–1971), on the Hollywood screenwriter; *FC* 8 (Summer 1972), on Hollywood cameramen; *FC* 10 (November–December 1974), on *Film Noir; Cinema* 7 (Fall 1971), large section on Joseph H. Lewis.

Videos

Film Noir (American Cinema; 7). Video/C3715. 55 min.

Index

Wallis, Hal, 50
Wall Street (N.Y.C.), 122, 125, 126, 128, 174
Walsh, Raoul, 342–43n.6, 346–47n.7
  High Sierra and, 63, 72, 74, 77–78, 164, 342n.5
  Roaring Twenties and, 62, 78, 164
  White Heat and, 51, 163–67, 172, 173
war, 53, 62. *See also* war movies; World War II
Warden, Jack, 298
Warhol, Andy, 149
war movies, 24, 79
Warner Bros., 167, 317, 323, 324
Washington, D.C., 174
Wayne, John, 24, 239
Wellman, William, 22, 35, 50–52, 54–61
  Blondie Johnson and, 323–24
Wenders, Wim, 274
Western films, 4, 7, 19, 26, 177, 285
Where the Sidewalk Ends (1949/1950), 21, 146
White Heat (1949), 51, 114, 144, 145, 148–49, 162, 178, 183, 340–41n.1, 343n.8, 346n.1
  critical exposition of, 163–75
Widmark, Richard, 108, 111, *111*, 199, 297, 325
Wilde, Oscar, 193
Wilder, Gene, 248–49
Wild One, The (1954), 347–48n.1
Wiles, Gordon, 19, 305
Williams, Treat, 295
Wilson, Scott, 324
Wind and the Lion, The (1975), 269
Winters, Shelley, 28
Woman Under the Influence, A (1975), 142
women, 23
  in *The Big Combo*, 348n.2
  in *The Big Heat*, 348n.2
  in *The Brothers Rico*, 207, 208, 211, 213, 217
  in *Criss Cross*, 317–18, 319–20
  in *D.O.A.*, 151, 152–53, 154, 158

fifties film portrayals of, 179, 182
  as *film noir* characters, 23, 94, 106
  in *Force of Evil*, 120, 121–24
  as gangsters/criminals, 17, 131–44, 244–53
  in *The Godfather* films, 272
  in *Gun Crazy*, 131–33
  in *High Sierra*, 63–64, 70–76, 78
  in *I Walk Alone*, 281
  in *The Killers*, 82–87, 89, 91, 94–95, 97, 111, 344n.11
  in *Kiss Me Deadly*, 222, 225–27, 229–30, 233–34
  in *Kiss of Death*, 111–13, 115–16
  in *Little Caesar*, 39
  in *99 River Street*, 197–200, 202, 349n.8
  in *Once upon a Time in America*, 286, 289, 290–91
  in *Pickup on South Street*, 187–90, 192, 193, 348n.2
  in *Point Blank*, 255–56, 259–60, 263–64, 352n.11
  in *The Public Enemy*, 55, 56–57
  stereotyping of, 182
  in *Things to Do in Denver When You're Dead*, 293
  wartime and postwar film roles for, 141
  in *White Heat*, 168, 169, 170, 172–73
  See also love relationships; mothers
women's pictures, 79
Woo, John, 17
Woods, Eddie, 50
Woods, James, 286, 287
World War II, 62, 65, 66, 79

xenophobia, 345n.2

Yellow Sky (1948), 64
You Only Live Once (1937), 345n.12

Zamfir (musician), 287
Zanuck, Darryl, 50, 51